Contents

Contributors

Ellen Arnold is Assistant Professor of English at East Carolina University. She received her PhD in Interdisciplinary Studies from Emory University's Institute of the Liberal Arts. She has published articles on Native American literature and film, and an interview with Leslie Marmon Silko. Her collection of interviews with Silko will be published by the University Press of Mississippi in autumn 2000. Her website can be accessed at www.ccu.edu.

Chris Berry is an Associate Professor in the Film Studies Program at the University of California at Berkeley. The author of *A Bit on the Side: East–West Topographies of Desire* (Sydney: EMPress, 1994), he has a strong interest in issues of sexuality and the media in East Asia, as well as the cinema in East Asia. In 1999, he visited Seoul on a Korea Foundation fellowship to work with students and faculty at the Korean National University of Arts on an academic website devoted to the late Korean director Kim Ki-young: www.knua.ac.kr/cinema/index.htm.

Charles Cheung is a PhD candidate at the University of Leeds. His interests include audience studies, youth subcultures, masculinity and cultural identities. He has co-edited the book *The Study of Popular Culture in Hong Kong: A Reader,* a comprehensive collection of articles on Hong Kong television, cinema, comics, popular music, consumption, youth subculture and cultural identities (forthcoming 2000, in Chinese; co-editor Dr Ng Chun Hung, University of Hong Kong). Website: www.leeds.ac.uk/ics/cheung.htm.

James Cornford is a Senior Research Associate at the University of Newcastle upon Tyne's Centre for Urban and Regional Development Studies (CURDS: www.ncl.ac.uk/curds). His most recent publications include 'New media', in J. Stokes and A. Reading (eds), *The Media in Britain: Current Debates and Developments*, London: Macmillan, 1999 (with Kevin Robins), and 'Counting computers, or why we are not well informed about the information society', in D. Dorling and L. Simpson, (eds), *Statistics and Society* (London: Arnold, 1999).

Daniel Curzon-Brown believes in free speech. As a gay writer who walked the minefields when it was far from trendy, indeed was very dangerous, he has devoted his writing career to 'telling as much truth as he can get away with'. His works include *Godot Arrives,* for which he won the 1999 USA National New Play Award, as well as a new book of politically impolite and often funny short stories called *Not Necessarily Nice,* and a novel about siring a child with a lesbian couple, *Only the Good Parts.*

Stephen Driver is a Senior Lecturer in Sociology and Social Policy at the University of Surrey Roehampton. In the early 1990s, he did research at CURDS on British magazine publishing. For the past five years, he has been working on the rise of 'New' Labour. His book, written with Luke Martell, *New Labour: Politics after Thatcherism* (Cambridge: Polity), was published in 1998. A follow-up, *Blair's Britain,* is due out in 2001.

JoAnn di Filippo is a doctoral candidate at the University of Arizona. She has conducted in-depth research within the adult website industry over a number of years.

David Gauntlett is Lecturer in Social Communications at the Institute of Communications Studies, University of Leeds. His interest in the social impact of communications is reflected in his previous books: *Moving Experiences* (John Libbey, 1995), a critique of media effects studies; *Video Critical* (John Libbey Media, 1997), which presented a new audience research method; and *TV Living: Television, Culture and Everyday Life* (with Annette Hill, Routledge, 1999), a study of diaries kept by 500 people over five years. His next book will be *Media, Gender and Identity: A New Introduction* (Routledge, forthcoming). He produces the websites www.theory.org.uk and www.newmediastudies.com.

Gerard Goggin is Lecturer in Media Studies at the School of Humanities, Media and Cultural Studies, Southern Cross University, Lismore, Australia. He holds a doctorate in literature from the English Department, University of Sydney. Gerard has written extensively on telecommunications policy and the cultural formations of new media. With Christopher Newell, University of Tasmania, he is currently writing a book on new media and disability, provisionally entitled *Digital Disability.* His website is at www.goggin.wattle.id.au.

Wendy Harcourt is the Director of Programmes, Society for International Development, Rome. She has edited three volumes published by ZED Books: *Feminist Perspectives on Sustainable Development* (1993), *Power, Reproduction and Gender* (1997) and *Women@Internet: Creating New Cultures in Cyberspace* (1999). Her current interests are on women and cyberculture, and reproductive rights. In both areas she is leading a dynamic international group of women and men setting new political agendas.

Amy Happ is pursuing her MFA in Cinema at San Francisco State University. She makes social issue documentaries, and works at the SFSU library. She helps promote teacherreview.com both at City College of San Francisco and San Francisco State University because she believes in freedom of expression.

Ryan Lathouwers is a software engineer who lives in San Francisco. While attending City College of San Francisco he created a website, www.teacherreview.com, which empowered his fellow students to help each other have a more rewarding educational experience. It also caused some controversy. He went on to engineer www.teacherreviews.com, which took the concept of the original site and expanded it to cover over 6,000 universities in over 150 countries. He's also an avid bicyclist and vegetarian. His homepage is http://home.pacbell.net/ryanlath.

Stephen Lax is Lecturer in Communications Technology at the Institute of Communications Studies, University of Leeds. He is interested in the social role of communications technologies and claims about the transformative or revolutionary potential of such developments, and co-ordinated the ESRC *Informed or Forewarned* Seminar Series at the Institute from 1996 to 1998. He is author of *Beyond the Horizon: Communications Technologies Past Present and Future* (John Libbey, 1997) and editor of *Access Denied: Exclusion in the Information Age* (Macmillan, 2000). Website: www.leeds.ac.uk/ics/sl1.htm.

Madhavi Mallapragada is a doctoral candidate in the Media and Cultural Studies Division of the Department of Communication Arts at the University of Wisconsin-Madison. Her research interests include South Asian media, new technologies and diaspora studies.

Fran Martin is a PhD candidate and a Sessional Lecturer in Cultural Studies at the University of Melbourne. She has published articles on contemporary lesbian and gay writing and social movements in Taiwan in *Positions, GLQ, Communal/Plural and Critical InQueeries*. She has also published translations of recent lesbian and gay fiction from Taiwan.

Vincent Miller is currently finishing his PhD in Sociology at Lancaster University. His research is an investigation of enclave, lifeworld and identity within the social structure of cities. The contribution for this volume is a result of his time spent as a Research Associate on the 'Biographies of Cultural Products' project at Lancaster University, from which he has also published 'What happens if nothing happens? Staging Euro 96', with Jeremy Valentine. Website: www.comp.lancs.ac.uk/sociology/vince.html.

Richard Naylor is a Research Associate at the University of Newcastle upon Tyne's Centre for Urban and Regional Development Studies (CURDS: www.ncl.ac.uk/curds). His most recent publications include 'Multimedia and uneven urban and regional development: the internet industry in The Netherlands' in Braczyk, Fuchs and Wolf (eds), *Multimedia and Regional Economic Restructuring* (Routledge, 1999) and a forthcoming paper (with James Cornford) for the journal *Environment and Planning A*, on the business and geography of computer and video games in the UK.

Eva Pariser is an artist and writer, and teaches at Long Island University. She earned a Doctor of Arts degree from New York University and is author of the forthcoming book *Contemporary Self-Referential Art Constructs*, a study of self-referential expression in the visual arts. She also lectures nationally and internationally on the various aspects of self-referential art.

Darcy C. Plymire is an Adjunct Instructor in the Department of Interdisciplinary Studies and Women's Studies at Appalachian State University. She teaches classes on sport, the body and media; she also designed Appalachian's first Lesbian, Gay and Bisexual studies course. She recently co-authored *Breaking the Silence: Lesbian Fans, the Internet, and the Sexual Politics of Women's Sports* with Pamela J. Forman.

Kirsten Pullen is a PhD candidate in the departments of Theatre Research, and Media and Culture at the University of Wisconsin-Madison. Her dissertation research considers links between prostitution and performance. She has contributed chapters to the anthologies *Sex, Media, and Religion* (2001), and *Jane Sexes It Up: Feminist Confessions of Desire* (2001).

Howard Rheingold is author of *The Virtual Community* (1993, new edition, MIT Press, 2000), the groundbreaking book about the cultural and political implications of a new communications medium, as well as several other books including *Tools for Thought* (1984, new edition, MIT Press, 2000) and *Virtual Reality* (1991). In 1994, he was the first Executive Editor of *HotWired*. He launched *Electric Minds* in 1996, and *Brainstorms* in 1997. He remains the world's favourite virtual communities guru. Details of all this at www.rheingold.com.

David Rieder teaches in the English Department at the University of Texas at Arlington where he is a PhD candidate in rhetoric. David is an avid Web-based programmer, specializing in Javascript- and PHP-based projects. He is co-founding editor of *Enculturation: An Electronic Journal for Rhetoric, Writing, and Culture* (www.uta.edu/enculturation). His research is focused on the eighteenth-century thinkers George Campbell and David Hume, and the late twentieth-century philosopher Gilles Deleuze. Website: www.uta.edu/english/daver.

David Silver is a doctoral candidate in American studies at the University of Maryland and founder of the Resource Center for Cyberculture Studies. He is currently completing his dissertation, a comparative analysis between the Blacksburg Electronic Village and the Seattle Community Network, and working on his first book, *Critical Cyberculture Studies: Essays and Annotations on an Emerging Field of Study,* to be published by Sage in 2001. For further details, see www.glue.umd.edu/ ~dsilver.

Christopher R. Smit is a Carrol Arnold fellow in Communication Studies at the University of Iowa. His essay 'The creation and corruption of diversity in MTV's *The Real World*' appeared in *Studies In Popular Culture* (October 1999). In 1999 he organized a conference which is documented in his essay 'Notes on *Screening Disability*: A conference on film and disability' to be published in *Disability Studies Quarterly* in 2000. He also has a chapter in Ray Browne's next book, *Public Reaction To Disaster*, entitled 'Deconstructing the King: Death narratives of Elvis Presley in the 1980s'.

Donald Snyder is a doctoral student in American Studies at the University of Maryland. His research interests include webcams, online journals, race and gender in cyberspace and comic books. Website: www.wam.umd.edu/~djkay.

Philip M. Taylor is Professor of International Communications and Director of the Institute of Communications at the University of Leeds. He is the author of numerous articles on aspects of propaganda and his latest book is *British Propaganda in the Twentieth Century: Selling Democracy* (Edinburgh University Press, 1999). For further details see www.leeds.ac.uk/ics/phil.

Douglas Thomas is Assistant Professor of Communication at the Anneberg School for Communication at the University of Southern California. He is author of *Reading Nietzsche Rhetorically* (Guilford, 1999) and *Hacking Culture* (Minnesota, forthcoming) and co-editor (with Brian Loader) of *CyberCrime: Law Enforcement, Security and Surveillance in the Information Age* (Routledge, 2000). Website: www.rcf.usc.edu/~douglast.

Nina Wakeford is Foundation Fund Lecturer in sociology at the Department of Sociology at the University of Surrey, and a research associate of EC2 at the Annenberg Center at the University of Southern California. She recently completed an Economic and Social Research Council postdoctoral fellowship on women and new technologies, which will be published in *Networks of Desire: Gender, Sexuality and Computing Culture*. In her current research she is experimenting with the use of video and multimedia in an ethnography of a new media company.

Acknowledgements

Putting together this book took a large amount of time within a small number of months. Therefore most of these thanks are simply for people who were kind and made life a bit easier for me. Bonus points are awarded for intellectual contributions. Top of this league, then, comes Susan Giblin, sunny companion and political theory star, with whom I had hundreds of useful discussions. David Silver has become a great friend, although we have never met, who was always ready to discuss Web issues – or the most appropriately insulting summary of them – by e-mail.

Thanks to everyone at the Institute of Communications Studies, University of Leeds. Graham Roberts, the punk legend and film scholar, is a fantastic colleague. Phil Taylor was very supportive and helpful. Jayne Rodgers, Robin Brown and Steve Lax provided entertaining insights. Thank you once again to Communications Theory, Internet Communications, and Media, Gender and Identity students with whom I have discussed ideas, including Verdine Etoria, Lizzy Say, Nicola Kenny, Mark Riley and Jude Wayte.

Annette Hill was helpful about many things, as always. Slantgirl (www.worsethanqueer.com) inspired me Web-wise, as did Emily of *Emily's Madonna Spotlight* (www.mlvc.org/spotlight), Spacegirl (www.spacegirl.org) and numerous other Web artists. Kirsten Pullen generously helped me to do some last-minute rewriting on another contribution. Howard Rheingold lived up to his genial reputation. And my parents were very kind over Christmas 1999, as I wrote my chapters.

Many thanks to Lesley Riddle, Emma Heyworth-Dunn and Wendy Rooke of Arnold for their help, enthusiasm and support during the production of this book, and also to the copy-editor, Lynn Brown.

Finally, and rather obviously, a big thank you to all of the contributors, for being so helpful – and prompt – and for turning in such diverse, creative and useful chapters.

David Gauntlett
June 2000

Picture credits

Every effort has been made to gain permission for the reproduction of images. Owners of uncredited copyright material reproduced here are invited to contact the publisher to receive appropriate credit in future editions.

David Gauntlett produced, and holds copyright in, the following images: *Powercut* magazine, the *New Media Studies* website, the *Theory.org.uk* website (Chapter 1), a shark eating the Web (Chapter 12), a capitalist (Chapter 13), Web-related graffiti in Leeds (Chapter 18) and tiny devices of the future (Chapter 24). Reproduced by kind permission.

Chapter 3 – The image of Netscan output is reproduced by kind permission of Marc Smith (http://netscan.research.microsoft.com). The image of Loom output is reproduced by kind permission of Judith Donath.

Chapter 4 – Images from Spacegirl's website are reproduced by kind permission of Angela Martini (www.spacegirl.org).

Chapter 5 – Images from the *Xena: Warrior Princess* website are TM & Copyright © 2000, Studios USA LLC.

Chapter 6 – Images of the websites discussed in this chapter are reproduced by kind permission of the respective artists.

Chapter 7 – Images from the Jennicam website are reproduced by kind permission of Jennifer Kaye Ringley (www.jennicam.org). Images from the Anacam website are reproduced by kind permission of Ana Voog (www.anacam.com).

Chapter 9 – Samples from the websites of the movies *Bringing out the Dead* and *Sleepy Hollow*, TM & Copyright © 2000 by Paramount Pictures. A page from *The Internet Movie Database* is reproduced by kind permission (www.imdb.com).

Chapter 14 – Samples from *Club Virtual* (www.clubvirtual.com), © Internet Supply, Inc. 1999–2000.

Chapter 16 – Samples from BBC Online, TM & Copyright © 2000, British Broadcasting Corporation.

Chapter 24 – The picture of a 'Dustbin Dalek' is reproduced by kind permission of Nathan A. Skreslet (http://members.xoom.com/Skreslet).

Further resources on new media can be found at David Gauntlett's web site:

Part I

WEB STUDIES

1

Web Studies:
A User's Guide

David Gauntlett

Let me tell you a secret: in 1995, two years after the Mosaic browser had grabbed the attention of the world and made the Web an interesting place to hang out, I hated all the hype about the internet. Bloody internet: full of computer geeks swapping episode guides to TV shows. We laughed about the guy down the corridor who spent hours every day wandering around the net. We said that it was like wandering around an amateur library, gazing admiringly at the shelves, but with no idea where to find anything useful. Which, as far as I could tell, it was.

I was interested in popular mass media and the way they might change people's lives. Therefore, I thought, the internet was of little interest. Of course, I was wrong. Even whilst I was scowling about it, the Web was careering out of the hands of computer scientists and becoming, well, a form of popular mass media that might change people's lives.

Within three years it became impossible to think about life without the Web. By 1999 I was producing the websites www.theory.org.uk and www.newmediastudies.com, and was sending and receiving e-mails all over the world every day. This was nothing special – just the new face of academic life. Academic journals and conferences, which had always veered towards the tedious, were now quite clearly preposterous anachronisms. Why let an article go out of date by two years waiting for a journal to publish it? Put it on the Web today. Why fly thousands of miles only to hang around with lots of middle-aged, unhappy academics? Instead, chat with them within the welcome confines of e-mail, and then do the international travel to explore other cultures.

This book, for example, came together entirely on the internet. I have never spoken to most of the contributors, nor written to them by conventional mail. But we've exchanged a lot of e-mails. I invited some people to write chapters because I'd seen their work on the Web, or in books. (Books are still good.) A couple of contributors were part of the community that had developed around my websites and ones related to them. I also put out a call for contributions, once, on just one e-mail discussion list, and the net's grapevine effect meant that

www.NewMediaStudies.com
Web culture, design and reviews a go-go

New | Reviews | Resources | Guide | Art | Debates
Effects | Design | Marketing | Rubbish | Statistics
The book | About | Dave | Feedback | Theory

Developed at the Institute of Communications Studies, University of Leeds

1.1 *New Media Studies*, home of useful Web things.

I received 140 proposals for chapters – mostly from academics and postgraduate students – within a month. Obviously, I had to reject most of them. Once commissioned, the chapters were sent and discussed by e-mail. I checked facts and dates on reliable websites, and gave away bits of the forthcoming book at newmediastudies.com in a bid to raise interest. Of course, the good thing about the Web is that it's not just full of academics. It's the *diversity* of creative participation that keeps it alive.

Media studies was nearly dead: long live new media studies

By the end of the twentieth century, media studies research within developed western societies had entered a middle-aged, stodgy period and wasn't really sure what it could say about things any more. Thank goodness the Web came along. See where media studies had got to . . .

☞ Studies of media texts, such as a 'critical reading' of a film which identified a bunch of 'meanings' the director hadn't intended and which nobody else had noticed, were clearly a waste of time.

☞ Similarly, people had noticed that semiotic analysis and psychoanalytic approaches were all about saying that something had a hidden cause or meaning, but you couldn't prove it, so it became embarrassing.

☞ Audience studies had run out of steam. Unable to show that the media had a clear and identifiable impact upon people's behaviour, audience researchers had been trying to make some descriptions of how people *use* the media look interesting, with little success.

☞ The 1990s theoretical view that we had to consider media usage within the very broad context of everyday life had actually ruptured the impetus for research, since nobody could afford, or be bothered, to do such wide-scale, in-depth, qualitative research. And even if anyone did get all that data, it wasn't clear what they would have to do with it.

☞ Studies of media effects and influences had shown that the mass media do not have predictable effects on audiences. Nevertheless, the right-wing psychologists who argued (for reasons best known to themselves) that the mass media were responsible for the decline of western civilization seemed to be winning the argument (within the public sphere, anyway). Cue despair, resignation and boredom amongst researchers in this area.

☞ Historical studies of the mass media justified themselves by saying that we could learn from history when planning the future. But nobody ever did.

☞ Most importantly, media products and the organized use of communications technologies had become so knowing, clever and sophisticated that academic critics were looking increasingly redundant. In other words, media products, and their producers, had themselves become self-analysing and multi-layered. It is difficult to say something about Tony Blair's clever use of political communications, for example, which is *more* clever, as a theory, than the actual practice. To make an intelligent film like *The Matrix* (Wachowski Brothers, 1999) or *Fight Club* (Fincher, 1999) is a substantial achievement, whereas writing a typical academic article about it is, in comparison, pathetic. Even mainstream TV shows like *Who Wants to be a Millionaire* (a UK format sold to numerous other countries) were already, in themselves, super-analysed dissections of the style and culture of populist TV. All academics could do was write obvious explanations of what the producers were up to (boring and ultimately sycophantic), or make predictable critiques of what such shows tell us about capitalist or postmodern society (which you could do in your sleep).

Media studies, then, needed something interesting to do, and fast. Happily, the area of new media is vibrant, exploding and developing, and nobody is certain of the best way to do things. There is change (look at how the Web was just three years ago) and there is conflict (look at the Microsoft trial and the impassioned feelings it provoked). New good ideas and new bad ideas appear every week, and we don't know how it's going to pan out. Even better, academics and students can *participate* in the new media explosion, not just watch from the sidelines – and we can argue that they have a responsibility to do so. So it's an exciting time again.

First, though, we'd better rewind to the basics.

Origins of the Web

This is the internet

The internet is a global network of interconnected computers. Rumours that it started life as a sinister US military experiment may be somewhat exaggerated, although a computer network called ARPANET run by the US Defense Department from 1969 was a primary component of the super-network which would eventually become the internet, and the US Government was definitely interested in a network that could withstand nuclear attack. In fact the first talk about an internet can be traced back to 1962, when J.C.R. Licklider of MIT wrote a number of memos about his idea of a 'Galactic Network' linking computers worldwide (see www.isoc.org/internet/history/brief.html).

The first event in the life of the internet as we know it today came in 1974, when Vint Cerf and Bob Khan defined the Transmission Control Protocol (TCP) and Internet Protocol (IP) by which information could be put into a 'packet' and addressed so that computers on the network would pass it along, in the right direction, until it arrived at its destination. Various tests and demonstrations were conducted successfully, and internet-style networks started to take off, but it was 10 years before the TCP/IP-based internet rolled out across the USA in 1983. And then it would primarily remain the domain of academics and scientists for another 10 years.

So what is the World Wide Web?

The World Wide Web is a user-friendly interface on to the internet. It was developed by Tim Berners-Lee (www.w3.org/People/Berners-Lee) in 1990–91, and caught on in 1993, when a freely available Web browser called Mosaic, written by Marc Andreessen and Eric Bina, started the 'Web revolution'. (Mosaic went on to become Netscape Navigator, and Andreessen went on to become very rich.) Berners-Lee is sometimes mistakenly credited with inventing the internet. But his actual achievement was perhaps more socially significant: he recognized that the internet was 'too much of a hassle for a noncomputer expert' (Berners-Lee, 1999: 20), and created an elegant solution.

Berners-Lee's idea was to create a set of agreed protocols and standards so that documents could be stored on Web servers anywhere in the world, but could be brought up on a computer screen by anyone who wanted them, using a simple address. Central to Berners-Lee's dream was the use of hyperlinks, so that Web pages would be full of highlighted words or phrases, which would be links to other relevant pages elsewhere. (Today, many websites only link up their own 'internal' pages, with 'external' links offered on a separate 'links page', if at all. Berners-Lee had really wanted everyone to be much more liberal in their inter-linking across these boundaries.)

Also at the core of the idea of the World Wide Web was *collaboration* – Berners-Lee wanted Web users to be involved in a two-way process, not only reading Web pages, but also adding to and amending them, creating links, and, of course, creating new pages. The Web's creator did not expect Web browsing to be a one-way experience, but the browser software which became popular, from Mosaic onwards, would only read and present Web pages, not alter them. The World Wide Web Consortium, the advisory body Berners-Lee established and still directs, has developed its own browser/editor, Amaya, which will both read and edit Web pages. But it hasn't really caught on. (See the Consortium's website, www.w3.org, for the latest, and Berners-Lee's book, *Weaving the Web*, 1999, for the story of the Web's development.)

Summarizing his 'vision' of what the Web should be about, Tim Berners-Lee says:

> The dream behind the Web is of a common information space in which we communicate by sharing information. Its universality is essential: the fact that a hypertext link can point to anything, be it personal, local or global, be it draft or highly polished. There was a second part of the dream, too, dependent on the Web being so generally used that it became a realistic mirror (or in fact the primary embodiment) of the ways in which we work and play and socialize. That was that once the state of our interactions was on line, we could then use computers to help us analyse it, make sense of what we are doing, where we individually fit in, and how we can better work together.
>
> (From 'The World Wide Web: A very short personal history' at www.w3.org/People/Berners-Lee)

Why the Web isn't the same thing as the internet

To clarify: the Web is something that runs on the internet. It is the popular face of the internet. It is not, however, the *same* as the internet. The internet is the network of networked computers. Since it is basically all cables, wires and micro-processors, the internet can carry any kind of data, such as e-mail, and computer programs. The Web, however, is made up of a particular type of (easy to use, universally readable) data. At its heart is Hypertext Markup Language, HTML, a simple computer language which can be used to create Web pages which include links, graphics, and multimedia components. (Watch out, however, for its advanced sibling, XML, lumbering on to the scene around now.) Even more central is HTTP, the protocol which tells Web browsers where to find Web pages and their components. All this clever stuff runs *over* the internet.

Basic Web geography

The Web, of course, has no central point, no capital city. But most people find their way around by starting with Yahoo! (www.yahoo.com), a massive Web directory compiled by humans, or one of the search engines, such as AltaVista (www.altavista.com) or Google (www.google.com). Other options are offered by those sites that interrogate several search engines at once, such as Ask Jeeves (www.askjeeves.com) or Metacrawler (www.metacrawler.com).

A bit of thought is required to work out which kind of search facility will give you the kind of information you need. If you want a whole, permanent website about a certain topic, turn to a directory like Yahoo! If you are looking for any page that contains a particular name or phrase, use a search engine like AltaVista.

Once you have found a website on a certain topic, it should offer you links to other relevant sites. Some creators of websites can't bear the thought of you going elsewhere, however, so this doesn't always happen. In which case you just have to search harder. This is how everyone finds their way around the Web. Apart from perfecting your use of search phrases – so that you can find that site about the Dust Brothers without sifting through pages of people who are merely dusty or related – there are no other secrets to learn.

Today's Web, not yesterday's net

While the developed world quickly adopted the World Wide Web as its internet medium of choice, many internet scholars tried to ignore it because they had found a niche for themselves making repetitive arguments about 'Multi-User Dungeons' (MUDs) and other text-based interactive areas, in the early 1990s, and refused to move on. One of the aims of this book is to shift forwards scholarly discussion about the internet, so that it fully considers the multi-faceted and popular Web, instead of contenting itself with publishing yet another article about how no one knows who you are in cyberspace. (Which is an interesting, if rather obvious, point – but how many books do we need to tell us this?) I am talking here about the books aimed at students and academics about 'cyberculture' or 'internet culture' or 'virtual society'; some popular and business books have been more on the ball, whilst several of the more sophisticated internet magazines – available from your local newsagent – seem to publish articles with more depth and insight every month. To be fair, we should note that alongside the half-baked and slightly out-of-date pieces on identity in cyberspace, academics have also produced numerous half-baked and slightly out-of-date pieces on how the internet is going to transform democracy, politics, relationships and other stuff.

Anyway, the internet scholars who aren't very interested in the Web have more recently found a new excuse to ignore it: 'the Web has been taken over by big business'. It is certainly true that the percentage of corporate websites, and Web traffic going to them, has massively increased since the mid-1990s and the turn of the century. However, since the number of websites has also shot up exponentially, this doesn't mean that fewer people are using the Web for interesting non-business purposes – quite the opposite, in fact. More on this later.

First of all let's consider the interface between Web creativity and real-world money. There's no escaping it.

The Web and money

The news is full of stories about people getting rich from the internet. This sometimes confuses news viewers and internet users – how do people make money by giving information away free on the Web? And how have people become rich from their loss-making e-commerce websites?

How people become millionaires by making free websites

David Filo and Jerry Yang, who created the Web directory Yahoo!, for example, became millionaires (see 'company info' at www.yahoo.com). But you may wonder how one becomes a millionaire by providing a useful free service on the Web. In fact, there are now many people who have become millionaires by devising websites people want to visit. Their money-making secret is quite simple: advertising and sponsorship. It's just the same as with commercial TV: you don't pay to watch the programmes. The programmes are paid for by advertisers, who, in return, get to display their ads to audiences alongside the shows.

In the same way, you get to access Web services, such as the Yahoo! directory, for free. The only 'price' you pay is being exposed to some modestly sized but inescapable adverts. Yahoo! is in a great position to scoop up advertising revenues, because it can 'deliver' adverts to people who are actually interested in particular things. For example, the kind of people who search for information about cats in Yahoo! are exactly the people that cat food manufacturers want to address. People looking for Web pages about chocolate will be subjected to mouth-watering chocolate ads . . . and so on. Since Yahoo! lists everything under the sun, that's a lot of targeted advertising space to sell.

Numerous other Web services, such as free e-mail and free Web space, are paid for in the same way. The user is pleased to get these handy services for no money, the advertiser is pleased to be able to flash its messages at the user (and, in the case of free Web space, that user's website visitors), and the service provider is pleased to take money from the advertiser.

Not all of these services are actually making a profit at the moment, though. And in fact, Yang and Filo's millions haven't actually arrived as payment from advertisers. Their high value is a stock market value – the same kind of value enjoyed by the many Web businesses that haven't even turned a profit yet.

How people have become millionaires with loss-making Web businesses

Investors value Web companies based on an expectation of how powerful they think those companies will be in the future. So, for example, in the late 1990s the well-known internet bookshop Amazon.com had not yet made a profit, but shares in the company had a very high value, because it was widely expected that the company's leading position in the ever-expanding world of e-commerce would bring in huge profits . . . sometime quite soon.

Similarly, any website that is well known and visited by millions of people – such as Yahoo!, or any popular Web service – has a high value simply because that's a lot of eyeballs to sell to advertisers, and everyone expects that as the Web is always increasing in popularity, that will mean even more eyeballs in future.

A particularly good way to become a millionaire is to start a small but innovative Web company, and get it noticed. (You may need to get some people to invest in it at the start for this to happen on a sufficient scale.) Then sell it to one of the big conglomerates for loads of money. This happens all the time. In a broader sense, it is a shame because all of the little internet companies get swallowed up by the same old big companies. But if you're a millionaire you most likely won't be worrying about that.

Why people won't pay to access a Web page

In the earlier days of the Web, it was thought that the providers of online content would be able to charge users directly. Some newspapers, for example, started to put their content on the Web for free, but this was so that they could build an audience, and then start to charge an annual fee for site access. However, the latter part of this plan never became possible. Since there was so much useful information available on the Web for free, it was discovered that no one wanted to pay for it.

A few sites offering specialist information, such as stock market 'insider' news or unique reports of interest to businesses or professional people, have been able to charge for access to their websites (see Schwartz, 1999). But the only other websites that have successfully charged for access, and perhaps the *only* sites to have made big business out of it, are pornography sites. They make substantial profits by charging subscription fees for access to their content. Unlike everyday news or poetry, porn is something people are willing to pay for (see di Filippo's chapter in this book). In addition, porn merchants can say that they are helpfully protecting children from their content by requiring visitors to give their credit card numbers. They're not stupid, although they may hope that *you* are.

Other examples of paid-for content are rare. The *Encyclopaedia Britannica* used to charge US$5 (£3) per month for full online access. But since October 1999 the famous encyclopaedia, which until recently came in the form of a mountain of books (current cost: US$1,250), has been available for free on the Web. In a move which must have made some Britannica managers feel quite ill, all 44 million words are now free. Advertising, sponsorship and e-commerce will be the new ways in which Britannica pays her rent – in line with most other Web services.

How businesses hope to scrape back some cash

Some internet content providers are pinning their hopes on the idea of 'micropayments', which means they want to devise a system which will be able to charge you small amounts for bits of content. It's based on the idea that, whilst nobody wants to have to type in their credit card number just to look at some bit of information, most people wouldn't mind spending a few cents or pence to read an article or listen to a pop song. What the businesses want to develop is an extremely easy system for charging small amounts. This might fail though – people are already used to getting their information for free.

Giving it away free

Internet businesses, then, have discovered that giving things away for free – not promotional balloons, but whole products – can actually lead to riches. Netscape, for example, built up a huge user base for its Web browser by giving it away. In

1994, it was a small start-up company that you would expect would want to sell its milestone product. But by giving it away free over the internet, it got its software on to millions of computers. That brought power and fame, enabled the company to sell other products (such as Web server software) from a prominent position, and gave it a huge stock market value in less than a year.

Later, once Netscape had started charging non-educational users for its browser, Microsoft demolished Netscape's domination by giving its own new browser away free to everyone. (Big business wasn't used to this idea: according to one book about Microsoft, when someone suggested to Bill Gates that his company should give away its Internet Explorer browser, he exploded and called the man a 'communist' (Wallace, 1997: 266).) Lots of other success has followed people giving stuff away.

The attention economy: quality content wins?

Michael Goldhaber (1997) argues that what we have on the internet is an 'attention economy'. The scarce resource which everybody with a presence on the Web is struggling for is *attention*. On the internet, money is not the most important scarce resource, for reasons we will turn to in a moment. And information certainly isn't a scarce resource – the Web contains oceans of it. The Web's scarce resource is attention, because there is so much information out there, and everyone has so little time to look at it. To triumph on the Web is to have lots of people giving attention to your site, instead of giving it to someone else's. Attention is what everyone wants. So it's an *attention economy*.

Big companies don't automatically get attention on the Web simply because they have a lot of money. Having money can enable a company to make a diverting multimedia website, and generate awareness of it through conventional media and promotions, but if the website has no engaging content it will not win attention. Meanwhile, individuals and small groups are relatively empowered in this medium, because if they produce a website deserving of attention then, hopefully and ideally, word will spread around the internet and lots of people's attention will be drawn to that site.

A commercial website, set up to promote a chocolate bar or a book publishing company, say, has the great advantage that it can promote its website address on all of its adverts and all of its products. A non-commercial website does not usually have such an opportunity, and so is at a disadvantage. (The publishing company is also in a good position because it can give away bits of its product directly, on its website, as a 'taster' for the full product, whereas the chocolate manufacturer usually has to settle for offering news, games and quizzes associated with the product.)

However, if the commercial website does not have any interesting content, other websites will not link to it, it will not be talked about in e-mail discussions or on newsgroups, and will only ever be visited by curious individuals (and the company's employees, partners or competitors) who have seen the address advertised and who visit the site – once.

Meanwhile, any website which is full of appealing and regularly updated content has a better chance of getting attention. This is something that has to be worked on – usually by sending lots of personal e-mails to potentially interested, and ideally influential, people. The whole thing takes effort, but not a lot of money. By getting linked to and from other websites, and listed in directories, search engines and magazines, a website can come to command a lot of attention. And without attention, on the Web, you're nothing.

Goldhaber says: 'Money flows to attention, and much less well does attention flow to money.' In other words, you can't buy attention. You can pay someone to listen to you, but you can't make them *interested* in what you have to say, unless they actually find the content of what you have to say engaging. So money is less powerful than usual on the Web.

But if you can gather a lot of attention, you can then, potentially, translate it into money. Look at the following examples:

☞ Netscape, as we have seen, got lots of attention by giving away its Web browser, and then was able to capitalize on its swiftly established position as the best-known brand on the Web. Trying to sell the browser didn't work, but companies were keen to buy Netscape Web server software because Netscape had become synonymous with the Web in the mid-1990s. In November 1998, America Online (AOL) bought Netscape for US$4.2 billion.

☞ Vincent Flanders set up a website called WebPagesThatSuck.com, grabbing loads of attention from all those people struggling to design nice websites. Through website links, e-mails, newsgroups and ordinary conversation, word spread quickly about this witty site where you could 'learn good design by looking at bad design'. People gave it so much attention that Flanders could make money from selling advertising space on his site, and by turning it into a best-selling book, and by charging companies money just to hear him speak.

☞ Linus Torvalds invented Linux, a reliable operating system for computers – an alternative to Microsoft's dominant Windows environment – which is distributed free over the internet. Its 'open source' software, which means that anyone can use, amend and improve the code, is becoming increasingly popular: Bill Gates says he's not feeling threatened by it, but commentators say that shows what a big threat it is. Torvalds wouldn't make any money directly from Linux, then, but he has such a stock of attention that translating it into money (by offering his consultancy services, say) would be easy, if he wanted to. But Torvalds doesn't seem to be motivated by money.

All of the above examples are about people who start off with attention-grabbing content, but no money. Money flows to attention. Meanwhile, there are many examples of companies who have thought that their money would translate, on the Web, into attention and success. But they made boring websites, and failed. Attention doesn't just flow to money.

Doesn't money provide a considerable advantage?

There is, of course, a problem with this optimistic view. It is all very well to say that anybody can make a great website and become an online and offline success, but having money certainly helps. It remains the case that if a company has money to spend, it can pay talented people to create an attention-grabbing website, full of useful, frequently updated content. And at the same time, the company can advertise its site in the mainstream mass media, and on its own products and packaging. Therefore, money provides a considerable advantage.

Nevertheless, it remains the case that any websites with interesting content can become well known around the Web, and be linked to a lot, and talked about, and therefore grab a lot of attention. Because internet content is the broadest of fields – it can be about anything – there will not be corporate 'competition' in

1.2 Web success *The Onion*, the disturbingly funny news spoof.

all areas. For example, you wouldn't want to set up another news site, or search engine, or internet bookshop, because these areas are already dominated by professional, well-resourced organizations. But you could set up a website about, say, the art of creative writing, and it might become very popular – because lots of people around the world are struggling to write their first novel. Since it's not the most obviously commercial idea, you probably wouldn't have to worry too much about Microsoft trying to capture all of the online-advice-about-creative-writing market (though you never know).

To take a real-life example, Harry Knowles – an ordinary, hairy, twentysomething guy from Austin, Texas – has received much attention with his *Ain't It Cool News* (www.aint-it-cool-news.com), a website providing daily Hollywood gossip and movie previews from a network of 'spies' (industry insiders and people who infiltrate test screenings). Knowles identified a niche where there is a great appetite for information amongst the public, but where mainstream film magazines and websites would be too cautious, and too slow, to tread. Knowles is now very well known and much in demand. Similarly, *The Onion* (www.theonion.com) was a brilliant but little-known satirical weekly newspaper run by a group of reasonably penniless ex-students from the University of Wisconsin. But then it went on the Web and became a massive international success (see http://mediakit.theonion.com).

Why people say big business has killed the Web

The business end of the Web can provide some spectacular news stories, with multi-million dollar battles, deals and stock floatations. Tim Berners-Lee may have thought that the Web would foster co-operation and understanding, but brash new e-commerce ventures are all anybody seems to talk about regarding the internet these days.

Nevertheless, the part of the Web which is concerned with sharing ideas and information is still there, and indeed is getting bigger along with everything else in cyberspace. So maybe it is more helpful to think of the Web now having different spheres, existing alongside each other, but used for different things.

For example, let's say your town has an excellent public library which you enjoy using. One day a company opens a large supermarket next to the library. The library continues to be good and well stocked, and indeed picks up more users from the influx of supermarket customers. Now, if your friend said, 'I see the supermarket has destroyed the library', you would think they were a bit of an idiot.

In the same way, the commercial and non-commercial parts of the internet ought to be able to exist side by side. The problem, alas, is that in this town, we would probably see marketing people from the supermarket sneaking into the library, taking down the community notices in the foyer, and replacing them with adverts. They would also interfere with the library catalogue, so that it told library users that the answers to their questions would be found in the super-market. Such forces obviously need to be kept in check.

Is money dead?

Goldhaber argues that, in the future, money will become unimportant, and that attention will be the new wealth. But since money shows little sign of extinction at the moment, perhaps it's a better use of the basic argument to say that atten-tion certainly does equal wealth in the new economy, but that's because you can always translate it into good old-fashioned money, which everyone still thinks is pretty handy stuff.

An outline of this book

The first, introductory part of this book consists of three chapters: this introduc-tion, an overview of the development of cyberculture studies during the last 10 years and an outline of methodologies for studying the Web. This is followed by the first themed section, 'Web Life, Arts and Culture', which looks at a range of creative uses of the Web by everyday people, creating new cultures and interacting with existing ones. We consider personal homepages and websites by fans, artists and webcam owners, as well as use of the internet by gay, lesbian and bisexual people, by students writing 'reviews' of their tutors and by movie-goers. The next section, 'Web Business', looks at the ways in which commercial interests have affected – and continue to influence – the development of the Web. We focus in particular on search engines and portal sites, Web pornography, how *fascination* entices audiences, and how the BBC – a major public-service TV broadcaster with commercial aspirations – adapted to the challenge of the Web. The final themed section, 'Global Web Communities, Politics and Protest', is about people coming together, for political or social reasons, on the net, and the ways in which the Web might change those polit-ical relationships and processes. We look at communities built around political inter-ests, women's activist groups, ethnic identities and certain websites. We also see how the internet is used in contemporary warfare, and study the political, criminal and social activities of hackers. Finally, the last chapter takes a brief look at some possible futures of the internet and 'wired society'.

Some of the main issues

This section outlines some of the main issues in Web studies. These are key themes which will recur in other chapters throughout the book.

The Web allows people to express themselves

The Web offers people an opportunity to produce creative, expressive media products (or texts, or art works, if you prefer) and display them to a global audience. Without question, this is a new and significant development. We may be able to produce a painting, or a poem, or an amateur 'magazine', but without the Web, most of us would not have the opportunity or resources to find an audience for our work. We could force our family and friends to admire our masterpiece, but that would be about it.

When I was at school, I made a 'magazine' for a (hopeless) musical 'group' that I was in. My materials were biro and paper. I was aged 12 and photocopiers weren't very accessible, so the single edition of each issue had to be passed around between members of its audience – approximately four people.

1.3 *Powercut* magazine: futuristic self-expression from the paper and ink days.

When I was a student, I published a fanzine (or 'small press magazine') with an anti-sexist theme, *Powercut*, which was reproduced by a professional printer (in exchange for a significant chunk of my humble student finances). Producing and printing the thing was the easy part: it was the *distribution* that would eat up my life. I spent hundreds of hours visiting and writing to bookshops, and getting magazines and newspapers to write about it – with ordering details – so that I could spend yet more hours responding to mail-order requests. I published two issues and, for each one, it took me a year to shift 800 copies. This was regarded as a considerable success in small press circles.

Today, like many people, I can write a review or article, stick it on the Web, then sit back and relax in the knowledge that 800 people will have read it – well, *seen* it – within a couple of days. I largely enjoyed the *Powercut* experience, back in 1991–93, but think how much simpler my life would have been – and how much more of a life I would have had! – if Tim Berners-Lee had bothered to invent the World Wide Web just a few years earlier than he did.

A website can be your own magazine and gallery. Anything that can be put into words or pictures – or animation, video or music – can be put there. Nobody can tell me this isn't fantastic.

The only potential flaw to this glorious revolution is: what if nobody visits your site? Frankly, this isn't a very powerful argument. If you put some effort into the site content, and then put a bit more effort into establishing links with other sites, and getting it covered by search engines and directories, then there are sufficient millions of Web users out there that some of them will come and visit. The Web, then, offers a fantastic explosion of opportunity for creativity and expression. Less than a decade ago, almost all readily accessible media was made by a small bunch of companies (and the lucky people who had got jobs with them). Now look at it.

The Web brings people together, building communities

Since Howard Rheingold published *The Virtual Community* in 1993, much has been written about communities on the internet. The basic point is simple enough: before the internet, communities were people who lived or worked close to each other. If you were lucky, you might have a community of *like-minded people*, although it was unlikely that you would get a very compatible bunch all in the same place. The global internet transforms this – for those, as always, who have access to it – because it enables like-minded people to form communities regardless of where they are located in the physical world. Before the internet, scientists working in a particular field might have little contact with each other, and needed to organize expensive conferences in order to have a meeting of minds. Meanwhile, fans of obscure bands would have little to do with their counterparts elsewhere, and people interested in certain hobbies, or artists, or skills, could only feed their interest through one-way communication processes such as reading a magazine or newsletter about it.

Again, the internet changed all that. Now, regardless of where they are in the world, people with similar interests, or with similar backgrounds, or with similar attitudes, can join communities of like-minded people, share views, exchange information and build relationships.

In practice, what these communities look like are people sending electronic text to each other. Most of the studies of virtual communities are about groups exchanging messages on newsgroups and e-mail discussion lists, or groups who often meet in the same chatrooms. The studies seem, so far, to have ignored the communities that develop amongst similarly themed websites and their creators, which in many ways may be stronger and more permanent. Participants in chattering groups may come and go, whereas the bonds of friendship and interdependence which the Web, by its interconnected nature, breeds amongst website creators – expressed in public links and personal e-mails – may be more compelling.

The more websites there are, the more complex these community webs may be. Some of us are quite moralistic about use of the Web, and feel that you must *contribute*, and not merely 'surf'. Everyone who uses the Web should, ideally, have a website, where they endeavour to put some stuff that may be of interest to someone else. It is difficult to take seriously, for example, internet scholars who don't even have their own website. You might say that we don't expect film critics to have their own movie studio, but this is rather different – making a website requires some effort, but not much in terms of material resources.

Whilst the net's global friendship-building is valuable, there is, as usual, a downside. As with any open-access communications medium, the Web can be used in ways we may find distasteful. If the internet can foster communities of like-minded artists and poets, it can also give a home to groups of like-minded Nazis and child molesters. Many countries already have laws to deal with the real-world actions of such people, but we can't stop them talking to each other. It is important not to confuse the medium with the message: newspaper stories still appear which seek to show how evil the internet is because unsavoury characters communicate using it. But when unpleasant people appear on TV, or make use of the telephone, we don't normally blame the box of electronics. We can hope that the opportunities for education and creativity the Web offers will lead to a kind of human society which can find ways to get along without causing harm to others. That's the optimistic view, obviously.

Anonymity and identity play in cyberspace

Since the early days of the internet there have been bulletin boards and 'chat' spaces where users can interact online and, today, many websites include chat or discussion rooms where visitors can interact in real time. Since participants cannot see each other, and are not obliged to reveal their real name or physical location, there is considerable scope for people to reveal secrets, discuss problems, or even enact whole 'identities' which they would never do in the real world, not even with their closest friends – in some cases, *especially* not with their closest friends. These secrets or identities may, of course, be 'real', or might be completely made up. In cyberspace, as the saying goes, no one can tell if you're talking complete garbage.

Some aspects of this 'identity play' can be annoying, such as the sad middle-aged man who pretends to be a movie star in the hope of attracting the online attention of a young woman (who, in the real world, may be another sad middle-aged man). Other aspects can be criminal – paedophiles have been known to present themselves as friendly children online, so that they can arrange meetings with (what they hope are) other children. Sometimes, they might find that they have unintentionally arranged a meeting with another paedophile; sometimes it can turn out to be a police officer. (Some police services employ staff to wander around chatrooms pretending to be children to see if anyone asks to meet them.)

Some internet chat stories are more heart-warming: men and women who have thought they may be gay, but have been afraid to come out in the 'real world', have 'tested' this identity online. They have been so happy to be able to express their 'true' selves – and to receive such a supportive (and perhaps erotic) response – that this has given them the courage to come out in their everyday real-world lives as well.

And, of course, people of all sexual orientations have used the internet for 'cybersex', which involves people telling each other what they are doing to each other (within their shared cyber-imagination) as they fumble their way towards sexual satisfaction. More recently, webcams have allowed participants to see each other; but they might not want to – that might not be the point.

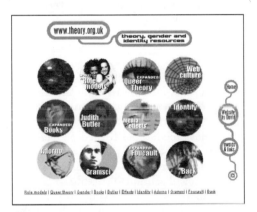

1.4 Queer theory and other resources at www.theory.org.uk.

The internet's scope for anonymous interaction, and therefore identity play, is significant for the way in which it fits in with contemporary queer theory. Queer theory suggests that people do not have a fixed 'essence', and that identity is a performance (Butler, 1990a; www.theory.org.uk/queer). We may be so used to inhabiting one 'identity' that it seems to be 'natural' to us, but it's a kind of performance none the less. Because the internet breaks the connection between outward expressions of identity and the physical body which (in the real world) makes those expressions, it can be seen as a space where queer theory's approach to identity can really come to life.

Having said that, there is not really any excuse for the large number of very similar, tedious and repetitive academic articles that basically all say 'cyberspace . . . you can play with identity . . . nobody knows who you really are . . . gosh . . .', but fail to develop any theoretical insights beyond this once-engaging thought.

Furthermore, these chat-type interactions aren't the primary use of the internet these days anyway. Attention should be turning more, I feel, towards studying expressions of identity, and community developments, within and between people's websites.

The Web and big business

The Web has created a wealth of new business opportunities, some of which we have discussed above. Recent years have also seen existing businesses racing to establish an internet presence. The chief executives' fear that their companies may die if they aren't on the internet is well founded. Of course, if they do not plan carefully how to do their business using the Web, and simply rush into doing anything that looks impressive to a board of directors, there are still broad opportunities for failure.

Alongside the fears of the internet's potential being scuppered by heavy-handed interventions by the big businesses who would like to use the Web as a big marketing fair, there is another type of corporate threat to the good health of the Web – single, powerful software companies who might try to make the whole Web into something that works best with its own products. Microsoft's domination of the field in the 1990s led to a lengthy court battle with the US Department of Justice, culminating in the order, in June 2000, that the software giant should be broken in two. But Microsoft thinks it will escape, on appeal, from even this major blow.

The Web is changing politics and international relations

The internet, as many people have noted already, had the potential to create links between people and groups with shared political interests – and for them to promote their ideas to others. By increasing access to information – or propaganda – the internet may bring about a greater engagement and interaction between the individual and larger political processes.

The public sphere

In an argument related to the idea of virtual communities, discussed above, internet scholars often relate the net to the idea of the 'public sphere', as developed by Jurgen Habermas (see, for example, Habermas, 1989). In an ideal public sphere, citizens would discuss issues of concern and arrive at a consensus for the common good. Habermas did not feel that we have an effective public sphere in western societies, partly because commercial mass media had turned people into *consumers* of information and entertainment, rather than *participants* in an interactive democratic process. Now: you can see where this is heading. In the 1990s, internet enthusiasts noted the kinds of discussions taking place in newsgroups (text discussion forums), and argued that, when even more people had access, the net would bring about a healthy public sphere. (Even recent books like Wise (2000) point to newsgroups as evidence of promising public sphere debate, although he seems to have reservations.)

The shortcomings of this view are equally obvious. Increasing numbers of people *do* have internet access, but most of them are roaming the Web these days and, of course, the popular internet technologies and interfaces are liable to change again. But one thing seems certain: intense discussion spaces, like newsgroups, will remain the province of the minorities of individuals who are so interested in a particular area that they want to spend their time debating specific issues. Most people won't bother.

Not as dead as it looks

This conclusion, for those internet academics who have been paying enough attention to reach it, led to the feeling that, damn, the internet won't help to foster a healthy public sphere after all. But that may not be true either. If we look carefully at the interactions between and around the thousands of websites which can be called 'political' in the broadest of senses, we do find cultures of engagement and discussion. The fact that people who are concerned about an issue can create a website about it, and then find themselves in e-mail conversations (or, in the future, perhaps in different forms of electronic conference) with people who are interested, curious or opposed to their views, or who run related sites, *does* create a climate of greater public discussion. Compare it to the days when all you could do was read about an issue in a mass-produced newspaper, and then discuss it with a handful of friends in a pub. This Web-based political culture is not, of course, the same as a democratic online meeting where every member of society chips in with their view, but that was never going to happen anyway (how do several million people chat about an issue at once? The only workable method would be . . . voting). As always, there is also the problem that only interested people participate, which will always be the case. We can hope that the greater engagement with political issues which the Web can bring will mean that more people become interested in politics generally, but this is far from guaranteed.

How to succeed in Web studies

Make your own

Unless you want to be a very detached critic who argues that all new media developments are really bad and that we're all doomed, in which case you won't really need to understand the Web very well anyway, then you'll need to experience the agony and ecstasy of building and promoting your own website.

You'll find instructions on how to do this in numerous books and magazines, and, of course, on various websites. The design and marketing guides at www.newmediastudies.com should get you started. In the print world, cheap books are often as good as expensive ones; for example, the very good *Simple Guide to Creating Your Own Web Page* (Dreyfus, 2000) costs £6.99 in the UK. The best book on Web design – and I've seen a lot of them – is definitely *Web Pages That Suck* (Flanders and Willis, 1998), the book based on the website mentioned earlier, which unfortunately costs £30 (US$39) and comes with a CD that's not as useful as the ones you get free with internet magazines every month. Nevertheless, it's easy to read, full of valuable advice, and the authors' idea that you can 'learn good design by looking at bad design' is both instructive and enjoyable.

To make a website really quickly, visit Yahoo! GeoCities (www.geocities.com) or Lycos Tripod (www.tripod.com), where they not only give you webspace for free, but have clever page-building facilities where you construct and publish your Web page(s) on the spot, within the website, with no extra software required (apart from the recent Web browser you need to use the site). To make a really good website, though, you'll need Web design software (Netscape Composer is OK and is free; Macromedia Dreamweaver is the best, but costs money, although you may be able to get a perfectly good early version for free) and graphics software (such as Paint Shop Pro, if you're paying, or use free demo versions or shareware of that or other packages).

Keep up to date

As well as making your own site, and then getting it noticed on the Web, you will also need to keep abreast of what's going on in the ever-changing new media world. One way of doing this is to subscribe (for free) to the excellent *Wired News* e-mail service, which will send you a daily message listing headlines and short summaries, with links to the full stories on its website (see www.wired.com/news). Another method is to buy the more intelligent internet magazines, such as *.Net* and *Internet Magazine* in the UK, or *Internet World, NetGuide*, and *Yahoo! Internet Life* in the USA. These magazines usually come with free CDs containing copies of the latest Web browsers and plug-ins, other free software, and demo versions of new professional packages. Soon your home will be adorned with lots of these shiny discs, doubling as coasters, mobiles and Christmas decorations.

Here we go . . .

I hope that you find this book useful. Please send your comments to david@newmediastudies.com.

USEFUL WEBSITES

New Media Studies: **www.newmediastudies.com**
The website for the study of new media, produced by David Gauntlett, with articles, reviews, Web design and marketing guides, Web art and culture, and other resources.

Yahoo!: **www.yahoo.com**
The most popular and comprehensive Web directory.

The World Wide Web Consortium: **www.w3.org**
Lots of useful basic (and advanced) information about the World Wide Web, with Tim Berners-Lee's interesting Frequently Asked Questions page at www.w3.org/People/Berners-Lee/FAQ.html.

Resource Centre for Cyberculture Studies: **www.otal.umd.edu/~rccs**
Produced by David Silver, RCCS is 'an online, not-for-profit organization whose purpose is to research, study, teach, support, and create diverse and dynamic elements of cyberculture'. Full of useful information.

Spark: **www.spark-online.com**
Lovingly designed online magazine, about culture, mass media and new media, made by nice creative folk for no money.

Wired News: www.wired.com/news
Daily articles about internet developments, regulations, and innovations, with an excellent searchable archive where you can find an article on anything Web-related.

A Brief History of the Internet and Related Networks:
www.isoc.org/internet/history/cerf.html
Useful short history of the internet by Vint Cerf.

Web Pages That Suck: **www.webpagesthatsuck.com**
The excellent Web design guide.

2

Looking Backwards, Looking Forwards: Cyberculture Studies 1990–2000

David Silver

While still an emerging field of scholarship, the study of cyberculture flourished throughout the last half of the 1990s, as witnessed in the countless monographs and anthologies published by both academic and popular presses, and the growing number of papers and panels presented at scholarly conferences from across the disciplines and around the world. Significantly, the field of study has developed, formed, reformed and transformed, adding new topics and theories when needed, testing new methods when applicable.

In an attempt to contextualize the chapters found in this volume, this one traces the major works of scholarship on cyberculture from the last 10 years, seen in three stages or generations. The first stage, *popular cyberculture*, is marked by its journalistic origins and characterized by its descriptive nature, limited dualism and use of the internet-as-frontier metaphor. The second stage, *cyberculture studies*, focuses largely on virtual communities and online identities, and benefits from an influx of academic scholars. The third stage, *critical cyberculture studies*, expands the notion of cyberculture to include four areas of study – online interactions, digital discourses, access and denial to the internet, and interface design of cyberspace – and explores the intersections and interdependencies between any and all four domains.

Popular cyberculture

Our disciplinary lineage begins with what I call *popular cyberculture*, a collection of essays, columns and books written by particularly wired journalists and early adapters. Starting in the early 1990s, these cultural critics began filing stories on the internet, cyberspace and the 'information superhighway' for major American newspapers and magazines. Significantly, what began as an occasional column in a newspaper's technology section soon developed into feature articles

2.1 *Wired* magazine, lifestyle porn for technofuturists.

appearing on the front page, in the business section and in lifestyle supplements, as well as within the new media/cyberspace beat of many mainstream magazines. Between 1993 and 1994, for example, *Time* magazine published two cover stories on the internet while *Newsweek* released the cover story 'Men, Women, and Computers'. Moreover, in 1994, the second editions of the popular how-to books *The Internet for Dummies* and *The Whole Internet* became bestsellers.

Popular cyberculture writings were generally descriptive. Usually required to follow the term internet with the parenthetical phrase 'the global computer network system', these journalists had the unenviable task of introducing non-technical readers to the largely technical, pre-World Wide Web version of cyberspace. Accordingly, much of this work included lengthy descriptions, explanations and applications of early net technologies such as file transfer protocol, gopher, lynx, UNIX configurations, telnet and Usenet.

In addition to being overly descriptive, early popular cyberculture often suffered from a limited dualism. As a number of scholars (Jones, 1997; Kinney, 1996; Kling, 1996; Rosenzweig, 1999) have noted, early popular cyberculture often took the form of dystopian rants or utopian raves. From one side, cultural critics blamed the net for deteriorating literacy, political and economic alienation, and social fragmentation. For example, Birkerts (1994) warned that the internet, hypertext and a host of electronic technologies would produce declining literacy and a less than grounded sense of reality. Sale (1995) drove home the points he made in his book *Rebels Against the Future: The Luddites and Their War on the Industrial Revolution: Lessons for the Computer Age* by smashing computers while on a promotional tour, and Stoll, upon shifting career tracks from a cyber-hyper computer hacker to a cyber-griper Cassandra, begged cybernauts to log off, reminding us that 'life in the real world is far more interesting, far more important, far richer, than anything you'll ever find on a computer screen' (1995: 13).

Conversely, a vocal group of writers, investors and politicians loosely referred to as the *technofuturists* declared cyberspace a new frontier of civilization, a digital domain that could and would bring down big business, foster democratic participation, and end economic and social inequities. While finding platforms within major American newspapers and popular magazines, among nascent organizations like the Electronic Frontier Foundation, and throughout newsgroups, listservs and websites, their primary pulpit was a new line of 'technozines' – glossy, visually impairing magazines with names like *Mondo 2000*, *bOing bOing* and *Wired*. Encapsulating the utopian rhetoric of the technofuturists, *Wired's* publisher Louis Rossetto likened cyberspace to 'a new economy, a new counter culture, and beyond politics'; the magazine's executive editor Kevin Kelly proclaimed 'technology is absolutely, 100 per cent, positive' (Keegan, 1995:

39–42); and contributing editor John Perry Barlow argued 'with the development of the internet, and with the increasing pervasiveness of communication between networked computers, we are in the middle of the most transforming technical event since the capture of fire' (1995: 36).

Not surprisingly, many politicians joined their ranks. Speaking at a conference in Buenos Aires, Vice President Al Gore (1995) remarked:

> These highways – or, more accurately, networks of distributed intelligence – will allow us to share information, to connect, and to communicate as a global community. From these connections we will derive robust and sustainable economic progress, strong democracies, better solutions to global and local environmental challenges, improved health care, and – ultimately – a greater sense of shared stewardship of our small planet.

Finally, in addition to its descriptive nature and rhetorical dualisms, early popular cyberculturalists employed the frontier as its reigning metaphor. William Gibson (1984) famously coined the term 'cyberspace' in his groundbreaking novel *Neuromancer*: 'Cyberspace. A consensual hallucination experienced daily by billions of legitimate operators. . . . A graphic representation of data abstracted from the banks of every computer in the human system. Unthinkable complexity' (51). In *Neuromancer* a new frontier emerges, one whose currency rests less in geographic space and more in digital information.

It did not take long for activists, writers and scholars to latch on to and reify the metaphor. In the now canonical essay 'Across the electronic frontier', Kapor and Barlow (1990) described the net in the following terms: 'In its present condition, cyberspace is a frontier region, populated by the few hardy technologists who can tolerate the austerity of its savage computer interfaces, incompatible communication protocols, proprietary barricades, cultural and legal ambiguities, and general lack of useful maps or metaphors.' The 'frontier' metaphor stuck. Rheingold (1993a) observed: 'The pioneers are still out there exploring the frontier, the borders of the domain have yet to be determined, or even the shape of it, or the best way to find one's way in it' (58). Rushkoff (1994) noted, 'Nowhere has the American pioneer spirit been more revitalized than on the electronic frontier' (235). Whittle (1997), discussing the future of the internet, waxes poetic: 'The pioneers, settlers, and squatters of the virgin territories of cyberspace have divided some of that land into plots of social order and plowed it into furrows of discipline – for the simple reason that . . . natural resources can only be found in the mind and have great value if shared' (420).

Cyberculture studies

Like most generations, mine bleed. Indeed, a significant portion of our second generation of cyberculture scholarship, *cyberculture studies*, can be characterized by its descriptive nature, binary dualism and frontier metaphors, and, as such, could easily be referred to as 'popular cyberculture'. Conversely, some of the early journalists made important explorations into, and observations about, cyberspace, thereby allowing them membership into the second generation. One such journalist was Julian Dibbell, whose provocatively titled 'A rape in cyberspace; or how an evil clown, a Haitian trickster spirit, two wizards, and a cast of dozens turned a database into a society', appeared in *The Village Voice* in 1993. In the article, Dibbell presents the now endlessly recounted tale of 'Mr Bungle', a member of LambdaMOO (a popular multi-user domain, or MUD) who uses a voodoo doll –

a program that allows one user to control the online 'actions' of another – to rape, violently attack and force unwanted liaisons upon a number of LambdaMOOers. Dibbell describes the attack, the violated users' emotional reactions, the community's outrage and the public discussion of Mr Bungle's punishment, including the possibility of 'toading', a process by which an MUD wizard turns a player into a toad, eliminating the player's identity and description. Noting that the chief wizard of the MUD recently revoked the toading process in an attempt to foster self-governance, Dibbell traces the steps of one user, JoeFeedback, who decides on his own to eliminate the Mr Bungle character. Besides offering readers a provocative glimpse into the online environment, Dibbell brilliantly portrays the complex individual and social negotiations existing within LambdaMOO, negotiations which, when viewed together, constitute very real identities and communities.

Using Dibbell as a starting point, we can characterize our second generation with a single passage by cybertheorist Allucquere Rosanne Stone (1991) who defines cyberspace as 'incontrovertibly social spaces in which people still meet face-to-face, but under new definitions of both "meet" and "face" ' (85). In other words, while cyberspace may lack for the most part the physical geography found in, say, a neighbourhood, city or country, it offers users very real opportunities for collective communities and individual identities. It is upon these twin pillars – virtual communities and online identities – that cyberculture studies rests.

One of the earliest and certainly the most referenced articulators of the virtual communities idea is Howard Rheingold (see his chapter in this book). Building upon Stone, Rheingold (1993a) defines a virtual community as follows.

> A group of people who may or may not meet one another face-to-face, and who exchange words and ideas through the mediation of computer bulletin boards and networks. In cyberspace, we chat and argue, engage in intellectual discourse, perform acts of commerce, exchange knowledge, share emotional support, make plans, brainstorm, gossip, feud, fall in love, find friends and lose them, play games and metagames, flirt, create a little high art and a lot of idle talk. We do everything people do when people get together, but we do it with words on computer screens, leaving our bodies behind (58).

A few months later, Rheingold published *The Virtual Community* (1993b), a significant expansion upon his earlier essay which would quickly become one of the principal texts of cyberculture studies. In the book, Rheingold provides a brief history of the internet, a social history of a particular online community – the Whole Earth 'Lectronic Link (the WELL) – and countless examples of online interactions which take place within both the WELL and the internet. Although the author concludes with a cautionary chapter detailing the potential perils of an overly commodified internet, online surveillance and cyber-induced hyperreality, Rheingold's enthusiasm dominates:

2.2 Howard Rheingold.

We temporarily have access to a tool that could bring conviviality and understanding into our lives and might help revitalize the public sphere. The same tool, improperly controlled and wielded, could become an instrument of tyranny. The vision of a citizen-designed, citizen-controlled worldwide communications network is a version of technological utopianism that could be called the vision of 'the electronic agora' (14).

If Rheingold's *The Virtual Community* is the first pillar of cyberculture studies, the second is Sherry Turkle's *Life on the Screen: Identity in the Age of the Internet* (1995). Turkle addresses the idea of online identities by exploring ethnographically a number of virtual environments, including MUDs. She finds that while some use cyberspace to repress an otherwise less-than-functional 'real' or offline life, most use the digital domain to exercise a more true identity, or a multiplicity of identities. In each case, users are free to pick and choose genders, sexualities and personalities within what Bruckman (1992) labels an 'identity workshop'.

Like Rheingold, Turkle's take on cyberspace is largely enthusiastic. Through a number of case studies, the author reveals how users of MUDs create online identities to help navigate their offline lives. For example, Turkle introduces Ava, a graduate student who lost her leg in a car accident. During her recuperation process, Ava began to MUD, and created a one-legged character. Soon after, her character became romantically involved with another, and they began to make virtual love (or, as it was then commonly referred to, have 'tinysex'). According to Turkle, these online interactions led Ava to become more comfortable with her offline body, leading her to note: 'Virtuality need not be a prison. It can be the raft, the ladder, the transitional space, the moratorium, that is discarded after reaching greater freedom. We don't have to reject life on the screen, but we don't have to treat it as an alternate life either' (263).

By the mid-1990s, cyberculture studies was well under way, focused primarily on virtual communities and online identities. Further, as a result of the enthusiasm found in the work of Rheingold and Turkle, cyberculture was often articulated as a site of empowerment, an online space reserved for construction, creativity and community. Fortunately, however, this simplification was matched by the richness found in the nascent field's welcoming of interdisciplinarity. With the growing popularity of user-friendly internet service providers such as AOL and CompuServe and the widespread adoption of Netscape, by the mid-1990s, the great internet rush was on. Significantly, the introduction of the Web was not only a *technological* breakthrough but also a *user* breakthrough. Replacing tricky file transfer protocol and burdensome gopher with a simple, point-and-click graphical interface, the Web helped to foster a less technical, more mainstream internet populace. Coupled with these technological breakthroughs were academic considerations. In addition to a concerted effort on the part of university administrators to get 'faculty wired', scholarly conferences, papers, archives and discussions came online, leading all but the most technophobic academics to the net.

⊙ **2.3** Sherry Turkle.

As expected, new scholars brought new methods and theories. For example, while some sociologists approach virtual communities as 'social networks' (Wellman, 1997; Wellman *et al.*, 1996), others employ the sociological traditions of interactionism and collective action dilemma theory (Kollock and Smith, 1996; Smith and Kollock, 1999). Within anthropology, scholars began formulating a new subfield, cyborg anthropology, devoted to exploring the intersections between individuals, society and networked computers (Downey and Dumit, 1998; Escobar, 1996). Researchers from a related field, ethnography, took their cue from Turkle and began to study what users do within diverse online environments, ranging from online lesbian bars and Usenet newsgroups to Web-based 'tele-gardens' and online cities (Baym, 1995a, 1995b and 1997; Correll, 1995; McLaughlin, *et al.*, 1997; Collins-Jarvis, 1993; Silver, forthcoming).

At the same time, linguists began to study the writing styles, netiquettes, and (inter)textual codes used within online environments (Danet *et al.*, 1997; Herring, 1996a, 1996b, 1996c and 1996d). Similarly, feminist and women's studies researchers have used textual analysis and feminist theory to locate, construct and deconstruct gender within cyberspace (Cherny and Weise, 1996; Consalvo, 1997; Dietrich, 1997; Ebben and Kramarae, 1993; Hall, 1996). Further, a collection of community activists and scholars began to explore the intersection of real and virtual communities in the form of community networks, including the Public Electronic Network (PEN) in Santa Monica, California, the Blacksburg Electronic Village (BEV) in Blacksburg, Virginia, and the Seattle Community Network (SCN) in Seattle, Washington (Cisler, 1993; Cohill and Kavanaugh, 1997; Schmitz, 1997; Schuler, 1994 and 1996; Silver, 1996, 1999a, 1999b).

Critical cyberculture studies

By the late 1990s, the study of cyberculture had arrived. Indeed, in the second half of the 1990s, many academic and popular presses published dozens of monographs, edited volumes and anthologies devoted to the growing field of cyberculture. Reflecting this growth, recent scholars take a broader view of what constitutes cyberculture. No longer limiting the field to merely virtual communities and online identities, a third generation of scholarship, or what I call *critical cyberculture studies*, has emerged. As with all emerging fields of study, the landscape and contours of critical cyberculture studies are, at best, chaotic and difficult to map. That said, I wish to argue that critical cyberculture studies contains four major areas of focus – each, as we will see, interdependent on one another.

As revealed in the last few pages, the perspectives and priorities of the first and second generations of cyberculture scholars differ significantly. Instead of approaching cyberspace as an entity to describe, contemporary cyberculture scholars view it as a place to contextualize, and seek to offer more complex, more problematized findings. In general, four dominant areas of focus have emerged. Taken together, these areas serve as the foundation for critical cyberculture studies:

☞ critical cyberculture studies explores the social, cultural and economic interactions that take place online
☞ critical cyberculture studies unfolds and examines the stories we tell about such interactions
☞ critical cyberculture studies analyses a range of social, cultural, political and economic considerations that encourage, make possible and/or thwart individual and group access to such interactions

☞ critical cyberculture assesses the deliberate, accidental and alternative technological decision- and design-processes which, when implemented, form the interface between the network and its users.

Critical cyberculture studies, in its most rich manifestation, explores the intersections between any and all four of these focal points.

Contextualizing online interactions

While critical cyberculture studies scholars acknowledge the importance of virtual communities and online identities, they take a step back and contextualize their topics. For example, Jones (1995a) sets the stage for what could be called the social construction of online reality. Unlike so many cyberculturalists who approach their topic as a brave new world, Jones contextualizes cyberspace within the more traditional paradigms of communication and community studies, including James Carey's work on the electronic sublime, James Beniger's notions of pseudo-communities, and David Harvey's theories of postmodern geographies. From there, the author reminds us of the cultural construction of cyberspace and warns us not to celebrate uncritically its potential. Two years later, Jones (1997) continued this necessary process of contextualizing by problematizing some of the key definitions and directions of cyberculture studies. Drawing on the work of Benedict Anderson, Richard Sennet and, once again, James Carey, Jones historically locates popular rhetoric heralding the net's potential to transcend time and space. Next, commenting on Rheingold's *The Virtual Community*, he questions the all-too-unproblematized notion of virtual communities. Substituting neo-Luddism with critical caution, Jones calls for a healthy re-evaluation of cyberspace, noting that the 'internet is another in a line of modern technologies that undermine traditional notions of civil society that require unity and shun multiplicity while giving impressions that they in fact re-create such a society' (25).

In addition to contextualizing virtual communities and online identities, many scholars have gone beyond merely recanting the findings of Rheingold and Turkle to make critical explorations and discoveries of their own. For example, McLaughlin *et al.* (1995) attempt to establish general, online codes of conduct by collecting all messages posted to five newsgroups within a three-week period and analysing them for normative discourse. From the data, they deduce seven categories of reproachable behaviour, including novice use of technology, bandwidth waste, ethical violations, and inappropriate language. Next, they note the ways in which 'rules of conduct on Usenet as currently constituted can be understood as a complex set of guidelines driven by economic, cultural, social-psychological, and discursive factors' (107). Much more than a simple set of 'netiquette', the authors' findings trace the intricate parameters and factors that help to support the relative success or failure of online communities. Similar scholarship (Kollock and Smith, 1996; MacKinnon, 1995, 1997 and 1998; Phillips, 1996) focuses on the parameters and punishments that serve to establish acceptable and unacceptable behaviour within online environments.

At the same time, Baym (1995b) has used ethnographic methods to better understand the nature of virtual communities. Baym explores the well-trafficked Usenet newsgroup rec.arts.tv.soaps, or r.a.t.s., and suggests that online communities emerge out of a complex intersection between five factors: external contexts, temporal structures, system infrastructure, group purposes and participant characteristics. Applying such factors to r.a.t.s., Baym concludes that:

> ... participants in [computer-mediated communication] develop forms of expression which enable them to communicate social information and to create and codify group-specific meanings, socially negotiate group-specific identities, form relationships which span from the playfully antagonistic to the deeply romantic and which move between the network and face-to-face interaction, and create norms which serve to organize interaction and to maintain desirable social climates (161).

Another important yet largely unexplored element of contextualizing online interactions is to trace the history and development of virtual communities. While past scholars approached online communities as already existing digital environments, critical cyberculture studies scholars (Dibbell, 1998; Horn, 1998; Silver, 1996 and 1999a) have begun to analyse their brief yet crucial histories.

Discoursing cyberspace

Like all forms of culture, cyberculture is, in part, a product of the stories we tell about it. Indeed, the tales we tell over coffee, read in *Wired, Newsweek,* and *The New York Times*, and watch in movies like *The Net, The Matrix,* and *Disclosure* inform the ways in which we engage in cyberculture. Further, these stories – and lack of stories – can potentially discourage and dissuade would-be cybernauts from going online. Thus, for some scholars (Borsook, 1996; Sobchack, 1993; Ross, 1991), cyberspace is not only a site for communication and community but also a generator of discourse, a very real and very imagined place where a variety of interests claim its origins, its myths, and its future directions. As many third generation cyberculture studies scholars have noted, two disturbing discourses of cyberspace have emerged: the net as frontier and cyberspace as boystown.

For example, Miller notes the ways in which the net-as-frontier metaphor serves to construct cyberspace as a place of manly hostility, a space unsafe for women and children. She argues that 'the idea that women merit special protections in an environment as incorporeal as the net is intimately bound up with the idea that women's minds are weak, fragile, and unsuited to the rough and tumble of public discourse' (L. Miller, 1995: 57). Further, as Doheny-Farina (1996) argues, the metaphor reinvokes the American myth of the individual and 'conjures up traditional American images of the individual lighting out from the territories, independent and hopeful, to make a life' (16).

In addition to the net as frontier metaphor, a dominant discourse found in magazines and movies is cyberspace as boystown. Understanding cyberculture to be not only online interactions but also the stories told about such interactions, scholars have performed feminist readings on such technozines as *Wired* and *Mondo 2000*. For example, Borsook (1996) analyses the ways in which the trendy magazine has appropriated countercultural themes in the name of testosterone-driven commercialism:

> *Wired* has consistently and accurately been compared in the national media to *Playboy*. It contains the same glossy pictures of certified nerd-suave things to buy – which, since it's the nineties, includes cool hand-held scanners as well as audio equipment and cars – and idolatrous profiles of (generally) male moguls and muckymucks whose hagiography is not that different from what might have appeared in *Fortune*. It is the wishbook of material desire for young men (26).

Online access and barriers

While cyberculture studies celebrates the existence of online communities, critical cyberculture studies seeks to better understand their participants. Although important work in the field of online marginality has begun, much more is needed. Indeed, while scholars from across the disciplines flock to the general topic of cyberculture, few have made their way into the margins to explore issues of race, ethnicity and sexuality online.

One step in the right direction is the work of the National Telecommunications and Information Administration, or NTIA, an agency of the US Department of Commerce. In a three-part series of studies entitled 'Falling Through the Net,' the NTIA examines what it calls the 'digital divide', a growing gap between information haves and have-nots, and the economic, social, cultural and geographic elements contributing to the gap. For example, in 'Falling through the net: A survey of the 'have nots' in rural and urban America' (1995), the NTIA concludes that class, race, age and education contributed significantly to online access. In 'Falling through the net II: New data on the digital divide' (1998), the NTIA expanded its study to find that although Americans, as a nation, accessed the internet in increasing numbers:

> ... the 'digital divide' between certain groups of Americans has *increased* between 1994 and 1997 so that there is now an even greater disparity in penetration levels among some groups. There is a widening gap, for example, between those at upper and lower income levels. Additionally, even though all racial groups now own more computers than they did in 1994, Blacks and Hispanics now lag *even further behind* Whites in their levels of PC-ownership and on-line access.

Finally, in 'Falling through the net: Defining the digital divide' (1999), the NTIA reveals that the digital divide had increased further, leading Larry Irving, assistant secretary of Commerce for Telecommunications, to remark that 'America's digital divide is fast becoming a "racial ravine".' As before, the report notes that while Americans, as a nation, continue to flock to the net, disparities based on race, class and region contribute to the growing gap between information haves and have-nots.

In addition to the barriers discussed by the National Telecommunications and Information Administration, there are other, more cultural ones. Performance artist and writer Guillermo Gómez-Peña (1996) recounts his and his collaborator Roberto Sifuentes' 1994 entrance into cyberspace, a digital space already largely 'settled' by ethnocentrism:

> We were also perplexed by the 'benign (not naive) ethnocentrism' permeating the debates around art and digital technology. The unquestioned lingua franca was of course English, 'the official language of international communications'; the vocabulary utilized in these discussions was hyper-specialized and depoliticized; and if Chicanos and Mexicans didn't participate enough in the Net, it was solely because of lack of information or interest (not money or access), or again because we were 'culturally unfit' (178).

Along similar lines, Bailey (1996) argues that shared customs such as netiquette and acronyms constitute 'newbie snobbery', producing an unwelcoming terrain for marginalized cultures. He notes that 'the Net nation deploys shared knowledge and language to unite against outsiders: Net jargon extends beyond technical language to acronyms both benign (BTW, "By the way") and snippy (RTFM, "Read the fucking manual"). It includes neologisms, text-graphical hybrids called emoticons, and a thoroughgoing anti-"newbie" snobbery. Like any other community, it uses language to erect barriers to membership' (38).

This is not to suggest that traditionally marginalized cultural groups have not taken to the wires as a means for communication, community and empowerment. Indeed, a number of contemporary cyberculturalists explore marginalized cultural groups' attempts to establish self-defined, self-determined virtual spaces. For example, Mitra (1997) analyses the discursive practices of contributors to the Usenet newsgroup, soc.culture.indian. While acknowledging strong 'segmenting forces', especially when users cross-post messages to soc.culture.pakistan, Mitra argues that the online community generates 'centralizing tendencies' for Indian users: 'these diasporic people, geographically displaced and distributed across large areas, are gaining access to [internet] technologies and are increasingly using these technologies to re-create a sense of virtual community through a rediscovery of their commonality' (58). Other scholars (Shaw, 1997; Correll, 1995) make similar arguments regarding gay and lesbian online communities.

As many scholars have noted, males tend to dominate online discussions, regardless of the topic. Recently, however, female users have countered this domination – not to mention hostility – by creating online spaces of their own. As Camp (1996) recounts, Systers, a mailing list of women in computer science and related disciplines, was established in response to male-dominated discussions about women taking place in Usenet newsgroups like soc.women. The solution was to 'withdraw to a room of our own – to mailing lists' (115). Able to control and moderate the list, members of Systers discuss the issues most relevant to them. These online spaces also include, of course, the Web. These sites are as diverse as the population they hope to represent, ranging from academic sites like the *Women's Studies Database* (www.inform.umd.edu/EdRes/Topic/WomensStudies) and the *Center for Women and Information Technology* (www.umbc.edu/cwit), to hipper, do-it-yourself sites like *Geekgirl* (www.geekgirl.com.au) and *AngstGrrl!* (www.angstgrrl.com). Not to be left out of growing markets, feminist-leaning websites like *iVillage.com* (www.ivillage.com), *Oxygen* (www.oxygen.com) and *Women.com* (www.women.com) fuse timely women's issues with targeted cybermarketing.

Digital design

Second-generation cyberculturalists admirably explored the kinds of community and identity found on the internet. Yet too often they all but ignored the ways in which the digital design of online spaces informs the types of interaction made possible. One exception is the significant attention literary scholars paid to hypertext, or what is commonly refereed to as *hypertext studies*. Focusing more on early hypertext software like HyperCard than on online networks such as the internet and the Web, hypertext scholars (Bolter, 1991; Landow, 1992 and 1994) compared the new media to contemporary critical theory and considered the ways in which hypertext reconfigures the text, writer and reader.

More recently, however, conversations between computer scientists, community activists and ethnographers have produced new insights into the complex relationships between humans and computers. Commonly referred to as *human-computer interaction*, or HCI, such work approaches the interface as a critical site for interaction. The design of an interface – as designers have known for years – can have a substantial impact on the relative success of a site's intentions. For example, as Kollock (1996) notes in 'Design principles for online communities', online environments should be designed to encourage user co-operation, maintain a community-based institutional memory and include elements of the physical environment through which users travel. Currently, a number of scholars (Baecker, 1997; Kim, 1999) are developing models for discussing and assessing online interfaces. The pursuit has also been one of the key sites of study for a number of research institutes, including the Graphics, Visualization and Usability Center (www.cc.gatech.edu/gvu) at the Georgia Institute of Technology, the Human-Computer Interaction Lab (HCIL) (www.cs.umd.edu/hcil) at the University of Maryland, and the Knowledge Media Design Institute (www.kmdi.org) at the University of Toronto.

Issues of design and participation come together in the relatively new field *participatory design*, an approach pioneered in Scandinavia and currently making waves in the United States. As Schuler and Namioka (1993) note, participatory design 'represents a new approach towards computer systems design in which the people destined to *use* the system play a critical role in *designing* it' (xi). With support from the Computer Professionals for Social Responsibility, participatory design has been debated and adopted by both scholars and designers (Muller *et al.*, 1992; Shneiderman and Rose, 1997; Trigg *et al.*, 1994).

Conclusion: bringing it all together

As previously noted, critical cyberculture studies at its best does not focus simply on one of its four key areas. Instead, it seeks to comprehend the relationships, intersections and interdependencies between multiple areas. To better understand this point, we turn quickly to the work of Nakamura (1999) and Collins-Jarvis (1993). Brief yet penetrating, Nakamura's 'Race in/for cyberspace: Identity tourism and racial passing on the internet' explores the ways in which race is written within the popular MUD, LambdaMOO. She observes that while users are required to specify their genders, there is no such option for race: 'It is not even on the menu,' Nakamura notes (444). Instead, the formation of racial identity is limited to the selection of already established characters. Focusing specifically on Asian identity formation, Nakamura notes that the vast majority of such characters – Mr Sulu, Bruce Lee, Little Dragon and Akira, for example – fall within familiar discourses of racial stereotyping: 'The Orientalized male persona, complete with sword, confirms the idea of the male Oriental as potent, antique, exotic, and anachronistic' (445).

Countering optimists who view cyberspace as a space where race does not matter, Nakamura argues that not only does it matter, but it has been designed out of the network, or what I call routed around. Significantly, this process is largely a *design* issue; the interface of LambdaMOO is designed without race-based user identities. Instead, users are forced to assume one of the default identities – identities which for Asian-Americans reinforce stereotypes. Nakamura's work is important, therefore, because it reveals the interdependent relationships between interface design and user identities.

The issues of access, discursive communities and insider/outsider dynamics come together in an article on one of the first community networks in the world, Santa Monica's Public Electronic Networking system, or PEN. In her article 'Gender representation in an electronic city hall: Female adoption of Santa Monica's PEN system', Collins-Jarvis examines the reasons why the percentage of female PEN users (30 per cent) was, for the early 1990s, unusually high. Significantly, Collins-Jarvis offers three answers: PEN's public terminals, the availability of socially and politically related discussions and forums related to 'female interests', and the ability for women to take part in the network's design and implementation.

According to Collins-Jarvis, female users of PEN required not only access to get involved, they also needed a reason to participate: 'Computing systems which appeal to women's norms and interests (e.g. by providing a channel to enact participatory political norms) can indeed increase female adoption rates' (61). Further, when faced with often hostile flaming and a dearth of 'women-specific' forums, female users of PEN assumed the responsibility of reinventing rather than rejecting the network. This reinvention took the form of creating a number of conference topics and user groups devoted specifically to issues of their own. Like Nakamura, Collins-Jarvis correctly understands online interactions to be a product of many offline factors, including design, content and outreach.

As Nakamura and Collins-Jarvis suggest, cyberculture is best comprehended as a series of negotiations that take place both online and off. In this light, it is crucial to broach issues of discourse, access and design. In the new millennium, it is the task of cyberculture scholars to acknowledge, reveal and critique these negotiations to better understand what takes place within the wires.

USEFUL WEBSITES

Center for Women and Information Technology:
www.umbc.edu/cwit
The Center for Women and Information Technology, established at the University of Maryland Baltimore County in July, 1998, seeks to address and rectify women's under-representation in IT and to enhance our understanding of the relationship between gender and IT.

Cybersociology: **www.socio.demon.co.uk/magazine**
Cybersociology is a non-profit multi-disciplinary webzine dedicated to the critical discussion of the internet, cyberspace, cyberculture and life online. Edited by Robin Hamman of the Hypermedia Research Centre at the University of Westminster, London, *Cybersociology* often substitutes academic analysis with anecdotal experiences, making for somewhat engaging, yet rather shallow, treatments.

The Psychology of Cyberspace:
www.rider.edu/users/suler/psycyber/psycyber.html
Written and put together by John Suler, a professor of Psychology at Rider University, *The Psychology of Cyberspace* is an online book which explores the psychological dimensions of environments created by computers and online networks.

Resource Center for Cyberculture Studies: **www.otal.umd.edu/~rccs**
The Resource Center for Cyberculture Studies, produced by David Silver, is an online, not-for-profit organization whose purpose is to research, study, teach, support, and create diverse and dynamic elements of cyberculture. Collaborative in nature, RCCS seeks to establish and support ongoing conversations about the emerging field, to foster a community of students, scholars, teachers, explorers, and builders of cyberculture, and to showcase various models, works-in-progress, and on-line projects.

3

New Media, New Methodologies: Studying the Web

Nina Wakeford

One of the most confusing aspects of doing research about the Web, as with any media form, is that it can be understood at many levels. Web pages are simultaneously computer code, cultural representations, material objects for consumption and the outcome of skilled labour. Although it is possible to do a fine-grained reading of an individual Web page as 'cultural text', it is equally feasible to take a broad view of the way in which the Web is becoming part of global culture and commerce. This requires a different set of data and methods than would a purely online study. At the same time the Web often involves experiences that take on a distinctive local flavour, such as Web browsing at a cybercafe, which can be explored in a place-based ethnography (Wakeford, 1999).

Currently there is no standard technique, in communications studies or in allied social science disciplines, for studying the Web. Rather it is case of plundering existing research for emerging methodological ideas which have been developed in the course of diverse research projects, and weighing up whether they can be used or adapted for our own study. If this chapter seems eclectic, it simply reflects the scattered nature of the enterprises in the field up to this point (see Lyman and Wakeford, 1999). Whatever technique we use, we cannot presume in advance that the cultural significance of the Web can be read off its current popularity. The relationship between the Web and the rest of the social world cannot be presumed, but must be investigated.

How do we do this? A database of maps of the Web is being developed by Martin Dodge at www.cybergeography.com, providing views of the topology of the electronic networks. These maps provide a macro-level bird's eye view of the structure of Web and can rarely provide us with information about the kinds of communication that are happening there. What if we wanted to know about the Web in terms of users' daily practice? Counting access 'hits' on a site via the URL is a relatively simple way to analyse the Web, and one frequently reported in the media and on the 'counters' of the Web pages themselves. Yet these *hits* do not measure the number of individual *users*. A single user may hit the same page more than once during one session, access the site on several occasions and log on from different machines. Most of the work on server log files looking at users is undertaken by market research companies. As well as the more established companies such as Nielsen, new Web trend forecasting is provided by companies such as Media Metrix (www.mediametrix.com). Websites are frequently ranked in terms of their popularity; using these formulae gives us tables of the 'top sites' in terms of unique users and minutes per use. For example, in December 1999, Nielsen/NetRatings reported that the 'top shopping sites' were Amazon.com (4.4 million unique visitors; average stay 11 minutes), Ebay.com (3.9 million unique visitors; average stay 52 minutes) and Etoys.com (1.8 million unique visitors; average stay 11 minutes) in the week ending 28 November (*Los Angeles Times*, C4, 12 December, 1999).

The range of variables that can be collected is shown in a study in which researchers sought to measure the 'internet audience' of a Web-based online art museum (McLaughlin *et al.*, 1999). These researchers used the server log files of Web pages to assess the characteristics of the users. Using the software WebTrends, they identified the total number of hits, the total number of user sessions, how many US and international user sessions, and average user session length. (These are the kinds of statistics relied upon by most website producers.) The investigators then created profiles of the kinds of users who had accessed the museum, and combined this with the analysis of the interactive 'chat' features of the site.

Techniques for analysis of these 'access statistics' are of great importance to companies who wish to prove that sites are visited by large quantities of users. They are also useful for a broad overview of the behaviour and location of those accessing the site. They are of less use when studying the cultural importance of the Web, at least when used as a stand-alone technique. Statistical rankings tell us only a limited amount about the use of the Web (although they may tell us plenty about the culture of market research). Just as we would not want to judge the social impact of television viewing by only looking at audience figures, we cannot rely on 'hits' to tell us about the cultural significance of the Web. There are, however, several ways in which we might go beyond counting hits, and begin to develop sociological and cultural approaches for the study of this new media.

In thinking about which methodological frameworks we have at our disposal to study the Web, it is advisable to bear in mind that what is considered as legitimate methodology is itself always in flux. Alongside the rise in new information and communication technologies over the last 10 years a substantial body of work has emerged which questions orthodox methodological practices (see Denzin and Lincoln, 1994; Denzin, 1997). In qualitative sociology in particular there have been extensive debates about the possibility and desirability of feminist methodology (Oelson, 1994) and alternative measures of validity (Lather, 1993). Another intervention is the rise of writing as a method of enquiry (Richardson, 1994) which often draws on the notion of reflexivity (Woolgar, 1988). Several branches of social science are advancing the use of visual material, which holds much promise for the investigation of the graphics-laden new media. These branches range from a long-standing tradition of using photography and film in anthropology (Banks and Morphy, 1997) to newer developments in visual sociology (Harper, 1994) and computer-assisted analysis of qualitative material (Fielding and Lee, 1998). All of these developments can be used as a resource for new studies of new media while at the same time acknowledging that questions of research design, sample or participant selection, choice of site to be studied, methods of data collection and analysis, ethical practice and the use of theoretical frameworks are all just as relevant, and cannot be sidestepped however 'virtual' the data collection.

Some of the methodological challenges of researching the Web resemble those involved in studying other systems of mass communication, but there *are* distinctive technical features of the Web which allow the collection of particular kinds of data. For example certain kinds of relationships between individuals or groups can be tracked by following hypertext links from one website to the next. Ananda Mitra and Elisia Cohen (1999) set out six special characteristics of Web text. First, it is overtly intertextual through the presence of 'links'. Second, it rarely has the linearity of more conventional texts. Third, the reader becomes the author, in a sense, as he or she actively selects which links to follow. Fourth, the Web is a multimedia text. Fifth, it has a global reach, albeit constrained by access and language. Sixth, the Web is characterized by the ephemeral and impermanent nature of many of its texts, files and filenames.

Nevertheless, the Web's new features bring completely new methodological problems. Web pages appear to allow us the possibility of conducting fast and cheap global surveys by administering an electronic rather than paper questionnaire. Yet we cannot rely on the same respondent behaviour online as we would on 'pencil and paper' questionnaires (Witmer *et al.*, 1999). The quantity of information that may be generated, and the speed at which responses can be collected, can result in pleasing piles of data – but we should be wary of being seduced by sheer quantity; data is only useful if it is representative of the larger population (Jones, 1999).

The apparently unproblematic model of Web pages as public documents cannot be taken for granted (Chandler, 1998). Furthermore, Web search engine databases themselves are rarely neutral; rather they are constructed in such a way that advertising and other commercial values play a significant role in what is retrieved after a word search (Goguen, 1999). Such issues direct us back to the inseparability of methodology with *ethics* and *politics* (Star, 1994; Goguen, 1999). Studying the Web is a matter of moving back and forth between these long-standing debates and the distinctive form they take in new electronically mediated research.

The short history of social science research in this area has tended to relegate study of the Web as secondary to the study of interactive communication spaces (see David Silver's chapter in this volume). Much of the early communication research about the social aspects of the internet focused on 'computer mediated communication' and the irritatingly over-used acronym 'CMC' (see, for example, Baym, 1995b). Several authors examined the types of social world that existed online by studying the textual interactions that constituted so-called 'virtual communities' or 'cybersocieties' (Jones, 1995a). At this stage the Web did not appear to overlap with newsgroups, bulletin board services or e-mail discussion lists, which were the sites considered in this first generation of research.

Chat or e-mail exchanges remain a key topic of research in communication studies, but as the Web develops, increasingly e-mail accounts and chat spaces are integrated into Web browser capabilities. As this happens it is likely that the boundaries between the Web and other internet spaces will continue to blur. As a result the research projects described below, which are currently creating new ways to investigate the social networks of newsgroups and group chat, will be able to be used to investigate the multiple social worlds of the Web. Of course, just as important as these technical changes will be studies which question whether users indeed experience the Web as such an integrative interface.

In addition to these changes in Web interfaces, developments in related communication technologies are constantly changing the way in which the Web is produced, represented and consumed. The overlaps of television, the internet and personal computing have led to the rhetoric of technological 'convergence' as well as corporate mergers such as the purchase of Time Warner by America Online (AOL) in January 2000. In this way the Web is poised to generate the convergence of previously segregated media technologies. Delivery devices are also in a state of radical upheaval. Wireless technologies, such as mobile phones, uncouple Web access from the desktop and the personal computer, and such technological developments are likely to have methodological consequences.

Web pages as cultural representations

The essence of the Web is countless linked Web pages. It takes a relatively short amount of time accessing these pages to realize that the variety of purposes and formats cannot easily be summarized. Some are clearly advertisements, others are for public information. Some are transparent as to their authorship and location, and others appear to float free of any identifiable geographical base, and/or the authorship is unclear. In the face of such diversity, there is a need for a researcher to be as specific as possible about the types of page that are under investigation. One way to do this is to use a list of generic features which can operate as a template against which to analyse a specific page. Daniel Chandler has devised a framework for the analysis of one type of Web page, the personal homepage (Chandler, 1997 and 1998; Chandler and Roberts-Young, 1998). Homepages generally have one author, and the subject of the page is often the author him/herself. Chandler's aim is to enable us to think about the cultural significance of these pages in terms of the systems of signs they display, and it is closely associated with the semiotic readings that one could make of texts such as films or literature. Chandler's 'Generic Features' list is divided into five primary sections: themes, formulaic structures, technical features, iconography and modes of address. Although these were devised for personal homepages, the organization of these sections is a practical starting point for a study of other kinds, or genres, of Web pages. In this case the themes would be expanded beyond the central organizing question of 'Who am I?' which provides the pivot of a personal page. Similarly, the formulaic structures would be supplemented by the culturally resonant forms of content for the group or organization under investigation. For a commercial site, for example, the catalogue, stockroom or shopping cart would be more appropriate than the diary or curriculum vitae. And, of course, the technology, iconography and modes of address of a site will change considerably over time, and across different types of site.

As a methodological device Chandler's list can be used to systematically analyse a single website (perhaps over time), and to compare sites in a particular sector or market, or investigate cross-national dimensions of website design. How do the websites of national museums differ? Or those of governments providing 'online democracy'? In themselves, these descriptions could be pointless, and probably tedious, but happily Chandler combines his own close textual analysis with interviews. Authors are asked for their own explanations for the particular features of their homepages, and their answers are used to explore his thesis of the public/private transformation made possible by Web pages. Through the collection of such interview material, a methodological strategy, which initially relied purely on an online system of signs, is expanded in terms of the interpretations of personal pages given by their producers. There are several ways in which these ideas of context could be further elaborated. As well as Web page authors, we can interview members of the 'posited audience'. In this way a researcher can move from studying a system of signs that is detached from a user's interpretation of them, towards an approach that integrates the readings intended by an author and those accomplished by the people consuming the Web pages.

In his essay on how a visual sociologist would approach a photograph, compared to the way in which a photojournalist or a documentary photographer would undertake the same task, Howard Becker (1998a) points out that when sociologists look at a picture they search for contextual information such as explicit statements about cultural patterns and social structure. How can we make statements about cultural patterns and social structure as part of studies of the Web? One way is to expand the boundaries of our data collection beyond textual or semiotic analysis, and to consider the technical, social and political infrastructure of Web pages. Web pages are always located on a server, and this server exists in a real physical place and has a private or institutional owner. A study with a focus on infrastructure might investigate the significance of who carries out such 'hosting' of Web pages, and the relationship between the content of the site, the author and the server on which is it housed. What is the role of internet service providers in the creation of the Web? Who is paying for the Web page, and why? Are some images or words filtered or censored? Students who house their personal homepage on university servers, for example, are often bound by the regulations of the university which may prohibit certain types of image and language.

Querying how the process of representation is linked to the social and political infrastructure, as well as to technical standards, can lead to a methodological approach which Leigh Star has called an 'ethnography of infrastructure' (Star, 1999). Although infrastructure sounds (and often *is*, according to Star) quite unexciting, by *not* studying infrastructure we risk overlooking other discourses. 'Study an information system and neglect its standards, wires and settings, and you miss equally essential aspects of aesthetics, justice and change' (Star, 1999: 379). As an information system the Web has its own distinctive 'standards, wires and settings', including those whose skills are to build them. Using the ethnography of infrastructure framework as we scrutinize Web pages we might be tempted to ask about the skills necessary to create such a page and how they are distributed within a population. I will return to frameworks that link offline and online methods of studying the Web, including research on Web page designers, after exploring how some researchers have created ways of visualizing the social networks of computer-mediated communication.

Visualizing social networks online

The kind of semiotic methodological strategy described in the previous section does not deploy the networked features of Web documents. The analysis is 'read off' the Web page and its links. Unlike other documents and texts that might undergo similar analysis (letters, photographs, advertisements), Web pages can be thought of as representations in themselves and at the same time their computer code can be a resource for methodological innovation. Unlike television and radio, the capacity for monitoring use (including 'cookies') and browsing behaviour is built into the structure of many Web pages (although the skill and opportunity to operate this monitoring is not as widespread as the ability to build a Web page). Several mapping techniques are currently being developed which use the technical features of electronic networks to model the kinds of sociability that can occur in electronic textual chat. Such chat is increasingly happening over the Web.

The methodological importance of these projects is that they enable visualization of parts of the network, either through tracking users or the text they contribute to a discussion. Rather than attempting to map the whole of the Web as is the aim of some of the projects at the www.cybergeography.org site, social science researchers have teamed up with computer scientists to build software that will facilitate looking at smaller sections of the Web user population. The 'Sociable Web' project has pioneered a way of seeing who else is simultaneously accessing a Web page while a user is browsing that page (Donath and Robertson, 1994). A custom browser allows each user to see the e-mail identifier or graphical icon of other users who are viewing the same page. The researchers hope that this is a way in which users can 'sense the presence of each other'. It could also be used for research purposes both to look at the dynamics of usage and group activity on the Web, as it allows people to browse the Web as a group. The user is required to create and present some information about him/herself either in terms of an identifying address or a pictorial representation. The researcher can monitor not only the behaviour of moving between sites, but also the relationship between the kinds of identities that are created by the user and their browsing behaviour.

Large-scale conversations on the internet can seem overwhelmingly huge and chaotic. Increasingly tools are available to discern the topical 'threads' of a conversation in one isolated group, but many discussion groups and newsgroups are connected to other sites or groups on the Web. Netscan is a piece of software which allows a researcher to view associations between newsgroups that would not be obvious from a standard newsgroup viewer. Netscan has been developed by Marc Smith and is currently a project of Microsoft Research (http://netscan.research.microsoft.com). The relationship between newsgroups is assessed via the cross-posting of messages between newsgroups. (A sample of output of a Netscan visualization is shown in Figure 3.1.)

This figure shows a network diagram of the newsgroups neighbouring and linking *alt.fan.bill-gates* and *alt.destroy.microsoft* through cross-posted messages. In this diagram, the size of each block indicates the relative size of the group in terms of number of messages. The shade/colour of each block represents the poster to post ratio for the group. Figure 3.1 demonstrates how groups we would expect to have independent topics and audiences are associated. When patterns of association have been established a researcher is able to retrieve the postings and conduct a content analysis of the messages that have been posted.

Cross-posting occurs between newsgroups – however, responses can be copied not only to whole groups, but also to individuals within the same group as part of a pattern of responding to the questions and comments of interlocutors. Warren Sack has developed 'Conversation Map' which is 'an interface for very large scale conversations' over the internet. In essence, Conversation Map is a newsgroup browser that analyses the content and the relationships between messages and then uses

3.1 Connections between newsgroups drawn by Netscan.

the results to create a graphical interface (Sack, 1999). It produces three
types of graphical analysis, showing
the *social networks* (detailing who is
responding to and/or citing whom in
the newsgroup), the *discussion themes*
(based on frequently occurring terms
in the newsgroup archive) and the
semantic networks (representing the
main terms under discussion and their
relationships to one another).

Software which allows us to
inspect the content of the conversations can also be programmed to
search for language patterns in the
text that may give us clues about the
social conventions being created in
that space. The Loom tool shows the
role of a user in the community by
plotting dots to represent individual

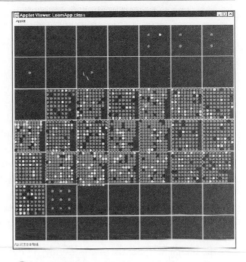

3.2 Newsgroup postings analysed by the Loom tool.

postings (Donath *et al.*, 1999). The most methodologically adventurous feature is
one that attempts to plot message content in terms of affective states (such as
angry or peaceful). The results of automatic calculations, based on language and
grammar in the post, are then represented graphically and colour coded. Red dots
are used to represent angry postings, for example. Figure 3.2 shows the results
of one such Loom plot.

Sociable Web, Netscan, Conversation Map and Loom are all tools that can
be used by researchers as the Web increasingly becomes a place in which conversations occur and awareness of co-presence becomes possible. Most of the projects
use methodological assumptions developed in quantitative sociology and compu-
tational linguistics. Marc Smith's Netscan was inspired by earlier attempts by
sociologists to look at the patterns of short interactions between strangers on
busy street corners (Smith and Kollock, 1999). Plotting all interactions over a
long time period can provide some unexpected results. The exact points at which
people loiter are not at all where we might predict. In the same way the promise
of the programmes outlined in this section is that they too will provide us with
previously unnoticed patterns or sites of interaction. Most of the programmes
aim to give us maps of networks which we would not be able to see using other
methods. They have the advantage of being developed in an open dialogue with
their users through websites which are themselves dedicated to their use. Yet
still the greatest risk in their use is seduction by the data itself, as reasonably
unimportant patterns identified by the software may lead the researcher to draw
odd conclusions. This, of course, is not an inherent problem with online data, but
is an issue for all those researchers dealing with large quantitative datasets.

Researching the Web offline

Whether we are examining the semiotics of individual Web pages or mapping
interactions between thousands in Web chat spaces, asking users about the
meanings they associate with their actions will provide us with interpretations
which may not be always what we expect from the server log files or the network

diagrams. As well as interviews, such as those used by Chandler (1998), the development of online focus groups is another way in which data about user experiences may be collected online. Ted Gaiser has discussed the mechanics of organizing and interpreting online focus group methodology (Gaiser, 1998); however, many researchers find it beneficial to combine online research with face-to-face meetings, interviews and/or ethnography. We can think of this as 'offline' research about the Web.

In most disciplines, combining online and offline data collection will challenge the boundaries of traditional fieldwork, which is located in a particular *place*. A team of anthropologists working on the meanings of genetic knowledge (such as that produced via the Human Genome Project) have been working with a methodology centred around 'multi-site ethnography' (Marcus, 1995) in which participant observation at laboratories, clinics and support groups was combined with data collected from websites and other internet spaces (Heath *et al.*, 1999). This kind of approach contrasts with traditional anthropological practice in which a practitioner claimed a geographically defined place of research on the basis of long-term residency or contact. It also has methodological consequences. Individuals with genetic conditions who were initially contacted through their websites were later met face to face. Overall this was advantageous; the researchers discovered that since leaving university (and losing her computer access) Karen, who has a blistering skin disorder, had been using the computers at the research laboratory where she was being treated to create her own independent informational Web pages about the disorder. 'Without these face to face interactions with Karen, we would not have recognized the extent to which her online work was entwined with the work of the university dermatology department where we were conducting fieldwork' (453). It was nowhere evident on her Web page.

This approach also generated research dilemmas. The team members realized that they could not isolate what they had learned (or assumed) from information on a participant's Web page from subsequent encounters. Reflecting on the subsequent meetings with Karen the researchers write about these methodological tensions:

> When we first met her, we wanted to interact with the woman that she presented to us in person and not with the woman that she presented to the public online. No matter how hard we tried, however, it seemed as if we could not disentangle the conversation from our earlier knowledge of Karen's online work. We found ourselves (often unintentionally) asking questions that reflected these earlier understandings, forming opinions about her statements based on them, and even interjecting details to what she was telling us about her life.
>
> (Heath *et al.*, 1999: 454)

The practical resolution was to account for this kind of overlap rather than try avoid it. Heath and her colleagues outline a model of 'network ethics' to cope with these tensions. Writing about such methodological difficulties is a good sociological 'trick of the trade' (Becker, 1998a). Another trick this team developed is to view research as a 'modest intervention' of collaboration between the participant and researcher in which both sides 'reveal and transform the boundaries which separate online and face to face lifeworlds' (Heath *et al.*, 1999: 462).

As these researchers began to investigate in more depth how the boundaries between online and offline are continually crossed, any initial definition of what the Web might be became unstable. Here the Web is not merely a network of hyperlinks, but also represents an opportunity for Karen to claim access to computing resources, and negotiate her relationship with her condition through the construction of her own Web pages. So how do we construct the boundaries of a Web page? George Marcus has pointed out that the very subject of our research is determined by the connections we make between objects, people and stories during our fieldwork (Marcus, 1995). Taking this view, we constantly construct the Web as we conduct our research, rather than researching something that is already 'out there'. Although this perspective might seem confusing, it is merely another way of restating an earlier claim. Limiting Web studies at the outset to the collection and analysis of online data is restrictive, and in so doing we may miss the central features of the behaviour or group we are trying to describe.

Researching the Web offline includes conducting ethnographies in locations where the Web is used. A cybercafe is one location where such an ethnography has been carried out (Wakeford, 1999). In the ethnography, participant observation was conducted with the staff in the cafe who served the coffee and showed customers how to use the machines. It was found that the kinds of interaction that happened around the machines where customers accessed e-mail and the Web were influenced by much more than the technical capacity of the machine or the level of user skill. Rather the way in which the cafe functioned wove together its place in the London internet 'scene', its own spatial ordering, and the ideologies of age, race and gender that were perpetuated by both staff and customers. Use of the Web was not merely an experience of the human interaction with a terminal, but was filtered through a much broader experience of being one of the most well-established internet cafes in London.

Qualitative face-to-face studies of media usage in a domestic context are well established – including, for television (Morley, 1980; Gauntlett and Hill, 1999), radio (Tacchi, 1998) and personal computers (Silverstone and Hirsch, 1992). More recent studies are beginning to examine how the internet is used in households (see, for example, www.brunel.ac.uk/research/virtsoc). Ethnographers have shown that media devices are part of a world of material culture, which may operate in the background of other activities. Jo Tacchi explains that when it enters the home the sound of the radio is both material and social (Tacchi, 1998: 43). She comments 'The use of the radio adds to the sound texture of the domestic environment' (27). We can use this kind of research finding about other forms of media and communication to compare and contrast the entry of the internet into the household. How does the Web enter the different (sound, visual) textures of the household? Silverstone, Hirsch and Morley also claim that the computer becomes part of the 'moral economy of the household' in which households appropriate commodities into the domestic culture in accordance with the household's own values and interests (Silverstone and Hirsch, 1992: 16). How does the Web enter into this moral economy? Ethnographies of previous technologies in a whole variety of settings can be used to provide the techniques for future qualitative studies (Suchman *et al.*, 1999), as well as useful comparisons when the Web is under investigation in households with previously investigated technologies.

Offline research of the Web could also encompass the range of occupations that are associated with its production. What are the politics of identity involved in the production of the Web and how could we study them? Jerome McDonough interviewed the creators of Web-based and non-Web-based virtual worlds, and found that even when they had little contact with end users, programmers had clear visions of how to represent the user in graphical environments, and these took on particular gendered and racial forms which were associated with the programmers' identities as predominantly white and male (McDonough, 1999). At the other end of the process of creating the Web, workers on the chip assembly lines in Silicon Valley are preferred if they are 'small, foreign and female' (Hossfeld, 1994). Karen Hossfeld's study was conducted using over 200 interviews with workers, and their family members, employers, managers, union organizations and community leaders. The computer industry is embedded within the wider system of US social stratification. '[T]he racial division of labour in the Silicon Valley high-tech manufacturing work force originates in the racially structured labour market of the larger economy, and in the "racial logic" that employers use in hiring' (1994: 89). Clearly the production of the Web cannot be separated from the wider questions of justice and equality for all of those who create it.

Web designers are at the higher end of the scale of status and income in terms of Web production. Methods from historical sociology have been employed to look at the development of Web design skill among this group (Kotamraju, 1999). This study attempted to document the changes in the skills required by Web designers over a short period of rapid development (1994–98) in the San Francisco Bay Area. Kotamraju traced newspaper advertisements as well as recruitment sites on the Web. She also interviewed Web designers about their own changing skill sets and those of their colleagues in the Web development industry. The most interesting finding, methodologically, is that the history of Web design seemed to have largely disappeared. Most job openings had been filled by word of mouth or personal recommendation, and neither appeared in print nor electronically archived records. Neither were the practitioners themselves able to reconstruct the recent skill changes. Web designers themselves were not able to describe the changes in skills which producing the Web required.

> For the most part, the people I interviewed were not able to remember the details or impact of technical changes that occurred a mere 3 months ago. They could not remember what skills the early version of HTML demanded from them. Similarly, they were usually unable to remember how Website design changed when cascading style sheets were introduced, or that some versions of Internet Explorer and Netscape once handled JavaScript differently – events that had taken place within months of our interviews (1999: 468).

This research suggests that one of the puzzles of doing research on the Web may be trying to work out the appropriate place to study when online data yield no results. Kotamraju concludes that the problem is related to the topic of research itself: 'Data, the traces of technology-related phenomena, reflect Web technologies, and in doing so, increasingly mimic the high turnover, rapid obsolescence, and momentary existence of digital technologies' (1999: 468). Researchers need to be wary of the speed with which information about recent Web history may vanish into the haze of obsolete technology.

Offline research into online spaces can take numerous forms. We may want to spend time in places where the Web is being produced, or amongst those who produce it. Although Silicon Valley has been the site of much of the investment and activity in the development of digital technologies, other Silicon alleys, valleys and glens are emerging across the globe. But as Hossfeld's study makes clear, we cannot study these in isolation from the systems of economic and social stratification in each country. Interviews and participation in offline spaces can be combined with online data for new insights about the creation and reception of Web pages, as was shown by Heath and her colleagues. Whatever method is used for data collection offline, the technical features of the Web may still need to be taken into account, as Kotamraju's theory of the disappearance of data attests.

How we *define the subject* of research will always be strongly related to the choice of methodology. This is true both for what we represent as 'the Web' and the level at which we study it. In this chapter there has been the space to point only briefly at a range of techniques and frameworks for studying the every changing phenomenon which is the Web. Throughout I have emphasized that even though the Web appears to be about electronic communication, every component is also set within the *social and economic infrastructure* within which this communication/information network has emerged. This infrastructure, in turn, influences our methodological options. We should not rely on the technical abilities and infrastructure of the Web to drive all of our data collection, yet there are creative and useful tools being developed that can be used alongside well-established methods such as interviewing and ethnography. Susan Leigh Star has written that methodology is 'a way of surviving experience' (1994, 13). In the world of rapidly changing technological products, platforms and visions, we need as many ways of surviving experience as possible.

USEFUL WEBSITES

Computer Assisted Qualitative Data Analysis Software Networking Project: **www.soc.surrey.ac.uk/caqdas**
This project aims to disseminate an understanding of the practical skills needed to use software which has been designed to assist qualitative data analysis (e.g. field research, ethnography, text analysis). The website has links to software sites where free demo downloads of the products can be acquired. Many of these software products now allow use of audio, text and visual data. Useful bibliography.

Social Research Update: **www.soc.surrey.ac.uk/sru**
SRU is a newsletter resource for social scientists interested in keeping up to date with the latest methodological concerns in social research. Several issues are directly relevant to Web research: Issue 11 looked at 'Visual Methods' and Issue 21 dealt with 'Using Email as a Research Tool'.

Cyber Geography Research: **www.cybergeography.org**
This site provides a gateway into research which is concerned with the spatial mapping of the internet, including the Web. It provides access to a directory of 'Atlases of Cyberspaces', which includes links to many commercial and academic projects, and a regular research bulletin.

Media Metrix: **www.mediametrix.com**
Media Metrix advertises itself as a 'pioneer and leader in the field of internet and digital media measurement services'. See this site for a window on the commercial world of market research of the Web, including rankings of companies, a client list and indications of what Fortune 500 companies want to know about the Web.

Part II

WEB LIFE, ARTS AND CULTURE

4

A Home on the Web: Presentations of Self on Personal Homepages

Charles Cheung

When I was young, I loved Japanese animation and comics so much that I wanted to become a comic book artist myself. When I was 10, I made a book called 'The Comic Kingdom of Charles', which included a biography detailing my struggles to become a 10-year-old amateur comic producer, a two-page feature about my family, a scrapbook with photos of me and my school friends, and selected comic strips I had drawn. I wanted other kids to read my book, but I didn't have the money to publish it. I wanted to circulate it among my classmates, but I was afraid they'd laugh at my efforts. In the end, my only reader was a relative who wasn't very interested in comics. I still think it was a brilliant piece of work for a 10-year-old kid but, needless to say, it has never been published.

Today, my story would have a very different ending. When I was a little boy, access to a large reading public was limited to a privileged few. Writers could compose novels and short stories, academics could publish papers, artists could produce their work, successful business people might write autobiographies, and stars could 'confess all' to magazine journalists. The high production costs

How many personal homepages are there on the Web?

Although it is difficult to compile statistics indicating the dispersed and ever-changing number of homepages on the Web, a look at the press relations sections of a handful of the sites offering free Web space shows that the numbers must add up quickly: Tripod.com and Geocities.com claim over four million active homepage builders each, for example, and Xoom.com claims a further two million (January 2000). Millions more homepages reside in the numerous other free services, the webspace provided by Internet Service Providers, and within commercial and educational sites. Personal homepage websites have increasingly become a popular Web 'destination'. Surveys published by Media Metrix (www.mediametrix.com) during 1998-2000, recording the audience reach of websites, showed strong and fast growth in sites offering free personal homepage space, such as Angelfire.com, Xoom.com, Tripod.com and Geocities.com.

of the print media, however, kept these mediums of self-presentation beyond the reach of the general public. Of course, ordinary people could write diaries or keep family albums, but their readership was limited to relatives and friends. With the emergence of the personal homepage on the Web, however, things have started to change. Anyone with access to an internet-connected computer, and a certain degree of practice, can now present their creative work, biography, family photos, and opinions to net browsers around the world. Millions of people have already put up homepages with personal information about themselves and their interests, often featuring their families, friends and even their pets. Erickson (1996) rightly points out that, with the personal homepage, for the first time 'individuals can project huge amounts of detailed information about themselves to a mass audience'.

So what do people do with this fascinating medium? What strategic decisions do they make when transferring their 'real life' persona into its virtual equivalent in this public space? What do they get out of it? Who are their audiences? Should we believe everything we read on personal homepages? This chapter attempts to address these questions by focusing on the presentation of self and the way that self is 'read' on the personal homepage.

What is a personal homepage?

Before discussing self-presentation on personal homepages, I want to define what a personal homepage is:

> A personal homepage is a website produced by an individual (or couple, or family) which is centred around the personality and identity of its author(s).

The categories of personal information on a personal homepage may include:

☞ diary, journal, or autobiography
☞ 'description' of the author's personality
☞ views on personal, social, political and cultural issues
☞ personal photographs
☞ achievements and awards
☞ places of living and working
☞ information on and links to personal interests
☞ links to websites created by acquaintances, friends and family members
☞ links to websites created by organizations and schools with which the author is or has been affiliated.

Broadly speaking, there are two types of personal homepage. The first tells us directly about its author. It usually has a short biography, some of the author's views on certain matters, one or more pictures of the author (and his or her pets!), along with favourite hobbies or activities, and links to favourite sites. The second type introduces the author indirectly, by providing information about something that he or she is devoted to, such as a band, occupation, movie star, religion or hobby. It usually features an account of how the author has developed this particular area of interest, articles written by the author on that subject, a 'news' or 'events' section with the latest happenings, some links to other sites on the same topic, and a list of online bookstores or shops for purchasing relevant items. Although this kind of personal homepage gives little personal information about the author, it does suggest indirectly what the author may be like through the language, design, style and content of the site.

The motivations for making personal homepages are diverse. Some people use them primarily to communicate their news to friends and family, others want to share their beliefs or hobbies with like-minded individuals. Some people are searching for friendship or love, some simply want to learn HTML, others enjoy the creative process – and there can be many other motives (Roeder, 1997a; Buten, 1996).

Self-presentation on the personal homepage

Regardless of their content, and the motivations behind their production, all personal homepages inevitably involve self-presentation. The creative process starts with one question: 'What am I going to put on my page?' The homepage author asks, in effect, 'What aspects of my "selves" should I present on my webpage?' The concept of 'self' in late modernity is too complicated to be discussed at length here, so I will briefly summarize the arguments relevant to our discussion (for an accessible overview, see Hall, 1992).

☞ Late-modern society offers a range of possible social and cultural identities, including those based in gender identity, nationality, religion, family relationships, sexuality, occupation, leisure interests, political concerns and so on.

☞ We usually incorporate more than one of the aforementioned social and cultural identities to form our selves: the British-born Chinese feminist kick-boxing policewoman and mother who loves lesbian fiction and Tom Hanks movies, for example.

☞ Different identity categories may contradict each other. For example, a diligent lawyer is expected to work at evenings and weekends, but as a wife and mother she may find that her family expect to see a lot of her as well.

☞ Contradictions may also exist between the identity one wants and the identity one lives. A woman may identify as a traditional 'happy housewife', but her daily experience – unending chores, isolation from the outside world – may constantly contradict this aspirant identity.

☞ In sum, the 'selves' that we have are composed of multiple identities and the associated contradictory experiences. In late-modern society, it is almost impossible to have a fully unified, completed and coherent 'self'; rather, we all tend to have fleeting, multiple and contradictory selves.

We are not concerned here with the identities that specific individuals adopt in real life or with their associated experiences. Our point is rather that, by using the expressive resources of the personal homepage, authors can choose which aspects of their multiple and contradictory selves they wish to present. As Goffman (1959) suggests, in everyday encounters, the social settings and audiences we face always define the kinds of 'acceptable' selves we should present – we perform as hard-working students in front of teachers in class, as responsible employees in front of our bosses and colleagues, and as wild romantics in front of our lovers. However, homepage self-presentation is a wholly voluntary affair, where we choose our own target audience, or audiences, and decide which part(s) of our 'selves' are most suitable for presentation to them. A family making a site for grandparents may choose to present their happy family life, but conceal the fact that both parents recently got the sack. A girl writing a homepage to experiment with HTML may express nothing private on her site but she will still care about whether she looks like a keen amateur homepage programmer. An artist may hope to start up her own Web design business and so may choose to present herself as a single female artist on her homepage, thus deliberately omitting the identities of wife and mother she presents to her husband and kids in real life. A young man, however, may want to find love online, and so may 'honestly' present all aspects of his romantic life: being dumped recently, his ideal woman, his star sign and so on.

Lynda's homepage (www.crosswinds.net/~lyndavandenelzen/HOME.htm) illustrates this creative process. Using the different expressive resources of the personal homepage – in Lynda's case biography, links, fan activity and a newsletter, but also including music, sound effects, poetry, fiction, original artwork, graphics and desktop backgrounds – website authors present their 'multiple and contradictory' selves. As detailed below, several examples of this sort of expressive resource manipulation are evident from Lynda's homepage.

☞　The *biography* is a good place for homepage authors to present their multiple and contradictory selves in an orderly way. Lynda's section called 'Me, I, and Myself' is an example. Lynda first confesses to her readers that she falls short of the standard of being an 'exemplary student', as she doesn't study much or have long-range career plans. However, she is not particularly unhappy, as her diverse range of hobbies helps her to define herself as a 'young girl with eclectic taste'. She sets herself apart from her peers – as she says, 'I've always been different from everyone else, so why stop now?' Then she goes on to say that she is a mature 'optimist' who enjoys life, but is also a 'political cynic' and a keen 'individualist' who has some complaints about society. The multiple selves presented here are obvious.

☞　Site authors can use *Web page links* and devote a certain number of *sections* to highlighting certain aspects of their selves. In Lynda's case, we see this in the 'Links' and – you guessed it, Web fans – the 'X-Files Page'. In the 'Links' section, Lynda includes links to some websites about the writer T.S. Eliot, the SF television programme *The X-Files*, and the female singer-songwriters Tori Amos and Sarah McLachlan. In the 'X-Files' section, she includes episode transcripts (presumably 'lifted' from another site), a couple of X-Files desktop backgrounds and some pictures from the programme. The overall effect is that she presents herself as a young woman with eclectic taste who is also a fan of this popular TV series.

☞　If the *biography* is best for more organized self-presentation, the *diary*, *newsletter* and *journal* are more suitable for making an immediate record of spontaneous thoughts, random ideas and notes about recent encounters or events. In Lynda's homepage, she uses the 'Newsletter' section to record her complicated feelings towards life in general.

Lynda's homepage is just one example of the millions of personal homepages. In fact, people from all walks of life have started to use personal homepages to present positively their self-defined 'virtual' selves: cancer patients, retired scientists, kids with disabilities, vinyl collectors, kung fu movie lovers, transsexuals, DIY enthusiasts, pornographic movie lovers – virtually anyone with any identity. Listed in Yahoo! there are even hundreds of cats with their own homepages. The degree of creative freedom the medium of the personal homepage provides for net users to construct and present their 'selves' is enormous.

The personal homepage as an emancipatory medium

The personal homepage, as discussed above, allows ordinary people to present their 'selves' to the net public. But the emancipatory possibilities of the personal homepage are perhaps more important than the sheer size of the audience it can reach. This section will illustrate two other emancipatory characteristics of the personal homepage.

First, personal homepage production 'emancipates' the author because it allows a much more polished and elaborate delivery of impression management compared with face-to-face interaction. Goffman (1959: 34) suggests that, besides 'verbal assertions', there are many 'sign vehicles' that are widely recognized as expressions given off unintentionally by people, by which others can evaluate how successful or sincere the self-presentation is. Some sign vehicles, like sex, age and race, are extremely difficult to conceal or manipulate in face-to-face interaction. Although the rest – such as clothing, posture, speech pattern, facial expression, bodily gesture and intonation – are relatively more manipulatable, Goffman emphasizes the difficulties in exerting total control over these sign vehicles (14–18). In a nutshell,

4.1 Spacegirl's stylish homepage, with her art, photos, journal and more (www.spacegirl.org).

Goffman suggests that presentation of self in everyday life is a delicate enterprise, subject to moment-to-moment mishaps and unintentional misrepresentations.

Moreover, most self-presentation in everyday life is not like a formal job interview in which we can do a 3-minute self-introduction. On the contrary, most face-to-face interaction proceeds in a spontaneous manner, during which we will never have an assigned block of time to present ourselves in an orderly and systematic fashion. More often than not, we constantly have to adjust our presentation to the unexpected reactions of others: their suspicious gazes, their impatient gestures or their provocative questions. The selves we present are always much more unorganized and haphazard than we intend.

In contrast, the 'sign vehicles' used in homepage self-presentation are more subject to manipulation. For example, in real life we sometimes 'give off an impression' we regret. If we chortle when our boss is making an idiotic argument in a meeting, we cannot rewind the scene and remind ourselves not to chortle when they make the point again. On our personal homepage, however, we can manipulate all the elements until we are satisfied: we can always experiment with the background colour, choose the most presentable head shot, censor the foul language accidentally written in the biography draft, and ponder as long as we like before deciding whether to tell the readers that our partner just dumped us. If we have put our risqué swimsuit pictures on our page, but then worry if our parents or boss will stumble across them, we can just delete them. Even on a webcam through which other Web browsers can see us 24 hours a day, we can always 'dress up' in front of a carefully positioned camera. In other words, the personal homepage allows careful construction of our personal portrayal before its release to the audience. All the mishaps mentioned by Goffman that may affect one's self-presentation in everyday life can be avoided on the personal homepage.

Second, the personal homepage can be emancipatory because it insulates the author from direct embarrassment, rebuff and harassment. As all face-to-face interaction involves the co-presence of others, we always have the chance to experience rejection and shame. Miller argues that the personal homepage is immune to these two problems:

> On the Web you can put yourself up for interaction without being aware of a rebuff, and others can try you out without risking being involved further than they would wish. There is another liberation that can be negative, too. One of the regulating and controlling forces in face-to-face interaction is embarrassment. That is less likely to work on the Web. Others may find your Web page ridiculous, but you probably won't be aware of it. Those others who might be prompted to find ways to mend your presentation to reduce their own embarrassment in a face-to-face encounter are unlikely to feel pressure to smooth over the interaction between themselves and a Web page. So, in two senses, it is easy to make a fool of yourself on the Web: there is little to stop you doing it, but doing it will cause you little pain.
>
> (Miller, 1995)

Moreover, although much has been written on cyberstalkers, who track down Web contacts in the real world, the personal homepage is still a relatively safe environment. Homepage authors can easily maintain relative anonymity by leaving out certain bits of 'vital' personal data by which others would be able to identify their physical location. Furthermore, there is little evidence that any more than a tiny minority of homepage authors have experienced harassment from unknown audiences.

The above analysis clearly demonstrates why the personal homepage is very valuable for some people. First, it is emancipatory for those who feel they have difficulty presenting themselves in face-to-face interaction. Chandler and Roberts-Young (1998) rightly argue that we should not privilege 'the particular "reality" of face-to face interaction', as some people may 'feel more "at home" in representational media than in face-to-face interaction'. These homepage authors may feel better able to express themselves through the use of biographies, online writing, or their photos. The personal homepage liberates those who want to present their personal information to others but find it difficult to do so in real life.

Second, the personal homepage is emancipatory for those who want to present 'hidden' aspects of themselves – things they are cautious to reveal in 'real life' because of fear of rejection or embarrassment. Two case studies demonstrate that some gays and lesbians may use the personal homepage to present their identities while avoiding telling others face-to-face (Chandler, 1998).

☞ James, a British gay man, 'was out in cyberspace long before being out in daily life'. He found it useful to be able to say to people, 'Oh, didn't you know?', as if the issue was old news.

☞ Rob, living in London, commented that his Web page provided an easy way for him to come out. He would say to friends, 'Check out my website', and let them see his positive expressions of gay identity, and 'think about it before reacting'.

Of course, homepages are not only for providing 'difficult' information to people the author already knows. When personal homepages are linked to other websites about particular objects, ideas, or activities, visitors may 'surf on in' and be introduced to the homepage creator. The author of a website about comics, skateboarding or horses effectively says 'Hello, this is me' to all the visitors who follow the link within the site to its creator's personal page. If they like what they see, they may establish contact through e-mail, or via the site's guestbook or feedback forms. Cyberfriendships are made this way.

Homepage selves and real-life selves

We should also be aware of the danger of assuming that people are 'really' like the persona presented on their Web page, especially given the opportunity for impression management. In a 1996 US personal homepage survey by Buten (1996), homepage authors were asked: 'Do you present yourself as accurately as possible in your Web page?' Buten reports that almost all (91 per cent) reported that they felt they had presented themselves accurately in their homepages. But what did 'accurate' mean to the respondents? As I have argued above, the 'self' or 'selves' presented on personal homepages are highly contrived artefacts, since homepage authors consciously select particular parts of their selves for presentation. In this sense, they may still feel that they present themselves 'accurately', as long as they do not 'lie' in presenting those parts of their selves. In fact, as I have already shown, the work of impression management on personal homepages can be highly polished and elaborate.

Another reason for caution in reading the homepage 'self' is the issue of self-censorship. This can be illustrated by a survey of online diarists – people who maintain a diary or personal journal on the Web. The researcher Roeder (1997b) asked, 'Do you censor yourself in your online diary?' The result suggests that most diarists did censor their writing online: 87 per cent said they had done so, and only 13 per cent claimed they never had. Roeder also observes that sexual details were a 'relative rarity' in online diaries, even though sex could be expected to be a part of online diarists' lives. Although the survey was exploring a specific type of personal homepage – the online diary, it would not be unreasonable to expect self-censorship to occur in other types of personal homepage as well.

But why would authors self-censor? Goffman's idea of 'audience segregation' may help to explain this phenomenon. Goffman (1959: 135–40) argues that if a person is

● **4.2** Mahir Cagri's homepage (http://members.xoom.com/primall/mahir), which received millions of hits due to the popularity of its 'I kiss you!' message of worldly love.

caught presenting an unexpected aspect of herself to an unintended audience, that audience may become disillusioned not only about that aspect, but about the other 'self' more usually presented to them. For example, if a young girl who has been perceived as well behaved in school is then seen shouting abuse at elderly people outside the school gates, her image as a 'good' girl will be tarnished. In everyday life we rely on 'segregation of physical environment' to help us to play the game of 'segregation of audience'. Some men will only show their sentimental side to their partners at home, away from their male friends and bosses. Only when with their closest friends do some women disclose the intimate details of their relationships, telling secrets they may not even share with their partners. However, segregating physical environment and audience is more difficult to achieve on the personal homepage than in everyday life. Although homepage authors may only give their site address to a few friends, family members and colleagues, rather than submitting it to search engines, there is always a danger that unwanted audiences may accidentally stumble across it.

A certain degree of self-censorship must take place during homepage construction, then, as authors will always have information they are unwilling to reveal on the public Web: a girl may avoid mentioning her smoking habit in the 'hobby' section of her homepage (unwanted audience: her parents and teachers), a boy may suppress the fact that he has three girlfriends on his homepage about his philosophy of love (unwanted audience: his lovers, of course), and so on. This problem of self-censorship may be most prominent in the staff homepage section of institutional websites, because the company must insure that self-presentations do not run counter to the organization's carefully cultivated corporate image. Since staff homepages are usually subject to certain forms of surveillance from superiors, or even monitoring units, conscious or unconscious self-censorship of certain personal information is bound to occur (Wynn and Katz, 1999).

Cat Calls: One Cat's Stock Market Predictions

Prepared by Skye, D.S.H. (Domestic Short Hair)

The Canadian and U.S. markets have had a tremendous run over the last six years. Now, for the first time, the tide is turning. Growth in Canada has actually been *falling* for the most recent two months for which statistics are available. The main threat now, to both markets, is the Asian downturn. While greeted initially as a positive by investors who were concerned about the threat of inflation and rising interest rates, it is becoming clearer that deflation and not inflation poses the greatest threat.

Of course, hindsight is usually excellent, but could it be that the collapse in the price of gold we've seen during the last two years was the harbinger of a severe global downturn? It is beginning to look like it. Prices for oil, [...]

4.3 The personal homepage of Skye, a cat, who offers stock market tips. The logo at the top notes that the page is in the 'top 5 per cent of all cat financial websites'. Small print at the bottom warns 'Before investing in the stock or bond markets, you should consult a professional broker or investment advisor. Remember also that Skye is only a cat, and most cats are notoriously poor investors' (www.calcna.ab.ca/~kyasench/catcalls.html).

Conclusion

As we have seen, the personal homepage provides a range of ways in which net users can carefully select, polish and embellish aspects of their selves to present to their friends, families and unacquainted Web surfers, without risking the embarrassment or harassment that may be experienced in face-to-face interaction. Some internet commentators complain that personal homepages are filled with trivialized personal information unworthy of skimming (DiGovanna, 1995; Lem, 1999), but I would argue that the personal homepage is a very powerful medium for ordinary people to present the selves that may not otherwise be displayed in 'real life'. The media is flooded with stereotypical images and representations: the serious and aggressive businessman, the stupid teenager, the sexually available woman and numerous others. Individuals may feel that these stereotypes are unjust and the personal homepage provides an opportunity for people to present their 'selves' to the public (or net browsers, at least) beyond these crude images circulated in popular media: a businessman can express his repressed nurturing side, a woman may emphasize her professional achievements, and a teenager can argue that *A Tale of Two Cities* and the *Superman* comic are equally rewarding. There may be radio phone-ins and TV audience talk-back programmes for the 'users' of these media to express their points of view, but the limited access to these shows, as well as the pre-defined nature of their topics – and the commercial pressures that affect their selection – means that they never allow people the degree of creative freedom offered by the personal homepage. Although for some people the personal homepage may be a medium for presenting fabricated 'selves', the unavoidable existence of a certain degree of deception and overstatement is surely a price worth paying for this emancipatory medium. After all, it is the only medium in which most people are truly able to become 'authors', presenting their suppressed or misrepresented selves to audiences around the world.

Author's note   Thanks to David Gauntlett and Kirsten Pullen for their help with this chapter.

USEFUL WEBSITES

Unsurprisingly, *Yahoo!*'s list of personal homepages under 'Society and Culture > People > Personal Home Pages' is a good starting point . . . if you want thousands of unsorted pages to choose from.

About.com – Personal Web Pages: **http://personalweb.about.com**
A diverse range of articles about personal homepages: statistics, technical know-how, recommended books and selected sites.

Webring.org: **www.webring.org**
Webrings connect every type of homepage you could imagine – and some you would never dream of. Homepages with similar personal concerns are linked together in a 'ring' so that browsers can navigate through similar kinds of homepage.

The Meeting Place: **www.nis.net/meet**
Catalogue of personal homepages where authors can list their site within categories, with a graphic and a comment.

Word of Mouth:
www.glassdog.com/the_experience/word_of_mouth.html
Selected personal websites.

5

I-love-Xena.com: Creating Online Fan Communities

Kirsten Pullen

The relationship between the media text and the audience has been described within contemporary media studies as a dialogue: texts are presumed to be open to various interpretations, and audience members are presumed to interpret those texts in various ways and for various uses. Some audience members engage in this dialogue more aggressively and sustainedly than others: they are the fans. In the last ten years, several academic studies of fan communities have been undertaken, most focusing on science fiction fans taking part in conventions and producing print zines, or the hysteria surrounding certain musical groups, or the activities of sports fans. While those studies have defined and determined the boundaries of contemporary fandom, none thus far have considered the implications of the World Wide Web for this sphere of activity. This essay begins that enquiry, suggesting differences and similarities between traditional fans and fans on the Web. The online fans of the MCA/Universal syndicated hit, *Xena: Warrior Princess* and the strategies they use to create a community provide a case study of internet fan activity.

So what do fans do? How do you know a fan when you see one, on the Web or in the world? Media scholar Henry Jenkins (1992: 277–80) has identified five characteristics that fan communities share. First, fans watch and re-watch favourite programmes, looking for meaningful details, internal contradictions and ambiguity in order to find the gaps that suggest a space for intervention. Second, fans learn to understand and analyse texts in terms of the fan community. Watching this way, fans create what Jenkins calls a 'meta-text', one that has more information about characters, lifestyles, values and relationships than the original. Third, because fans have a particular investment in a programme, they often write letters about plot lines and characters, and have in some cases successfully lobbied to keep favoured series on the air; fans are active consumers. Fourth, fans create unique forms of cultural production, such as: zines publishing stories about major characters, information about actors' appearances, production schedules and gossip about the show; videos of moments from the series set to popular music and resembling music videos; fan artwork; and 'filk songs' about particular shows or characters and fan activity. On the Web, this cultural production includes websites dedicated to the programme or the programme's stars, online zines and posts to official and unofficial fan bulletin boards. Finally, fans create an alternative social community. In conversation and correspondence with other fans, viewers of a particular television text create a space that is more 'humane and democratic' than the everyday world. Brought together by their love of a particular programme, these fans form alliances with others who may have different political, social and economic backgrounds but are committed to the ideals expressed by their favoured television show. Within both

5.1 The official Xena website.

Web and traditional communities, fans frequently express pleasure and relief to find others who are like them; posts to official bulletin boards and individual websites often praise the support that online fandom provides. As one young Xena fan exclaimed on the official Xena bulletin board, 'I'm the only Xenite at my school, so it's really cool to come here and talk to all you guys! Rock on, Xena!'

Although fans are generally stereotyped as obsessive losers, lacking ties to the real world and living in a fantasy universe populated with characters from *Star Trek*, media scholars have reframed discussions of the fan, generally arguing that fan culture is unfairly maligned for a variety of reasons, often explicitly tied to class and gender. For example, John Fiske (1992) suggests that fandom is linked with aesthetic and cultural choices made by subordinate groups. In addition, Fiske points out that fan activity can include empowered social behaviour that merely substitutes for political and social action (30). For Fiske, then, fandom is a way for disenfranchised groups to engage with mass media products like television shows in a way that makes the content meaningful for them but does not necessarily offer models for political action. Similarly, media scholar Lawrence Grossberg (1992) suggests that fans of rock music and rock musicians choose to identify with certain behaviours and personalities in order to confirm their own sense of self. Identifying with 'rock and roll', rock fans borrow some of the anti-authoritarianism associated with rock culture in order to mark their own politics, behaviours, and identities (58–63). Thus, according to these analyses, fans are not fringe extremists with an unhealthy and unrealistic interest in a particular media text, but savvy consumers who are able to use popular culture to fulfil their desires and needs, often explicitly rearticulating that culture in unique and empowering ways.

Despite these scholars' attempts to celebrate and valorize fan activity, most academics have insisted on the marginality stereotypically associated with fandom. Though academic studies have included fans of musicians and athletes, the majority of work is focused on fan activity surrounding such cult favourites as *Dr Who, Beauty and the Beast*, and most famously *Star Trek* and its movies and spin-offs. And in fact, according to traditional accounts, fans of these programmes seem to most actively rework the meanings provided by the original texts and to create the most elaborate structures through which new meaning is circulated, thereby justifying the attentions of these scholars. Media scholars suggest that the choice of these particular programmes is not coincidental, as they specifically lend themselves to fan intervention. According to John Fiske, all television texts are polysemic – that is, open to interpretation and requiring viewers to make their own meanings – but some texts are more polysemic than others and are thus more likely to be appropriated and used by fans. Fiske defines these texts as 'producerly'. Producerly texts contain internal contradictions and ambiguities, providing opportunities for fans to fill in the gaps and make their own meaning (1992: 42). Shows set in the future or in alternate universes, such as science fiction programmes, and shows with a strong element of fantasy such as *Beauty and the Beast* lend themselves to being worked on and activated by fans: the fantasy included in the original text legitimizes the flights of fancy engaged in by the fans as they revise, continue and rework plot lines. According to Constance Penley's (1991) study of female *Star Trek* fans, science fiction and fantasy offer more freedom than other genres, because these texts allow for discussion of real-life issues unconstrained by real-life circumstances (138). Producerly texts invite fans to incorporate their own ideals and practices into the narratives provided.

The academic focus on marginal television programmes suggests that fans are equally marginal viewers, an assumption that belies a certain critical blindness to some of the limitations of fandom. According to traditional accounts, fans choose programmes that are presumably more open to interpretation and intervention than critically acclaimed and popular programmes. They are drawn to polysemic texts because they see something in them that critics and the mainstream audience have missed. Further, fans form an alternative community that rebels against mainstream norms and creates a space for the open communication of liberal, democratic ideals. Members of disenfranchised groups, such as women and the working class, find in favoured programmes a more equitable society and seek to replicate that society within the fan community. In fact, some media scholars (most notably Jenkins and Penley), express a certain romantic attachment for fan activity, uncritically assuming that fans who rework television's meanings are somehow better than the average viewer.

With the Web now readily available on college campuses, in public libraries and in a lot of middle-class homes, fan communities have taken their enthusiasms and discussions into cyberspace, and analyses of Web-based fan activity suggest important correctives to the assumptions made in traditional studies. Most important for Web-based fan communities are the distribution and production of fan-created texts and the sense of community talking about a favoured television programme can impart, even to viewers separated by thousands of miles. Further, the immediacy of the internet enables fans to get an immediate response to their interpretations of a particular text or fan production. Rather than waiting weeks and even months for a new zine or newsletter, within hours a fan can expect an internet reply. Xena fans can choose from and interact with nearly 200 websites devoted to the programme. These websites vary from pages with images from the television show and appearances by the stars on talk shows, news programmes and personal appearances, to sites devoted to fan fiction, sites about the charitable and community-based action of fans; and of course, most of the sites are hyperlinked to each other, often including plugs for other sites and the people who have created them. In addition, many of the sites offer tips for creating Web pages and offer the use of graphics to those designing new sites. By checking out a search engine and surfing the Web, even a fan new to either Xena or the internet can quickly find other fans and information about joining the online fan community.

Significantly, the publishing and networking capabilities of the internet have enabled more viewers to participate in activities usually associated with long-term, committed fandom. Literally anyone with access to a computer and modem can create a Web page, as many companies offer free Web space, and internet providers such as America Online furnish Web page instructions for all new members as well as space for individual Web pages. Because access to Web pages is virtually unlimited, counting the number of fan websites on the Web is nearly impossible. However, approximate data is available and suggests that there are thousands of fan websites. For example, in June 2000 the Yahoo! Web directory listed more than 33,000 websites about individual actors and actresses, television programmes and films. We can also assume that there will be thousands more sites not listed in Yahoo!, and even more by the time you read this. Traditional objects of fan culture are well represented on the Web (the ubiquitous *Star Trek* has over 1200 websites), but soap operas, talk shows, sitcoms and dramas all have internet fans.

In fact, it seems as though the Web has opened up the boundaries of fandom, allowing more people to participate in fan culture, and designating more television programmes, celebrities and films as worthy of fan activity. While traditional studies insist on the marginality of the television texts appropriated by fans, the Web offers a different model. Most television programmes and films now have internet addresses and official websites advertising themselves, providing information and serving as a clearing house for fan activity. Most of these websites provide the kind of information previously available only through fan clubs and fan activities such as newsletters and conventions. For example, CBS, NBC and ABC all have extensive websites for their daytime soap operas, which provide plot summaries, actor biographies, behind-the-scenes footage and information, and chatrooms. In the UK, the BBC and Channel 4 have provided similar websites for their top soaps. In addition, celebrities from all forms of media often host live, interactive online discussions with their fans, especially when promoting a new film, special television programme, new season, or music release. Previously, fans only spoke with celebrities at conventions or special appearances, and few celebrities participated in those kinds of fan outreach activities. America Online offers a different celebrity webcast nearly every week to its subscribers; therefore, even casual fans can chat with stars.

The ubiquity of film and television websites has blurred the boundaries between original fan activity and marketing ploys. Because movie studios in particular increasingly target the internet audience, websites advertising films are becoming more visually complex and interactive. Summer 1999 saw an increase in website and movie synergy. Both the billion-dollar *Star Wars* prequel, *Episode I: The Phantom Menace*, and the independent Artisan Entertainment release *The Blair Witch Project* depended on the Web for marketing. In the case of *Phantom Menace*, LucasFilms drew on an established fan community to make the film a hit before its actual release. *Blair Witch Project* took this strategy one step further. By establishing an enormous internet presence, with a detailed and inter-

5.2 One of several websites built to develop the *Blair Witch* myth.

active website, Artisan created fans of the movie before the movie even existed. In fact, many American reviewers have noted that the pre-movie internet buzz and film website were more interesting than the movie itself. The pre-release activity guaranteed huge opening weekends in the US for both films, and the success of these marketing techniques represents one of the most radical ways in which the Web has expanded definitions of fandom.

Within traditional accounts, fan fiction is often suggested as the basis for creative, interventionist fan activity. Fans write and circulate stories about particular television programmes, continuing narratives, creating alternate endings and, most frequently, suggesting romantic relationships not explicitly designated by the original text. According to Constance Penley, heterosexual female *Star Trek* fans write an explicitly pornographic relationship between Captain Kirk and Mr Spock. Penley argues that these stories may be used as models by the fan writers for more equitable heterosexual relationships (155). Penley asserts that the original, polysemic *Star Trek* text, explicitly invites this kind of rearticulation, and further that only texts like *Star Trek* offer the ambiguity necessary for such textual intervention (138). However, the fan fiction on the Web suggests otherwise. Yahoo! lists approximately 785 fan fiction sites, many with multiple stories and multiple authors. While marginal, presumably polysemic, texts like *La Femme Nikita*, *Babylon 5*, and *Silk Stalkings* – all syndicated US programmes – constitute the subject of most fan writing, mainstream and critical successes are also fictionalized. There are over a dozen fan fiction sites devoted to *The X-Files*, an Emmy-nominated programme with an active, more traditional fan community that suggests a bridge between the marginality usually associated with fan texts and the mainstream success most traditional fans eschew.

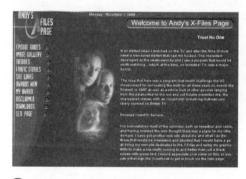

● **5.3** The truth is out there. Apparently.

Even solidly mainstream programmes have active internet fan communities. For example, the highest-rated, most expensive and most Emmy-nominated programme in the US, *ER*, has at least five fan fiction sites, with plots ranging from the imagined homosexual relationship between Dr Mark Greene and Dr Doug Ross, to cross-overs with other television characters such as the doctors on another hospital drama *Chicago Hope*, to alternate endings to the relationship between Dr Ross and nurse Carol Hathaway. In addition, the soap opera *Guiding Light* has at least one fan fiction site, focusing on the relationship between two of the principal characters, Danny and Michelle Santos. Though soap opera fans and traditional fan communities are generally considered distinct phenomena, and though mainstream texts have generally been considered closed to the plurality of readings necessary to fan activity, on the Web common fan practices emerge.

It seems as though the Web has mainstreamed fandom, allowing more viewers to participate in activities usually reserved for alternate communities interested in marginal texts; and fans' pervasive presence on the internet suggests that stereotypes of the fan as a fringe obsessive may give way to views of the fan as an average Web user. On the internet, it seems as though nearly everyone is a fan, and nearly everything is worthy of fan adulation. As the case study of *Xena: Warrior Princess* demonstrates, fan communities on the Web share characteristics with the exclusive, marginal populations in studies like Jenkins' and Penley's, and simultaneously provide a more inclusive and diffuse model.

Xena: Warrior Princess debuted in syndication in 1995. Produced by Renaissance Pictures, a production company owned by director Sam Raimi and distributed for syndication through MCA/Universal pictures, the programme is carried on several cable channels and local Fox affiliates; reruns are currently shown daily on the US cable network. *Xena: Warrior Princess* features New Zealand actors Lucy Lawless in the title role and Renee O'Connor as her trusty sidekick, the bard Gabrielle. Xena and Gabrielle travel around the Mediterranean countryside, protecting the innocent and punishing the wicked. In most typical plots, a poor village is under siege from a cruel and greedy warlord. Xena and Gabrielle help the villagers band together to oust the evil tyrant, using a combination of swordplay, fisticuffs and quasi-martial arts techniques. During their travels, Xena and Gabrielle have met King David, Helen of Troy, Caesar, Vishnu, the archangel Michael and various other gods, goddesses and monsters.

Xena is a relatively generic action/adventure show, albeit with a fair amount of campy humour, historical anachronism and female heroines. In John Fiske's terms, *Xena: Warrior Princess* is a particularly polysemic text. Its humour and fantasy lend themselves to the kind of fan activity associated with traditional fan communities. However, on the Web, Xena fans do not constitute a totally unified community: *Xena: Warrior Princess* is a text that is read from multiple and often contradictory positions within its fan communities, and fans put their investment and identification with Xena to a variety of uses.

The Web has a variety of sites devoted to *Xena: Warrior Princess*, ranging from Usenet groups to fan websites to the official MCA/Universal homepage. Further, these fan sites seem to differentiate along sex and gender lines. Xena fans can roughly be divided into lesbians, straight men, and straight women. When Xena first became a cult hit, these groups were often openly hostile towards one another, with lesbians and straight women in particular battling over the 'meaning' of the show and its depiction of the relationship between Xena and Gabrielle. Now, however, there seems to be more tolerance among Xena fans, with alliances between the groups visible on individual websites and on the official bulletin board. For example *The Ultimate Xena Fan Fiction Directory* (1999), includes heterosexual male and female writers and lesbian writers, all who seem to encourage and enjoy each others' output. In addition, *A Day in the Life . . . (of a Xena Addict)* (1999) a website maintained by a heterosexual female fan, includes links to several lesbian fan pages. In addition, lesbian fans have become more visible on the official website and now have more Web pages than any other group.

Lesbian websites generally focus on the relationship between Xena and Gabrielle, which most of the fans refer to as the 'subtext' of the show. Subtext fans watch the show for what one fan calls 'the electricity that runs just beneath the surface of *Xena*' (Dax) and some catalogue each instance of homoerotic contact on their individual websites. *Dax's Museum of Subtext* (1997) is such an archive, begun because the fan is 'tired of hearing the mental gymnastics created and executed by the 'phobes [homophobic fans] on other Xena lists'. In fact, recognition and discussion of the subtext makes up an important activity for many Xena fans. By acknowledging and celebrating the subtext, lesbian viewers create a critical framework for understanding the programme, one that distinguishes between fans and suggests at least a contingent political position.

5.4 More Xena fiction than you can shake a sword at.

In addition to recognizing the subtext in the original programme, lesbian viewers actively rearticulate the relationship between Xena and Gabrielle through fan fiction. *Xena: Warrior Princess* has dozens of fan fiction sites, and many develop a lesbian relationship between Xena, Gabrielle and other female characters. Lisa Jain Thompson's *Xenerotica* (1999) website includes original artwork, poems and short stories, most written by Thompson herself, but others contributed by fellow lesbian fans. This soft-core erotica is prefaced by a warning that if the viewer is under 18 or easily offended, they should 'stop reading now and go outside and play'. All of the erotic fan fiction sites have similar warnings, though it seems as if such warnings are used differently by different fans. In Thompson's case, it seems clear that she is attempting to protect herself from charges of distributing pornography to minors and to warn off fans who might denigrate her depiction of Xena and Gabrielle's relationship. Other fan fiction sites, such as Tim Wellman's *Alternative Fan Fiction Gallery* (1998) display warnings acknowledging that not all fans are interested in erotic fantasies and should therefore not read specific narratives.

Of course, not all fan fiction is erotic: stories about Xena and Gabrielle travelling through time to meet their fans, narratives that focus on the friendship between the women, and encounters with characters from other television shows, myths and historical episodes also exist on the Web. And not all erotic fan fiction is written by lesbians. Wellman's site includes both lesbian and heterosexual fan fiction, and categorizes the erotica depending on the sexual activity depicted. Interestingly, Wellman writes some lesbian fan fiction himself, and though these stories are presumably written by a straight man, they are virtually identical to lesbian fan fiction written by lesbians. Though in some ways lesbians maintain a distinct fan community on the Web, especially because they insist on the primacy of the subtext, within fan writing these distinctions blur.

Many heterosexual male fans take a similarly sexual approach to *Xena: Warrior Princess* as many of the lesbian sites. These websites parallel the kinds of pages dedicated to other female celebrities and contain many images of Lucy Lawless, Renee O'Connor, and other female stars from the show. *Chris Boehm's Xena Page* has been on the Web since 1995, and its content is fairly typical of male fan pages. Boehm's homepage asserts that he is Xena's '#1 fan' and alludes to other fans who don't have the same kind of respect and affinity for Xena that he does. In addition, he affirms that 'Lucy Lawless is one of the hottest stars on TV right now. (Yes, hotter than any *Baywatch* woman.) She is a class act and possesses every quality that an established star ought to have.'

Boehm's assertion that he is a true Xena fan and that others don't share the kinds of investment he has made is echoed on many other fan sites, regardless of gender or sexual orientation. Like the lesbian fans who focus on the show's subtext, other fans are determined to control multiple readings of *Xena: Warrior Princess*. Straight female fans, for example, are often hostile to subtext sites and bulletin board postings. Their websites include celebrations of the platonic friend-

ship between Xena and Gabrielle, and often discuss the influence the relationship has had on their lives: as a post to the official Xena bulletin board explains,
'This Forum has helped me along. . . . And the summer has been easier because
of the Wonderful Xenite's here . . .'. Despite the differences in meaning, Xena
Web pages are visually very similar, as nearly all include images, broadcast schedules, fan fiction, show gossip, guestbooks and links to other sites.

These fan sites draw on the official MCA/Universal website, inaugurated in
1995. The site includes programme summaries and air dates; cast, crew, and
producer biographies; an extensive database that promises information on any
theme, character, place, or prop from the show's texts; a collection of the 'Xena
Scrolls', documents supposedly found by an archaeologist that serve the basis for
the programme; an online shopping service for Xena memorabilia; and a bulletin
board. There are Xena games, online polls, a sweepstake, an archive of images,
a map of Xena and Gabrielle's travels, and downloadable graphics, sounds and
video. The official site itself encourages fan interaction, especially as it provides
material for fan websites and a bulletin board for discussions about the show and
actors.

However, the official site encourages only particular kinds of fan activity.
Despite their overwhelming presence on the Web, lesbian fans are virtually invisible on the official site and MCA/Universal never mentions Xena's subtext. Even
the database that promises unlimited information does not recognize the terms
'subtext' or 'lesbian'. In addition, the official site displays an uneasy relationship
between commercialism and fandom, offering both free graphics and expensive
memorabilia, all contained within the assumption that Xena exists and her world
is accessible to the viewer. For example, the separate category Web pages on the
site are headed with faux archaic text like 'Lay down your weapons and carry
instead treasures' for the online merchandise store. This archaic syntax is particularly interesting since the television programme includes anachronistic references to unauthorized biographies, fast food, the fitness craze and beauty
pageants. However, the official site purports to transmit the viewer into Xena's
world; the archaic language is presumably used to distance the viewer from such
crass, 'fanatical' activities as collecting memorabilia and to facilitate total immer-
sion in the online Xena experience.

The official site also maintains a bulletin board, or NetForum, with threaded
fan comments, which receives about 50 posts on the days Xena episodes are aired,
and about a dozen posts during the week. Posts are databased and archived, and
date back to 1995. Sentiments expressed include a love for and identification with
Xena and Gabrielle, production gossip, plugs for individual Web pages, and often-
contentious debates over meaning. Fans muse on the influence their posts have
on the show's content and worry that their comments are being monitored. In
general, fans are concerned that MCA/Universal will shut down the NetForum if
they express contradictory opinions and criticism, suggesting an antipathy
towards the production company. Heated exchanges frequently centre on Xena's
subtext:

> For all of you who think that Xena and Gabby are lesbians because of [the
> episode] *Is there a Doctor?* you need a more open mind and get a life.
> Gabby is giving Xena mouth to mouth resuscitation!!! They are not
> kissing!!! Grow up and get a life! That's not what the show is about!!!

This post was answered by a presumably lesbian fan: 'You need to get a life!!!
How do you KNOW they're not kissing!?! It sure looked like that to me!' The
official website, which seems to encourage some kinds of fan activity, does not

necessarily reflect a harmonious community making consistent meanings from *Xena: Warrior Princess*.

Despite different interpretations and disparate fan communities on the Web, a significant Xena unity is visible. One website, *Sword and Staff* (1997) is an online clearing house for charitable activity done in Xena's name. Fans are invited to donate to different charities and take part in auctions to raise money for a variety of causes. Generally, fans donate Xena merchandise and other celebrity memorabilia to auctions designated to a particular cause. Judging by the different charities and comments on the Sword and Staff site, a variety of fans are active in these philanthropic pursuits. Between May 1997 and October 1999, nearly US$105,000 was donated by Xena fans to children's hospitals, women's shelters, rainforest preservationists and AIDS organizations. This charitable activity is unprecedented in fan communities, and seems to demonstrate the opportunities for social action the Web might offer. The auctions, based on the wildly popular eBay site, suggest that Xena fans are harnessing Web technology to move beyond merely talking about a favoured television programme and the ideals it espouses to putting those ideals into practice.

Despite the aggressive, sustained fan activity visible on the Web, the internet should not be assumed to have created utopian fan communities. And despite the example of *Sword and Staff*, few internet fans have moved from imagination into action. As the examples in this chapter suggest, fandom on the Web is a complex phenomenon. More fans are able to take part in fan activity, and fan cultural production is more readily available to a larger community. However, fans do not always interpret texts, fan production, or fan positions and identifications similarly. Though the internet may have begun to mainstream fandom, it has not necessarily created a single, unified fan position or practice.

Author's note   Josh Heuman, Ann Linden and Jami Moss were particularly helpful during discussions about the impact of the World Wide Web on fan communities. In addition to these discussions, all three commented on earlier drafts of this chapter, and their input is gratefully acknowledged.

USEFUL WEBSITES

The Blair Witch Project: **www.blairwitch.com**
The official website for the independent film, the first movie marketed and hyped almost exclusively on the Web.

Countdown: The Ultimate Fan Site: **www.countingdown.com**
Professional fan site that serves as a clearing house for release dates, production gossip and celebrity appearances for many major motion pictures.

Dax's Museum of Xena Subtext:
http://members.aol.com/xenastry/subtext/subtext.htm
Scene-by-scene analysis of homoerotic content in each Xena episode from the first three seasons of the programme.

Storm and Spirit's Domain:
http://xantia.simplenet.com/LucyLawless/index.html
This site combines Xena fandom with lesbian and gay rights activism, and
includes several links to gay charities, political groups and discussion boards.

Sword and Staff: **www.sword-and-staff.com**
Online clearing house for charitable activities undertaken by Xena fans.
Includes online auctions, event schedules and personal messages for the
series' stars and producers.

Chris Boehm's Xena Page: **http://webspan.net/~ironman/xena.html**
On the Web since 1995, one of the longest-running and most extensive
individual fan sites.

The Ultimate Xena Fan Fiction Directory: **www.xenafanfiction.com**
Archived database with hundreds of Xena fan fiction stories, contributed by
heterosexual male, female and lesbian fans. Promises the most extensive
collection of Xena fiction.

Whoosh! International Association of Xena Studies:
http://whoosh.org
Online fan newsletter with articles about the meaning of the show, particularly interesting because it includes both scholarly and more traditional fan
perspectives.

Xena: Warrior Lesbian Links:
www.geocities.com/TelevisionCity/4580/links.html
List of links to dozens of lesbian fan sites.

Xena: Warrior Princess: **www.mca.com/tv/xena**
The official Xena website.

The X-Files: The Official X-Files Web Site: **www.thex-files.com**
Fox television's official website for the series. Contains air dates, plot
summaries, actor and crew biographies, a chronology and an explanation of
the show's mythology.

Andy's X-Files Page: **www.saxfp.f9.co.uk**
One of the most technologically intensive fan sites on the Web. In addition
to standard fan site content, Andy also provides links to downloadable audio
and video technology, original animation using stills from the programme
and a list of top ten X-Files sites, determined by online voting and updated
weekly.

The X-Files Romantic Fan Fiction Archive:
www.geocities.com/Area51/4261
Hundreds of stories, primarily exploring the relationship between Fox
Mulder and Dana Scully, although both lesbian and homosexual romantic
fantasies are included as well.

6 //

Artists' Websites: Declarations of Identity and Presentations of Self

Eva Pariser

Contemporary visual artists have embraced the Web, creating websites as a natural extension of their artistic output. These sites, while serving a multitude of purposes, exist as a vehicle for self-referential expression. Issues of identity, along with declarations of existence, constitute the motivational force behind self-referential art. Artists working within this mode of expression frequently incorporate in their work a combination of what may be self-images, images of other personally significant individuals, or objects and symbols directly associated with the artist.

Applying this definition to artist websites in their entirety, considering them an art form unto themselves, we encounter a unique example of self-referential expression particular to the medium of the internet. Any artist can create a website. The World Wide Web is an open forum where there are no quality controls, no art establishment guidelines to adhere to, and no institutional acceptance is required. With this in mind, the art represented in the websites selected for discussion here will not be subject to aesthetic judgements; rather the focus will be on the artist's self-conscious, self-promotion in creation of self-referential art particular to this new medium.

Most artist websites are highly self-referential. Certain artists create art works that are self-referential while others do not, yet the websites of the majority of artists on the internet are replete with references to the artist themselves. Not only is the visitor invited to become acquainted with the works of art, but also with the artist, often on a personal level. Self-revelation is quite common. Material of a personal, confessional or autobiographical nature is freely offered. Self-images are included in nearly all these sites. Sometimes friends and family members play a part as well. Even the family pet can make an appearance. Access to the artist via e-mail, telephone, fax or mail is readily available; comments and suggestions are encouraged. Privacy does not seem to be an issue for many artists choosing to promote themselves through the Web. What may have originated as a means of obtaining exposure and selling works of art has become a vehicle for personal expression, with declarations of identity and the marketing of the artists themselves.

The design of artist websites is as diverse as the art works offered. For the most part, artists create their own sites, sometimes with technical help from others, and view them as evolving art forms, reflections of themselves. Certain sites are straightforward and matter of fact, displaying images of the art and a curriculum vitae – the bare essentials – while others are dramatic, sophisticated, flamboyant or humorous. Presentations run the gamut from formal to informal. Most are in colour while a few are monochromatic or black and white. A number of sites include animation and/or sound. Others provide links to additional material of interest and some sites are easier to navigate than others. What becomes clear in viewing artist websites, is that nearly every site exhibits a distinct personality reflective of the artist and promotes not only works of art but the artist as well, on a professional and personal level.

6.1 Stephen Goodfellow welcomes visitors to his website.

One finds artists dealing with political issues on their sites that are personally relevant, such as racial and gender-related themes, while others, free of inhibition, discuss their family, relationships, illnesses, adoption and other personal circumstances that may or may not be relevant to their work. Numerous sites contain a photograph of the artist as 'artist', posed in the studio or standing before an example of their artwork, clearly establishing a statement of professional identity. Many sites, however, extend beyond the professional persona into a more private realm. The following discussion will focus on specific artist websites and their inherent self-referential expression.

An open invitation to enter the day-to-day life of the artist is incorporated in the websites of artists Stephen Goodfellow (http://goodfelloweb.com) and Lee Harrington (www.leeharrington.com). Among other features, these two artists have installed webcams in their studios displaying continuously updated pictures for their viewers. Goodfellow's site, *Goodfellow's Gate*, established in 1994, is quite sophisticated, displaying elaborate visual and audio effects. Self-referrals, in this site, take a number of different forms. Images of the artist appear throughout the site. The homepage consists of two self-images: one painted, the other a photograph. Included in the résumé is another photograph of Goodfellow as 'artist' with his art and computers. He even supplies us with an animated, spinning, self-image, *Stevie 3d,* complete with audio effects. One can visit Goodfellow's cottage and surroundings in all four seasons, and see his dog, Ricki. Reproductions of his work and photographs of friends appear along with information on Goodfellow's other areas of interest, music, travel and nature. This multifaceted site includes a crash course for artists, seasoned with humour, on Micropointillism and Radiative Primarism, techniques devised by the artist. He describes the website as an art form that 'slowly becomes a shadow of the artists' expression, personality . . .' and explains that his website is 'a shadow of me; it's the foot I want to put forward'. The webcam in his studio, according to Goodfel-

In light of the events at the Brooklyn Museum of Art, I offer this thought from R. A. Heinlein:
"When any government, or any church for that matter, undertakes to say to its subjects, 'This you may not read, this you must not see, this you are forbidden to know,' the end result is tyranny and oppression, no matter how holy the motives."
more thoughts on the subject

- Recent Artwork
- Self portrait
- Inspirational quotes
- Artist's Statement
- What time is it?

- Articles I've written on art.
- Mailing list for visual artists.
- Send me email

This is my 'live' and working art studio.
A web cam at the front of my web page is my comment on the internet mingling with art. The internet is, in my opinion, one of the greatest leaps in communication humanity has made in centuries. Since art is my means of communication to the world, I felt one way I could do this is to let you see into my art world day in, day out.
So here I am, getting my art done.
Thanks for dialing up my page. Stay tuned and have a great day!

6.2 Lee Harrington's site, with webcam showing her studio, live.

low, satisfies two functions: people can see him as he works, which forces him to work; and it allows prospective buyers to view the work before it hits the market. With regard to sharing personal information and being accessible via his website, Goodfellow believes in being wide open, considering it an artist's 'duty'.

Lee Harrington's website is rather simple in format and design, in keeping with the artist's preference for a 'clean, clear' presentation. The site is a reflection of herself which she describes as 'really me'. It is comprised of a self-portrait, the sole artwork reproduced, inspirational quotes, writings on her personal ideology regarding art and gender, a mailing list for visual artists and a front Web page containing updated pictures of her studio activity, allowing the visitor into her personal space. Her statement below the webcam photo reads:

> This is my 'live' and working art studio. A webcam at the front of my web page is my comment on the internet mingling with art. . . . Since art is my means of communication to the world, I felt one way I could do this is to let you see into my art world day in, day out. So here I am, getting my art done . . .

According to Harrington, she decided to use the webcam in her studio 'to allow the world to "peer" into my world, that of creating art. It is the ultimate voyeur/exhibitionist relationship.' She considers her studio a private place in which the physical presence of others is not always desired. A camera, therefore, allows her to selectively share herself with the world on her own terms.

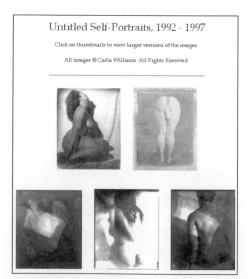

Untitled Self-Portraits, 1992 - 1997

Click on thumbnails to view larger versions of the images.

All images © Carla Williams. All Rights Reserved.

6.3 Self-portraits by Carla Williams.

Photographer and writer Carla Williams' artistic expression and website (www.carlagirl.net) are full of self-referrals. The initial motivation for creating her website, according to Williams, was to provide samples of her photographs and writings to those who expressed an interest. However, her site has expanded far beyond the initial intent, to become an in-depth artist page and resource. Due to her desire to offer researchers a reliable source of information, Williams chose a more formal presentation with a 'simple and clean' design. As with other artists, she considers her website an art form that she is continually altering 'because it is my interface with an audience, my audience'. Issues of racial and gender identity appear to be at the forefront of her art and subsequently her website. She explains, 'It is very important to me to declare my presence as a black woman artist and create a virtual space for other artists of color and interested individuals.' Williams' photography centres largely on herself as subject. In her artist's statement she reveals, 'I never used to think of the images as self-portraits, preferring instead to believe that I was using my own body to represent a type not specific, necessarily to me. I don't feel that way now, I see them as highly personal, almost diaristic visual note-taking that function in an ongoing continuum.' A link to a family tree website and her online journal, and a forum for her views on various subjects are extensions of her self-referential expression.

Williams also provides links to political and environmental causes she supports and to which she wishes to draw attention. Even her hobby of collecting vintage postcards, primarily of black subjects, to which she devotes a portion of her site, is in keeping with the self-referential climate of her entire website. While her work and site are most self-revelatory, Williams does seek to protect her privacy. She invites viewer comments and is accessible via e-mail and fax, averaging about two comments per week, yet is careful not to offer her home address or telephone number, although she has been contacted at work prompting her to include a 'Do not contact me at work' statement.

The subtle, elegant website of artist Ingrid Capozzoli, conceived in black, white and grey (http://members.xoom.com/icapozzoli), began as a portfolio of her fine art and digital work. Since then it has evolved into what the artist describes as 'an interactive art form' that is 'an extension of myself in the same way painting is'. Devoid of the self-images frequently seen in artists' websites, Capozzoli's site is an example of symbolic self-referential expression in which artists employ a stand-in to represent themselves. As Pablo

6.4 Ingrid Capozzoli's web of intertextual art.

Picasso adopted the minotaur and Belgian Surrealist Reneé Magritte the bowler-hatted man, Capozzoli has chosen the Mona Lisa to be her surrogate. She explains, 'I think of the Mona Lisa as a reflection of me and my interests and obsessions as an artist. She embodies my Italian heritage, love of classical figurative painting and my obsession with ... depicting images of women'. Photo-manipulations of the Mona Lisa appear throughout the site as a unifying design principle. Capozzoli views the manipulations as a blending of classical art with modernist design principles through new technology. In addition to symbolic self-representation, Capozzoli has included a brief artist statement, recognizing that her audience may want to know something about her and her art, but in e-mail correspondence she admits that the inclusion of this quite personal component remains a source of some discomfort for her. On the whole, to the uninformed viewer, the self-referrals in Capozzoli's site are not readily apparent, which clearly is the artist's intent.

The image and personality of cartoon artist Mitch O'Connell could not be more conspicuous in his website (www.mitchoconnell.com). O'Connell appears to have mastered the art of self-promotion and marketing, engaging his audience on many

6.5 Mitch O'Connell's tribute to 'the world's most beloved artist', himself.

levels. With humour and a somewhat egotistical approach, touting himself as the 'world's most beloved and respected artist', O'Connell meets the world. His informal, less than serious site contains pages of his writings and cartoon art, a section devoted to his wife's sewing studio, with a family snapshot, and other features of a more unusual nature. A 'Readers Page' (at the time of writing) pays homage to a tattoo artist, whose pierced and tattooed client sports an O'Connell cartoon figure on her arm. O'Connell writes, 'Imitation in the form of a permanent tattoo is the sincerest form of flattery', and adds, 'Anyone else who has paid me the compliment of using their flesh as a walking gallery of my doodles, please send a photo.' He promises to include it in his site and offers a 'swell gift'. 'Art for the masses', Mitch O'Connell T-shirts, are offered for sale in two designs, modelled by his wife and children with amusing captions. One photo has the 'help' on her knees, bucket and T-shirt in hand with a caption that reads, 'Along with being the most fashionable in casual attire, the unique texture of the cotton and silkscreen design works wonders for loosening up hard-to-get-off stains from your kitchen floor or appliances. Works on any surface!'

A 'What's Happenin' page keeps the browser up to date with announcements and updates on Mitch's art, books and other projects. One 'Item!' on this page announces the artist's *Newsweek* magazine cover, which appeared on the 5 July 1999 issue, and his reaction: 'A *Newsweek* cover at long last! Now I'm officially a Big Shot! For a solid week I spent all my time re-arranging newsstands throughout Chicago, making sure that this fine publication topped each of the stacks. Then I danced the dance of glee in front of them.' Leading into the 'Could Mitch Love You?' section is a comical picture of Mitch's head superimposed on a small body dressed in plaid shirt and pants. In a spoof on teen magazine quizzes, the artist offers a 'yes' or 'no' quiz, with answers, to help you find out if you could be the special girl in his life. For all its silliness and teen humour, O'Connell's site is a wonderful example of self-referential expression with the persona of the artist indelibly marked on every page. It is, however, understood that O'Connell does take his work seriously and the 'style' of his website reflects a clever marketing strategy.

Other sites representative of self-referential expression include Diana DeMille's *Dancing Tree Frog* (http://fp.tcsn.net/dianademille). DeMille, identifying herself as an artist and breast cancer survivor, uses her website as a 'healing' vehicle revealing her personal struggle with cancer through her art, writings and lectures. The site, with its pink headings and 'feminine' symbols, also serves as an information and support reference for women's health issues. The promotion of her art itself appears to be of somewhat less importance than the overall theme of her site. As with most artists, DeMille includes a number of self-images in her website.

Utilizing a straightforward, less creative format in his website, Dr Lai Kui-Fang, (http://home.pacific.net.sg/~drlai_kf), a painter and sculptor working in the classical tradition, promotes himself and his art in a strikingly formal manner. The recipient of numerous academic degrees, awards and prizes, Dr Lai presents his image in cap and gown, or adorned with medals, in addition to the standard 'artist' representation with brush in hand posed before a painting in progress.

Detailed accounts of his accomplishments, in large, bold-type bullet headings, along with a selection of articles about the artist are included. A visit to *Dr Lai's Art Museum* acquaints the viewer with his works of art. Dr Lai does not take full advantage of the interactive possibilities with his audience that websites can provide. Instead, it appears that of principal concern is the furnishing of information supporting a declaration of professional identity.

As seen in the foregoing examples of artist websites, self-referential expression is a fundamental component in this newly developed art form. Self-referrals, including self-images, highly personal information and personal symbolic references are found to a greater or lesser degree in nearly every artist website. While most artists explain that their initial purpose in creating their websites involved marketing concerns, for many, these sites have become much more than advertisements of art work. Given the opportunity to freely express themselves on many levels via their websites, a majority of these artists have chosen to provide their audience with a view of themselves that extends beyond their works of art. These artists, it appears, want to be known for who they are, how they live and what they believe in, in addition to their artistic creations. They desire direct contact with their audience and invite an exchange of ideas and information. Declaring their existence, identifying themselves as artists and unique individuals, is ultimately the primary motivation for their websites. The artists' personalities are clearly embedded in this ongoing art form, and the audience acquires a multi-dimensional knowledge of the artists and their creative output. The complete and total control they exert over their websites allows artists to present the precise image of themselves they wish to project. Therefore, artists' websites, an ever-changeable, evolving art form, in addition to functioning as a marketing tool, become a perfect vehicle for ongoing declarations of identity and presentations of self.

USEFUL WEBSITES

Through the Flower: **www.judychicago.com**
A non-profit arts organization built upon the desire to create a cultural legacy based on the vision of artist Judy Chicago through education, exhibition and preservation.

World Wide Arts Resources: **http://wwar.com**
Gateway to arts information and culture on the internet including artists, museums, galleries, art history, arts education and more.

UIAH Art Navigator: **www.uiah.fi/internetguide/navigator.html**
An extensive list of art and art-related sites on the Web.

Art on the Net: **www.art.net**
A collective of international artists joining together to share their work on the internet.

Art Star – Everything Art: **www.artstar.com**
Comprehensive art information including art news, search engine, directory and resource base, auctions, magazine, collector-to-collector sales, exhibitions consulting and more.

7

Webcam Women:
Life on Your Screen

Donald Snyder

What if you could open a window at any time of the day and see into your next-door neighbour's bedroom? What do you think you would see: your neighbour doing a crossword puzzle, or in a compromising situation? Or maybe just an empty room? Would you want to look, especially if the neighbour had created the window for the *purpose* of you looking?

The World Wide Web is becoming populated by people who are providing windows into their lives for the purpose of your viewing pleasure. Over the last couple of years, a growing number of people have been hooking up digital cameras to their personal computers and broadcasting scenes from their lives out to the internet, for anyone with access to see. Webcams – live cameras which send continuously updated pictures of a subject over the internet – are becoming extremely popular, both for people using the technology to place their life on a screen and for people wanting to open those windows and see how other people live their lives.

A large percentage of the 'webcam sites' on the internet feature women. How are these women being portrayed and how are they portraying themselves? Much has been written and discussed about the amount of pornography on the Web (see di Filippo elsewhere in this volume); are these webcams only reflective of that trend, or are they offering potential spaces for other women – people who want to keep their clothes on and use the webcam for more philosophical, artistic or creative ends? In the same regard, are women able to take control over their own bodies, and over the economic gain assigned to those bodies, with the aid of this new technology? What sort of power does the webcam offer to women who are interested in creating new kinds of art and exploring new ways of expressing their selves? Finally, who makes up the audience for these webcams, and what does the popularity of these sites say about that audience? It is necessary to examine several examples of this trend in order to find some answers to these questions.

Surveying some of the most popular websites of women running their own webcams, a pattern seems to emerge. Most of the webcams fit into one of three categories. In the first, the subject of the webcam – the site's 'star' – operates her site as a hobby, with little interest in economic gain. One of the best examples of this is *JenniCam* (www.jennicam.org). In the second category, the webcam's subject operates the site as a source of personal expression and potential economic gain. *AnaCam* represents a very successful example of someone forging a career in art using this technology (www.anacam.com). In the final and probably most prevalent category, a woman has set up a webcam in order to represent herself sexually for the sole purpose of making money. One example of this is *CollegeCutie* (www.collegecutie.com). While all three women are using webcam technology, the way each is using it reflects their different reasons and goals attached to living their life on the screen.

The most famous woman using webcam technology to document her body, and life, is Jennifer Kaye Ringley. In 1996 Jennifer was a student at Dickinson College in Pennsylvania. She quickly became an internet legend by creating a website named *JenniCam*, which was one of the first 24-hour-a-day cameras displaying a person that existed on the Web. Since then, Jennifer has graduated from college and moved to the Washington DC area, continuing *JenniCam* along the way. Currently, Jennifer has several cameras located throughout her apartment. One of these cameras, depending upon where Jennifer is, takes a picture and uploads it to the internet every minute if you are a member, and a little less frequently if you are not. When Jennifer began *JenniCam*, she attempted to keep the site 'private' by only telling a few of her friends. However, her friends told their friends, who told *their* friends, and after about 3 months of existence, 7,000 users were logged on to *JenniCam*. In 1998, Jennifer reported that her site was receiving over 100 million hits a week (Firth, 1998). (See the definition of 'hits' in the glossary of this book, though; the number of different *visitors* would be a fraction of this number.) To this day, *JenniCam* remains one of the most popular and interesting personal webcam sites on the internet.

To what extent is Jennifer presenting her real life on *JenniCam*, and to what extent is it a performance? In the very beginning of *JenniCam*, Jennifer was not aware that anyone was (necessarily) watching, so she easily ignored the camera. The camera was there to document her life and nothing more. After she learned of her success, Jennifer began to interact with the camera. Exploring her exhibitionist tendencies at the urging of her audience, she began putting on impromptu, and then planned, strip shows. Eventually, though, Jennifer decided to return *JenniCam* to the original idea of ignoring the camera. When accused of being an exhibitionist, Jennifer replied, 'The definition of an exhibitionist is someone who gets off on having people watch them. And the whole point of *JenniCam* is that I ignore the fact that the camera is there. So by that definition, I am not an exhibitionist' (E! Television, 1998).

● **7.1** Jennifer, of JenniCam, asleep when we dropped by (7 January 2000, 7am).

While Jennifer denies performing for an audience, she is still actively creating an image that attempts to counter the common image of women presented on screens. When asked about the success of *JenniCam*, Jennifer replied, 'People enjoy seeing what other people do. And I think it makes other people feel better about themselves to know that they are not the only ones out there not living these glamorous lives' (1998). She presents to the internet not just the spectacular events of her life, but also – and much more often – the mundane. The camera captures her 'normal' life, which might contain some nudity and sex, but more often than not captures a vision of a woman that is not only absent from the internet, but absent from all media. Jennifer attempts to show a vision of a 'real' woman, and not the celluloid, glamorous image presented on television, in movies and over most of the Web. Nevertheless, Jenni has inevitably become a celebrity of sorts, and her site has correspondingly come to look more like a standard (self-) exploitation site. She is certainly not afraid to store some of the more revealing shots in her permanent online archive, and she includes on her site the photo shoots taken to accompany magazine features about *JenniCam*.

7.2 One of many stylized images from Ana Voog's webcam.

One woman that *JenniCam* inspired is Ana Voog, who created *AnaCam*. Ana explains her site as 'a window into my house, into my life ... sometimes I'll be surfing the net, sometimes I'll be dancing wildly about my house to some disco music ... sometimes I might put on little skits for you or decide to cover myself in blue paint or something weird'. Ana attempts to take more control over her image than Jennifer does. While Jennifer ignores the camera, Ana constantly interacts with the camera, pretending that the camera is her friend and her audience. Where Jennifer tries to replace the image of the spectacular sexualized woman on the internet with the image of the 'normal' woman, Ana attempts to replace that same image with something *other* than woman. One of the reasons she does the site, she confesses, is to 'push boundaries of what people think a woman is and isn't'. Within *AnaCam*, Ana creates a cyberpunk image of herself. For example, in one series of shots she appears on the camera dressed in black leather, highlighted with metal. Her hair is spiked and dyed gold, while her eyebrows are dyed with silver sparkles. She is adorned with various piercings, and black face paint in the form of a cross. Unlike *Jenni-Cam*, *AnaCam* challenges predictable representations of womanhood, and Ana's art questions the common perceptions of women's bodies. Her art commonly manipulates the female body with digital imaging or paint in a way that attempts to resist or manipulate sexist notions present in society and on the internet.

Where Jennifer's performance in the front of her camera is supposedly the very opposite of self-conscious 'performance', Ana considers herself an artist, and *AnaCam* her art. In her FAQ section, in response to the question of what she does for a living, Ana replies, 'I do *AnaCam* for a living ... I am a singer/songwriter/performance artist. I am also a visual artist.' She uses the camera in a very different way to Jennifer, while still using the camera to present an alternative image of a woman on the Web. Ana does performance art for the camera and distributes her music through her site; she has been able to utilize the technology of the Web in order to announce herself as an artist. She has made the webcam a new tool for the artists' palette, and turned her website into her own private gallery. *AnaCam* enabled Ana to bypass the traditional art world on her path to becoming a successful and economically viable artist.

When discussing *AnaCam* as a project with an economic gain in mind, one major point must be reinforced: like *JenniCam, AnaCam* is a free site. The difference between the two is that Jennifer has treated her site as a hobby, whilst Ana sees her site as a career maker. *AnaCam* has provided Ana with a way to advertise her consumer products, most importantly as a way to sell and distribute her music. Ana also allows companies to advertise on *AnaCam*, whereas Jennifer has maintained an organization (not for profit) status for *JenniCam*. In addition, people can become members of both *JenniCam* and *AnaCam* and receive or gain access to added materials. In the case of *JenniCam*, for a small annual fee (US$15 in 2000, about £9), members are able to view a picture from the webcam at a more rapid rate than non-members. On *Ana2, AnaCam's* sister pay site, for a monthly fee almost equivalent to *JenniCam's* annual fee, members are able to view not just one cam every 5 minutes (the standard refresh time on *AnaCam*), but four cams every 30 seconds each. Ana occasionally uses one of these cams to document her life outside of her home, giving the viewer the ability to follow her throughout her day. Other features only members can access on *Ana2* include a picture archive, a members-only bulletin board system (BBS), and access to Ana's book while she is in the process of writing it. The appeal of these members-only benefits to Ana's audience has enabled her to use this new technology to build a successful business venture.

Much of Ana's success seems to be tied into how she has created a community of fans around her website. One way that Ana appeals to her audience is by including them as part of the artistic process that is *AnaCam*. The most successful aspect of this is apparent in the popularity of 'Anapix'. 'Anapix' are digitally or artistically manipulated images of Ana from *AnaCam*; Ana's viewers download pictures of Ana from the webcam and create their own imaginative works of art, and then send them to Ana where they are displayed in a special section of the website. The inclusion of an exclusive BBS in *Ana2* also works to reinforce the community of true *AnaCam* fans, who Ana refers to as a 'cool community of wonderful, creative and supportive people'. Ana's life and art has become an important aspect of her fans' lives, and Ana uses the technology to foster this fascination (see Smit's chapter elsewhere in this volume).

Where Ana was inspired by Jennifer to use the webcam to create a new artistic community built around her life and image, Carlota was inspired by Jennifer to use the webcam to sell a sexualized vision of her own body. Carlota created her webcam site *CollegeCutie* in 1998 as a source of income for her education. She writes, 'I got the idea for this from an article on (guess who) *JenniCam*. . . . I started grad school this fall and thought this would be a good way to help me out.' Like most webcam sites, *CollegeCutie* offers a free image from the camera, in this case one picture every 15 minutes. In most pictures, she is nude or in various states of undress. *CollegeCutie* also offers a free gallery of nine pictures where Carlota is posing in various sexual positions. This page promises that a new similar one is added weekly for members. But for the majority, this site, unlike *JenniCam* and to a lesser extent *AnaCam*, is not intended to be a free site at all. If you are not a member, there is really little to do or see. Jennifer and Ana provide several options for the non-member to click and explore the site; Carlota, however, shows the non-member a sample of her merchandise and promises more only if the non-member joins for a monthly fee similar to Ana's. *CollegeCutie* is not an experiment in art or life, it is a way to make money.

Two of the most interesting aspects of *CollegeCutie* relate to how Carlota is using technology in order to enhance the effect of traditional pornography. First of all, she offers a real-time camera. Where most webcams refresh every 15 seconds at quickest, a real-time camera presents the image continuously. As Carlota explains, this type of camera caters to the experience desired by her audience: 'You'll have access to my live webcam. . . . You'll be able to watch me shower, take a bath or just play around!' (In reality most personal computers do not have the capability to view the material in its intended quality; for the time being, most real-time cameras appear slow and disjointed.) The other way Carlota uses technology to appeal to her desired audience is that she provides a private chatroom. In this space, Carlota is able to interact with the people watching her, chatting and 'flirting' with them, or asking them what they would like her to do. She effectively builds a community around her website, using personal interaction to encourage her visitors to feel they are part of the experience (in line with Rheingold's community-building recommendations, in his chapter of this book).

The fact that Carlota views *CollegeCutie* as a source of income and not as a hobby is reflected in the fact that it is not a 24-hour site. The picture only changes when Carlota is on, and Carlota posts a schedule, on the site, of times she will be on the webcam. While this is not always the case on webcams where the main goal is to offer sexualized bodies, in this case it seems to comment on the difference between Carlota's commitment and that of Jennifer or Ana. In essence, Carlota is able to use the webcam as a 'convenient' and 'safe' way of continually selling images of her body to those who desire to see it. She controls the economic gains in every way; there is no magazine, club or entertainment service exploiting her. *CollegeCutie* provides Carlota with a way of completely capitalizing on her own body. Although Carlota is not challenging the stereotype of women and pornography on the internet, she is using webcam technology to challenge successfully the traditional way in which women's sexual bodies have been controlled in economic terms.

In all three webcam sites, *JenniCam, AnaCam* and *CollegeCutie*, a woman is performing for the camera. That performance is dictated by the way that these women view their sites and their audiences. They each understand the needs of their target audience and use the technology in ways to appeal to those needs. Jennifer feels that her viewers want images of reality, and so her performance involves giving the impression that she is not performing (which often, we can suppose, she is not), and her exhibitionism becomes not exhibitionism but 'real life'. She refuses the 'star' role and chooses not to romanticize her life. She becomes everywoman – a symbol of normalcy in a spectacular media-saturated world. Unlike Jennifer, Ana's appearances are self-styled performance art. Ana is appealing to those who are interested in seeing technology in extremely creative ways. Ana uses the webcam to turn the image of her body into a work of art. Whilst the site, by its nature, tends to position the viewer as voyeur and the artist as exhibitionist, these positions are challenged through the way Ana attempts to include her viewers in the creation of both the website and a strong community network of Ana fans. Once Ana's voyeurs begin to assist Ana in exhibiting the image of Ana, they too become exhibitionists of Ana's 'body'. Finally, Carlota uses the technology of the webcam to represent herself within the most traditional understanding of the exhibitionist-and-voyeur relationship. Because Carlota is interested in using the technology solely for economic gain, she offers what she feels most people seek and are willing to pay for: sex (or, more specifically, the digitized image of flesh). She exhibits her body for anyone willing to pay to view her. Her exhibitionism is a performance because a true exhibitionist would expose their body for the thrill, not for an income. Webcams are not always sites of exhibitionism, but if someone is watching, then they are always sites of voyeurism.

These three examples of women's webcams are interesting because of the ways they challenge the perceptions of what it means to be a woman on the World Wide Web. Webcams are an important trend on the internet and will continue to grow in popularity. There is a danger in writing off the webcam as only a new site for pornography; even when the subject is pornographic, there is much more being transmitted than pornography. With the recent popularity of reality television shows like *Cops*, and MTV's *The Real World* and *Road Rules* – an interest reflected in movies like *The Truman Show* and *EdTV* – 'reality' is becoming a controversial but legitimate and successful source of entertainment. Webcams are a perfect site for examining why 'reality' has become such an important subject for our culture and how this 'reality' is constructed. In finding out how and why people want to live their lives on our screens, we can begin to understand our need and desire to watch them.

USEFUL WEBSITES

NetGuide to Webcams:
www.netguide.com/special/internet/webcams/home.html
Useful introduction, including 'Nine creative uses for your webcam'.

Sam's Webcam Cookbook: www.teleport.com/ samc/bike
Well-linked guide to webcams, including other people's uses and how to set up your own.

AllCam: **www.allcam.com**
A 'free, family-oriented video community' giving users the opportunity to 'explore and share the possibilities of live internet video'. Has a big Yahoo!-style database of webcam sites.

WebCam World: **http://webcamworld.com**
Everything you would ever need to know about webcam technicalities, plus a webcams webring.

CamCities: **http://camcities.com**
Geographically arranged links to webcams around the world.

8

Queer 'n' Asian on – and off – the Net: the Role of Cyberspace in Queer Taiwan and Korea

Chris Berry and Fran Martin

Writing about community and internet communications back in 1995, Nancy Baym bemoaned a general lack of empirical field research (1995: 139). This situation still prevails regarding published research on lesbian, gay and bisexual internet use, even though queer people are among the net's most enthusiastic users (McLean and Schubert, 1995; Shaw, 1997). Although there are numerous philosophical discussions in this area, such as *The Domain-Matrix: Performing Lesbian at the End of Print Culture* (Case, 1997) and the disappointing *Cybersexualities* reader (Wolmark, 1999) – as well as popular handbooks such as *Gay and Lesbian Online* (Dawson, 1998) – actual fieldwork studies remain thin on the ground. Among the few items we have located are Tsang's examination (1996) of Asian-American men's use of a gay bulletin board system (BBS), Shaw's interview-based research on gay men's use of IRC (1997), and Phillips' study of how a lesbian and gay Usenet group fended off outsiders (1996). Our research based on field trips between August 1997 and January 1998 in South Korea and Taiwan helps to address this lack of data by examining the uses of net communication in lesbian, gay and queer communities there.[1] (To save space, we'll use the term 'queer' throughout this chapter to denote lesbian, gay and bisexual identities.)

8.1 Electronic postcards from *PlanetOut.com*, one of the most successful queer websites.

Furthermore, both the design of our study and its findings support and extend the re-orientation of net research and reconceptualization of cyberspace that has been ongoing since the mid-1990s. Fieldwork-based empirical research such as Baym's contradicts earlier lab-based findings which suggested that computer-mediated communication inhibits interpersonal communication and is not conducive to the formation of community. Given greater time than is usually available in lab experiments, internet users in the field overcome the lack of visual and aural channels and do form personal relationships and communities. These are often integrated with their lives off the net (Baym, 1995; Parks, 1996).

Bearing in mind findings such as these, Mantovani argues against the conceptualization of cyberspaces as 'other worlds', stating that they 'are not true alternative realities. They are within, not beyond, daily reality' (1996: 112). This rethinking lies behind our decision to examine net use in a broader context. Earlier studies including all those cited above start out from a focus on particular net groups or users as though they were autonomous and separate from 'daily reality'. In contrast, our study starts from individuals and communities in the context of real life to look at their particular uses of the net. We find that in Taiwan and Korea queer communities and subjects use computer-mediated communication to construct their identities and communities on and off the net in a dialectical and mutually informing manner.

Furthermore, queer subjects have a particular investment in retaining and further developing the connection between their on- and off-net lives. As people who usually have to make a conscious decision to form and maintain public identities and communities offline, the net can be an important tool in that ongoing struggle. Similarly, Marj Kibby notes that far from hiding their gender or their bodies, women on the net often use photographs that emphasize these in their homepages. In this way, she brings down to earth rapture-like fantasies of leaving the body behind as 'meat' while one ascends into cyberspace. She notes that 'The creator of the electronic persona is the self at the keyboard, the embodied self', and 'while this new medium allows the possibility of creating a new genderless self, the tools of creation are still those of gendered society' (1997: 41–42). She also quotes transgender activist and cyber enthusiast Allucquere Roseanne Stone's astute comment that 'Forgetting about the body is an old Cartesian trick, one that has unpleasant consequences for those bodies whose speech is silenced by the act of forgetting . . . usually women and minorities' (1991: 100).

With these thoughts in mind, perhaps it is not so surprising that all three field studies of queer net use cited above are decidedly local and pragmatic, showing activity connected to off-net life rather than separate from it. All three are US-based. Our study finds similar patterns in Taiwan and Korea. However, we were drawn to Taiwan and Korea as spaces where the emergence of public queer communities has been more or less contemporaneous with the availability of the net.[2] In these circumstances, instead of simply fitting into and extending pre-existing identities and communities, there is the possibility that the net might inform the character of the queer identities and communities that were being constructed (on and off the net) from their inception.[3]

Taiwan and South Korea have enough in common to provide a suitable comparative context for studies of sexuality and net use. Neither state has specific legal prohibitions on homosexuality.[4] However, kinship conventions emphasize heterosexual reproduction in both states, and until recently both were ruled by right-wing regimes under which the populations were strongly disciplined and the development of popular initiatives was harshly restrained (Wachman, 1994; Cumings, 1997). Now, those right-wing regimes have been replaced by democratic systems with pluralistic policies. Combined with economic growth that has made youth less reliant upon family, this has produced preconditions for the emergence of both public queer cultures and widespread internet use.

Discrete queer subcultures invisible to the general public existed in both states prior to more recent developments (Berry, 1996). However, a public culture emerged earlier in Taiwan than in South Korea. In Taiwan the first openly homosexual group was established in 1990, and by the mid-1990s there was a steady output of queer novels, films and magazines, whereas in South Korea, groups only began to be formed in the mid-1990s, and the first glossy magazine appeared in 1998. Various differences may account for this. First, whereas Taiwanese queer activists draw upon a long history of same-sex cultural activities and representations, this is currently not so in South Korea (see Hinsch, 1990; Pai, 1995; Chao, 1996; Rutt, 1969). Second, fundamentalist Christianity is far more influential in South Korea than in Taiwan (Song, 1990: 47–50; Palmer, 1986; Jordan, 1994). Third, while the dismantling of military rule began in Taiwan in the early 1980s, this period remained one of severe repression in Korea. Taiwan's desire to appear internationally as a modern democratic society has produced attempts at liberalization in many areas, including sexual politics (Patton, 1998). Political reform in Korea, meanwhile, has not extended to policy on sexuality. Traditional family values continue to be officially endorsed.

In our efforts to understand net use in these emergent Taiwan and South Korea queer cultures, we had significantly different research experiences. Our questionnaire went smoothly in Korea, where it was apparently the first such study. Responses were broken down into two groups, 'activists' and 'bargoers', according to whether the questionnaires had been returned from organized groups or bars.[5]

In Taiwan, the questionnaire failed. Warned of low return rates encountered by previous researchers using bars, we tried posting it at sites with a queer bulletin board system (BBS). However, we were advised to remove it, because another scholar had quoted BBS site conversations in a recent paper, making participants feel invaded.[6] Taiwan's queer BBS sites require participant registration, so they are small, local, intimate and suspicious of outsiders. Other contributing factors may include 'research fatigue' following extensive local academic interest. Also, the relatively developed state of Taiwan's queer internet and culture means that more assured queer subjects may care less about academic acknowledgement. Therefore, Taiwan data comes from other sources, including extensive interviews with frequent BBS users and site managers.[7] The Korean survey was also supplemented with interviews.

We found that the participants in the publicly visible queer cultures of Taiwan and South Korea are young, highly educated and, in many cases, still students. A total of 90 per cent of Korean survey respondents were tertiary educated, 60 per cent were in the 23- to 28-year-old age bracket, and almost three-quarters were men.[8] The most significant general demographic difference concerns domestic situation. Fully 64 per cent of Korean survey respondents were living with their parents. Taiwan interview responses indicate that many more queer-identified people live away from their families. Student dormitories are more common there, and deposits on rental apartments are prohibitively high in South Korea.

The queer population in both places has a very high level of computer access and usage. A total of 90 per cent of Korean survey respondents had regular access and 37 per cent were using a computer daily. Of course, frequent computer users might have been more inclined to complete the survey than non-users, but this still indicates a very high level of usage. There was notable gender difference around usage, with 40 per cent of total female respondents never using the computer although 90 per cent had access. Taiwan data indicates that computers are a 'boy thing' there, too. A 1997 government survey of 38,645 of Taiwan's internet users indicated that 68 per cent of those users are male.[9]

Gender differences around general computer use also correlate to gender difference around use of the computer for queer activities, which seem more common among gay men than lesbians in both places. Whereas 67 per cent of all Korean survey respondents with regular access were using it for queer activities, only 45 per cent of women with regular access were. However, we estimate a much higher overall level of computer use for queer activities than in, say, Australia.

When asked, 'What lesbian, gay or queer computer activities do you engage in?', the most popular response was 'Visiting chatrooms to meet lesbian, gay or queer people' (82 per cent within Korea, 17 per cent overseas), followed by 'Visiting internet sites for activist information' (63 per cent within Korea, and 26 per cent overseas). E-mailing friends was popular, and more than one in five said they e-mailed friends to spread activist information. The internet was also used for other kinds of conversation, information sharing, and for reading queer fiction. Only 12 per cent said they visited chatrooms for cybersex. Interviews indicate that all these activities were popular, to similar degrees, in Taiwan. One of the most significant findings was the low use of overseas queer sites, despite high levels of foreign language proficiency. Taiwan data indicated that this even applied to overseas sites in Chinese. This data makes sense in the light of our data on the most popular activities, namely extensions of the socializing activities you might find in bars, followed by information seeking. Interview responses in Korea indicated a desire to meet people on the net as a prelude to possible meetings in real space. Of course, local sites are best for this.

A note of caution should be sounded. In the Korean survey, many who acknowledged going to overseas sites claimed to be seeking 'activist information'; however, about 60 per cent of the overseas sites they nominated as popular were pornography sites. At a stretch, this might be construed as 'activist information'. But it also indicates under-reporting. As one Korean interviewee pointed out, no gay pornography is sold in Korea, so 'If few people are going to overseas sites, how come every guy here knows the names of American gay porn stars?'

Amongst this wide range and high level of activity, two particular patterns interested us. First, much of the activity in both Taiwan and Korea is focused on sites where high levels of interaction are possible. We believe this creates sizeable and substantial social formations within Taiwan and Korea's emergent queer cultures that we would call 'online discursive communities'.

In Taiwan, the most popular sites are university-based bulletin board systems (BBSs) known as MOTSS (members of the same sex) sites, of which there are now around 80. In Korea, university administrators seem less accommodating, and the most popular sites are at the Web homepages of major commercial ISPs. Chollian's *Queernet*, Nownuri's *Rainbow*, and Hitel's *Dosamo* are huge text-based sites incorporating multiple chatrooms, message boards and other subgroups. One interviewee estimated that one site gets up to 5,000 hits a day. Comparative lack of interactivity has made other Web pages less popular in both Taiwan and Korea.[10]

Several interviewees pointed out that many queer net users have no access to other aspects of queer culture. They may be too young or too poor to attend bars, or remote from the queer cultures of Taipei and Seoul. However, the range of activities pursued in these online discursive communities also indicates frequent integration with offline life.

The most common activities are social. As well as searching for partners, interviewees specified counselling and information exchange as particularly popular. 'When I was that age, we had to keep it to ourselves. We had no one to tell,' one Taipei woman explained about relationship break-ups. 'You'd just go and play basketball or whatever til you felt better. The kids today have it so good.' A Korean interviewee drew attention to a discussion thread, which 'warns about people who exploit young gays. They fall in love quickly, and those guys borrow money and then leave.' Interviewees also emphasized that many topics were discussed that had no direct relation to sexuality. A Taiwanese interviewee suggested this could be explained as a desire to speak freely on all topics safe in the knowledge that everyone chatting was queer.

These online discursive communities are not only integrated with existing offline activities but often also stimulate new offline connections. One interviewee in Taiwan cited birthday parties held by MOTSS members to which the condition of entry was membership of a particular MOTSS. Similarly, a Korean interviewee had posted a message when living in a small college town asking if there was anyone else online from the same town. After online exchanges, the group met to see a movie and began more regular social activities. Another Korean interviewee reported that a similar process had facilitated the rapid recent development of queer student groups across the whole country.

Queer online discursive communities also engage in the publication and dissemination of queer cyberfiction. Although no star writers have emerged yet in Korea, in Taiwan there is now a series of books composed of material that originated on the net.[11]

Finally, online discursive communities have proved important tools for queer activists. They use message boards to distribute information about activities and stimulate debate. A Korean activist explained, 'I set up a sub-group in Nownuri's *Rainbow* called Tank Girls and Tank Boys. My intention was to fight against stereotyped identities in the gay and lesbian community through discussion of popular culture.' This group met both on and off the net.

As examples of direct action, a petition was widely posted in 1997 protesting the Taipei Municipal Government's decision to outlaw prostitution, with the result of mobilizing an influential campaign of public protest. And while we were carrying out our survey, the First Seoul Queer Film and Video Festival was banned. News and petitions were circulated by fax, e-mail, snail mail and by hand. E-mail proved particularly effective internationally. A year later, a festival worker laughed, 'Now we are more famous overseas than the Pusan International Film Festival' – Korea's largest mainstream event.[12]

The second pattern that caught our interest related to the formation of identities. Mantovani has argued that instead of being used to escape from offline selves, the net may function as a testing ground for 'possible selves' that can then inform offline identity (1996: 123–27). In the case of queer subjects, who face very serious obstacles in the construction of offline identities, this may be particularly true.

In Taiwan, a common response to questions about the role of internet technology in shaping users' experience of their queer identities emphasizes how BBS boards allow queer subjects the rare opportunity to assert their sexual politics in the face of the homophobia of broader society. Bruce relates:

To me, 'queer politics' means something very progressive, active, positive, and proud. It's saying to people 'Yes, I'm here. ... I don't want your sympathy. I don't want your acceptance. What I want is *to be here*. That's my right. If you don't give it to me, I'll take it anyway.' Because of the net's anonymity and its speed, ... that kind of queer attitude has developed easily there ... as compared with other media or with 'real life'. Actually, I think I've learned my own queer politics and queer attitude from the net.[13]

Bruce's response goes beyond simply celebrating the freedoms of cyberspace, suggesting that his very sense of himself as identifying with the outspoken, anti-assimilationist politics of 'queer' arises from his experience as a net user.

Korean activists had similar stories to tell. But our interviews also indicated that the net facilitated identity formation in other less predictable ways. Our interview subject from outside Seoul with little connection to metropolitan queer culture had learnt from surfing the net to think of himself as a 'potato queen', given his preference for Caucasian sexual partners. However, he indicated no awareness of the far more derogatory equivalent slang terms used in Seoul. Deciding to study in the United States, he met other Korean gay men in the city he was travelling to on the net prior to departure. Fearing exposure back in Korea, they assumed English names and their online identities never included their individual Korean backgrounds. In a follow-up interview, our respondent told us this was still the case now he had met these friends in real life. The identities they constructed on the net have functioned successfully as 'possible selves' transferred offline.

A woman net user in Taiwan has an interesting point to make about how the net effects lesbians' experience of themselves as gendered according to the categories 'T' and '*po*', comparable to the English 'butch' and 'femme'. She says:

> To a girl, her name is very important, because the name she has grown up with was given to her by her father. On the net ... people are free to play language games with their real names and mix up the roles. ... A T may have a very 'feminine' name in real life, but on the net she can use a name she chooses herself ... taking on the role she prefers.[14]

This comment implies that for Taiwan's lesbians, the net enables an extension of the gendered relations of the 'T bar' (lesbian bar). In T bars, it is common practice for women to introduce themselves using fictitious nicknames – in the case of Ts, these names are often androgynous or masculine, symbolizing their rejection of traditional 'feminine' style (Chao, 1996). This woman's observation suggests that the net offers further possibilities for reworking feminine gender norms, enabling Ts actively to rename themselves, shaping new identities defined by their assertion of a specifically 'T' lesbian gender.

In conclusion, we would argue that our findings on online discursive communities and possible selves in queer net use in Taiwan

8.2 *The Other Queer Page*: resources from around the world.

and South Korea underline the need to rethink the ways in which we conceptualize internet communications. In the cases we have studied, the net is neither a substitute for nor an escape from real life. Nor is it simply an extension of existing offline communities and identities. Instead, it is part of lived culture, informed by and informing other parts of users' lives. And in the emergent queer cultures of Taiwan and South Korea, it is a particularly substantial and dynamic component.

USEFUL WEBSITES

The following websites relate to the study of lesbian, gay and queer life on the Web generally (not only in Taiwan and South Korea).

Freedom Pride: **www.freedompride.com**
Based in Geneva and available in five languages, *FreedomPride.com* is an information network which, it boasts, 'allows you to find every kind of Lesbian, Gay and Bisexual resource in the world'. Lots of information, daily news and interactive discussion.

PlanetOut: **www.planctout.com**
'*PlanetOut* is the leading Internet media company offering a vibrant, welcoming and safe community for all gay, lesbian, bisexual and transgender people as well as their family and friends.'

The Other Queer Page: **http://im1ru12.org/toqp**
A well-established queer Web directory, with an emphasis on information resources. It boasts 'over 1400 sorted links: to the best of gay, lesbian, bisexual and transgender resources available on the Web, ranging from coming out to getting involved in the fight for equal rights'.

Queer Arts Resource: **www.queer-arts.org**
Queer Cultural Center: **www.queerculturalcenter.org**
Attractive queer arts sites, with galleries and other features.

The Advocate: **www.advocate.com**
Website of the US news magazine for the gay and lesbian community, with substantial archive of news, features and reviews.

Theory.org.uk: **www.theory.org.uk**
David Gauntlett's other site which is concerned with the relationship between the mass media and gender and identity, but has a particular emphasis on queer theory and related resources, including pages of material on Judith Butler and Michel Foucault (including the illustrated tourists' guide *Foucault's Paris*).

Notes

1. We would like to thank Lee Chung-Woo, Seo Dong-Jin, and the staff members of the Seoul Queer Film and Video Festival for distributing and collecting survey forms. They

also helped translate the questionnaires together with Kim Hyun-Sook, who also helped with the design. We would also like to thank the respondents in both Korea and Taiwan. Thanks also to National Taiwan Central University's Center for the Study of Sexuality and Difference, as well as Grace, Bruce Chen, Davy Chi and Josette Tang in Taiwan, all of whom helped with the Taiwan research.

2. In speaking of 'queer subjects and communities' in the Taiwan and South Korean situations, we refer to the appearance of recognizable, public identities such as 'lesbian', 'gay', 'queer' or 'homosexual', in distinction to older, subcultural and less generally visible traditions around sexually non-normative behaviour.

3. Although it is not our main focus here, these issues also raise debates around what has been called 'global queering', for example by Dennis Altman in *The Australian Humanities Review*, No. 2, July-September 1996 (www.lib.latrobe.edu.au/AHR/home.html). The net is often linked explicitly with strongly homogenizing arguments about cultural globalization. So it might be expected that our project would align itself either in terms of the ways in which the net helps bring about the 'westernization' of homosexual identifications in these East Asian states or else in terms of 'indigenous' resistances to this process. Instead, as already indicated, the information we have gathered to date suggests a view more akin to Appadurai's 'heterogenizing' view of cultural globalization as a moment in which all forces involved are mutually (if unequally) transformed by it (see Appadurai, 1990). For a more extended discussion of the data presented here in relation to global queering, see Martin and Berry, 1998).

4. Same-sex sexual behaviour, however, has had scant public recognition in either place. And those who engage in it are liable to prosecution under laws regulating 'public obscenity' or 'hooliganism'.

5. These sites were chosen in an effort to target the emergent public queer culture. Of 1000 forms distributed, 'bargoers' returned 86 and 'activists' 109, an overall response rate of approximately 20 per cent. However, without reliable general data on Korea's queer population, representativeness cannot be claimed. Also, although forms were anonymous, we estimate that 70 per cent plus were filled in while the respondents were in bars or meetings. This undermines results such as those indicating few respondents participated in queer culture to find sexual partners.

6. This was Chen Cong-Qi's paper entitled 'Are you a Gay, Kuer or Tongzhi? Notes on the politics of hybrid sexual identity', presented at the Second International Conference on Sexuality Education, Sexology, Gender Studies and LesBiGay Studies, National Central University, Taiwan 31 May-1 June 1997. Interestingly, a near-identical debate was sparked at the 1998 International Conference, when a feminist scholar was berated for quoting from 'private' conversations on a feminist BBS site.

7. The Taiwan information comes also from: a regular column on lesbian net culture in a local lesbian monthly, *Nü Pengyou* (*Girlfriend*); attendance at the 1997 National Central University mini-conference; Chen (1997), Yang (1997) and Hung (1997); mainstream media articles on internet regulation; personal visits to queer sites; readings of local cyberfiction; and the 15 or so responses we did get to the questionnaire, although these last are clearly too few to be statistically meaningful.

8. In both places, the transgender scene is relatively separate, explaining the few transgender respondents.

9. *Taiwan 1997 Wanglu Shiyong Diaocha Huodong* ('The 1997 Taiwan Internet Use Survey'), http://taiwan.yam.org.tw/survey.

10. For an example of a more sophisticated and interactive Taiwanese Web page, see Dingo's lesbian pages and online pub at www.to-get-her.org/. There is also a list of links at www.dakini.org. For a list of Korean links see www.geocities.com/WestHollywood/Stonewall/6460.

11. 'Ask', *Xiao Mo* (Hong Kong: Huasheng Shudian, 1996), 'Garrido', *Meimei Wan'an* (Hong Kong: Huasheng Shudian, 1996).

12. For a report on the Second Seoul Queer Film and Video Festival, which was not banned, see Chris Berry, 'My Queer Korea' at http://wwwsshe.murdoch.edu.au/hum/as/intersections/current2/Berry.html.

13. Interview with Bruce, 20 January 1998, Chungli. 'Bruce' (Bu-lu-si) is the name his friends call him both on and off the net, but he also uses his birth name when necessary in pursuing his 'queer' activist politics.

14. Paper presented by 'Waiter' to National Central University's December 1997 mini-conference on lesbian/gay/queer internet activism.

9

The Web goes to the Pictures

David Gauntlett

Cinema is perhaps the popular medium *least* similar to the internet. The Web is quite like a set of magazines, say, with their static, colourful pages. We already have 'radio' stations on the internet, and the Web even has things in common with TV – a range of content, but not always easy to find something you like, and too many adverts. The form and speed of the Web, though, is not much like the rich widescreen visual experience we get at the movies.

Nevertheless, movie producers quickly embraced the Web as a publicity medium, and now we see independent and corporate short films being made especially for the internet. The Web also includes a mine of information about movies, and what people think about them. These three Web phenomena – movie publicity, original productions, and audience reviews – are surveyed in this chapter.

Movie promotion on the Web

Websites promoting specific movies are often uninteresting in their use of the Web, but may offer valuable information about a film to those interested in it, as one can usually expect to find an interview with the director, production details, pictures, the trailer, etc. Quality, even for major films, is variable. For example, the site for the 1999 hit *The Sixth Sense* (http://movies.go.com/sixthsense/) looked awful, offered two (two!) photos from the film and little else. It gave you the opportunity to send your review of the film to the site – but it would then vanish into cyberspace, and it was not possible to read other people's reviews. The movie was critically acclaimed as an intelligent and lavish production, but its website was just the opposite.

9.1 Promotional sites for Tim Burton's *Sleepy Hollow* and Martin Scorsese's *Bringing Out the Dead*.

On the other hand, the website for *The Matrix* (www.whatisthematrix.com), another big hit in the same year, was packed with pictures, interviews, a downloadable screensaver, and much information on production and effects. It also featured a (rather violent) arcade-style Shockwave game. The most distinctive corner of the site contained comic strips by well-known comic artists such as Neil Gaiman and Paul Chadwick. Each of these multi-page comics developed the universe and storylines of *The Matrix* in new directions, and so actually *added to* (rather than merely supplemented) the creative content of the film. Movie tie-in comics have been doing this for years, of course (the many *Star Wars* and *Aliens* comics spring to mind), and putting comics on the Web as simple graphics files is nothing groundbreaking, so it must be the fact that these are additional creative materials given free of charge – not to make money, except in the indirect way that the comics may strengthen fans' interest in the movie and related products – which makes this seem special.

The most notable movie promotion on the Web, in the twentieth century, was that for *The Blair Witch Project* (www.blairwitch.com and other sites), as mentioned in Chapter 5 of this book. The movie, made to look like a real amateur documentary, was supported by sites which began to appear more than a year before the movie was released, fostering the myth of the 'Blair Witch' and the 'missing' youngsters who had supposedly made the film. Word of mouth spread, amongst those who believed in this mysterious tragedy and those who just thought it would be a good movie, which meant that by the time the film was actually released, the Web had helped to generate an enormous amount of hype about this low-budget production.

However it is done, though, reading about cinema releases on the internet is not the best use of the Web's multimedia capabilities. Whereas if you could go to the pictures from the comfort of your computer screen . . . wouldn't that be good?

Films on the Web

At present, most people's internet connections are not nearly fast enough for them to be able to enjoy good-quality, feature-length films over the Web. Furthermore, most people wouldn't want to watch long shows on their computer screens anyway (although the integration of the internet and TV is changing this). In recognition of these factors, the 'short film' is enjoying a renaissance on the Web. Short films are seen as an art form in themselves, and also as a stepping stone – and calling card – for would-be movie directors. In the past, there were not many places that makers of short films could get their work seen, but the internet has changed that (albeit to a limited extent, because not all internet users are downloading short films). Whilst mass audiences remain elusive, these shorts may nevertheless be seen by the industry insiders and film enthusiasts who are important audiences to their creators.

In 1999, a number of sites emerged as talked-about homes for the short film. The *Internet Film Community* (www.inetfilm.com), for example, is a website 'built to showcase the artistry of independent filmmakers'. The site of *Atom Films* (www.atomfilms.com) offers short films and animations 'to every conceivable audience' (it says), noting pragmatically that 'short entertainment is perfectly suited to fast-paced lifestyles, Internet bandwidth constraints, and audiences seeking innovative alternatives to traditional forms of entertainment'. Another one is *Student Films* (www.studentfilms.com), which boasts that it 'gives everyone the means to have their storytelling voice heard around the world'.

Which is not wholly inaccurate.

Then in 2000, Stephen Spielberg and friends jumped on the bandwagon with *Pop.com* (from Hollywood big shots Imagine Entertainment and DreamWorks SKG). 'The content will be a mix of live action and animation, video on demand and live web events', their press release burbled. 'Most features will consist of one to six-minute episodic streaming video segments, or "pops", with an emphasis on comedy.' Jeffrey Katzenberg, one of the DreamWorks partners, said breathlessly, 'Just as MTV introduced a new entertainment forum for music videos, we think this new enterprise will offer a new form of entertainment for the rapidly growing population of internet users. *Pop.com* has the capability not only to offer a variety of entertainment options, but to tap into an as-yet-undiscovered talent pool that is as global as the internet itself.'

One of the best-known Web films is *Troops* (www.theforce.net/troops), a 10-minute mock documentary by Kevin Rubio about the everyday lives of *Star Wars* stormtroopers, which appeared online way back in February 1998, and has been seen by millions. The film cost less than US$2,000, took 6 months to make, and boasts impressive effects produced on a home computer. It was made for free Web distribution and is not (officially) available in other formats.

Whether or not short films take off on the Web, though, people will always want to discuss cinema releases on the internet, and that is the focus of the rest of this chapter.

Researching movie audiences – the armchair method

For a conference last summer, I had been asked to talk about *The Truman Show* (Peter Weir, 1998) to round out a panel of people talking about films about television. *The Truman Show*, as you probably know, stars Jim Carrey as Truman Burbank, a man who has spent his life unknowingly trapped in a prefabricated world which is televised, 24 hours a day, for the entertainment of the masses in the real world outside.

I'm not really a 'film studies' person. It struck me that, as with all film studies, one could either say the really obvious things about this film, which all members of the audience should have noticed ('It's an extension of the fly-on-the-wall TV shows popular today ... the producers exploit Truman in the name of entertainment'), or invent some pseudo-theoretical interpretation which almost no one else will have considered ('Truman's journey parallels that of the beleaguered hero in sixteenth-century Italian poetry and represents a meta-rhetorical quest for self-determination in a post-didactic society'). Since the first is banal and the second is pointless, I quickly realized that a Plan B was needed. How could I tell a conference audience what *The Truman Show* 'said' about the world of contemporary television, without it being something they knew already, or something they didn't know only because I'd just made it up?

Happily, I remembered the *Internet Movie Database* (www.imdb.com), where everyday movie-goers, and video-renters, review and rate movies. The site also contains a wealth of factual information about cast, crew, marketing, quotes, soundtrack details and so on, for most English-language films. (It's best on recent films and less good, unsurprisingly, on older films except for known 'classics'.) There are, of course, thousands of other websites about movies – see any Web directory for details – but the *Internet Movie Database* (*IMDb*) is built upon the input of its users and, since it is so well known, the contributions are huge in number and diverse in character. The *IMDb* is one of those websites that started as a hobby – before the Web was invented, in fact, using arcane internet technologies. The first Web version ran on the servers of Cardiff University in Wales. It was compiled and run for love, not money, but ultimately made its makers rich when they sold it, in 1998, to Amazon.com, on the condition that they could continue to offer the same free service to the internet community. In 1999 it was receiving 65 million requests for pages from over 3.5 million visitors every month. (See '*IMDb* history' in its help pages to find out more.)

9.2 The *Internet Movie Database*: All movie knowledge is here.

For *The Truman Show*, the site had 236 reviews written by *IMDb* users. (That was in July 1999; there were 50 more by January 2000, and this database just grows and grows.) In sociological terms it seems a poor sample, being a self-selected bunch of internet users who have the time and inclination to share their views with other *IMDb* visitors. However, the people who posted reviews were not, say, visitors to a Jim Carrey fan site, although some may be Jim Carrey fans. (Of course, views posted at a fan site would be great for a study of fan culture, but not good for sampling the views of 'the general audience'.) Most of the reviewers appeared to be people who regularly watched movies and liked to place their thoughts at this website.

The 236 reviews came to about 45,000 words, which I printed out, read and annotated. It's not a perfect cross-section of the audience for the film, but it's infinitely better than the singular, subjective, usually obscure 'reading' of a film by a film studies 'expert'. In fact the sample is as good as most used in qualitative research (funnily enough), and the data they presented is what they had chosen to write, unprompted, about the movie.

So what did they say? It has to be noted that most respondents loved *The Truman Show*. A small number had heard the hype and then found it disappointing. Some people just thought it wasn't very good and, of those, a lot felt that it didn't really explore the possibilities presented by its premise, and wasn't as clever as it thought it was. The complexities of their responses could only really be done justice in a longer chapter than this one, but I'll mention a few of the comments here. Some rejected the idea that the movie was 'deep': 'It's as sinister as a choc chip cookie,' said one. But others felt that this 'delicately beautiful' film 'should be applauded for bravery' for sending up the Hollywood media industries. Some liked the 'sly digs at product placement', and seemed to feel pleased that they had detected the 'important moral message' of this 'thinking person's movie'. But others resented this simple satire on an obvious target. One wrote: 'Can it be possible that the message of this movie is that we watch too much TV? That many of us have trouble distinguishing entertainment from reality? That everything in life is an illusion? If it isn't one of these hoary platitudes, what is it?' Someone else said: 'This film is a smug, simplistic, self-congratulatory exercise in Hollywood telling us what's wrong with Hollywood – and us. Go write your own screenplay on this theme. Anyone could do it better.' Other people had different agendas altogether. 'There were no particular funny scenes,' complained one: '*Dumb and Dumber* is so much more entertaining.'

The Truman Show wasn't necessarily the ideal subject for this kind of armchair research, though, since (as some people complained) it was a pretty straightforward film that some people would like and some would not. I was actually more interested to see what *IMDb* respondents made of *Starship Troopers*, Paul Verhoeven's expensive 1997 effects bonanza based on Robert A. Heinlein's 1959 novel. Almost all of the professional movie reviewers had read the film as a more or less enjoyable satire upon Heinlein's fascist utopia. But since *Starship Troopers* looks, in large part, like a typical sci-fi action movie, with only a sprinkling of overt satire, plus (arguably) some other levels of more subtle social comment, I was interested to see how it had played with the 'ordinary viewer'. (The professional critics' reason for liking it – because it subtly made fun of the book on which it was based – seemed, in particular, like a potentially unusual response.)

By January 2000, 302 people had posted reviews of *Starship Troopers* at the *IMDb*. First we should note that a number of respondents found the movie to be awful. One remarked, 'I have seen many bad films over the years. This is by far the worst film I have ever tried to sit through. In fact, to call this movie bad would be an insult to bad movies.' Another wrote: 'Like a message written in blood by a man taking his dying breath, I scrawl on the hallowed walls of the internet these words: *Don't ever see this movie if you value your intelligence.*' These were responses to what was seen as wooden acting, duff script and a stupid plot.

Others took the Nazi overtones at face value, and rejected the film for that reason: 'It is very difficult to express how greatly I loathe this film [which] should be re-named "Fascists in Space".' Several other respondents who admired Heinlein's 'excellent, serious' novel felt that Verhoeven had failed to take the book seriously (!) and had produced a moronic Hollywood version.

Most interestingly, a larger number of other people loved it for *this very reason*. 'If you think this film is shallow, you're watching it in a shallow way,' cautions one. 'It works on at least two levels at one and the same time; it's both an extravagantly gory, nasty action horror sci-fi flick, and a critique on modern American gung-ho attitudes to the rest of the world.' Another person adds, 'The proximity of this film to the ra-ra homecoming of American troops from the Gulf War should also not be ignored.' Someone else says, 'You will never see a better movie at explaining what it was like for World War II era Germans.'

Whilst those who disliked the movie would say that it lost what little political point it had because the acting and direction was so hammy, those who enjoyed it argued that the cheesy style was self-conscious and deliberate: 'Someone said that to make a good parody you either get very good actors, and tell them it's a parody, or save some money, get budget actors, and don't tell them anything. You can tell the director here has used the money he saved on actors for special effects. Very canny.'

In this interpretation, Denise Richards smiles throughout the movie and the other characters show so few emotions, *not* because the director has failed to spot that they are useless actors, but because this is part of his cunning plan. Another person, for example, said that there was 'so much to enjoy' in the 'acting and directing choices', such as the lack of grief shown by the leads – even when their families and friends have been brutally slaughtered – and their eagerness to flirt with each other at funerals.

Personally, it had not occurred to me that competent-but-weak acting might be part of a director's strategy, or that audiences would appreciate such an approach. But I'm very much in favour of researchers being taken by surprise by their 'subjects'.

These 'ordinary viewers' had found much *pleasure* in the film, and for many this was closely connected to a feeling that the film had serious intentions. 'By choosing an enemy that's unknown and traditionally considered dangerous, the film tricks us into accepting and even applauding the meaningless and sadistic scenes of violence, where essentially harmless aliens are being tortured and viciously murdered.' Another person noted, 'I suspect Verhoeven is challenging us to ask ourselves the question: would we have enjoyed the holocaust too – suitably presented, of course?'

Unsurprisingly, some people enjoyed the film on a simpler level: 'Some people like to consider the statements about society and war that the director is making. If you want to get all academic about this flick, fine, but I prefer to just enjoy all the guns, nukes, and flying body parts.'

Nevertheless, the range of responses – even along the simple love/hate divide – was extraordinary, and rather uplifting. If anyone ever tries to tell you that audiences generally have similar responses to media products, send them to the *Internet Movie Database* for some corrective instruction.

MORE USEFUL WEBSITES

Movie Critic: **www.moviecritic.com**
The *Critic* asks you to rate a set of movies and then uses clever interactive technology to tell you which films you'll like. And it's spookily accurate.

Drew's Script-O-Rama: **www.script-o-rama.com**
Hundreds of movie scripts and transcripts. Drew links to them, rather than storing them on his own site, which is good as it is difficult to run a website from prison.

International Film: **www.internationalfilm.org**
Articles and critical analysis of the world of international film.

Variety: **www.variety.com**
The latest Hollywood news, reviews and gossip.

Empire: **www.empireonline.co.uk**
Articles, interviews and reviews from the UK's top movie magazine.

Exposure: **www.exposure.co.uk**
The internet resource for young film-makers; excellent features on film structure, guerrilla movie-making, and more.

Film Education: **www.filmeducation.org**
A host of resources for teachers and students studying film across academic disciplines.

10 //

The *Teacher Review* Debate

Editor's note

The controversial Teacher Review *website gives students at the City College of San Francisco (and now other colleges) the opportunity to share reviews of their teachers, via a well-organized online database. We invited the site's creator, Ryan Lathouwers, and his colleague, Amy Happ, to write about why the site is a valuable resource for students. And we asked one of the site's most vehement critics, Daniel Curzon-Brown – a member of the teaching staff who considers himself a victim of student criticism – to say why the site is bad, which he does with a bitter vengeance. Since Lathouwers and Happ explain the intentions and rationale behind the site, it is logical to put their contribution first; but then Curzon-Brown seems to get the last word. You should read both arguments, and then visit www.teacherreview.com (and its newer global companion, www.teacherreviews.com) for yourself, before making a final judgement.*

10.1 Votes cast on *Teacher Review* are compiled to show which tutors are 'Making the Grade' or, less happily, 'Not cutting it'

Part I: Just what the Internet was made for
Ryan Lathouwers and Amy Happ

What student hasn't taken a class she regretted? What student hasn't sat in a class and wondered what planet his teacher came from? What student wouldn't like to know more about an instructor before enrolling in his or her classes? As students, we are always asking our peers for their opinions about their classroom experiences. Was Dr So-and-so a good lecturer? Were Professor What's-her-name's examinations fair? We've all used the word-of-mouth system to find the best instructors and have a more rewarding educational experience. Unfortunately, this method has its limitations. Because college students are a transient population and rarely spend more than four years at any one institution, developing a social network large enough to gather information on every instructor is time-consuming and unrealistic. We need a system that allows us to freely share our experiences and express our opinions with all current and prospective students.

In the summer of 1997, we decided to create such a system for the students at City College of San Francisco (CCSF), California. Although we liked the Web for its availability, accessibility and economy, we chose it as our medium for its democratic nature. Where else could a little know-how and a small monthly fee allow us to create a valuable resource where over 26,000 students could voice their opinions? We created an interactive, online resource where students can freely evaluate instructors' classroom performance, unhindered by the power dynamic of teacher-student relationships and the fear of retribution. We did it without having to ask for permission and without getting tangled in the stifling, unresponsive bureaucracy that is the American educational system. We created a website run entirely by and for students: www.teacherreview.com.

Teacher Review helps students pick classes that are more conducive to their preferred learning styles. Students get the best teachers for their needs and teachers get students who know what to expect. Students are therefore more eager to learn and participate in the classroom. The site also functions as a small step towards equalizing the huge power disparity between teachers and students by giving students more choice in their educational careers and by holding instructors accountable for their teaching practices on an informal level.

Since the site opened in September 1997, the response from students has been overwhelmingly positive. 'Great tool, it would have saved me from finding things out the hard way,' said a Liberal Studies major. 'I like the idea of a forum for students in which we can share ideas/opinions/suggestions about instructors. It will be a good resource when planning my next semester's schedule,' responded another student.

The response from the faculty has been more diverse. The majority of instructors who have contacted us appreciate the voice we have given students. Some related to when they had been students. 'As a student at [a local university] I depended heavily on the "word on the street" and I've always thought student opinions are not respected enough in the whole process.' Others recognize the benefits of empowering students. As Mike Solow, Professor of Chemistry at CCSF, said about *Teacher Review* in the April 1998 edition of *Union Action*, the college's teachers' union newsletter, 'We can improve a student's performance here if he or she feels greater control over his or her education and, as a result, greater responsibility for it.'

Some instructors have had a few qualms about the implementation. When a student leaves a review, he or she gives a letter grade and a written evaluation of the instructor's performance. Because of the honest nature of the critics (and the occasional typo), a small number of instructors have complained about students' poor writing skills, grammar and even illiteracy. Daniel Curzon-Brown, an English teacher at CCSF, has gone so far as to call the reviewers 'an embarrassment to our college'. Another concern with the written evaluations is that students will believe everything they read on the site and make irrational decisions. But, as one remarked, 'Students themselves can evaluate the comments for honesty, bias, or prejudice.' A few instructors have also complained of 'grade rage', the misguided notion that they might get bad reviews because they have given bad grades. They might be surprised to learn that some of the highest student-ranked instructors are also the most demanding.

A more serious complaint is that we have no way to verify the existence of a student. Since our site is off-campus and run privately by students, we have no access to the college's enrolment records and, therefore, no way of knowing if a person leaving a review is actually a student of the instructor in question. Of course, the question of anonymity is not specific to our site; it's an issue that has helped to make the internet both wildly popular as well as extremely controversial. Although there are a small number of people who try to undermine the integrity of the site by posting fake reviews, most students have accepted the responsibility that comes with anonymous postings.

A handful of instructors want the site closed down. Curzon-Brown has called the site 'Incompetence Manifest', 'The Holy Inquisition', and 'a disgusting, lie-filled, destructive force'. Charles Burke, Professor of Mathematics, has labelled the site 'CCSF's version of cyber-terrorism'. They've complained to every committee on campus and to their union. They have tried to convince the college to block access to the site from all computers on campus. So far, the intelligence of others has prevailed against them.

At best, their complaints are unfounded. They like to claim that instructors have no input on the site, that they have no voice. But every instructor is entitled to post an Instructor's Statement (a statement that appears before any of the student-written reviews and that can include anything the instructor wants to say about herself, her teaching methods or what she did last summer). Curzon-Brown even had one for a while, but later asked for it to be removed. They also assert that an avenue of feedback already exists and the site is redundant. They say this because the college has students fill out official evaluations of their teachers at the end of the semester. What they fail to mention is that we students have never seen the findings of these evaluations because the teachers' bargaining contract protects them from our eyes. They also like to paint the site as a smorgasbord of negativity. But the site is overwhelmingly positive: over half of all students give their instructor the best rating. In fact, if *Teacher Review*'s critics investigated the site they would discover that the majority of reviews are thoughtful and earnest, written by students who obviously care about their education and want to help their peers.

At worst, their criticism is an emotionally laden cry of 'libel and slander'. *Teacher Review* has a set of guidelines for the reviews. Anyone who feels a review has violated these guidelines, which condemn 'libel and slander', is encouraged to contact us so that a response can be considered. Occasionally pranksters will leave bogus reviews; we have removed them. Has any of the handful of instructors who so despise our site ever contacted us about a particular review? Not one. They confuse libel with opinion, slander with criticism, and dismiss students' right to freedom of speech when it doesn't suit them.

When they first threatened a lawsuit against City College for having a few links to the site, an article appeared on the front page of the *San Francisco Chronicle* quoting Carey Heckman, a Stanford University technology law expert: 'I think these teachers are living in a fantasy land. This is normal speech and we like this. This is exactly what you ought to teach students in a free society.' Daniel Curzon-Brown eventually filed a lawsuit against *Teacher Review* in late 1999. We are confident that *Teacher Review*'s right to exist as a forum of student opinion will be vindicated.

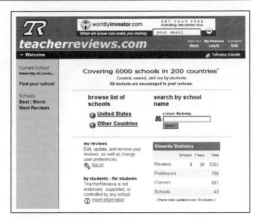

10.2 Teacher Reviews, the newer international site.

Is student opinion free speech or is it slanderous and vile filth? Is *Teacher Review* a menace to teachers or a valuable student resource? The greatest benefit of the internet is the untrammelled flow of diverse ideas in an open forum. By the time this chapter is published there will be a website of student reviews of teachers covering over '6,000 schools in 200 countries'. Decide for yourself after visiting www.teacherreviews.com.

Part II: The dark side of the internet

Daniel Curzon-Brown

How do you think you'd feel if your teachers put up a website in which they printed their opinions about you for the whole world to read? Not just your grades sent to you privately, but what they really think of you: 'A known plagiarist!'; 'Ugly as hell and probably a child molester!'; 'Whatever you do don't allow this horrible semi-human being to enroll in your class!' Future employers in particular should find these very useful in selecting – or not selecting – future employees. A little old grade doesn't begin to do the job.

How does it feel? Well, that's exactly the kind of 'reviews' teachers at City College of San Francisco (CCSF) have had to put up with for several years. The *Teacher Review* website is a disgusting, lie-filled, destructive force that has had the very opposite effect of its avowed purpose – to make education better. It is used for either mash notes or hate speech, neither of which is appropriate in a teacher-student relationship. It is also a place to demean ('. . . she loves to get freaked doggy-style') and threaten teachers ('I feel like killing her . . .'. 'This site has helped *so many* students out and if those $#@$# ever take it down, I will slice their car tires up myself . . .'). These are direct quotes, just three of hundreds.

Teacher Review provides no checks whatsoever on who submits reviews. People who are not students, or not students of the individuals being reviewed, can send in any comments they fancy. Some of them even say 'I've never had this teacher, but . . . '. How could such a situation be allowed for even a minute, let alone for years? It is also possible to lie about the grade you received and every other aspect of the 'information' requested of the 'reviewer'. So one dedicated, or pathological, person can spread disinformation, misinformation, half-truths, gossip and downright lies about any teacher on campus. 'God, Beavis, this is so cool!' People wishing to attend the school can find out the 'truth' about teachers by accessing the college's website. A reporter for the *Jerusalem Post*, of the so-called legitimate press, wrote an article quoting a negative comment about a teacher and then cited this as 'the practical use of the Internet as a productive, global sharing of views' (5 January, 1999).

It gets better. If you don't like somebody or you got a bad grade, go ahead – send in multiple reviews. No one will know you did it. It's totally anonymous, and maybe you can get somebody fired. After all, look at all those different people (you!) bad-mouthing him. It must be all be true or it wouldn't be there, right? Torquemada with technology.

God knows, no student ever lies about a teacher! No student is ever self-serving, cruel, or wrong. And wouldn't it be great if other teachers read those things and believed them and never bothered asking whether or not they were true. I mean, how could they even ask, when the charges are so awful?

And students, of course – not teachers – know what should be taught in colleges. That's why they're going to college. People who are remedial students barely able to express themselves in basic English are telling people with degrees how to teach specific courses, even what the subject matter should or should not be, and who to study from. ('He has a sence [sic] to [sic] racial discrimination. He ever [sic] asked a question like this: Why the English of students . . . are so bad?') Don't ask me why the English of students are so bad! After all, this comment wasn't made about me, just some other schmuck supposedly teaching *college* English. No wonder American education is so bad. And it is bad – inflated grades exceeded only by inflated 'self-esteem' and ignorance exceeded only by arrogance – with a sense of 'entitlement' for having merely paid tuition, as though you buy your grades! And now at last our educational system is actually teaching students to break the law (libel is a crime, punishable in court).

Even the tyrants of old did not have such quick and pervasive methods of ruining reputations, either through whim or grudge. It allows people to flame off angry, ill-considered, murderous comments, the same way someone can shoot off an Uzi. Just shoot and move on; there's no looking back, no removal of the damage inflicted. The cybervictims just lie there in the pool of blood forever. But, hey, it's not your blood. It's sorta like a video game. Cool.

If an accusation were true, let's say (who said teachers are perfect?), and the poor misguided teacher shaped up to the high standards being set for him or her, it still doesn't matter to *Teacher Review*. To call this 'free speech' is letting ideology run rampant over common sense. For some leftists it's the equivalent of the literal interpretation of the 'bible of right-wing fundamentalists'. But if you said such things to anyone, never mind a teacher, in person or left such comments on an answering machine, they would not be 'free speech'; they would be grounds for defamation lawsuits – or for expulsion from school. No newspaper can or would publish the remarks that *Teacher Review* is now publishing (and for a much larger audience).

Offline you cannot publish lies and distortions just because you feel like it and want to express your 'free speech'. This website has made generalizations about a teacher's 'competence' or 'incompetence' on as few as three or four reviews, thus misusing statistics with a mind-blowing incompetence that would cause these people to be fired in a non-remedial world – and yet such puffed-up self-importance about the free expression of opinion! It's not only their math that's terrible, either – their sense of history is too. They believe they are the Berkeley Free Speech Movement reincarnated, while they are actually the McCarthy Era, where the lie becomes a fact merely because it is stated and then restated and then stated again, and any denial or silence is taken as proof of the lie.

Of course the teachers are not permitted free expression, any response, to these so-called reviews. Teachers are expected to stand there and take the abuse and be 'professional'. Professional suckers, yes. Why would anybody want to go into a profession where they can be abused and humiliated publicly? Even more, why would you want to be able to defend yourself from this unholy inquisition: 'No, I didn't kick a pregnant woman out of class and send her to the hospital'; 'Please, please believe me. I am not a homo-maniac!'; 'No, no, I don't hire street hustlers!'

Hey, every job in the world should have a permanent website like this one, where people who've never worked with you, or who have worked with you for a few minutes, or people that you fired can write you up and send The Truth for the whole world to look at.

Well, certainly the people looking at the fabrications and lies can see through them, you say. Why, when they don't know the situations first hand, don't know the parties involved and only get to hear the prosecution's side? People need real information – not just the spite, fantasies, nonsense and viciousness the anonymity of the internet permits. With this kind of 'information base' the internet at its worst – the world is plugging right along towards the knowledge and wisdom we have heard so much about, but some of us are just crash-test dummies on the so-called superhighway.

The answer is not 'fixing' the flaws. We already have official student reviews of teachers in place. Most schools do. These are read by professional college evaluators and acted upon. No *Teacher Review* website of any kind without *Student Review* of exactly the same kind: what's sauce for the goose is sauce for the goddamned gander! (But does anyone really think this is the answer?) When you create a website that permits all these abuses (death threats, rumours, hearsay, grade rage, blackmail and distortions of fact) and then drapes itself in obscene pieties about 'free speech' and 'information', is it any wonder that teachers feel in danger, a danger that grows daily with every new internet user? It's just a matter of time before people act irresponsibly – violently – based on the irresponsible 'information' that is being disseminated by *Teacher Review*. Does someone actually have to die to see how monstrous this thing is? From *Teacher Review* – SFSU from November 1999: 'All I need now is a consensus of all the students who want me to go along and eliminate Mr . . . from the face of the earth. So . . . if you are with me, give me a 666.' We're supposed to say, 'What a boon to education!' Well, you can make me eat shit. You can probably make me eat a lot of shit. But you can't make me say it's delicious!

The illiteracy displayed on the site would seem to be reason enough to shut down this embarrassment to our college and to the world. ('She doesn't have the patients [sic] or understanding [sic] to be a teacher. . . . She's really disrespectful and really incapible [sic] of explaining what she means. Her class was a hugh [sic] aste [sic] of time.')

Who's wasting whose time here? Higher education??

It's time for this madness to end, some appropriate punishments for those who have created and enabled this travesty – and then some reparations for those who have been savaged by this immoral, indefensible hate site; or it will spread to all schools everywhere, with this result: 'Professor, you gave me a D on my first assignment. I showed it to my friends, and they think it's a B. I'd hate to see you written up online as a really bad teacher. Now I'd never do that myself, but my friends are threatening to. Oh, I'd try to stop them, but what could I do? They might even send in lots of reviews under different names and destroy your reputation and kill enrolment. I'd hate to see that happen. Wouldn't you? . . . Now about that A in the course . . . '

RELEVANT WEBSITES

Teacher Review: **www.teacherreview.com**
The original site, where San Francisco students review their teachers, and their classes, so that other students can make informed choices about which modules to select.

Teacher Reviews: **www.teacherreviews.com**
The new, more ambitious spin-off site, which offers students of colleges around the world the opportunity to use the *Teacher Review* system.

The Student Press Law Center: **www.splc.org**
A non-profit organization dedicated to providing legal help and information to the student media of US schools and colleges.

American Civil Liberties Union: **www.aclu.org**
The ACLU is the foremost advocate of individual rights in the USA – litigating, legislating and educating the public on a broad array of issues affecting individual freedom.

Part III

WEB
BUSINESS

11

Bad Web Design: The Internet's *Real* Addiction Problem

David Rieder

It starts as follows. You've been an outsider for months, maybe years. You've been surfing the Web as a user and you always assumed that Web page development was something beyond your capabilities. Suddenly, all of that changes. In a few hours you have learned how to build and upload a Web page. And now, you need to be sure it isn't a fluke, so you put as many examples of everything that you have ever seen around the Web in your first page: five animated GIFs that take 6 minutes to load; three image rollovers that don't work; two Java applets that keep crashing your browser and a 10-meg movie about UFOs that is 2 hours away from playing. In other words, you code a page with every cliché and hackneyed visual metaphor you can find. Why do you do it? Why do so many first-time Web designers reduce their creative potential to a few bells and whistles?

In 1964, decades before Tim Berners-Lee started to develop the World Wide Web, Marshall McLuhan, the Canadian media theorist, published a book entitled *Understanding Media: The Extensions of Man*. In the chapter entitled 'The Gadget Lover', McLuhan develops a theory that he calls the Narcissus Effect. It is an effect that new technologies, new mediums of communication, can have on their users. According to McLuhan, we are often so fascinated by our new technological capabilities that we stand paralysed before them. Many first-time Web designers succumb to this effect. Paradoxically, the new creative outlets that the digital medium affords reduce many designers to trite and uncreative output.

Narcissus famously fell in love with his reflection in a pool of water. As it is often told, he could not tear himself away from his own image and, himself, stood paralysed before it. Redescribing the details, McLuhan tells a slightly different story:

> The Greek myth of Narcissus is directly concerned with a fact of human experience, as the word *Narcissus* indicates. It is from the Greek word narcosis, or numbness. The youth Narcissus mistook his own reflection in the water for another person. This extension of himself by mirror numbed his perceptions until be became the servomechanism of his own extended or repeated image (1994: 41).

McLuhan goes on to explain that 'the point of this myth is the fact that men at once become fascinated by any extension of themselves in any material other than themselves' (41).

McLuhan therefore defines a medium as an extension of our human selves: quite literally, media extend our human capacities, our worldly capabilities. For example, a pair of binoculars is an extension of our eyes, the radio is an extension of our ears and, McLuhan would argue, digital media, like the internet, are extensions of our central nervous systems; we extend our thoughts and ideas across the globe with e-mail, chatrooms and the World Wide Web. Any artefact, any object can be a medium, from a pebble to a rocket.

Like Narcissus, we become captivated by our newly enlarged and extended self-images. We become, as McLuhan points out, 'inextricably linked to images of ourselves in material other than ourselves'. This is what seems to happen to many first-time designers. We are so excited to be able to code HTML – to have our creative potential extended by the new digital medium – that we shut down. The power of the Web renders us powerless to create. When this happens, first-time designers are reduced to servomechanisms of the medium: they become robot-like, parroting over-used phrases and visual metaphors without any sense of ingenuity or creative difference.

There are too many Web pages filled with trite, overused gadgets. There are too many first-time designers building Web pages numbed-out and paralysed by the effects of the medium. It's time to shake off this narcosis. It's time to break free of the initial narcissistic impulse that renders so many first-timers bad Web designers. Wake up: it's time to learn good design by recognizing what's bad.

Gadget loving for dummies

There are dozens of sites devoted to the critique of 'bad' Web design. Their titles reflect the concern and sensitivity with which their authors approach the topic: *Web Pages That Suck, How To Tell If You Have a Sucky Homepage, How to Build Lame Web Sites* and *The Worst of the Web*. My personal favourite is *The BadWickedEvil Web Page* (www. secret-passage.com/bwe), which posts the following warning: 'For entertainment, education, or sheer horror, *The BadWickedEvil Page* is a force to be reckoned with.'

Some of these sites are essentially soapboxes for disgruntled users with a bone to pick. One fairly tame example is entitled *Employment Agency Websites That Suck* (Grumer, 1999). The site is little more than a rant about the problems a professional Web administrator experienced while looking for a job online in 1998. The majority of these sites, however, are maintained by authors of books on Web design, lecturers on the same topic and professional Web designers who have devoted a few pages linked

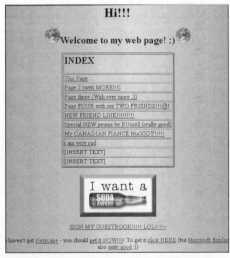

11.1 The deliberately awful *BadWickedEvil Page.*

to their home pages as a resource and an implicit ad space. An example of the latter is Jeffrey M. Glover's *Sucky To Savvy* tutorial (http://jeffglover.com/sucky_to_savvy. html). Glover is a website manager in San Francisco, California. His site is a 20-page tutorial of design tips, from bad to good. Glover's site distinguishes itself from all others by being translated into nine languages including French, German, Russian and Swedish (see Glover, 1999).

One of the most comprehensive sites devoted to all things that suck is Vincent Flanders' *Web Pages That Suck* (www.webpagesthatsuck.com), as mentioned in the introduction to this book. Author of a best-selling book on Web design, lecturer and columnist Flanders has the following claim posted on the front page of his site: 'Enter here to learn good design by looking at bad design.' As mentioned above, several sites approach good Web design in this manner, and they are some of the funniest. In his article, *How to Build Lame Web Sites* (http://webdevelopersjournal.co.uk/columns/perpend1.html), Charlie Morris presents a descriptive outline of everything you need to do to fail miserably; obviously, he is hoping you will stay away from everything on his list. *How to Make an Annoying Webpage* (www.users.nac.net/falken/annoying/main.html) is another example in this pedagogical genre, as is (again) *The BadWickedEvil Web Page*. The latter is a museum of bad design that the authors have copied and pasted from real sites all over the Web.

With this in mind, what are some of the worst and suckiest design elements listed? The following are five classics that are found on almost every site devoted to the critique of horrible Web design.

Under construction

Dating back to 1994, the claim, 'This page is under construction' may be the quintessential cliché in Web design. Almost every site on bad Web design cites this numbingly outdated 'bumper sticker' of incompletion. The basic argument against the cliché is its obviousness. 'The whole idea of the Web as a place 'under construction' is getting very old.' Scoring nine out of ten on his Suck-O-Meter, Glover writes, 'I think we all know that pages are always under construction!'

The worst examples of this cliché are bookended by static or animated graphics of shovels, hard hats, jackhammers and bulldozers. Some animated graphics of jackhammering-happy men are so blatantly sexualized that you don't need a degree in psychoanalysis to find them disturbing. In an article on the top ten signs of amateur Web design, Charlie Morris (1999) writes, 'Some newbies get pretty elaborate with this nonsense, even including cute animated graphics of a highway barrier with a flashing light, like a little klaxon bleating, "... Amateur! ... Amateur! ... Amateur!"'

Frames

If you were surfing the Web in 1996, you might remember the numerous 'anti-frames' clubs and campaigns. They included the 'I Hate Frames Club', the 'Campaign against Frames' and the 'Official Frames Free Ribbon Campaign'. Many of the sites connected to these campaigns are sorely out of date. For example, the author of 'I HATE Frames' evokes a cold-war rhetoric attributing their narcotic use to a communist plot (http://web2.airmail.net/atapaz/www/frames). Part of the reason for this is given in Jakob Nielsen's (1999) update to his often-cited 1996 article 'Top Ten Mistakes in Web Design'. He writes, 'Frames are no longer the disaster they were in 1995 and early 1996 due to some advances in browser technology.' Nevertheless, frames are a classic gadget lover's mistake.

They steal precious 'screen real estate' with their scrolling bars and borders, they do not work on all browsers, they are difficult to bookmark correctly and they confuse search engines.

Blinking text

Blinking text is a Netscape-only gadget which has been around since its first browser, Navigator 1. Simply stated, using the <blink> tag in a Web page is a sure sign of a newbie at best and a narcissistic, paralytic gadget lover at worst. Curiously, the explanations for their sucky status are universally terse: 'Don't use them. Thank you'; 'They suck'; and, next to a ten out of ten on Glover's Suck-O-Meter, 'nuff said'. Blinking text is another over-used and visually distressing element in the medium.

Counters

The following is written at the top of Jordan Mendelson's *Evil Counters* page: 'You've seen them before, they litter the Web like trash on the side walk. They are hit counters, and they suck' (www.thirdwave.net/~jordy/counters.html). Counters are pure, unadulterated narcissism. There are numerous reputable companies that will gather statistics on your Web pages from the back-end or server-side. In other words, there is no reason to count hits 'out loud' on the front page of your site. Charlie Morris writes, 'It's another piece of visual clutter that serves no purpose, and is considered one of the classic signs of a tyro's site.' Besides, half of the time they are broken.

Pop-up windows

This isn't a classic, but it's just a matter of time. Jakob Nielsen writes, 'Opening up new browser windows is like a vacuum cleaner sales person who starts a visit by emptying an ash tray on the customer's carpet.' These are some of the most annoying new gadgets, creating what Nielsen calls 'user-hostility' when they take over your browser. The worst examples pop up when you are trying to leave the site: they empty an ash tray on your carpet while they are leaving.

There are many more classics: obnoxious background music; headache-inducing backgrounds; useless Java applets; an animated 'Get Netscape Now' or 'Best Viewed with Internet Explorer' graphic; a 10-meg movie of your high-school prom; and a JavaScript alert box that says, 'Welcome to my first homepage!' The point is to shake off the narcosis and stop using gadgets as if you are creatively paralysed. As I said earlier, it's time to break away from the self-serving, servo-mechanistic love affair so many of us have with a new medium like the Web. Apple Computer has been saying it for a decade: 'Think different.' Robert Frost wrote about it in his poem, 'The Road Less Traveled'. But, if you are not sure how to be different or where to find Frost's backroad, the least you can do is the following: begin shaking off the Narcissus Effect by parodying the very gadgets to which you are lovingly drawn.

Clearing the cache

On Federico Canzian's *Fake Counter Homepage*, you will always be the 8,349,262,107th visitor (Canzian, 1999). This is because the number never

11.2 Some parody Web campaigns, courtesy of *Boodle Box*.

changes. Federico hosts an international site for fake Web counters. It is divided in two parts. On Federico's 'Counter Gallery' page, he has over two dozen self-creations that you are welcome to steal. On his 'Fake Counter Hall of Fame' page, he publishes a list of fake counters on the Web by country. There are users from nearly a hundred countries faking counters on his list.

Parodies of bad design abound on the Web. In addition to fake counters, you can find fake awards, fake software buttons and fake 'under construction' signs. Examples of all of these are on the website, *Boodle Box* (Saul, 1999). For example, this list of fake Web page awards includes 'Official Bottom 5% of All Web Sites', 'Middle 5% of the Web' and my favourite, 'This Web Site SUCKS'; why beat about the bush?

Ironically, campaigns like the aforementioned anti-frames initiatives can also contribute to the worst of the Web. On *Boodle Box*, you can parody the narcissistic urge to join an online club with the following announcements: the free-the-fruit campaign entitled, 'Free Peaches Online'; the 'Smoke Free Web Site' campaign; and the 'No Blue M&Ms, I'm a Friend of Tan' campaign. You can even protest the very concept of a ribbon campaign with the 'Official Anti-Ribbon Campaign' campaign.

Related to campaign parodies are fake software buttons. Often, Web developers will advertise their allegiance to the products with which they create a site – a practice that has become less than original. In place of RealAudio, there are 'FakeAudio' and 'RealAroma'. Parodying the 'Intel Inside' logo is the alternative, 'Satan Inside' and, from a slightly different parodic angle, 'Made From 100% Recycled Electrons' and 'Made From 100% Unregistered Software'.

The problem with many of these parodic initiatives is their tendency to slip back into narcissism. (How eye opening is a 'Smoke Free Web Site' campaign, after all?) They are a good first try, but if you are not careful, they will pull you right back into the narcotic fold. Assuming that a primary goal of amateur Web design is to break free of the Narcissus Effect, there is only one thing left to do. It is time to study the most wide-eyed, wired Web designs of today: the World Wide Web is your creative medium and the Web page is your canvas.

Sites like the Center for Communication and Culture's *C3* (www.c3.hu) and *Wired* magazine's *RGB Gallery* (www.hotwired.com/rgb) – which are devoted to post-narcotic, eye-opening Web design – abound on the Web; you just have to know how to find them. Often they are connected to university programmes devoted to art and media studies. For example, *C3* in Budapest, Hungary, awards grants to digital artists and hosts a series of workshops for discovery and invention. Its online presence is extensive, including a 'Collections' page with links to a variety of projects dating back to 1996. One 'old school' project listed on this page is Alexei Shulgin's 'Form Art Competition' page. It is a good example of ingenuity using very basic elements of HTML. The competitors in Shulgin's 1997 competition use some of the most everyday and seemingly uninteresting elements of the browsing environment to develop their ideas. Using submit buttons, horizontal text fields, checkboxes, and radio buttons, they stretch the conventions of Web page design to the limit. Many of the competitors in Shulgin's competition create original interfaces that have no intrinsic or functional value. This is design for design's sake: radio buttons dancing across the screen; checkboxes checking and unchecking in pulsing waves; items in drop-down menus that pop open windows displaying poetry, sound and original graphics. Shulgin's contestants go well beyond the values of 'good' or 'bad' Web design. They aren't interested in what *should* be. For these designers, the Web can and should be stretched to see what happens: that is their criteria for 'good' Web design.

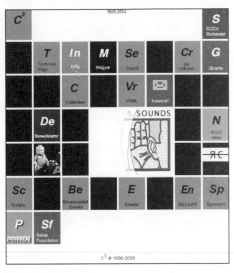

Wired magazine's aforementioned well-known *RGB Gallery* is

● **11.3** The artful *C3* site.

another example of Web design that pushes the limits of the medium. The introductory statement reads: 'Browse our entire collection of Web-based multimedia art from around the world. Each piece is a clever interactive experiment – a multi-sensory adventure. So let your mouse do the walking through this series of otherworldly exhibits. It's an experience you won't soon forget.' Instead of learning what is good from what is bad, here you can learn what is good from what is over the top. The sites linked to from *RGB Gallery* are exciting to read and watch. One project, entitled, 'My Place', is composed of dozens of photographs taken by secondary-school students in a rural northern California community. The piece 'reads' like an auto-ethnographic account of each student's world. David Opp's '4YB-002' is an 'elaborate meditation on the Macintosh interface' leading you through a 'noisy, clickable labyrinth'. And 'TEXT.URE', created by Nam Szeto, Steve Cannon and Jeffrey Piazza, is described as 'a fluid synthesis of text, visual abstraction, and user-interface interaction'. All of these projects are part of *RGB Gallery*'s permanent collection – and these are the 'low end' contributions, for basic browsers. (More complex animated interactive artworks, using the facilities offered by plug-ins such as Shockwave, are also available.)

For the first-time Web designer, sites hosted on *C3* and the *RGB Gallery* are probably too advanced to emulate, but they are very useful for sparking the imagination. These sites help designers at all levels of expertise generate original ideas. Working from these sites, first-time designers can learn how to use colour schemes effectively, how to experiment with layout and how to develop content around a theme – concepts that are essential to post-narcotic design techniques.

Often the narcissistic moment in Web design occurs when amateur developers code without a project in mind. Sitting at the keyboard, HTML manual in hand, they are so excited to code that they pull the most obvious content they can find into their pages: their personal lives. If there was ever a case of narcissistic Web design, it would be this rag-tag army of self-involved 'home' pages. Maybe I'm being unfair, but there really are too many pages 'under construction', hosting a series of badly scanned pictures of pets, with a disjointed version of the Macarena playing in the background. If the answer to the question 'Who will care about this site?' is a lonely 'Me', watch out. You might be falling victim to the Narcissus Effect – in which case you should pack up your gratuitous blink tags, scrolling frames, and background music and 'clear the cache'.

Ultimately, the only 'bad' Web design is no Web design. The critics will tell you otherwise, but the majority of them are motivated by a well-known design principle: form follows function. This modern aesthetic is a basic morality in many aspects of our lives, so it is no surprise that the critics rely upon it. But it is important to realize that there are a lot of great websites that are designed to be non-functional and impractical. The *RGB Gallery* and the variety of found-object Web artists testify to this. The difference between the 'postmodern' styles of impractical and non-functional design and most first-time Web design is one of focus and purpose: *RGB* and found-object artists have shaken themselves free of the rush of first-timer's power. In its place they experiment with the extended foundations of thought and feeling as reflected in the strange, other-worldly material of the World Wide Web.

USEFUL WEBSITES

Use It: **www.useit.com**
Enormously useful, very regularly updated website on Web usability by Jakob Nielsen, which favours simple and clear design. See www.useit.com/alterbox/990530.html for 'The Top Ten Mistakes in Web Design'.

The Worst of the Web: **www.worstoftheweb.com**
Celebrating horrible websites.

Web Developers Journal: **http://webdevelopersjournal.co.uk**
Lots of useful articles. With Charlie Morris's 'Amateur Web Sites – the Top Ten Signs' at http://webdevelopersjournal.co.uk/columns/abc-mistakes.html.

Good and Bad Web Design Features: **www.ratz.com/features.html**
Straightforward lists of good and bad Web design features.

12

Pay Per Browse? The Web's Commercial Futures

Gerard Goggin

From public to private on the internet

The 1990s has seen an explosion of commerce on the internet. Commercial interests are now fundamentally reshaping the multiple mediascapes of the internet, a phenomenon most apparent in the World Wide Web. This represents a radical departure for a worldwide communications system developed, run and funded for much of its life by governments, not-for-profit research institutions, universities, individuals and associations working on a voluntary basis. Thus commercialization poses distinct challenges for the way that public spheres of citizen interaction on the internet have and can be conceived.

The internet was initially created and, for many years, funded by the US Department of Defense, starting with the creation of its Advanced Research Projects Agency (ARPA) in 1957 and the commissioning of the first of the internet's networks in 1969. In 1979, the National Science Foundation (NSF) began to play a leading role, establishing the fast NSFNET in 1985, with five university-based super-computing centres. By the mid-1990s, the NSF had privatized the backbone network of the internet, and the US government had stepped back from funding and governing it. In countries other than the USA, university and research organizations also joined with government agencies to play a crucial role in the early spread of the internet.

The role of public-spirited individuals was also crucial in internet matters until very recently. A celebrated instance is the role of Jon Postel and his team, based at the University of Southern California's Information Sciences Institute, who took responsibility for internet protocol parameters under the rubric of the Internet Assigned Numbers Authority (IANA). Domain names were also allocated by individuals in different countries operating on a

12.1 Will the business sharks gobble up the Web?

custodianship basis, chosen by Postel largely on a first-come, first-served basis (Gillet and Kapor, 1997: 21–22). In other areas, much of internet policy and standards were set by scientists, researchers and enthusiasts on a decentralized model, epitomized in the Request For Comment (RFC) model initiated by Steve Crocker in 1969 for collaborative discussion on software (Hafner and Lyon, 1996: 144–45). The RFC model allowed anyone involved in the ARPA sites to comment on technical proposals, initially by post, but soon, of course, by e-mail.

Thus through its leading funders and developers in the public spheres of education and research – and its leading pioneers devoting much of their time for free – for its first two decades, the internet was explicitly fashioned as an educational space for the exchange of knowledge. This did not stop users routinely and gleefully devising all manner of recreations, in addition to research and educational exchanges. However, commerce and trade were explicitly prohibited through a ban on using the internet for personal gain, codified in an 'acceptable use' policy.

This was sustainable when the majority of users were based in educational and research settings, where the public-good characteristics of the nascent computing networks could be championed and safeguarded. Interested citizens who were not primarily researchers, academics or students could join the internet without too much problem, as long as they were happy to adapt to its ethos and master its interfaces. In this sense, the internet has long been considered to have a public character with distinct attributes: a highly decentralized structure; a valorization of public ends over private means; a dissenting temper; a commitment to free and frank speech; and a friendly, participatory ethos. This public culture of the net was significantly shaped by allied computer networking movements, such as the bulletin board systems (BBSs) from the 1980s onwards – such as FidoNet (1983), and the celebrated Whole Earth 'Lectronic Link (WELL – www.thewell.com), created by Steward Brand in 1985 and contributing a distinctively hippie countercultural politics of understanding the public sphere online. The emergence of 'hackers' was also important to net culture, an avowedly anti-corporate grouping devoted to disrupting corporate and computer control of computing (Raymond 1998a; see also Thomas's chapter in this volume).

The invention of World Wide Web protocol by Tim Berners-Lee in 1990–91 made the internet much easier to use, bringing together different information transfer systems. When Marc Andreessen developed the protocol into an easy-to-use graphic user interface in devising the Mosaic browser in 1992, this dispensed with the need to master complex text-based interfaces. The commercial deployment of the Mosaic browser, which then became the Netscape Navigator browser owned by Andreessen himself, coincided with the spread of other graphic user interfaces, especially with the IBM-compatible Windows software, but also with programs for e-mail and dial-up access. As a result, internet usage started to grow exponentially in more developed countries from 1993.

Slow to appreciate the virtues of an often anarchic, communal, public-spirited and text-intensive internet culture, it was the advent of the Web that spurred profit-making corporations to finally get wired. Business started to encroach on to the internet, but it was not until 1992 that the National Science Foundation Act was amended to allow a variation to the acceptable use policy to allow commercial traffic to be carried. In boardrooms around the world, senior executives of major corporations – notorious newbies on the net – initially demurred, then by the end of the decade rushed to gain an internet presence in the hope of helping themselves and shareholders to huge profits. The corporate sector finally saw the potential in the immense audiences and numbers of customers online, and the World Wide Web became the closest thing to a 'killer application' seen for some time.

The dawn of business on the net went hand in glove with significant rethinking of the internet by governments. By the mid-1990s, the vision of internet as publicly owned and freely accessible for non-profit research and information sharing was felt to be unsustainable by many policy-makers around the world. With government budgets shrinking, telecommunications reforms in progress and hundreds of millions of people logging on to the Net, the private sector was seen as the appropriate source of funding to unclog data traffic by financing the upgrade of internet technologies, including next-generation fast-data internet services. By the end of the 1990s, access to the internet was largely in the gift of a bewildering array of commercial internet service providers and telecommunications companies. The importance placed on an internet transformed through the operations of commerce was palpably exhibited in the sensational stock market fortunes of e-industry leaders such as Amazon.com and Yahoo!, as well as many other fledgling internet-based corporations whose profits were very much virtual at the time of listing.

Commercial interests and the Web

Prior to the widespread adoption of the Web, business leaders – especially early adopters – had been interested in the commercial potential for interactive data technologies, but had primarily vested their hopes in videotext (in the 1980s), existing private computer networks, electronic data interchange (EDI) or the potential of new technologies, such as interactive television, to allow home shopping or purchases of goods and services. The text-based interfaces discouraged businesses as much as other users. The ability of the Web to weave together disparate programs as well as text, images, sound and video proved very attractive. Concerns remained about the security of electronic transactions, and these were not satisfactorily addressed until the development and adoption of encrypted communications (such as secure Web servers).

Instead of just owning a server and having a ftp address where files could be downloaded, the Web allowed businesses to have a shopfront on the net. Even more impressive was the potential of the website as shopfront to combine many of the existing ways of interacting with customers – signage, catalogues, product information and pictures, advertising, a virtual tour, contacting a business, meeting staff. Better still, a business could be available 24 hours a day every day. Once the popularity of the Web become evident, there was a scramble by businesses to establish themselves on the net – one of those claiming early line honours, with mixed success, was *Wired* magazine's *HotWired* site (www.hotwired.com), established in October 1994. As well as making *Wired* magazine and other original content available online ('content channels', such as *Signal*, with articles, e-mails and gossip about the internet), *HotWired* styled itself as a pioneer of business models and communication forms. The free site featured a membership system, saw chat and forum activities as integral to its content, and developed a range of technology-related news and information services.

As with other real estate, an easily found and remembered location became important. Like phone numbers, Web addresses, or Uniform Resource Locators (URLs), can be given in letters as well as internet protocol (IP) numbers. A domain name system had been introduced in 1984, with domains including .edu (educational institutions), .org (for not-for-profit organizations), .mil (military), .net (internet organizations) and also .com for commercial organizations. An interesting thing about this domain name system is the conceptualization of the internet as having different sorts of spheres: civil (such as .edu or .org) and state (such as .gov or .mil) as well as commercial (.com).

The first domain name assigned was Symbolic.com, registered in 1985, ahead even of educational domain names such as cmu.edu or government names such as css.gov (Hobbes, 1999). Once the ban on commerce on the internet had been fully lifted and the Web commercialized, companies rushed to secure a URL based on their trading name or another evocative, easily remembered word. With the intense commercial pressure on the system of domain name registration, and ensuing legal battles over copyright and ownership of trademarks, it is not surprising that much recent attention has been given to its reform.

One of the first signs of commerce's presence on the internet was the controversial appearance of advertising. The netiquette of most online forums, such as newsgroup and mail lists, frowned upon blatant promotion or advertising of commercial material. The US law firm Canter and Siegel discovered this in 1994 when it posted an ad for immigration advice on green cards to thousands of newsgroups – the resulting tens of thousands of flames (abusive replies) saw its Internet Service Provider (ISP) crash many times the following day and its account cancelled. This netiquette still holds sway over many internet-based discussion forums, the members of which permit self-effacing promotion of an individual's product if relevant to the thread of the discussion – but mostly do not allow unsolicited commercial e-mails, known as 'spam'. Accordingly, many ISPs have been keen to provide their users with protection against spamming. In two separate cases in May 1997, CompuServe and EarthLink (following the lead of America Online) won court cases against notorious direct marketing firm CyberPromotions.

Some effort, however, is going into the evolution of the norms of internet culture to address concerns of commerce. For instance, advertising and commercial promotion via e-mail is acceptable for many internet users, provided consent has already been sought and granted. The norms of this sort of commercially oriented advertising have become modelled on the rules acceptable for direct marketing by post or telephone. As online advertising becomes an integral part of a company's advertising 'spend', so advertising agencies have made a great effort to understand how electronic communities work. Web-based advertising has built upon and extended traditions of billboard, newspaper, television and radio advertising to fashion pervasive and dynamic new forms of multimedia advertising. *HotWired* was one of the first to advertise on the Web, as a service dependent on advertising revenue (Zeff and Aronson, 1999: 15–16). Those who launched *Hotwired* had the advantage of already having an established advertising presence and sales force with *Wired* magazine.

For the next two years, many advertisers, along with other corporations, waited to see how consumers would adopt and use the internet. Though there remain many sceptics in the industry, advertising has been firmly and ubiquitously established. New genres of ads have emerged, such as the banner ad (interactive and 'rich media' banners are believed by some to have greater impact than static or crudely animated ones); buttons; text links; 'pop-ups', which are a much more in-your-face form of advertising, relying on windows to pop up and seize the attention of the Web surfer; interstitials, an 'in between' advertising page or image, which appears while the user waits for another page to load; and the sponsored website or Web event. Also important is the way technologies such as the World Wide Web allow the collection, stockpiling and interpretation of detailed information on a consumer's buying habits. Zef and Aronson point to four features of internet advertising which position it at the intersection of traditional advertising and direct marketing: targetability, tracking, deliverability and flexibility. Those hosting websites are finding their own distinctive opportunities to sell audiences to advertisers.

Debates over advertising, especially spam, illustrate a recurrent problem in internet commerce – the inability of the majority of businesses to understand internet culture. This is viewed as one of the main obstacles to e-commerce becoming successful (Clarke, 1999). A more recent development with striking similarities to spam is 'push technology', where instead of internet users choosing which sites they wish to visit, news, advertising and entertainment is sent to their desktop whenever they log on. With applications like PointCast and Castanet, 'push technology' was hailed by some as the ultimate way to market to consumers, taking back into the content provider's hands the ability to dictate what users received (Kelly and Wolf, 1997). While 'push technology' doubtless has important benefits – as for instance in the original Multicast Backbone (MBone) video broadcasting – to date it has tended to function on a one-way broadcasting model rather than the interactive communication model favoured by net users (Clarke, 1999). Not surprisingly, most net users have, to date, given the 'push' model the shove.

As well as establishing their own business shopfront on the Web and advertising their wares, profit-oriented corporations have also sought to have a financial stake in, and control of, spaces where different sorts of valued transactions can take place. Certain spaces on the internet are being dominated by commercial interests because they are the main transactional spaces – the 'central' points where much Web-surfing action takes place (White, 1996). Especially important are those sites, servers and search engines that offer help in navigating the internet's wealth of information and recreations. Given this, battles over transactional space on the internet have revolved increasingly around popular search engines and the commercial opportunities they offer. These 'portals' have become one of the most distinctive translations of the shopping centre or 'mall' to the net (see Miller's chapter in this volume).

In addition to the commercialization of the major public transactional spaces of the internet, another allied phenomenon is the intense commercial interest in valued information and cultural product. The Web provides a multitude of distribution points and communications channels which potentially allow a range of options for providing information and entertainment in digital form. However, as the means of distribution open up with the spread of the internet, so the premium placed on valued information rises. Transnational media corporations seeking a presence across both older and newer media forms (especially the internet) have invested greater sums of money into buying control of 'content': the archives of the most popular images, movies, books and music. The expense of creating new multimedia product and high-quality websites can also be prohibitive, and so commercial organizations are now well placed – as they finally start to take the internet seriously – to produce, mount and maintain high-end, high-functionality websites.

As the internet content has become more commercial, so too has access. To use the internet in the early years, enthusiasts needed to have access to a university, military or government account. When the number of users grew and became more widespread, it was possible for users to dial-up and connect to the internet for free. The costs to the dial-up user at this stage were the cost of purchasing a computer and modem, and the price of phone calls billed to their phone company. Commercial alternatives to the internet existed from the late 1970s onwards with bulletin board systems (BBSs), private computer networks (such as Prodigy, CompuServe and America Online), and data services offered by telecommunications companies favoured by business.

Once the Web and internet were commercialized, many universities stepped back from providing free access and privately owned ISPs came to the fore. The first of these was The World (world.std.com) in 1990 (Hobbes, 1999). A bewildering range of possibilities for connecting to the internet then came about, allowing customers to pay for a mix of attributes such as customer service, quality of service, bandwidth, hours of connection, download quota, and/or additional private sites to access. The basic infrastructure underlying the internet now comprises a much greater number of commercially owned networks, especially a much greater market-based approach to telecommunications worldwide. Designed to carry voice traffic, telephone networks are being redesigned to carry digital data services, and so there is a mix of cable, wireless and satellite networks being developed.

Finally, the design, manufacture and distribution of computer software used to access the internet has become more commercial in its nature. Especially as the commercial prospects of the internet have become clearer, information technology corporations and telecommunications companies have demonstrated a fundamental suspicion towards the fair use, open standard, 'information must be free' ethos of internet culture. Many companies still desire to control access to the internet itself through pay-per-use strategies, but these have not been very successful to date. Instead, companies are vying to be the dominant providers of elements of the communications infrastructure – such as set-top boxes, the telecommunications connection to the household, or computer operating systems – which are strategically important for access to the internet.

One of the grand battles over access software has been, unsurprisingly, focused on Web wherewithal – whose browser internet users turn to, and how it conditions and constrains their entry to the Web. A case in point here is Microsoft's attempt to control access to the internet through proprietary software. Microsoft has a significant potential commercial advantage through its dominance of the computer operating system market with its Windows product, which it has parleyed into a king-size share of the software market (with its Office suite), positioning it as the gatekeeper to the internet for many. Microsoft first tried to sideline the internet and promote its own separate network, MSN. When MSN was slow to grow, Microsoft entered into a period of suspicious rapprochement with internet culture. While Netscape gave away its popular Navigator browser (and in March 1998, the source code for Navigator 5.0), Microsoft held on for a long while to bundling its Internet Explorer browsers with its Windows software, seeking to be the browser of choice for the PC user.

The browser wars represent a break from the open standards approach, which resulted in the development and free availability of the network and Web protocols of the internet. As Gillett and Kapor suggest, open standards have been critical to the internet's public character, 'key to the internet's juxtaposition of interoperability with distributed power and control' (1997: 9). Building on the heritage of the anti-commercial ethos of those who developed AT&T's Unix and pre-commercial internet software, the free software movement (see www.fsf.org or www.gnu.org), with its 'General Public License', and the more pragmatic 'open source' (www.opensource.org) software grouping have been a rich and contradictory resource for those seeking to keep software development and use in public hands (Raymond, 1998b).

Maintaining public visions

The rapid commercialization of the internet, coinciding with its frenzied diffusion worldwide, raises a set of questions about its future as a public space. Do private corporations spoil the Web for everybody? Are such commercial uses of the internet a threat to internet users who would more often than not prefer to be digital citizens, rather than cookie-infested consumers? Does commercialization make the internet more accessible for a greater range of purposes, such as providing alternative media and distribution outlets for innovative small business, leading to greater choice? Or is commerce on the Web already well on the way to being dominated by the same media barons who already control much of the world's media, and who wish to consolidate their digital futures in emerging, interlocking applications such as internet television, digital broadcasting and newspapers online?

As the internet was initiated and developed by publicly funded organizations until comparatively recently, citizens theoretically had a direct stake in it through their elected representatives and government officials, and an indirect stake through the not-for-profit public service mission of universities and research institutions. The *ownership* of the internet has shifted dramatically into private hands at every level; and much of the *control* of the internet has gone the same way. Transnational corporations now desire to own and control strategic zones of the internet in order to secure markets – a symptom of which is the hyperinflationary fortunes of internet stocks (which themselves are increasingly traded online).

There is indeed much evidence for the claim that the prospects for a diverse, democratic, creative internet are being threatened by the desire of transnational and other corporations to turn it into a global electronic market-place, dominated by the profit motive. Herman and McChesney have pointed out the dominance of the global media market by roughly ten vertically integrated media conglomerates, most based in the USA (Herman and McChesney, 1997; see also McChesney, 1999) – the same transnational corporations who are steadily adding strategic parts of the internet to their portfolios. Herman puts this starkly when he argues that the 'public sphere is shrinking globally under the impact of a triumphant market system, which is putting more and more public space to profitable use, as defined by the advertising community' (Herman, 1998). In this light, internet developments need also to be placed within the context of an ensemble of capital's initiatives in new digital media, dubbed by some 'electronic empires' (Thussu, 1998).

What is very difficult at this point in the internet's development is how to situate and separate out the baleful from the beneficial effects of commercialization. A starting point is the recognition that commerce and its threats are not monolithic. This may be appreciated by a closer, more sceptical re-examination of the internet's myths of origin. It is not so easy to discern the dividing line between commerce and government in the second half of the twentieth century, especially in the case of military industries and research (a phenomenon often referred to as the 'military-industrial complex'), which developed the foundations of the internet. One might point to the way that the research and computing arms of private companies were very much involved in the development of the internet. Significant aspects of the early internet were provided by private corporations, the prime example being the private consulting firm Bolt Beranek and Newman (BBN), which was awarded a contract crucial to the start-up of the internet in 1968. Phone company AT&T provided the datalines to connect far-flung computers at this stage, its famous Bell Labs provided the Unix language, and even though IBM passed up the contract BBN won, it also provided critical infrastructure for the internet at different phases of its expansion. The mixture of public and private property, goals and projects may also be discerned in universities, many of which are privately owned in the USA, though predominantly publicly owned in Europe, Australia and elsewhere. Research organizations too have private corporations as substantial stakeholders of their applied and basic research. In addition, engineers who trained in universities on APRANET established successful businesses in networking (3Com), computers (Sun) and networking equipment (Cisco).

With the privatization of government-owned telecommunications enterprises and accompanying deregulation through the 1980s and 1990s around the world, allied with technical invention in the area of computing and networks – especially with personal computers and advances in software, but also with mix-and-match technologies such as routers, network and terminal equipment – the blurring of governmental and commercial zones of influences has become even more pronounced. This has cast into relief the importance of the early decisions which the US regulator, the Federal Communications Commission (FCC), took in its Computer Inquiries in the late 1960s and early 1970s not to regulate the emerging computer data industry or modems. This played a key role in establishing computer networking as a market outside the then more restrictive monopoly arrangements applying to the telecommunications industry (Oxman, 1999).

Further, although the internet has been viewed as public space, for much of the time it was funded and controlled by government, university and research entities, it was actually in effect a *private* network of networks with public aspirations and public good characteristics (Spurgeon, 1998). Until the mid-1990s, the general, non-technically literate public was not involved in policy-making about the internet; and the internet itself, for all its public significance and use, did not feature in public debate on communications policy as an important infrastructure alongside other media. Before this time, the public had a latent stake in the internet, but in reality much decision-making on the internet took place in specialized forums, albeit in reasonably democratic, decentralized and innovative ways.

Commerce on the internet has also had enabling, productive effects. The commercialization of the internet has intensified its reach and its possibilities, though these are dependent on citizens enjoying reasonable access and sufficient disposable income (both preconditions problematic in poorer countries, and for poorer members of richer countries). Many companies are pushing for better infrastructure, deployment of new technologies, increased bandwidth and an end to the 'World Wide Wait'. The internet has also provided an alternative, flexible distribution network, which allows smaller or inexperienced producers to market goods and services, and challenge the power of established corporations and older industrial interests. Of great interest to many also are the opportunities for different sorts of non-exploitative economic exchange to be developed through the internet – such as community networking, the formation of new voluntary organizations, the rejuvenation of civil society, the sustaining of social and countercultural movements.

It is important too to recognize how internet users and public not-for-profit organizations, groups, collectives and small businesses have responded to the commodification of the internet by dominant private corporations. Diverse coalitions have been formed to advocate for the interests of ordinary netizens in the face of domination by commercial interests. One of the overarching concerns has been the need for public spheres on the net, just as public spheres have existed in broadcasting (with the funding of public and community broadcasting, for instance), print and other existing media. This demand was often expressed as a plea for an 'electronic commons', eliciting widespread agreement that public spheres on the net must be provided alongside trading places.

Consumer, public interest, community and not-for-profit groups have also formed strategic alliances with corporations on issues of mutual concern. This type of net politics can be seen in interventions by individuals and organizations around debates on how domain names will be managed, where activists such as Ronda Hauben (Hauben, 1998a and 1998b), and consumer organizations featuring luminaries such as Ralph Nader, widely publicized their views (see Nader, 1999). The new Internet Corporation for Assigned Names and Numbers (ICANN – www.icann.org) has acquired its own watchdog (ICANNWatch at www.icannwatch.org). Much attention has also been given to citizen and community initiatives on the internet to promote equality of access among marginalized groups, address rural communications, and promote worthy non-profit projects (see Benton Foundation, 1998). The internet itself provides an excellent tool for resisting the encroachment of commercial interests – alternative views and campaigns can be widely and cheaply circulated using the most basic of internet technologies: plain text e-mail.

This underlines the fact that one of the prime sources of resistance to commercial dominance of the internet is the very open and deterritorialized nature of the internet as technological, social and cultural system. Despite the leaden-footed attempts of Microsoft, Time Warner, Disney and News Corporation to buy up the internet distribution chain from screen to server and beyond, the extraordinary complexity of the networks has made it very difficult for capital, like government, to gain even partial control. That the constituent parts of most internet industries are in flux, and that new players are able to challenge old with minimal start-up capital (at least until they are taken over by a bigger player) means that no one fraction of capital has yet really established its dominance over the whole system. There is a very real sense in which internet users are choosing where they wish to go, and what software they wish to use, so staying one step ahead of those wishing to build online empires.

Furthermore, it is yet to be seen in what sense commercial interests are able to 'take over' the Web. The explosion of networks, access lines, servers, software and users has so far meant that commerce is well established on the internet and dramatically increasing. However, this feverish trading takes place alongside a hot(wired) bed of educational, political, cultural and individual activity. Some of the traditional public spaces have been reinvented and reconceived online, often deliberately so – whether libraries, community or self-help groups, public broadcasters, news, public service announcements or information services. An individual or group's ability to make a space for themselves on the internet – public or private – is still arguably far greater than in other media. There is a real sense in which, given access and basic computer knowledge, anyone can mount their own personal Web pages (although these may be of dubious quality if time is not spent learning techniques and styles). 'Free' Web pages and e-mail are offered by a number of different companies, non-government and governmental organizations, although the commercial offerings are paid for by advertising and data collection – which is why the innovative Hotmail service, for example, was eventually swallowed by Microsoft, and GeoCities was bought by Yahoo!

To see the internet in terms of a simple opposition between commerce (bad) and the public interest (good) is to refuse a more difficult but necessary task – looking at the complex, contradictory and overlapping relationships between commercial and non-commercial interests on the Web. Neither easy denunciation of capital's reshaping of the internet, nor wholesale embrace of electronic democratic capitalism, is helpful here. Nor should we let our hopes rest too easily on a vision of the internet as a decentred anarchic cyberpolity, a zone too inherently diffuse and slippery to be completely colonized by commercial interests.

There is a very real need to re-examine and rewire our public visions for the internet of the new millennium. Many economically conservative governments are supporting policies which may result in commercial interests reserving control of the internet for themselves. We need to be sure that governments and corporations extend citizens the right to participate in the development and governance of the internet. The traditional institutions of the internet have already signalled their desire to influence its continuing development, by strategic initiatives such as the US university community's Internet2 initiative (www.internet2.edu), and the US Government's Next Generation Internet (NGI) Initiative (www.ngi.gov).

Key to a rejuvenated public vision of the internet must be a commitment to communication and information as a right. Corporations need to respect the fact that the internet is very much a *public* network, even when it is privately owned. Like the telephone or television, the internet is not just a hamburger for packaging and sale, but an essential communication service – a medium that should be available for the use of all citizens. Moreover there need to be well funded culturally diverse and politically challenging public spheres on the internet, as much in the .com as in the .org, .edu, and .gov domains. Putting this principle into practice on the internet in a myriad of global and local ways will go a long way to keeping as much of the internet as possible as a commerce-free zone – a healthy mix of public aspirations and private interests. Such public visions will stand to the benefit of all members of the browsing public, not just those who can afford to pay.

Author's note   Thanks to Fiona Martin and Justine Lloyd for their helpful comments on an earlier draft of this chapter, and to members of the Link discussion list for their assistance.

USEFUL WEBSITES

Electronic Frontiers Foundation: **http://eff.org**
Indispensable site of the best-known cyberspace civil liberties organization.

Computer Professionals for Social Responsibility: **www.cpsr.org**
Website of public-interest alliance of computer scientists and others concerned about the impact of computer technology on society, with useful documents, links, journals and archives.

ISWorld Net's Electronic Commerce Course:
www.isworld.org/isworld/ecourse
Very comprehensive collection of links on commerce on the internet maintained by Professor Blake Ives of Louisiana State University.

The Benton Foundation's Communications Policy and Practice Program: **www.benton.org**
Website of independent organization which promotes public interest values and non-commercial services for the internet.

Consumer Technology Project: **www.cptech.org**
Website of Ralph Nader's technology watchdog, giving information on consumer advocacy in electronic commerce, internet governance, anti-trust and telecommunications.

13

Search Engines, Portals and Global Capitalism

Vincent Miller

In *Virtual Capitalism: Monopoly Capital, Marketing, and the Information Highway*, Michael Dawson and John Bellamy Foster argue that the internet will fail to produce a perfect market-place. 'One of the great technological myths of our time,' they assert, 'is that the entire system of organized capitalism is being displaced by a new "electronic republic"' (1998: 51). The popular idea that the internet will provide consumers with a wealth of knowledge about products which will lead to 'Friction-Free Capitalism' is, they suggest, quite bogus. Their scepticism lies in the political and economic history of communications, which, as in most areas of economic life, is one increasingly dominated by oligopoly – a state of limited competition between a few powerful companies. They believe that the information highway will be no exception to this trend, especially given its current attractiveness to global capital.

For Dawson and Foster, this attractiveness, and indeed the rhetoric of the internet as the 'saviour' of economic growth, is born out of the stagnation of advanced capitalist economies around the world. Charting the stagnation of the (monopolistic) economies of the West with the rise of marketing, they effectively argue that with decreasing competition, the central problem for a business is not a competitive struggle between firms' products or prices, but a struggle to get consumers to buy more, thereby generating economic growth through an 'artificial stimulation of demand'. In other words: marketing. Put simply, products are no longer just produced and then sold to the general public; now research into consumers creates the basis for a product which can then be sold to a targeted market niche.

The argument is that this ability to target consumers is what makes the internet attractive to business. By its very nature – interactivity – the information highway and internet offers the possibility of much more effective 'artificial stimulation of demand':

> There is no doubt that the main reason for corporate interest in the information highway lies in the fact that it is seen as opening up vast new markets, which also means expanding the range and effectiveness of targeting, motivation research, product management, and sales communication – that is, a total marketing strategy.
>
> (Dawson and Foster, 1998: 58)

This chapter[1] is in effect an examination of the above points, using internet search engines (or portals) as an archetypal expression of some of these concerns. Thus, I will look at:

☞ how search engines have developed and helped shape the internet
☞ search services, marketing and the paradox of interactivity
☞ portals – from means to ends, to ends in themselves
☞ internet portals, investment and convergence.

My point will be that it is in the development of portals that we can actually see Foster and Dawson's thesis played out. These companies show how the development of the internet has been one of commercial interests, how they have the potential to be powerful marketing tools and how their continuing financial saga is evidence of a trend towards oligopoly on the information highway.

A brief history of search engines

The Web search engines of today have a history going back to 1991. The earliest internet search engine was Archie, based at McGill University. Archie allowed keyword searches of filenames listed on internet sites (Poulter, 1997). The advent of gopher (a forerunner of the World Wide Web) in 1992 brought the Veronica search engine into existence, which allowed multi-word and Boolean searches (using operators such as 'and' and 'or'). Despite these early developments, it was 1994 which was to be a watershed year for the internet, not only because it was the year that the Web got off the ground, but because in that year two projects appeared, open to the public as free services – both would change the course of the internet's development.

By 1994, the two main types of search engine that dominate the Web today, keyword and subject directory, had become established (Poulter, 1997). The first of the successful 'full text' keyword search engines, Webcrawler, was introduced and became the most successful of the early 'Web Robots'.[2] This approach to finding information on the Web proved popular, with Brian Pinkerton's Webcrawler soon followed by now more famous names such as Lycos and AltaVista.

That year also saw the rise of subject directory search tools with the Yahoo! search service. These types of search tools rely on human categorization of Web pages in a hierarchical ontology of subject headings. Pages are linked and given tags labelling them within this fixed hierarchy of categories. By the end of 1994, Yahoo! was a venture-capital backed brand, arguably the first and most powerful brand on the internet.[3]

While Yahoo! and Webcrawler are the extremes in both types of search service, many of the more prominent 'engines' of today rely on a combination of robot searching and human classification. This is true of the now-popular names such as Excite! and Infoseek.

These two (and other) search services had a huge impact on the Web. They made it negotiable and accessible to consumers and, by so doing, created traffic – but, most importantly, traffic that was reliable. No longer did consumers need to know what information they were looking for and where to find it, they could start their search for information at a central point and then branch out from there.

Webcrawler and Yahoo! continued to provide these search services for free, and while Webcrawler never really capitalized commercially on its name recognition, Yahoo! used its early loyal customer base to create a powerful brand and a strong commercial presence. After a few months the Yahoo! business model started to take shape, and out of three potential options to create revenue – subscriptions, pay per search and advertising – the latter was chosen. This decision was also fundamental to the Web as we know it, to keep services and content 'free' while earning revenue from advertisers. This created conditions for the World Wide Web to develop not as a 'glass-bottomed boat' where advertisements for products in the 'real world' are displayed,[4] but more along the lines of a model in which a large amount of information, goods and services are given away for free.

> I think what we're doing is giving validity to what the Web has to offer. Instead of going on-line and seeing a whole bunch of lists of things that are *available* in the real world, you actually *get* the stuff. ... I mean I think that the craze of financial information on the Web has made investors out of housewives, grandmothers, and college students. They weren't in a position to do that a year ago, so I think it's probably one of the ways in which Yahoo!'s role in the internet is probably benefiting [users].
>
> (Adrian Lurssen, Managing Editorial, Yahoo!)[5]

Searching and marketing potential

Search engines have arguably become the most supported commercial enterprises on the internet thus far. One can argue that this is because search engines (potentially) do two things that make them desirable to those willing and able to invest in the information highway: they help to direct internet traffic and they increase the potential for customer profiling.

Search services themselves make the internet practical. By corralling sources of information on any desired topic, search engines greatly increase the chances that a user can find the information they are looking for in the infinite space of the Web. And for those who produce websites, search engines are extremely important as the means by which their pages might actually be found by an audience. This has dramatic consequences, as it paves the way for advertising opportunities, which in turn means that content, funded by advertisers, can be provided free to the consumer.

Search engines provide entry points that users periodically return to several times when 'surfing'. Thus the idea of wandering around a 'net' is replaced by more of a 'hub and spoke' model, where traffic emerges from one central point and, more often than not, returns to that hub before going out again. What this does is to create nodes of traffic, which are predictable and therefore marketable to advertisers.

Search services also have the potential to contribute to more effective forms of marketing. The act of searching is itself an act that targets consumers. Most search services are based on hierarchies of categories (such as news, sports, finance, technology) of one form or another – which is one reason why they all look the same. These more general categories are divided into more and more specific ones (for example, sports into different sports, associations, equipment and the like). As the user moves on to more and more specific categories within their search, he or she also becomes a more precise target at which to aim advertising. Because these advertisements are more targeted, they have the potential to be much more effective, consequently advertisers are willing to pay search companies more for more directed ads.

> If I'm looking for golf, I'm not gonna mind seeing a golf ad, and I'm gonna like that. If I'm looking for a new car, I probably do wanna see advertisements for cars, because if I link up to a site and check out General Motors, check out Saturn, or whatever, [I can] see what cars are around. And so there are times when I think they do mesh, and that's one thing we can do that is difficult in the media. We can do a lot more targeting and advertising to people, hopefully in a good way, and then we can also track how successful things are, and so you can tell instantaneously what people respond to and what they don't respond to. What they like, what their complaints are, all these things.
>
> (David Filo, Co-founder, Yahoo!)[6]

Search services have the ability to collect an unprecedented amount of information about their audiences, amassing data on what a user searches for, as well as what sites they visit and how long they spend there. This is done in a variety of ways, but one important aspect is the use of 'cookies'. These are contained in a small information file on a Web user's hard drive, in order to supply information about that user's internet activities back to its original source Web page or a designated other. Most commercial sites, not just search sites, now send cookies, and usually their purpose is to obtain more complete profiling information about a potential consumer, hobbies, interests and the like. Search services use the information collected to assist them in judging what advertisements a consumer may be more interested in, and therefore more susceptible to. This information also puts them in a better position to market themselves to potential advertisers.

These last two points in particular work with one of the major strengths that new media in general, and the internet in particular, have to offer to the commercial world: interactivity. This has shown itself in search services particularly in the form of personalization. Most of the major search companies have varying degrees of personalization, where a user can now customize his or her preferred search service by being able to log on to a search interface which the user themselves can construct, focusing on their interests and what they find aesthetically pleasing in design. This creates an interesting paradox in Web space, one in which, simultaneously, the user is increasingly empowered and yet dominated.

On the one hand, the consumer is empowered by being able to customize his or her own space within an interactive environment, but on the other hand, this is done, in most cases, with the knowledge on the part of the user that this also makes them clearer targets to advertisers. Interactivity, especially in the form of personalization, means giving up more information to advertisers so that they can then better understand the user and what motivates him or her. In search engines, controlling your own environment also means your environment having a stronger commercial impact on you, as we can see in this excerpt from the *My Yahoo!* registration form below:

> My Yahoo! delivers customized headline news, sports scores, stock quotes, weather reports, web resources, your own personalized version of the Yahoo! directory, and more ... but first we need a little information.

> Yahoo! makes its money from advertising. The information below allows us to target our advertising and charge advertising rates that are better for Yahoo!. This helps us to provide you with more free features!

The information you provide on this page will only be used by Yahoo! to pick which advertisements to display.

We will not make this information . . . or your portfolio information available to our advertisers or anyone else.

Portals and the emergence of branding

I have always thought that a search engine that works well is like a silent author of a book. When you read a book, the story makes sense and – unless it is self-conscious and meant to be – you don't really notice the writer. . . . It never calls attention to itself, and it never says 'we are a destination unto ourself', we are simply a vehicle for getting from point A to point B.

(Adrian Lurssen, Managing Editorial, Yahoo!)

By the spring of 1998 a new bit of vocabulary had entered the new media world: 'portal' or 'Web portal'. Companies that had formerly been known as search engine companies or Web directories started to call themselves by, and to be referred to as, this new term. The idea of a portal site is that all your Web journeys should start there.

The switch from search engine to portal was based on the adoption of a 'consumer service model' by search services. This was done through the provision of an increasing amount of free services to build upon the search technology already given successfully for free. The first basic steps in this direction were the provision of free e-mail (for example, Yahoo!'s offering in late 1997), chat services and news. As of late, these services have expanded to include online auctions, shopping, free Web pages, and financial information and transactions. Now most portals are able to act as internet service providers, allowing internet access for very modest fees and often for free.

The aim of all this is to increase the amount of 'eyeballs' gazing at portal sites by attracting and concentrating internet traffic more effectively than through search services alone. In effect, portals want to be all things to all people. They are in a position to achieve this through taking advantage of the fact that they are located at the 'choke points' on the information superhighway, whether as search tools, default browser sites (such as Netscape or Microsoft), or ISP networks such as America Online.

This conglomeration of internet traffic through service provision can be achieved in two ways; through providing the service 'in house' and via partnerships as has been Yahoo!'s strategy, or through purchasing companies that are already established, as Lycos has done through an aggressive campaign, purchasing *Tripod* (a leading internet community site), *Guestworld* (providing free homepage facilities), *Wired Digital* (news and searching), *Quote.com* (a major player in online stock quotes) and *WhoWhere*, which provides extended personal and business searching capabilities, free e-mail and homepages. Here Lycos demonstrates explicitly the strategy of 'purchasing eyeballs to add to their collection of eyeballs' (Wong, 1998). Under the circumstances of huge market capitalization in portal shares, these small companies are given literally billions of dollars to invest in new services and buy out existing companies.

It is this process that O'Leary (1998) says is demonstrative of the 'Law of Merging Models', where, over time, online services come to resemble each other.[7]

Although they may begin with different models, they borrow successful and popular features – databases, services, search operators – from each other, until it is hard to tell them apart. With the development of portals this has clearly been the case. Yahoo!, Infoseek, Netscape and Microsoft all started their sites with different intentions, purposes and markets, but during 1997 to 1999, amidst buyouts, service introductions and partnerships, they have all changed to adopt (and build on) the basic set of features offered by America Online, the first portal. All portals now look very similar, and provide the same five basic services for free: information (news), communication (chat and e-mail), shopping (online retail links and auctions), Web pages and online games. In internet circles this phenomenon is starting to become known as the 'AOLing of the Web'. This tendency can be summed up by the following quote from David Filo, co-founder of Yahoo!:

> Whereas we started out as a directory and search [site], purely as this kind of navigation thing, we realized that there are other things we can provide, like news feeds and stock quotes and classifieds and whatever. Early on we looked at AOL and thought that the net, in order to be successful needed something like AOL. . . . AOL is in fact our biggest competitor because once they get the user, they kind of own the user, and they can provide any service they want to the user, and they really control all that the user does.

Throughout all of this, it must be remembered that the essence of the portal lies not in the production of information, but mainly in its distribution. 'Distribution is a powerful force in media-related industries,' Gurley (1998) notes. 'Sometimes it's hard to know which is worth more, the content or the pipes in which it flows.' Portals by their very nature produce very little, but what they do is aggregate content from other sources – newswire services, stock pages, online retailers and the like – and distribute it in a more readily available format. Through this aggregation they add value to their own sites. Somewhat beyond the 'silent author' referred to in the earlier quote, the presence of the portal creates a value that is more than the sum of its parts.

The added value created by the portal is the result of branding, and I would argue that the change that transformed search engines into portals has heralded the age of internet branding. Unlike search engines, whose purpose was to get a customer from point A to point B as quickly as possible, the purpose of the portal its to *attract* the customer and to keep them longer, looking at as many advertisements as possible, and then to move the user on to increasingly anonymous content providers. Where once content was primary and searching anonymous, now the searching process itself has become a prominent feature. This is because, as portals have moved towards commodity status, they have become gradually similar, and the only forum for competition involves 'non-product' elements, of which marketing and branding play a huge part (O'Leary, 1998). This process of course once again echoes Dawson and Foster's central argument, that competition and growth in global capitalism is based on marketing, not on the goods themselves.

Portals, investment capital and convergence

There has been a tendency among internet enthusiasts in academic and popular literature to emphasize the decentralized nature of the internet, by merit of its inherently 'anarchic' structure. For example, Poster (1995: 33) argues that 'The shift to a decentralized network of communications makes senders receivers, producers consumers, rulers ruled, upsetting the logic of understanding of the first media age.' This, it is argued, promotes two things: a disruption of hierarchies, placing 'senders and addressees in symmetrical relations' by disrupting the privileged position of hierarchical structures such as the integrity of the nation-state, or multinational corporations. Second, such a process encourages fragmentation by allowing for the proliferation of 'stories' from those smaller voices previously silenced under monopolies and nation-states. These developments, it is said, suggest a more democratic future where 'choice' replaces monopoly.

However, recent events, and particularly the development of portals show how these claims may be overly optimistic. The history and pattern of portal investment suggests that the World Wide Web is centralizing and adopting an oligopolistic structure which is very much influenced by multinational 'old media' firms, as well as future 'new media' giants.

13.1 A capitalist, yesterday.

The change in terminology from 'search engine' to portal signalled another change, which was to have a notable impact on recent internet history, in the form of the value of stocks. As I pointed out in the last section, newly formed portal companies engaged in a competition to attract eyeballs through developing and acquiring additional consumer services. This new-found aggressiveness was soon looked upon favourably by markets and investors, who saw portals as a chance to provide stability and workable business models for the Web. Indeed, after the use of the word 'portal' became common in early 1998, such companies saw their stocks rise quite dramatically in the first 6 months of that year. In that time Infoseek stock rose 223 per cent, Excite! 164 per cent, AOL 139 per cent, CNET 125 per cent and Yahoo! 120 per cent (Bass, 1998).[8] This trend came to a head and all but erupted in June 1998, when 'old media' giant Disney bought a controlling interest in Infoseek and television conglomerate NBC bought a considerable stake in Snap!, a CNET portal. From then on portal shares soared to heights that not even seasoned stock market veterans could understand or justify, given the fact that all but Yahoo! and AOL were consistently losing money at the time.

So what creates a situation where a company, such as Yahoo!, which currently earns in the area of US$100 million in quarterly revenue and has roughly 1200 employees worldwide, can have a market capitalization of over US$45 billion, more than Xerox or Boeing? What usually contributes to the value of a stock are tangible assets such as book value, current earnings and projected earnings growth. Internet companies confound these measures by having no, or few, tangible assets, few (usually negative) earnings, and a future growth that is unpredictable at best (Fox, 1999). So why are these companies worth so much?

The answer lies in two different forms of speculation. First, these portal companies are being valued on faith. Faith that the internet 'is the future', and that portals, more than any other type of internet company, have the potential to 'monetize eyeball time' – to capture viewers and hold them long enough to look at advertisements. The common conception among internet analysts in 1999 was that within the next year or two there would be a day of reckoning when the Web would eventually support only three or four portals. These three or four survivors will be in the enviable position of being global internet brands that have loyal access to the eyeballs, hobbies and interests of hundreds of millions of viewers worldwide. Investors in portal stocks are in part speculating that one or the other portal will make this cut to the magic three or four.

Second, and perhaps more cynically, investors are speculating that the majority of these portal companies will be bought out (at a favourable share price) by large 'old media' firms who are increasingly interested in 'hedging their bets' with the internet phenomenon. This has already been the case with media giants such as Disney, NBC, CBS, AT&T, and Time Warner – now AOL Time Warner. Furthermore, it only takes rumours that a large company such as Bertelsmann is interested in a portal for share prices to increase dramatically. Of course, these acquisitions are getting more and more difficult, as portal market values have become so high that many of the larger firms are far too pricey for even traditional media giants to buy outright. However, the trend is clear: portals are being pushed into partnerships with large media companies and analysts are expressing concern that those (such as Lycos and Yahoo!) that do not have a big media partner will not be competitive in the long run.

Here we can see the bias in the market. Investors and markets prefer oligopoly, as it is a sign of stability. This internet – particularly portal – stock boom shows how those companies that have the potential to converge the internet are rewarded with high market capitalization, giving them further resources to buy out smaller firms and aggregate World Wide Web traffic. At the same time, investors and markets also like to see traditional oligopolist firms investing, providing even further perceived stability and centralization of a potentially decentralized mode of communication. In short, the markets, through portals, have displaced the idea of the internet as a democratic, decentralized medium and put in motion its domination by a few very large old and new media firms.

USEFUL WEBSITES

Traffick (the guide to portals): **www.traffick.com**
The Web has so many portals that now there's this site *about* portals. 'Our mission,' it says, 'is to ... provide the user with timely, informative and helpful analysis on the world of portals.'

Then there are the big portals themselves, which include the following.

Yahoo!: **www.yahoo.com (and My Yahoo!: http://my.yahoo.com)**
Lycos: **www.lycos.com**
Excite!: **www.excite.com**
AltaVista: **www.altavista.com**
Infoseek (now part of the Infoseek/Disney Go network): **www.infoseek.com**

Handbag: **www.handbag.com**
Handbag is an example of a more targeted portal – this one is aimed at women.

Notes

1. This paper draws on research interviews conducted in California and London with Yahoo!, Yahoo!UK, Infoseek, Netscape and BBC Online in December 1997 and May 1988. This research was funded under the much larger ESRC (#L126251005) 'Biographies of cultural products' project at the Department of Sociology, Lancaster University. I would like to thank the people interviewed, the ESRC and project members Dede Boden, Dan Shapiro, Celia Lury, Jeremy Valentine and Scott Lash for their contributions.

2. A Web Robot is a program that essentially traverses the Web, following links between pages and reading the pages themselves. Each page found is copied to create a database which is then searchable by keyword.

3. In addition, a last category of search engines are what Poulter (1997) has called 'simultaneous unified search services'. These services access other search engines within one search. Such examples here include Metacrawler and Dogpile. Their comparative lack of commercial and user success suggests that there is more to a search service than simply complete searching.

4. Thanks to Adrian Lurssen of Yahoo! for the imagery.

5. From an interview conducted on 2 December 1997.

6. From an interview conducted on 2 December 1997.

7. In organization theory this process is akin to 'institutional isomorphism'.

8. To get a longer-term example, between 1996 and mid-1999, Yahoo!'s stock rose by 3135 per cent.

14

Pornography on the Web

JoAnn di Filippo

In cyberspace, the frontiers of technology and human capacity are continually expanding. One of the multiple possibilities on offer is the rapidly changing business of adult entertainment on the World Wide Web – a growing multi-billion-dollar operation. During the past 5 years, online sex has experienced phenomenal growth in sales and audience participation. It has also been the controversial focus of the feminist porn wars. Nevertheless, the technology shifts rapidly, offering dynamic online dimensions to innovative adult entertainment sites. These sites range from sophisticated multi-million-dollar corporate creations to amateur productions created with in-home disc cameras, scanners and video recorders. This hi-tech mode of adult entertainment has, of course, been seen as disgusting and obscene by some, whilst others argue that it is erotic and sexually liberating. Furthermore, commentators with no extreme views on that scale are nevertheless concerned about the accessibility of such material to children.

What actually constitutes pornographic material? How is it differentiated from erotica? John Preston, a gay pornographer and social critic, asserts that 'there isn't any workable definition of what is pornography vs what is erotica' (1993: 36). What Preston suggests instead is that we consider the production of the content: 'What goes as erotica is usually material that's packaged between hard covers or some other more expensive means of production and sold through more acceptable channels. The same book that would be called erotic if it were presented in a supposedly literary bookstore, bearing the trademark of a major publishing house, would be dismissed as pornography if it were found with inexpensive paper covers in an adult bookstore' (1993: 36). While Preston has offered a definition based on commodity differentia-

14.1 The Web's dodgy district welcomes you.

tion, I would rather refer to Wendy McElroy's value-neutral definition: 'Pornography is the explicit artistic depictions of men and/or women as sexual beings' (1995: 51). But no matter how you label or categorize sexual material, the basic *modus operandi* of adult entertainment websites is to make money by selling sexual images and representations of men and women to internet audiences.

In this chapter, I refer to research conducted from 1996 to the present among adult entertainment site developers, in order to provide a historical account and overview of the industry and its implications for society as a whole. I have no desire to enter the debates surrounding the issues of obscenity and child pornography on the internet, but rather to report on my research findings regarding adult entertainment sites. It should be noted that all names and personal references have been omitted to protect the rights of those individuals involved in my research. We should also be aware that, given legitimate fears about the AIDS epidemic and other sexually transmitted diseases, the demand for adult entertainment sites promises to expand in the twenty-first century. The growing demand and continued success of these operations will undoubtedly call for a new interpretation of society's treatment of sexual attitudes. Overall, it should be remembered that while the adult entertainment industry is reaping substantial financial gains from a sexual commodity, the pendulum continues to swing in both directions: these adult sites can be seen as dangerous and potentially damaging to women and men alike, or as representations of self-expression and sexual fulfilment, offering an unprecedented resource for enhancing one's sex life. While the courts continue to battle these legal and jurisdictional issues, the adult entertainment business continues to explode.

Background: the mechanics of site development

Erotic literature, images and art have always held great appeal for a primarily male readership and gaze. Early in the 1990s, however, a small group of innovative business people – some from highly lucrative careers in the fantasy telephone line industry – realized the tremendous opportunity for adult entertainment on the internet. A new genre emerged, and continues to be one of the fastest-growing businesses on the internet today: the adult entertainment site.

I first became aware of adult entertainment sites in the early 1990s while living in San Francisco, one of the major technology centres for website development and a leader in the sex fantasy telephone business. It is estimated that, in California alone, this industry generates annual revenues exceeding more than US$45 million. Two distinct types of adult entertainment site began to emerge. Those who had the necessary capital developed full-service adult entertainment sites complete with interactive components and highly specialized graphics. Production costs for these labour-intensive sites could run as high as US$250,000 for software, graphic and material content development. The other type of site was developed with a limited budget and often consisted of amateur material ranging from scanned photos and video clips, to 'hot chatting' on bulletin board systems (BBSs). Sites of this nature could be produced for less than US$10,000.

This produced a new wave of income for internet businesses dependent on charging weekly, monthly, annual or lifetime membership fees for entering their respective adult entertainment sites. Simultaneously, online chat offered the opportunity to enter new worlds and engage in sexual escapades completely unlike any you may have encountered in your offline life. There was hope for everyone to live out their sexual fantasies, and the possibility of meeting their ultimate sex partner online. What became alluring and seductive for many was the availability of sex within the relative privacy of cyberspace. Over the past 5 years, the design and implementation of adult sites has improved dramatically, eliminating the technical hitches which would sometimes affect early users.

Then as now, the key to any profitable adult entertainment site is the strength and technical expertise of its systems administrators, site technicians and graphic developers. Equally important is the ability to secure adequate content material – adult photographs and videos – and to develop relations with other adult site service providers, in order to create an alluring adult internet labyrinth. Five years ago, when the industry was still very young, adult sites varied considerably in their quality and professionalism. Anyone clicking into *clublove.com* or *adultplayground.com* could ascertain that these industry leaders had spent considerable sums of money developing graphically intense and technologically advanced sites – the cream of adult entertainment sites. Other hopeful entrepreneurs, many no longer in business today, have been known to project short video clips from adult foreign films over the internet by means of a television/VCR connection to a computer network. The advantage of deriving content from adult foreign films was an attempt to bypass strict US copyright infringement codes and costly royalty fees.

The major obstacles site developers faced in the early years were:

☞ how to prevent unwanted and authorized viewers visiting the site, and staying on the right side of the law
☞ how to secure technicians and graphic artists who could develop an adult site with innovative graphics while keeping download times to a minimum
☞ how to process membership and renewal fees
☞ how to deal with legitimate and fraudulent credit card transactions and refunds
☞ how to secure enough adult content to justify the promotion of a 24-hour internet operation.

Based on my experience with several adult site developers, these obstacles were overcome, but often at considerable expense. One critical issue, then as now, is the issue of censorship. The Communications Decency Act (CDA), passed in the USA in late 1995, sought to tackle free speech and censorship online with such broad strokes that even sites focusing on breast cancer awareness, responsible sex education or renaissance art became potentially illegal. Only two years later, the Supreme Court ruled that the CDA was so overwhelmingly vague that it was clearly in violation of the First Amendment. The legal pendulum had attempted to correct itself but was torn between oppositional viewpoints. The debates about internet censorship continue today, and it remains unclear who has jurisdiction over what in the increasingly globalized market-place. Virtually all adult site developers seek to protect themselves from the long arm of the law by inserting warning labels – often with terms and conditions which the user must click on to accept – on their homepages. Another control implemented to prohibit under-age access was through credit card membership agreements, which stated that the individual was at least 18 years of age and must be the holder of the credit card. While these two moves provided no absolute guarantee of unauthorized use by under-age individuals, they did provide a measure of security.

Attracting potential viewers to your site was another difficulty developers needed to resolve. A scheme devised by adult site developers was to embed 'hidden' sex-related words within the HTML of their homepage, in a bid to get a higher ranking in search engines (which in the early days were oblivious to such tricks – this technique works less well now). This is why internet searches for innocent-sounding things can return listings of adult sites, because a match has been made with a word like 'women', 'fantasy' or 'action'. This again poses problems for those who would like to censor or filter Web content.

One of the advantages of internet business is the flexibility in working relations; adult sites are no exception to that rule. Situating an excellent technician or graphic artist is no obstacle; they can reside anywhere in the world and build your site with you through the use of e-mail, zipped files and telephone communications. While working with one group of San Francisco developers, I discovered they had never personally met their site technicians and graphic artists, who were in Texas; they ultimately developed one of the most technologically advanced sites available during that time period. (The site has since closed.) Critical obstacles they encountered were the processing of credit card transactions and how to deal with charge backs (people calling back to state that they did not authorize the original charge). In late 1996, the choices were somewhat limited: you could opt for processing in-house, or pay a percentage fee to a brokerage house for processing all transactions. Cash flow was generally the deciding factor.

As for material content, the more connections you could establish in the wholesale sex industry, the more you could offer on your site. You could purchase a professional photographer's private collection CD of 100 photos of women and men in various sexual positions, with unlimited use, but restricted only to your site. If you opted for live performances, you could purchase the material from video wholesalers located primarily in New York and Los Angeles, splice the performances to short clip segments which could then be transmitted over the internet via Quicktime, blocky RealVideo, or another form of videostreaming. More aggressive and technically advanced sites could redirect and link you to a site operating out of The Netherlands, where there is less censorship. Specialized graphic design continues to be vital for luring potential viewers to your site. In order to minimize site development costs and maximize site exposure, it was fairly common – and still is today – to develop multiple homepages linked to a universal site structure. In doing so, each URL will read as a specific location; however, as you continue past the homepage you will be directed to the universal interior scheme shared by all URLs registered to that developer, or linked co-operative developers. One very successful group I researched had registered 50 different domains, all sharing the same content inside each site – a technique simply referred to as the 'art of multiple linking'.

There is no doubt that the demand for adult entertainment sites led to a competitive race for technology in the world of e-commerce. Many of the innovative designs and technological advancements created, developed and refined by adult site entrepreneurs can now be found as an everyday part of non-adult sites. Mechanisms for online shopping, credit card processing, banner advertising, chatrooms, videostreaming and general Web marketing were often pioneered by adult site developers.

Adult online entertainment today

Only 5 years later, at the start of a new century, the business of adult entertainment on the internet has become even more sophisticated, and boasts some of the most comprehensive news networks available. However, the mystique of

developing adult entertainment sites is rapidly disappearing. If you are able to learn HTML coding – as renowned porn star Asia Carrera (www.asiacarrera.com) has done – you can take advantage of new emerging full-service site development operations, such as www.ibroadcast.com, that cater to webmasters of adult sites. At this location, webmasters can purchase various types of ready-to-go adult video packages. The leading trade publication for video porn (www.avn.com) provides a multitude of internet services including late-breaking adult video news, upcoming events, site reviews, support for video store retailers, an online zine, adult industry statistics, archives, webmasters' resources and employment opportunities.

As the demand for adult entertainment sites has increased since the mid-1990s, so has the need for business-to-business services. Adult entertainment sites which had developed database tracking software, credit card processing facilities, online shopping cart programs and Web-based shopping malls, as well as original content, could now repackage their assets for sale in the secondary market – to other adult entertainment sites or potential developers of adult sites. Simultaneously, other sex industry corporations who could offer similar material targeted their sales at potential and existing adult sites. Strong competition developed, and some adult site developers opted for buyouts of their adult sites, so that they could develop credit card and client database programs using workers in Thailand and Korea, where labour is less costly. Database development can be more profitable than the adult site business, which requires continuous updating, maintenance and marketing.

Nevertheless, individuals and corporations continue to develop and promote adult entertainment sites, with aspirations to 'get rich quick'. One example from my research provides a vivid illustration of this: the case of a 26-year-old single mother raising a 2-year-old daughter. Faced with the prospect of single parenthood and possessing a less than average knowledge of computers, this mother purchased 20 books from a local bookstore on designing websites and writing HTML. Within a relatively short time, she was operating a mildly successful adult entertainment site. When asked how she could participate in such a business, her response was that it provided for her and her daughter, and allowed the opportunity to provide savings for the future. She further indicated that she tried not to think about she was doing, or when she was doing it, because otherwise she could not have continued. She later indicated that if her young daughter was older, and she was forced to explain the nature of her business, she would not be happy having to talk about this area of her life.

The social and cultural implications of internet pornography

> It is very hard to look at a picture of a woman's body and not see it with the perception that her body is being exploited.
>
> Andrea Dworkin (1981)

> Pornography is part of a healthy free flow of information about sex. This is information our society badly needs. It is a freedom women need. A woman's body, a woman's right.
>
> Wendy McElroy (1995)

Strong arguments are made both for and against pornography and its appearance in adult entertainment sites. Prevailing opinions include those of feminists such as Andrea Dworkin (1981, 1988 and 1997), Catharine MacKinnon (1987, 1993 and 1997), Diana Russell (1993), and Sheila Jeffreys (1990 and 1993), who stress the sexual danger and negative effects of pornography made for men; feminists like Susie Bright (1992), and Pat Califia (1994), who emphasize the need for freedom of speech so that women's sexual desire may be expressed; and still others like Anne Semans and Cathy Winks (1999), who consider the Web to be an 'amazing sex toy' for people to become sexually informed and satisfied individuals. Rather than align myself with either the pro-pornography feminists or the anti-pornography feminists, I intend to examine this alleged division between the two positions and the effects they place on contemporary society.

Catherine MacKinnon, in particular, in her statements regarding the anti-pornography civil rights ordinances of 1999, and in her argument that 'pornography, in the feminist view, is a form of forced sex' (1987: 148), obscures the division between the representation of the sexual image and the sexual act. For MacKinnnon, whose arguments have been supported by pro-censorship conservative legislators, depictions of sex have become synonymous with actual sex. Recent statements made by MacKinnon and Dworkin throughout the course of the pornography civil rights hearings, have firmly supported anti-pornography ordinances on the grounds that it gives 'pornography's victims back some measure of the dignity and hope that the pornography, with its pervasive social and legal support, takes away' (1999: 5).

The anti-pornography campaigners, with conservative legislative support, have been reasonably successful in exercising their objections. Through their persuasive efforts, the Senate in September 1989 passed a bill forbidding the National Endowment for the Arts to fund artistic projects that depict 'obscenity'. This restriction is grounded primarily on the development of American obscenity law and the 'prurient interest' clause which deems images to be obscene either because they cause real-life effects or because they depict sexual acts that are illegal under other sections of the criminal code (www.moralityinmedia.org). Dworkin and MacKinnon's claims are based on the premise that sexuality is the basis for the constitution of power relations in our society. In relying on the assumption that 'the social relation between the sexes is organized so that men may dominate and women must submit', MacKinnon concludes that this 'relation is sexual – in fact, is sex' (1987: 3).

Others simply do not agree, and suggest that in constructing a definition of sexuality in terms of oppression, this view fosters what Judith Butler argues is an unfounded association of 'masculinity with agency and aggression, and femininity with passivity and injury' (1990b: 113). Further, theorists such as

Alice Echols (1983), Marianne Valverde (1989), and Lynne Segal (1993) – as well as Kempadoo's interviews with exotic dancers in *Global Sex Workers* (1998) – suggest that we provide no alternative for women to construct their sexual desires, when the argument is grounded in the assumption that female sexuality is uniformly powerless and constructed within the confines of a patriarchal system. Semans and Winks' *The Woman's Guide to Sex on the Web* (1999) adds to the argument by asserting that there is a critical element missing in previous debates: the fact that 'the Web is actually an unprecedented resource for enhancing women's sex lives' (xi). Nowhere else can women of all ages, backgrounds, cultures and social groups, gather to 'create and explore sexually explicit materials that express their authentic desires . . . and [find a] sense of community that is changing their lives' (xii).

Conclusion

We are now faced with a new question: In light of the global reach of the internet, and given the fact that within this economy are social and cultural constructions of distinction, similarity and difference, how can people's rights to freedom and protection be upheld and preserved within the letter of the law and the moral conscience of humanity? Can this end-result be achieved, or will we continue to see these same debates, relocated and reargued within the realm of each future technological advancement? To reduce the power dimensions within adult entertainment and pornography to one dichotomy – the oppressor and the oppressed – is to deny any influence of individual consent, for whatever reason. In the end, perhaps there is no one solution, but rather a necessity for consciousness-raising within this controversial state of affairs.

USEFUL WEBSITES

Morality in Media: **www.moralityinmedia.org**
A national, not-for-profit, inter-faith organization established in 1962 to combat obscenity and uphold decency standards in the media. Maintains the National Obscenity Law Center and conducts public information programmes to educate and involve concerned citizens.

The National Obscenity Law Center:
www.moralityinmedia.org/nolc
Privately funded organization that acts as a national clearing house in obscenity law. A case bank index is maintained and the Center has copies of all reported obscenity cases since 1800. Assists prosecutors in enforcing obscenity laws and provides publications regarding current obscenity laws.

Anne and Cathy: The Women's Guide to Sex on the Web:
www.anneandcathy.com
A site dedicated to get the word out that SEX is fun. It's even more fun when you can learn about it easily, talk about it comfortably, think about it freely and actually have it without looking over your shoulder wondering: 'Am I normal?' A guide to the wide world of sex information and entertain-

ment; dispenses advice, sex trivia and reviews of the best sex-related sites on the Web.

Adult Video News: www.avn.com
Network featuring adult industry news, legal resources and employment opportunities.

Sex Laws: www.geocities.com/CapitolHill/2269
Collection of links to assorted state, federal and international penal codes related to sex crimes.

Web by Women for Women: www.io.com/~wwwomen
Site compiled by a group of women outraged by the fact that topics such as breast cancer, abortion and contraception were temporarily declared 'indecent' after the CDA was passed. Site includes articles and essays regarding women's health and sexual well-being.

Sexual Assault Information Page:
www.cs.utk.edu/~bartley/saInfoPage.html
Links to information concerning rape, child sexual abuse and assault, incest, ritual abuse, sexual assault and sexual harassment provided on this non-profit site.

Sex Homepage: www.sexhomepage.com
A resource for the study and understanding of human sexuality.

Online Harassment Resources:
www.io.com/-barton/harassment.html
General safety tips and anti-harassment resources for women online.)

15

Fascination: the Modern Allure of the Internet

Christopher R. Smit

Editor's note

This chapter may be more complex than some of the others, but I was interested to introduce new areas of Web theory. Here, Christopher Smit begins to develop a theory regarding the 'draw' of the internet, based in the idea of 'fascination'. The approach can, I hope, say something about Web surfing in general, and not just about those interested in pornographic, voyeuristic or 'freak show' sites.

The road from early nineteenth-century American freak shows to contemporary internet browsing is not a long one. Both activities depend(ed) on the consumer's fascination with difference, or the Other, and both were driven by commercial gain and commodified allurement. The rise of freak shows between 1840 and 1940 points to an era of unprecedented fascination with human oddity in the American public sphere. Stifled by guilt and the dawn of the deliberate concern for political correctness, the American public has stopped viewing freaks in sideshow venues and has instead moved them to film screens, televisions and, most recently, into homes via personal computer monitors. Thanks to the internet and the World Wide Web, voyeurs of all types can be fascinated 24 hours a day by practically anything they can imagine. The only difference between the participants of cyber-freak shows and the sideshows of tents and bearded ladies is that ticket buyers no longer wait in lines with other spectators: fascination has been personalized, and multitudes of freaks have been made immediately accessible. The world of fascination has been computerized.

What do we mean by fascination? Such a definition is necessary, for the term often carries with it a sense of shame. Might there be other possible implications for cultural fascination, other than perversion or deviance? To place the term 'fascination' in a negative and narrow slot is to deny that other outcomes exist for those who are fascinated. Fascination, put plainly, is a moment of enchantment, an allure, an irresistible appeal. There are reasons to be cautious when fascination enters the arena of cultural activity, due to its common association

15.1 Gateway to an internet freak show.

with objectification, yet I would like to suggest that it is not imperative to attribute negative connotations to the act of being fascinated.

It is important that the historical precedent of contemporary electronic fascination be established. Recent scholarship on the relationship between mainstream culture and the Other (i.e. those different from the cultural norm), along with the now-canonical texts regarding the freak have, however, sidestepped the element of *fascination*; while these authors use the term, they have failed to conceptualize its significance within the play between spectator and spectacle. The absence of an articulation of fascination within the newly developed freakology brings us to the question in hand: What are the current manifestations of cultural fascination seen in today's electronic and visual media? Furthermore, how do these manifestations resemble the historical models of fascination seen in the American freak show? Finally, what are the alternative, non-negative outcomes of fascination? To answer such questions would be to understand fascination not only as a contingent apparatus of the spectacular, but as a human response to difference; in short, such answers would urge us to understand fascination as a multi-faceted catalyst for human behaviour.

Fascination and technology: the force and challenge of contemporary media

In the nineteenth century, America was hit with 'cartomania', a compulsion to collect photographs. When scenic landscapes and family portraits grew dull to the privileged collector, an interest in the photography of freaks and circus performers took hold, and effectively initiated the first real surge in American commercialized fascination with the Other. Such pictures accompanied the exhibition of particular freaks, and proved to be the best source of capital for performers and proprietors alike. However, it was not until the freak show, which previously had travelled alone, was added to the circus by Barnum and Bailey in 1903, that the financial gains of freaks and their managers truly began. Among their 47 sideshow attractions, Barnum and Bailey hired Eli Bowen ('The Legless Wonder'), the Hovarth midgets and Henry Johnson ('What Is It?'), all of whom sold countless pictures from the turn of the century until the 1940s (Bogdan, 1990).

The role of the freak show in understanding contemporary models of fascination points to a vitally important classification that must be addressed further. Fascination, when harnessed through modes of production and consumption, converts the spectacle into a realm of cultural performance wherein the spectacle (i.e. freak) can become art. Two points of the freak show formula demand this identification. First, while on stage, the freak often amazed audiences by performing daily tasks using his or her unique physical abilities. Such displays moved the freak from mere object to performer. Second, and most important, the photographs of the freak performers, which were sold by the freaks as extensions of their performances, must be considered as artistic representations, strategically constructed to entertain the spectator after the experience of the freak show event.

Understanding the freak as performance and product, via photography, allows an understanding of the role played by fascination in contemporary media. As Walter Benjamin (1968: 218) points out, when the methods of mechanical reproduction of images are mastered by the modern culture, the 'politics of art' are reshaped. Contemporary manifestations of that reshaping affect three major elements of cultural fascination: the availability of images, the responsibility in production, and the ethical and moral decisions of the spectator. By looking at each of these notions of cultural activity vis-à-vis fascination, the various outcomes of fascination moments can be further identified.

First, one must consider the notion of availability with regard to contemporary fascination. Electronic media (via the internet and the World Wide Web) have made multiple images much more accessible to the viewer; digital photography, video, digital sound and webcams all provide images and sounds of the Other. In this context, the Other stands for any human site of viewer fascination: pornographic performers, popular music stars (such as Marilyn Manson), and internet fetish photography, are all to be considered the Other in contemporary popular culture. Such availability of images of the Other has drastically changed the nature of art, wherein the technology 'enables the original to meet the beholder half way, be it in the form of a photograph or a phonograph record' (Benjamin 1968: 220). By pointing this out, Benjamin is commenting on issues of authenticity and artificiality in art. He is addressing the manner in which technology manipulates the space between the art object and the audience. When applied to the idea of the freak as art, this conception explains the transfer of the Other from its original location to a middle ground shared by the viewer.

Second, in light of the distance between the original art object and the viewer, one must further consider the issues of production responsibility. Inside the 'middle ground' (i.e. the computer monitor), where the art object and audience meet, 'what is really jeopardized . . . is the authority of the object' (Benjamin 1968: 221). When the authority of an art object is violated in this way, its producer is subtracted from the transaction taking place between the spectacle and spectator. While accessing video links and online photography, the viewer is rarely aware of the creator of the images; what matters is the spectacular dynamic of the accessed image. This event releases the producer of internet pornography, shock photography and sensational advertising techniques from responsibility in production and distribution. Left in the abyss of ambiguous production, these creators are free to manipulate the Other for the fascinated viewer in a variety of ways.

Third, this variety of manipulations has a direct effect on the manner in which the viewer makes his or her ethical and moral decisions regarding fascination consumption. Because of technology's expansion of the social arenas of fascination, what Marc Augé (1998) has called the 'non-places of supermodernity', spectators can now access and view the Other in a much more privatized fashion. One need only log on to any of the countless search engines online to understand the outlet for computerized fascination. One could argue that such accessibility to images in a private setting isolates today's viewer from reality. Rather than attending a public display where other spectators would play a physical, communal part in the fascination event, the online viewer enjoys a guiltless gaze on the Other. The decision to gaze is thus freed from social pressures, be they positive or negative.

Mass production of electronic images, through the advent of the World Wide Web, have altered contemporary moments of fascination and hold true to Benjamin's assertion that, 'During long periods of history, the mode of human sense perception changes with humanity's entire mode of existence' (1968: 222). Caught up in the fast pace of modernity, e-mail and 'surfing the Web' have become daily rituals of time management. Such dependence urges the viewer to fascinate, or fetishize, his or her desires online.

Consider the recent website *Voyeur Dorm*, which has gained a great deal of media attention. *Voyeur Dorm* advertises itself as the hottest thing on the internet, allowing complete and unadulterated, unedited and uncensored video feeds of eight, sexy college co-eds, captured by 40 'secret' cameras for the home viewer's pleasure. Thinking about the three elements of mass production discussed above, *Voyeur Dorm* confirms for us the notions of availability, responsibility and moral decisions. Live video links of eight women are constantly *available* for the consumer willing to pay US$34 a month. Because these women, the Other, are available as images, they are seen as objects, thus freeing the producers of *Voyeur*

15.2 Voyeur sites draw audiences with the promise of live or hidden webcams.

Dorm from any *responsibility* to the women being portrayed. And finally, the *decisions* of the internet browser, to meet the images of these women in the 'middle ground' of their computer screen, is thus freed from moral conscience, due to the fact that he or she is alone, without a physical community to guide his or her actions.

Contemporary media images of the Other answer 'the desire of contemporary masses to bring things closer' (Benjamin 1968: 223). Because of this lack of distance between the object and the viewer, spectator satisfaction is only a mouse click away. The computer keyboard becomes the key that unlocks the autonomy and isolation of electronic interaction. That fascination is at the heart of this technological mass production of images is obvious, yet the definition of the term needs further consideration beyond the cultural isolation and ambiguity attributed to it above. Fascination needs to be separated from such negative connotations, in order for the concept to usher in new ways of reading these planes of interaction. What follows are two possible alternatives to understanding the contemporary sites of fascination.

Towards an open definition of fascination

We have seen that fascination is a term worthy of more attention. As suggested, the mode in which the term is used in many studies of cultural objectification carries with it a sense of separation, shame and isolation. When the other qualities of fascination, which I will discuss here, are ignored, there is a weighted analysis of the term's cultural effect. The alternative variations that follow aim to lighten such preconceptions. Seeing fascination as a means to identity and as a reflection and identification of the players involved (i.e. spectacle and spectator) will expand our use of the term, and endow fascination with a new vitality within the study of cultural practice. The first section presents an alternative understanding to the American freak show, which uses the concept of fascination as a creator of opportunity and freak identity. We return to the freak show in order to justify the historical need for a re-evaluation of cultural fascination, which precedes our main focus in electronic fascination.

While it is debatable whether or not the financial gains of marketing oneself as a 'freak' outweighed the objectification of these performers, such discussion is not important here. What is relevant, however, is the way in which fascination in the American freak show created an environment for a social, economic and personal definition of the Other. First, by establishing the freak as a purchased artefact, as in the pictures discussed above, the Other became part of the social action of production and consumption. In this economic sense, American freaks held a place within the cultural activities of their surroundings.

Second, because of this cultural activity, freaks were able to be dependent on their own economic fortitude. This was exemplified in the careers of Charles Sherwood Stratton, also known as General Tom Thumb, and his wife Lavinia Warren. Stratton 'sold thousands of . . . pictures, and because the markup was good, profits were high' (Bogdan, 1990: 14). Added to Stratton's profit was his wife's enormous capability to sell pictures of her own deformed body. 'She ordered fifty thousand pictures of herself at a time and these were widely available from photography vendors' (Bogdan, 1990: 15). The couple also found a great deal of success in the circus and private exhibition market, often teaming up with the Ringling Brothers' organization as well as Barnum and Bailey. Such a livelihood, made possible through the outcome of fascination, points to the claiming of identity by the Other.

Finally, the culmination of economic and social benefits led to the creation of what could be called a freak-identity. Able to function within a society by means of self-objectification, the Other was granted a self-consciousness, albeit a twisted one. Using the spectators' fascination to define an independent identity gave the freak show performer a position of cultural power. This is not to say that the status of the freak in America was a completely positive label. It is important to see the identification of a commodified, empowering 'identity' for freaks as a departure from the predominantly negative critiques of the American freak show. Such critiques often cite the phenomenon of isolation and objectification when discussing the freak's social existence. However, by using the term 'fascination' in a more neutral manner, it is possible to see other outcomes of the freak show. This conclusion points to a much-needed alteration and redefinition of the term 'fascination', and its use in analysing cultural interaction.

As we now turn to the modes of contemporary fascination seen in electronic media and in the results of what Benjamin understands as a drastic change in the politics of art, it is important that the same variations be applied. The role of the spectator within the moment of fascination, however, becomes more important as we make the shift from freak shows under tents to those under the 'big top' of the World Wide Web. Rosemarie Garland Thomson has briefly pointed out that, 'the extraordinary body symbolized a potential for individual freedom denied by cultural pressures toward standardization' (1997: 68). While attending the freak show, the spectator may have felt a connection to, or at least an understanding of, the freak performer as an example of American freedom. Such a freedom is alluded to in my distinctions regarding the freak-identity; under the blanket of democratic society, the freak may have symbolized an option, among many, for the pursuit of a productive and self-created lifestyle.

Taking these suggestions further, Garland Thomson also admits that 'some onlookers probably used the shows to explore the limits of human variation' (1996: 43). While she eventually dismisses the positive possibilities of this speculation in her final analysis, it is relevant here to extend them into the realm of contemporary fascination. In fact, I further propose that the suggestion that fascination is an avenue for exploring difference in order to understand one's own eccentricities and human needs, may offer a new understanding of online spectacle. First, it has already been established that the spectators of online fascination are somewhat freed from the producer of the objects they are viewing. Within that freedom, their gaze is denied the added pressure of personal contact with the images they are encountering. What follows, then, is a moment of exploration that affects both the spectacle and the spectator. The ramifications of such a moment for the Other have already been explored. The spectator, following his or her curiosity, delves into his or her own uniqueness – a trait that is subconsciously examined through fascination.

The use of the World Wide Web to access celebrity Web pages offers a good example of fascination working for the spectator as much as for the spectacle. Obviously, the outcome of capturing a viewer's attention with a particular star image, like Marilyn Manson, is commercially beneficial for Manson due to the publicity involved. However, this resulting publicity, when viewed through the model of fascination suggested above, may also hold positive effects for the viewer. When the spectator finds a commonality with the Other, and this 'star' quality is added, the justification of 'difference' is established at a completely new level; the viewer, attributing a celebrity's success – both personal and financial – to that performer's oddity, begins to define his or her own peculiarity as a potential for self-betterment.

A brief discussion of Marilyn Manson leads to a final alternative option for contemporary, electronic fascination. Manson, whose album *Antichrist Superstar* topped the charts in 1997, has been the target of criticism by several parent organizations and religious groups over the past 3 years. In addition to playing with norms of identity, spirituality and Christianity, as did Iggy Pop, Alice Cooper, David Bowie and Kiss before him, Manson utilizes the grotesque, transgendered aggression of 'shock rock' to lure audiences, listeners and Web surfers. It is fair to say that Manson himself is as fascinated with the religious groups that are against him as much as they are no doubt fascinated by him. This mode of shared fascination is the dominant model of contemporary cultural activity; when one is fascinated by the Other, they use that moment as a reflection of themselves, in which they can define who they are and who they are not. Thus, fascination moments on the internet can provide the catalyst for self-definition. Moreover, this definition of the spectator is consciously done with the presence of another human being, rather than an objectified image of the Other; the relationship to the Other is thus altered to offer shared humanity as a moment of connection rather than difference.

Moments of fascination have allowed people an avenue into understanding the political, ethical and cultural dynamics of the articulation of racial, sexual and physical difference. However, fascination often carries with it a dark tone, an element of shame, something that historical memory wishes to forget. While this may be partially true, such a one-sided use and critique of fascination ignores the cultural clues the term holds. Understood through an articulation of electronic media, the internet and the World Wide Web, fascination points towards a multitude of cultural responses. Pushed further, contemporary fascination may enable us to transcend ideas of the relationship between spectacle and spectator, and usher us into a new moment of social realization based in an equality of curiosity and admiration of human difference.

RELEVANT WEBSITES

The Side Show: **www.nurple.com/sideshow**
The online equivalent to Barnum's sideshow and freak show attractions.

Voyeur sites: **www.voyeurdorm.com; www.dudedorm.com; www.1hiddenvoyeurcamera.com**
Examples of the use of online voyeurism to fascinate the internet browser. (Web directories list hundreds more voyeur sites.)

Marilyn Manson: **www.marilynmanson.com**
Website of the gothic, gender-bending rock star feared by Middle America.

16

The BBC goes Online: Public Service Broadcasting in the New Media Age

Richard Naylor, Stephen Driver and James Cornford

The emergence of the World Wide Web is widely seen as having dramatic implications for media industries and media companies as we have come to know them in the twentieth century. For some writers – those who concentrate on the sheer technical capabilities of the technology – it is an avalanche that will sweep away the existing media landscape, radically undermining the power of existing media gatekeepers to create a new, decentralized and more democratic media environment. The most celebrated exponent of this view is Nicolas Negroponte, co-founder of MIT's MediaLab. For Negroponte, the advent of digital media will have dramatic consequences for media structures: 'if,' he asks, 'moving these bits [of information] around is so effortless, what advantage would the large media companies have over you and me?' (Negroponte, 1995: 19). 'Wholly new content will emerge from being digital, as will new players, new economic models and a likely cottage industry of information and entertainment providers' (1995: 18). The future is one in which the mass media that we have known are replaced with a myriad of small, specialist information and entertainment providers as 'the monolithic empires of mass media are dissolving into an array of cottage industries' (1995: 57).

From another perspective – one that concentrates on the social, economic and political contexts within which the Web is developing, and which are shaping that development – it is a very different story. For these authors, the development of the Web is increasingly driven and controlled by the very media empires that Negroponte imagines to be disappearing. One look at the highest-ranking North American 'digital media properties' (www.mediametrix.com) for instance, confirms the presence of major media corporations such as News Corporation, Time Warner and MSNBC (a joint venture between General Electric's NBC and Microsoft) on the Web. What the Web does, these authors argue, is provide these key players with new tools with which to pursue strategies of control and indeed expansion. From this perspective, the advent of the Web is seen not so much as a break with traditional media structures, but rather as 'the refinement, extension and embellishment of traditional media' (Cornford and Robins, 1999: 124; see also McChesney et al., 1998).

In this chapter, we want to explore some of the implications the emergence of the Web has had for one 'media empire', the British Broadcasting Corporation (BBC). The BBC is, however, a quite singular media empire. Unlike the entertainment and computing conglomerates mentioned above, the BBC is predominantly publicly funded, and charged with providing a public service. Indeed, it is arguably the largest and most successful example of public service broadcasting in the world, with income of £2.8 billion in 1999 and a payroll that currently numbers the equivalent of over 23,100 full-time employees.

How, then, has this public service monolith adapted to the more commercially and technologically fluid online environment? In audience terms, the Corporation has been very successful: the BBC is now a key player in new media on a UK, European and even global scale, and new media figures centrally in the Corporation's strategies for the future. Both of the Corporation's principal Web activities, those publicly financed and brought together under the BBC Online brand at www.bbc.co.uk, and the commercial joint venture, *beeb.com*, are highly popular websites. For example, according to the UK Audit Bureau of Circulation (www.abc.org.uk/electronic), in March 1999, BBC Online sites served up a total of 80 million Web pages in response to requests from 3 million users while the commercial *beeb.com*, served up 8.7 million pages to 400,000 users. The only other UK-audited site close to matching this performance is Yahoo! with 67 million pages served up in April 1999.

Yet it could be easy to view the BBC's Web activities as relatively peripheral to its 'core business' – when considering the Corporation as a whole. The BBC's 1998/1999 Annual Report suggests that the corporation spent just £23 million of its £2,155 million licence fee income on BBC Online. Only a small part of the £254.6-million turnover derived from 'publishing and new media' by the Corporation's commercial arm, BBC Worldwide, represents the activities of *beeb.com*. These, however, are only directly attributable costs and we would argue that the impact of the Web on the BBC's organization, working practices, culture and corporate strategy goes far deeper than these, or other figures alone, can suggest. This chapter will examine in detail how the Corporation has attained a leading status in the development of the Web in the UK and beyond, what it means for the way in which the BBC is organized, and how it impacts on the BBC's external relations with government and other players in the media and communications industries.

The chapter is in three sections. Our starting point is the political economy of public service broadcasting as it is instituted in the BBC. The first section briefly outlines the way in which the BBC has developed as an institution and the key structures, compromises and mechanisms by which that has occurred. The second section, based on interviews with a number of BBC managers, charts the development of the BBC's online initiatives and some of the ways in which the emergence of new media technologies are challenging the institution of the BBC. A final section considers the ways in which the Corporation is seeking to deal with the stresses and strains imposed by new media while upholding the concept of public service in the digital age.

The institution of the BBC

The BBC is a very particular institution whose aims are often summarized as to 'educate, inform and entertain', a phrase coined by John Reith, the first Director General of the Corporation. Traditionally, the privileged position of the BBC was shored up by the notion of spectrum scarcity – the limited amount of the technically usable radio spectrum made available by the government. Broadcast-

Table 16.1 The funding/geography matrix for the BBC (with turnover/budget for 1998/99 in brackets)

		Domestic	*International*
Commercial		Worldwide (e.g., magazines, BBC World TV Channel, *beeb.com*, etc.) (turnover = £446m including joint ventures, employees = 1,583)	
Non-commercial	Licence fee	BBC Home Services and Resources (e.g., BBC1 and 2 TV, Radios 1–5 and local radio) (income £2,155m, employees = 20,052)	
	Grant-in-aid		World Service (£161.5m, employees = 1,484)

Source: BBC Report and Accounts 1998/99

ing was, therefore, believed to be naturally monopolistic or oligopolistic and thus unsuitable for competitive market regulation, paving the way for public provision (the BBC), and highly regulated commercial services (independent television and local radio). (For informed accounts of the Corporation's development see Briggs, 1979 and 1985; and Scannel and Cardiff, 1982.)

However, with the advent of new delivery platforms (cable, satellite) and the increasingly efficient usage of the radio spectrum, the notion of spectrum scarcity has waned. In this context, new arguments have had to be put forward to maintain the BBC's privileged status. Perhaps the most persuasive has been the view that a licence-fee funded BBC, free of the pressures operating on commercial broadcasters, can help to set high standards, both technically and in terms of programme content and programme diversity. Analysts have described this as a process whereby the BBC triggers a 'virtuous circle' in which commercial broadcasters follow the Corporation's lead by producing distinctive programming of their own (see, e.g., McKinsey *et al.*, 1999). A similarly positive view of the existence of the BBC in its present form has been expressed specifically in relation to the emerging multimedia markets (Graham and Davies, 1997). The Corporation's present activities are summarized in Table 16.1.

What it is important to understand is that the BBC rests on a set of more or less stable compromises and a set of internal and external boundaries designed to maintain those compromises. The principal boundaries are as follows.

☞ An external division between the Corporation, as the sole beneficiary of the licence fee (and of grant-in-aid for the BBC's World Service radio broadcasts), and commercially funded broadcasters, who are obliged to finance their provision through advertising, sponsorship or subscription.

☞ An internal division between the licence fee-funded activities of the Corporation and its more commercial activities (symbolized by what is known as the 'Chinese wall' between the BBC's commercial arm, BBC Worldwide, and the rest of the Corporation).

☞ A related territorial division between the domestic focus of the bulk of the Corporation's licence fee-funded activity (which is paid for by its UK audiences) and its global ambitions (the increasingly overseas-oriented BBC Worldwide, funded commercially).

In addition, the 1990s has seen the BBC undergo a modernization programme – in response to government prompting and regulatory dictate – that has become known as the 'Birtian Revolution', so named after its instigator, Sir John Birt, the BBC's Director General from 1992 to January 2000. The thrust of this continuing restructuring is to make the corporation more economically efficient. Two of the most important transformations have been the imposition of a statutory minimum quota of non-news and current affairs programming that must be outsourced to independent companies, and the establishment of an 'internal market' within the BBC itself. Programme commissioning has been separated from programme production, with the two now consolidated into BBC Broadcast and BBC Production respectively.

Early moves online

The BBC's first incursions into the online world can be traced back to 1994 when it established a public Web server, and a number of more or less *ad hoc* websites and online projects were launched. Most of these early sites were programme or region specific and produced either by hobbyist producers, or created more formally in conjunction with the BBC's Multimedia Centre. The Multimedia Centre was a short-lived initiative, designed as a centre of excellence to investigate the possibilities of multimedia technologies. While some online work did take place, the Centre was still, if anything, biased towards CD-Roms, although a number of its staff did subsequently move into BBC Online.

In 1995, BBC Education (which is a substantial sub-department of Broadcast) launched the BBC Networking Club, one of the first internet service providers (ISPs) for consumers in the UK. Within BBC Education, the digital revolution in interactive media had provoked much interest. It was seen as a way of enhancing its educational brief, thus reinforcing the BBC's public service role. The idea behind the Networking Club was to 'lead people by the hand' to the (then) alien and intimidating internet, by way of the 'warm, fuzzy BBC brand', as one BBC Online manager recounted. Although not strictly within the bounds of the BBC's Royal Charter, the Networking Club was undertaken on a cost-recovery basis as a project that would help to kick-start the uptake of the internet in the UK. A precedent had been set in the previous decade, when the BBC had successfully achieved a similar goal with the launch of the BBC's own-brand 'Micro' for the home computer market. Once the Networking Club broke even during 1996, the service was terminated.

So, by the mid-1990s, the BBC had already developed a number of varied online initiatives. However, this activity had taken place within what seemed to be an internal policy vacuum, with no established vision from top-level BBC management (the Corporate Strategy department). The Corporation seemed more focused on the upcoming developments within its established media – specifically high-definition television and digital services – than the opportunities provided by the World Wide Web. In part, the lack of strategy was due to the understandable inability of the BBC's long-term planning and investment horizons to respond quickly to the very rapid expansion of the Web. But, additionally, one BBC executive suggested that there was an initial reluctance to claim the Web as part of the corporation's public service mission, as it was privately feared that the terms of the upcoming renewal of the BBC's Royal Charter in 1996 would prove unfavourable. With uncertainty regarding both the future operational parameters of the BBC, and the nature and level of the corporation's income, top-level management had in fact quietly decided that any new media activities would, ultimately, have to be commercially funded.

Despite appearances to the contrary, then, the BBC signposted its original online intentions as early as 1994 when BBC Worldwide assembled a team to write a tender for what would become *beeb.com*, a joint Web venture with a commercial partner. The deal would be short term, given that nobody knew where the market or technology was leading, and a short contract would also give the BBC an exit point. The criteria for choosing private-sector partners was 'what they could bring to the table', a phrase that can be translated as a combination of technical expertise and hard cash. The search for partners took two years and encompassed major UK and overseas companies from the telecommunications, online service provision and computer software sectors. A three-year deal was eventually struck with the computer services giant ICL (part of Fujitsu) in early 1996; and *beeb.com* was officially launched later that year.

Beeb.com

The BBC's joint venture with ICL ran for a three-year period that finished at the end of 1999. Under the deal, the BBC holds all the Intellectual Property Rights (IPRs) attached to *beeb.com*. In addition to ICL's strong technical track record, the BBC's partner has funded all of the investment for the joint venture; a figure that has not been made public but has been described by a senior *beeb.com* manager as 'running into the high single millions' per annum.

The website itself is intended as a 'focused webzine' with, at present, 10 entertainment and lifestyle channels that utilize and exploit content and branding from existing BBC TV programmes (e.g., a music channel modelled on the popular music television show *Top of the Pops*), or from existing BBC publications (e.g., a Web version of the radio and television listings guide *Radio Times*). The site is put together by a staff of over 80 full-time employees, making *beeb.com* one of the largest online content production units in the UK. Without income from the licence fee, *beeb.com* is a commercial online business that generates income from three main sources: the sale of advertising on its own site, licensing of *beeb* content to other online publishers (the first deal of this kind was agreed with MSN UK in March 1999) and through transactions – selling BBC videos, books, merchandising and so on.

16.1 Some *beeb.com* pages, heavily shopping-orientated in spring 2000.

At the heart of *beeb.com*'s identity lies the question of content. For ICL not least, *beeb.com* is nothing without BBC-originated content – and the BBC brand. The fact that content from licence fee-funded television and radio programmes, such as a car review from the popular BBC2 television motoring show *Top Gear*, can appear on what is a dedicated commercial website has aroused strong criticism. Other commercial broadcasters and online providers have argued that licence fee money is subsidizing the content of a commercial media enterprise and that this therefore constitutes unfair trading, as witnessed in submissions to the House of Commons Select Committee on Culture, Media and Sport's report on the multimedia revolution (House of Commons Select Committee on Culture, Media and Sport, 1998). The UK's telecommunications regulator Oftel and the Independent Television Network (ITN) argued that cross-subsidy was inevitable as the BBC's commercial activities, like *beeb.com,* exploited the 'brand identity' developed by the publicly funded corporation. ITN also noted the ease with which users of BBC Online, the public service site, could switch to the commercial *beeb.com*.

The BBC has so far avoided censure over *beeb.com*'s use of licence fee-originated content by arguing successfully that the material is used 'for promotional purposes', thereby only accruing what could be described as 'peppercorn rents'. What this means is that rather than *beeb.com* paying BBC Broadcast to use certain programme material – and then in return charging BBC Broadcast a fee that reflects the degree of exposure and promotion that its content will receive on the *beeb* site – both parties agree to undertake the transaction at zero cost, as the two charges would simply cancel each other out. *Beeb.com* has been able to demonstrate the validity of this system to the BBC auditors, as it was a system first established in relation to external content deals with, for example, the actor's union Equity, which agreed to waive fees for actors appearing on *beeb.com* due to the exposure and promotion the online site provided.

BBC Online

The development of the commercial *beeb.com* is indicative of the BBC's new mixed economy in which commercial activities take their place alongside the Corporation's traditional public service fare. The development of a public service site, BBC Online, soon after the *beeb.com* launch has not only proved a great success, but it has also become central to the arguments over the future of the BBC and public service broadcasting in the new media age. It is, as John Birt told MPs, the corporation's new 'third medium': the development of which, within the public service remit, is analogous with the corporation's decision as a radio broadcaster in the 1930s to invest in television. The BBC's argument is that only a publicly funded organization could have sanctioned investment in such a marginal medium as television, and that public service programming was essential for driving the uptake of the medium and underpinning the

16.2 BBC Online offers sites on news, soaps, music, education and almost everything else, within family-friendly limits.

emergence of a commercial market. The BBC believes that the Web represents a similar scenario and the Corporation's Chairman, Sir Christopher Bland, has added that the new site ought to be regarded as 'an integral part of our public service offering' and should be funded accordingly from the licence fee (in evidence to Select Committee on Culture, Media and Sport, 20 October 1998).

The BBC's decision to commit, as a senior Online manager put it, 'a more strategic investment of public service assets online', occurred in early 1997. By this time, the Web had expanded and developed beyond a transitory niche medium and, co-incidentally or not, the BBC's Royal Charter had just been renewed. The corporation thus applied to the government for approval to establish BBC Online and began producing in-house Online content from December of the same year. Full official government approval for BBC Online was only granted in November 1998.

Unlike *beeb.com*, Online is not intended primarily as a centre of excellence in online production. Rather, it exists as a sub-department within Broadcast to commission, co-ordinate and provide a 'strategic steer' for the online activities of the BBC's non-commercial departments (in this instance, predominantly News and Current Affairs, Broadcast, and the World Service). In addition to standardizing interface design and improving navigational structures, BBC Online has been responsible for the development of a common content production system that has harmonized the technical environment across all BBC departments, including *beeb.com*. Previously, all departments with Web ambitions had developed their own content production systems independently from, and in competition with, one another. BBC Online has thus acted to reduce duplication between sites and departments, and to bring down production costs.

In providing a unified interface, the BBC now claims that Online gives access to 'over 200 BBC sites', each of which 'measure up to the same editorial standards that apply to all BBC programmes and services' (BBC Annual Report and Accounts, 1998/99). Since its launch, BBC Online has quickly become the most visited content site in Europe. The runaway success to date has been News Online, whose site regularly accounts for over 50 per cent of BBC's Online's total page impressions. News Online is put together by a separate team of around 100 staff working alongside their radio and television colleagues in London. The UK-based team draws on the BBC's comprehensive worldwide network of journalists and reporters to produce a website that, the Corporation claims, hosts around 300 different stories each day. Achieving such a high level of success has, of course, incurred considerable expenditure – £18.7 million in the 1997–98 financial year alone to establish BBC Online. The BBC spent a further £23 million to run Online in the financial year 1998–99.

A tale of two sites

The success of Online owes much to the battle it has won with *beeb.com* over BBC-originated branding and content, in addition to the substantial (and free) cross-promotion that BBC Online receives from the Corporation's radio and television output. The contract that ICL signed with the BBC for *beeb.com* has proved to be somewhat open-ended as regards content. One might infer that it was written by a Corporation conscious of allowing room for the possibility of a public service website at a later date. Thus, when the BBC did decide to fully commit itself to the Web, it was still well within the terms of the *beeb* contract to claim News and Current Affairs and Education as central to the BBC's public service role. As such, News and Education became the preserve of BBC Online rather than *beeb.com*. Further, Online has since successfully claimed the large and vague category of the BBC's 'current output' for itself, leaving *beeb.com* to be portrayed in some quarters as Online's 'poor cousin' (*The Economist*, 1999a).

The division of BBC content, then, has been the necessary consequence of having two competing websites within the one Corporation. Confusion and duplication has often been the result, as the two have produced opposing sites for events such as the Edinburgh Festival and the football World Cup, and even for TV shows such as *Dr Who*. Very often, *The Economist* notes, 'the two sides of the Chinese wall go their own way' (1999a).

In tacit recognition that no adequate mechanism has existed for allocating content between the two websites, *beeb.com* has shifted its focus away from content, towards a more transactional model. As well as the joint venture's entry into the UK's free ISP market in September 1999, with a service called 'freebeeb.net', it is now intended that the website will ultimately become an aggregator of online shopping, selling goods associated with BBC brands. A central element of this restructuring task, is the removal of BBC-originated content (*Top of the Pops, Top Gear* etc.) from the *beeb*.site and its transfer to BBC Online's public service sites.

A clearer separation between the Corporation's public service and commercial websites might be expected to have improved the BBC's relationships with its private-sector rivals. But early indications suggest that this will not be the case. For instance, an alliance of major Web publishers, the British Internet Publishers Association (BIPA), has already lobbied the Secretary of State for Culture, Media and Sport, Chris Smith, regarding what it sees as the seriously adverse effect that freebeeb will have on the country's commercial ISP market. It would seem, then, that *beeb.com*'s new, more commercially aggressive strategy has brought the BBC into more direct conflict with commercial Web ventures in the UK than ever before.

The challenge of the Web

While the previous sections indicate some of the more visible difficulties that the BBC has experienced in the online world, these are indicative of more underlying challenges that the Web poses to the institutional arrangements and geography by which the BBC is currently managed, financed and through which it relates to other commercial media companies. First, the Web offers a noticeable challenge to aspects of the BBC's organization and culture – and, indeed, that of the wider media culture – upon which the BBC's commissioning policy rests.

Organization and culture

It is important to stress that both the BBC's internal market, and the commissioning of television and radio production from external companies, crucially depends on both shared knowledge and shared values. The commissioners of programmes need to understand and have knowledge of the production process, not least of its costs and milestones (milestones being the stages that a programme passes through before completion, such as treatment, script, rough cut, fine cut and so on). Commissioners and producers also need to share similar values ('BBC values') on programme content as independent TV producers have to recognize the peculiar characteristics of public service broadcasting and act accordingly; 'they need to know what can and can't be done', as one BBC executive put it. However, with the experience of in-house online production and, more pertinently, a number of early experiments with the outsourcing of entire programme-specific websites, the BBC has discovered that the Web has short-circuited this cosy shared culture.

Most fundamentally, the infancy of the medium coupled with its speed of change means that, as with many commercial online publishers, BBC commissioners are uncertain as to exactly what to expect when commissioning online content: 'it changes everyday' and 'where does it end?' as one Online manager put it, 'and how much does it cost?' Added to the lack of recognizable milestones and a lack of shared understanding as regards accepted market rates, there is also a value divide between the largely BBC-trained commissioners and producers and the new media producers, both external and (on occasions) internal. It seems that, for the present at least, net culture and the responsibilities that come with public service media, make for uneasy bedfellows, as a senior BBC Education manager explains:

> The people doing television have all come into television through particular routes, mostly having been trained at the BBC or another big broadcaster. And they know the rules. . . . However, with online you've got a load of people who are just out of university, who are having a great time and playing around and to them it's just like doing their own site. But it happens to be for the BBC! And keeping a handle on that is quite hard . . .

The combination of uncertain costs, quality and editorial concerns, a lack of trust and the necessity to constantly update and maintain a website, means that neither the BBC's internal market nor the 25 per cent independent quota applies with regard to the Web. Instead, BBC Online and *beeb.com* work on the basis of co-location, with commissioners and producers working directly alongside one another, 'learning together'. Outsourcing, meanwhile, is now strictly limited to piecemeal activities such as a few lines of computer code or certain design elements. The absence of an internal market for Online is somewhat ironic given that the BBC announced the policy ('BBC gears up to deliver digital dividend', press release, 7 June 1996) as a mechanism to help the Corporation 'address the strategic challenges of the digital age'.

The desire for tight editorial control in safeguarding what is perceived as the good name of the BBC has been one of Online's main purposes. Establishing this quality control has involved a degree of centralization with, for instance, the reigning-in of the BBC regions (which were initially free to pursue their Web strategies as they saw fit) as well as individual programme producers. However, this process has been neither easy nor entirely successful. A BBC Education manager indicated that the ease and speed of publishing on the Web, allied with the replacement of the BBC's traditional 'command and control' hierarchy with a modernized, decentralized model of editorial management has made Web content hard to police:

> I often think it's like that Dutch story about the boy with his fingers in the dam; if you've got all sorts of information and just *stuff*, the BBC has its fingers in the dam trying to stop it all leaking out through all these people doing websites! – Because editorial control has been devolved down.

Finance

The entry of the BBC into online publishing and the launch of new digital television and radio services is also pushing the Corporation into uncharted territory in financial terms. First, despite the publicly quoted sums regarding BBC Online, BBC managers concede that there are, and will increasingly be, significant problems in properly identifying and demarcating costs. 'The thing is,' a BBC Education manager ponders, 'once you've started some digital channels then there's a sort of funny overlap between what's interactive TV, what's CD and what's online. . . . And the BBC hasn't really got to grips with this yet in the way that it finances things.' As the Corporation moves further towards an interoperable content environment where all material – text, video, audio, stills and graphics – is held on centralized databases to be used and re-used, for different audiences in varying combinations in accordance with the chosen delivery platform, then the dividing line between the BBC's public service obligations and its commercial activities becomes ever more blurred. The Corporation's 'Chinese wall' and the detailed Commercial Policy guidelines established with the Office of Fair Trading seem to belong to a bygone era, whose 'rules are crumbling', as one BBC interviewee put it.

Finally, the most oft-repeated charge levelled at the BBC's online presence centres on the crumbling of what was once the BBC's central obligation to make its services universally available to everyone in the UK, in return for the government-sanctioned licence fee. Clearly, as the Corporation has expanded its services beyond radio, this is no longer the case. In response, the BBC has qualified the concept of universality with that of 'high reach': basically, that the BBC now provides a bundle of services, of which some will always be universally available and that it will continue to provide something for everyone. From the 'high reach' perspective, then, the BBC has a duty to provide Online, thus ensuring that 'the users of the internet have a public service choice in the digital age' (BBC Annual Report and Accounts, 1998/99).

However, the Corporation's rhetoric of 'high reach', and the parallel that it draws with television, does not answer the Corporation's critics. Fundamental differences, it is argued, exist between the BBC's pioneering investment in television and its pioneering investment in the Web. First, the early BBC television service was genuinely developed in a commercial vacuum, while this is not (and has never been) the case with the Web. Perhaps more importantly – certainly for the BBC's immediate self-interest – the difference also lies in the global reach and accessibility of the Web, which dramatically changes the geography of the BBC's audience. The bind that the Corporation now finds itself in is that, unlike BBC television, people from across the globe can legally consume the BBC's high-quality websites at no additional cost – websites that have been financed (effectively) from UK tax receipts. While it should be noted that the majority of visitors to all BBC websites are still UK-based, a very significant minority are not, particularly for the News Online site where around a third of all users reside in the United States.

Global ambition

> I often read that Britain needs a major media global player. Britain *has* a
> major media global player; and it is the BBC.
>
> (John Birt, Director-General, BBC, 1999)

Aside from 'high reach' and the BBC's declaration of the Web as its third medium, we would argue that there are other, less publicly espoused reasons for the scale of the BBC's Web activities (both *beeb.com* and Online). These motives relate directly to a long-term squeeze on the BBC's core funding (the licence fee) and the concomitant pressures on the Corporation to increase commercial revenues dramatically.

Recurring struggles with government regarding the level and existence of the licence fee have been an abiding feature of the Corporation's existence since the election of Margaret Thatcher's Conservative administration in 1979, if not from the publication of the Annan Report in 1977. Disagreements between the present New Labour administration and the BBC have recently been brought to a head, with the reporting in August 1999 of the Davies Committee's investigation into 'The Future Funding of the BBC'. The key conclusion of the government-convened Davies report is a rejection of the BBC's claim for an additional £650 million of public money to support the Corporation's expansion plans for online and, in particular, digital television and radio services. In their place, the Davies Report suggests more modest (and short-lived) proposals for a digital supplement to the television licence fee that would net the BBC less than a third of the Corporation's target sum. In response, the BBC is presently lobbying the government not to accept the Davies Report's recommendations.

While the level of public funding for the BBC remains a politically sensitive issue, high expectations regarding the BBC's output remain undiminished, as demonstrated by the government's Secretary of State for Culture, Media and Sport, Chris Smith, when announcing the terms for the BBC's funding review at the Royal Television Society Symposium in London:

> It [the BBC] must continue to be seen as a benchmark for quality, provide something for everybody, inform, educate and entertain . . . [in short] to continue to fulfil its public service obligations effectively whilst ensuring that it retains the ability to operate effectively in the market place.
> (www.worldserver.pipex.com/coi/depts/GHE/coi6686e.ok,
> 14 October 1998)

The Culture Secretary's concluding remarks are perhaps the most telling, for if the BBC is not to be the recipient of a publicly funded digital bonanza, the onus on the Corporation to increase its commercial revenues becomes more urgent.

Since the Birtian Revolution, the BBC has already dramatically intensified its commercialization strategy. The expansion has witnessed high-profile joint ventures with Flextech in Europe and Discovery in America; the launch of additional subscription-based domestic television services (such as BBC Choice and BBC Parliament), and a much stronger push into global markets (such as the recently launched television channels BBC America and BBC World). Given the BBC's desire to sell more products through more channels into more territories, one of the purposes of *beeb.com* as stated by a senior *beeb* manager, is 'to promote global brand awareness for the BBC'. That the Web is beginning to feature as an integral element of the BBC's marketing push is due to the relatively low cost and global reach of the medium. Hence *beeb* management describe the Web as providing the Corporation with 'more of a level playing field' than traditional offline media.

We should restate that the above viewpoint emanates from within a BBC commercial joint venture. However, the cross-promotional benefits of, for instance, News Online's substantial US audience cannot have been lost on a Corporation seeking to sell its television programming into US homes through its cable joint venture with Discovery. Indeed, the BBC launched its first co-ordinated online campaign to inform business travellers of its global business brands (World Service, BBC World and BBC Online) in October 1999. The Corporation's Web activities, then, are also integral elements in the BBC's ongoing transformation from a domestic public service broadcaster into a more complex, more overseas-oriented, 'marketing aware' organization.

Conclusion

What does the Web mean for the BBC as an institution, and for public service media more generally? What is clear is that the advent of the Web as a major medium has certainly had a destabilizing effect on the basic compromises – regulatory, financial and managerial – on which the institution of the BBC is founded, transgressing the set of internal and external barriers and borders that have been so carefully constructed. Specifically, the coming of the Web has desta- bilized the boundary between the BBC and the commercial media; it has eroded the internal boundaries between different media and between the Corporation's commercial and publicly funded activities; and, finally, it has eroded the link between the licence fee and the national audience. The process of going online has clearly been a painful and destabilizing one for the Corporation.

Yet it is also apparent that the BBC has not been the passive object of this process. Rather, the Corporation has reacted increasingly vigorously to the challenge of the Web. In some cases, it has sought to re-establish the borders between its various domains and to police them more rigorously, for example, in the case of the distinction between its commercial activities and its licence fee-funded work. In others, it has sought to establish new barriers and bulwarks, for example, by bring- ing much of its Web development work in-house and centralizing its public service offering in the form of BBC Online. While the new pattern is far from established, and many issues remain problematic and unresolved, the Corporation has clearly produced a hugely popular public service website, an advertising-free enclave within what is an increasingly commercialized online environment.

Author's note   This chapter is based around interviews with senior managers within BBC Online, BBC Education and beeb.com, undertaken for the UK Economic and Social Research Council (ESRC) project, New Media and Urban and Regional Development Oppor- tunities in the UK (Grant No. R000237747). The authors would also like to thank Fiona Martin, School of Humanities, Media and Cultural Studies, Southern Cross University, Australia, for her helpful comments on an early draft of this chapter.

USEFUL WEBSITES

BBC Online: **www.bbc.co.uk**
The overflowing public service website.

beeb.com: **www.beeb.com**
The unimpressive commercial site.

BBC Corporate Information: **http://bbc.co.uk/info**
Everything BBC, including Annual Reports, packed with critical analysis (not really).

The Future of the BBC: **www.newsunlimited.co.uk/BBC**
Lots of analysis in this special area of the *Guardian* newspaper's *Newsun- limited* website.

Part IV

GLOBAL WEB COMMUNITIES, POLITICS AND PROTEST

17

World Wide Women and the Web

Wendy Harcourt

Women's weavings on the Web

Popular imagery tends to exclude women as participants in cyberspace, with the typical image of the Web user as a middle-class (white) male 'techie'. And, if we were to believe all of the media hype about pornography and consumerism on the internet it would seem that women are more caught in the Web than weaving it themselves. But from my experience, working with women all over the world, this is not so. Women are actively engaged in the cyberdialogue, creating on the internet strategic information links, lobbying and advocating for change, and building up solidarity among groups that share the same goal even if they never meet face to face. Women's groups are using the internet as a way to break down barriers, exclusions and silences. The internet is fast becoming a tool for empowerment changing women's daily lives, their hopes and their future.

In this chapter I map out briefly some of the ways women are working, and networking, on the internet. My focus is on the positive side – to counter the images of women as objects rather than subjects of cyberspace. I also focus on women working in the global south to counter another prevalent image of the internet as exclusively the tool of the north. Our journey in cyberspace will

Is the internet dominated by men?

According to the statistics source NUA Internet Surveys (www.nua.ie/surveys), more than 200 million people were online by 2000. (NUA's 'how many online' figure is compiled from numerous surveys, and is defined as adults and children who have accessed the Internet at least once during the 3 months prior to being surveyed.) More than half of these were in the USA and Canada, and of those, 46 per cent were women: almost, but not quite, half the online population.

The percentage of women online in North America continues to rise, and elsewhere we have come to expect net demographics to lag a year or more behind (although cultural differences will affect the gender divide in different countries). But in 1999, women made up 44 per cent of Australia's online population and 42 per cent of France's, for example, and the ratio of women to men continues to become more balanced.

So it's wrong to see the internet as a 'male domain'. As always, for the latest statistics, you'll have to check the Web . . .

take up three examples of how women are using the Web in innovative ways. First, we will look at how women are using the Web to help stop violence against women. Second, at how the internet has enabled a vast outreach in women's networking and organizing. And, third, at how women are creating new cross-cultural connections on the Web through the group I co-ordinate, Women on the Net. I conclude the chapter with a warning note about the limitations of 'women and the cyber-revolution'. But I aim to show how women are using the Web to support their political work around women's rights, and in so doing are creating new cultures across time and space.

The cyberfight to stop violence against women

As you surf the hundreds of colourful and professional websites set up by women in every continent – *ISIS Manila* in the Philippines, *Aviva* in the UK, *FeMiNa* in the USA, *Women's Net* in South Africa, *Q Web* in Sweden to name but a few – you are struck immediately by the numbers of women using the Web for campaigns around violence against women. Similarly, as anyone hooked into this cyberworld knows, e-mail petitions are fast becoming one of the most common and effective lobbying tools used by women's groups to prevent violations against women. From all of this activity you can see how the Web provides a unique tool to empower women by opening up the possibility for international support in the struggle for women's rights locally.

Let us take some examples of women's groups in the global south using cyberspace for support. In Rajasthan, one of the most economically poor areas in India, Bal Rashmi (a non-governmental organization (NGO) based in Jaipur) is actively involved in the struggle against women's sexual exploitation by such means as rape, dowry deaths and torture. Its work drew the negative attention of the (corrupt) state government dominated by a Hindu right-wing party. The government filed bogus criminal cases and had the leaders of the NGO arrested. In fighting back, Bal Rashmi members used the Web immediately to contact international human rights and women's networks in India, South Asia, Europe and North America. Their call set off an appeal that within a few weeks led to faxes and letters flooding into the National Human Rights Commission, and the Rajasthan state and national governments. The internet campaign forced an investigation of the cases and within a few months five cases were quashed.

Another story comes from Mexico, where Claudia Rodriguez spent over a year in prison for the homicide of her would-be rapist, awaiting trial and the possibility of 15 years in prison. Women's organizations and activists in Mexico mobilized support for her case, declaring her innocence and recognizing the precedent a guilty verdict would represent for all women. Their slogan was 'As long as Claudia is a prisoner, we are all prisoners'.

17.1 *Women's Net* of South Africa.

The women's e-mail activist network Modemmujer sent out Claudia's words and situation over the internet to hundreds of women and women's organizations in Mexico, Latin America and North America, with calls for letters to the President, the Secretary of State and the Department of Justice. Mobilization by women's organizations in Mexico City resulted in women coming to the hearing process and making public protests. Letters were sent from all over Mexico, Cuba, Argentina, Colombia, Bolivia, Canada and the United States. Claudia was freed, though the verdict review stated that she used 'excessive force'. The judge refrained from sentencing her to an additional 5 years in jail (see www.connected.org/women/erika.html).

One more example comes from Shirkat Gah, based in Lahore, Pakistan, one of the very few human rights and environment women's organizations in Pakistan with the resources and connections to be able to make effective use of e-mail. Using trusted international websites (such as the GREAT network based in East Anglia, UK, with 550 organizations and individuals working on women and gender issues), it has mobilized around the prosecution of honour killings. As in Rajasthan, because of its work Shirkat Gah is also fighting for its legitimacy and survival through international cybersupport. It used its Web contacts to solicit support against threatened closure when Punjab police and state authorities went to press claiming that Shirkat Gah had illegally received millions of dollars of funds from the World Bank.

What is interesting in these stories (and I could also give examples from Uganda, Senegal, the Philippines, Kenya and Russia) is how women all around the world have been able to use the internet to support their networking, information and communication needs. Through international support, women's groups and individuals under threat locally are able to hold their ground. And in the process of mobilizing support, they have created a series of networks that quickly and strategically links women's local concerns with the global movement.

Another point to note is that, perhaps differently than is the case with other groups using the net for political organizing, women operate by creating safe personalized cyber spaces. The cyber network Modemmujer, which engineered the e-mail campaign that saved Claudia, maintains a close relationship with the 400 women's organizations and individuals in Latin America that are part of its list, keeping them up to date with information in Mexican women's movements and their counterparts in the global south. Shirkat Gah works with Women Living Under Muslim Law to keep key strategic information circulating in its network. Bal Rashami is part of the international women's human rights movement linked worldwide through the Web. These cyber networks do not flood women's groups with information, which would often be too impersonal and distant to local needs to be of interest, but rather focus on creating a safe and intimate space for women. That is why the campaigns can work. The women on the listservs (e-mail lists) know and trust the message sender and will quickly respond to such urgent requests.

Cyberorganizing for women's rights: the Beijing experience

The work around violence against women is just one facet of women's work on the Web. E-mail petitions, interlinked websites, chatrooms, listservs and sharing up-to-date information enable women's groups to empower themselves with information flowing in and among countries, regions and internationally, building structures for change and mobilizing struggles for peace, equality and gender justice. Women are using the internet to network, plan and strategize on a level that could never have been imagined just a few years ago. Perhaps the most impressive effort during the 1990s has been around the United Nations Fourth World Conference on Women, held in Beijing in September 1995. The event itself was one of the most well attended UN Conferences ever (thousands of women actually made it to Beijing) and the repercussions of the discussions and agreements were felt far and wide thanks to the internet. As reported by Alice Gittler, 'Electronic communication allowed women to bypass mainstream media and still reach thousands. . . . Women who met on-line found an immediate network. . . . One hundred thousand visits were made to the APC Website on the Conference. . . . When the International Women's Health Tribune Global FaxNet was posted on the Web, over 80,000 hits were recorded in the week before the Beijing Meetings' (Harcourt, 1999).

One of the key instigators of Web networking radiating out from Beijing was the International Women's Tribune Centre (IWTC), based in New York. The IWTC really launched the information technology process in Beijing. One hundred thousand women worldwide could learn about a problem instantly, making women a very powerful international lobby at the Conference which has repercussions still for UN policy-making bodies taking up gender and women's interests, feeling that the world's women are watching. For the 5-year review of post-Beijing progress, the IWTC with other partners has set up a website and embarked on 'cyberorganizing' with a 16-member coalition launching a global network of websites to share information and track progress. This is also connected to *WomenWatch*, the website for UN activities related to women. The global website (www.womenaction.org) will link regional sites in Asia/Pacific, Africa, North America, Latin America/the Caribbean and Europe.

These Web activities involve women who would otherwise never be able to link up – including women who due to their culture or locality would not be in a position to voice their opinions. Arab women, for example, are entering the space created by the net in the face of cultural silencing and questioning of any western medium. They have to fight the protectionist response of the Arab world to mass media as well as all manners of gender bias. Nevertheless, the internet enables them to express themselves and comment on contentious issues, which would be impossible – even dangerous – in the public sphere. With the impetus and opportunity provided by the Beijing process, religious debate as well as other issues relevant to women's rights and democracy – and subject to government suppression – can be carried on the Web, and Arab women are able to network in order to develop their ideas and activities further. As Lamis Alshejni observes, women's NGOs established to promote women's awareness and advocacy for gender political, social and economic equity are increasingly using the internet, and they have realized the importance of this tool for communication even if their usage is still largely of e-mail rather than the Web (Harcourt, 1999).

Another marginal group is indigenous women living in the 'liquid continent' (their evocative word for the Pacific islands). 'Netwarrior' Kekula Bray Crawford, working with other wired indigenous groups, has been connecting women's groups based in geographically isolated islands through the Web, aiming 'to expand the voice of cultures and peoples' through electronic forums into international arenas. She is creating a cyberculture where she hopes that women's indigenous wisdom can achieve greater recognition through international Web support. In an internet conversation in 1998, Kekula states, 'Including technology in our agendas is imperative in my theory to stand face to face, shoulder to shoulder, back to back with our sisters . . . we can join hands in peace, virtual space can allow us to do it.'

Women on the net: an experiment in women's cyberculture

Kekula is one of my cybercolleagues in the Women on the Net (WoN) project set up originally by the Society for International Development with UNESCO funding. WoN was set up to do several things. First, to encourage women – particularly in the south and in marginal groups in the global north (and central and eastern Europe) – to use the internet more easily as their space in an effort to 'empower' women to use technology as a political tool. Second, to open up and contribute to a new culture on the internet from a gender perspective that is simultaneously local and global. Third, to bring together individual women and men working from different institutional bases (women's NGOs, information technology networks, academia, women activists) to explore a transnational women's movement agenda in response to and shaping evolving telecommunication policies. And, fourth, to create a resource base that could be tapped into by different women's groups for analysis, knowledge and internet skills.

It has been a powerful and unique experience, professionally and personally, hinting at what the Web can do to strengthen women's political and analytical work. The dynamic that has evolved via the WoN online and in face-to-face interactions is somewhere between the personal, political and professional. The dialogues and meetings have been intense over the crossing of academic and activist knowledge terrain, over language and meanings, over concepts of place and identity. The lively discussions have brought out new ideas and concepts, and it is another illustration of the type of cyberculture women are creating, as people were communicating with one another as technicians, academics, activists and UN professionals from close to 40 countries.

WoN discussions on technical and political agendas are mixed with personal and intimate histories and happenings. The frustrations of being women working in a male-dominated environment are shared along with the pleasures: five babies have been born during the group's existence. Health difficulties, managing professional and political life with children and new and old partners are part of the culture being created, creating an intimacy which the solitary act of typing into a keyboard in front of a screen belies, but which the ethos of WoN embraces (see Harcourt 1999).

Women breaking down the boundaries

What can we learn from this very brief look at how women are using the internet? Women are empowering themselves through the net by breaking down traditional boundaries on many levels. Let us begin with the gender divide. Although it is true that fewer women use the internet due to economic, cultural and social reasons – though the gap is lessening daily – once they have used it (and finding time, overcoming fears of the technology, etc., may not be easy) they find that the virtual encounters can be easier than those of the face-to-face variety. As many commentators have noted, when we encounter people virtually we do not know what they look like in the flesh, who they 'are' just on sight; so a vital element of communication – physical attraction – does not play a role (except, perhaps, in the imagination). Not knowing the gender or the look of someone is a virtual robbing of some of the richness of communication, but it also offers the possibility for neutral, tolerant interchange. Women in particular respond to this possibility and, at least from my experience, the personal and even poetic enters to express who 'I am really' beyond the typing on the screen. Particularly when speaking about issues like violence against women this neutrality is important, as is the chance to express emotions. The speed of reaction is also vital as the three examples above from Pakistan, India and Mexico attest.

Another boundary that is being crossed continually is that between intellectual and activist. Labels become fluid as people find the words to understand each other divorced from concrete ways of judging – in cyberspace there is no actual classroom, no trades union hall, no ancestral ground to defend, no government office to lobby. These remain virtual points of reference that are imagined, not actually embraced and shared. Those who would not otherwise meet with professors or high-level policy-makers find themselves in correspondence with them via e-mail. Papers that would never have reached an African NGO in rural Senegal are translated and sent in a few days of delivery at a scientific or inter-governmental event. Women who will never meet exchange on a daily basis their worries about the men and children in their lives. Women engrossed in their own battles for survival suddenly find that groups living in other countries share the same concerns and they exchange valuable strategic knowledge. Academics and activists engage in a vigorous debate that each will use in different contexts enriched by what they have exchanged.

Then there is the crossing of personal and professional boundaries. For those who have access to the equipment and can find the time (even if squeezed between family needs), the internet offers a sense of being able to share your life more easily. People provide the personal in an e-mail communication – something that perhaps would never be placed in a fax or letter. There is something wonderful about this – news of a baby born to a never-met transnational group of cyber-friends, breast-feeding problems discussed among women isolated in rural settings, urgent messages sent by refugee Afghan women throughout the globe.

As is evident from all the networking women are engaged in around the Beijing process, the most obvious and celebrated crossed boundary is the geo-political one – thousands of kilometres fade in chats across the screen. The Web allows communication across time zones instantly, as the once-critical time difference disappears with access to terminals possible at all hours in homes or cyber-cafes, allowing messages to reach the Pacific, Asia, Europe, North America, Africa, Latin America and the Middle East instantaneously for the price of a telephone call.

The downside . . .

But here we need to raise the less positive side of the cyber-revolution for women. Beyond the fact that many women do not live in places that can afford or have access to the technical infrastructure, the continual crossing of the here and now divide can give an unreality to cyberpolitics. There is a strong need, felt by many women, to anchor the happenings of their real-life community to the virtual global discourse in order for the cybercommunication to have meaning. Where do all these online dialogues go (the time spent, people fleetingly met)? How are we 'really' relating to others on the Web? Women can feel overloaded with information and demands from others, and precious time may be spent responding to superfluous e-mails. There are also the dangers of never-ending conversations running into other issues, messages too quickly sent, tempers flaring, and unwisely shared fears and hopes.

A further issue is about who is masterminding the Web (see elsewhere in this book). It is important to chart how women are, more and more, using the

Web in order to open up new political spaces. Nevertheless it seems a tiny area that women are inhabiting, and usually controlled and designed by others. The nagging questions remain: are women truly connected, or just scratching at the surface of a fast-changing world that is evolving without their needs, or ideas, in mind? If you venture into the world of decision-making and policy agenda-setting on telecommunications and other areas affecting access and use of the internet, where are the women? As Sophia Huyer indicates, there are some brave women charting the ground, but women are yet to venture there as a critical mass (Harcourt, 1999). The world of Microsoft, high finance and telecommunications businesses are not the spaces in which women or those pushing for an alternative agenda easily find a voice.

More difficult still is the question of access. Many people are marginalized or excluded from cyberspace: the non-English-speaking nations, 'irrelevant' nations and peoples, national, religious and ideological minorities, the poor in poor countries and the poor in rich countries (the majority of whom are women), most old people and those with disabilities, and almost all children (although certainly not western 'screenagers'). The women I have featured here are the educated political elite of their countries (south but also north). The majority of the world's women are poor, illiterate and cannot hope to have access to this virtual world. The infrastructure is still not there, and the control of who has access is a political as well as economic question.

Future challenges for worldwide women on the Web

The challenge for women activists in search of gender justice is to use the Web not only as an immediate empowering tool for their strategic needs but to open up its potential to others. The form of the internet and Web lends itself well to women's traditional support role, and to networking. As women begin to train others and learn to create new software, more interactive, more user-friendly new types of communication technologies could emerge. A more women-designed Web-weaving could reflect women's sense of community and steer us away from the consumer-focused, alienated individual interaction that appears so much on the Web today, and back towards the more fully linked-up Web envisioned by Tim Berners-Lee less than 10 years ago. Women and other marginal groups should begin to *design* internet software and resources, not merely use existing ones, for their own empowerment. They have to be part of the design (the 'knowledge ware') and use process.

Sohail Inayatullah and Ivana Milojevic argue that the challenge for women is to search for ways to transform information to communication (going far beyond the 'interactivity' the Web promises), creating not a knowledge economy which silences differences of wealth, but a *communicative economy* – where differences are explored, some unveiled, others left to be (Harcourt, 1999).

17.2 The Women's Environment and Development Organization, linking women around the world.

To end on an upbeat note: even if many women are excluded from Web weavings, the potential for shared communication futures has been tapped and needs to be made stronger and more inclusive. In the future let us hope that the sense of enthusiasm and empowerment that Peggy Antrobus, a respected leader of the inter-regional southern women's group DAWN (Development Alternatives with Women in a New Era), can be shared by *all* women:

> The internet most of all . . . has empowered us, by giving us the information, the analysis, the sense of solidarity, the experience of shared achievements, the encouragement and moral support that comes from being part of a network, a movement with common goals and visions.
>
> (Personal cyberconversation, September 1999)

WoN, in a modest way, has begun that process with small training workshops on the politics of cyberspace with community women's groups. At a meeting held in September 1999 on the beautiful island of Zanzibar off the east coast of Africa (in both Kiswahili and English), members of WoN discussed with local women the whole nature of the 'virtual world', its possibilities and potential to communicate across the traditional divides of gender, class, culture and nation. Women who were veiled and had never seen a computer before were given two days to learn how to 'run with' the cyber-revolution. These women are now meeting virtually (and face to face) to tackle themes such as domestic violence, women and empowerment, social justice, and sex education. They draw on the internet to gain knowledge on production processes, health, teaching and cultural industries. They have tapped into a new world: one where they can contribute, create and participate.

USEFUL WEBSITES

International action Web pages

Aviva: **www.aviva.org**
A dynamic site aiming to keep information flowing on women's activism around the world. Based in the UK.

FeMiNa: **www.FeMiNa.com**
Informed and well-connected site on critical issues ranging from human rights to young women's needs. Based in the USA.

Q Web Sweden: **www.qweb.kvinnoforum.se**
Based in Sweden, with a particular focus on reproductive rights and empowerment. Very well linked on all major issues concerning women.

Beijing and UN websites

Beijing +5 Global Forum: **www.un.org/womenwatch/forum**
Official updates on the Beijing process, from the UN headquarters.

United Nations Development Fund for Women:
www.unifem.undp.org
A very dynamic site on all areas of UNIFEM's work, particularly on violence against women.

WomenAction: **www.womenaction.org**
A truly international site with input from women's networks around the world. Features well-organized and interactive content on all aspects of NGO participation around the Beijing process.

Other sites of interest

Isis International: **http://isiswomen.org**
Links up Asian and international women's organizations on a host of issues. Based in the Philippines.

Society for International Development: **www.sidint.org**
International organization hosting the Society for International Development – Women in Development network, and the SID-UNESCO *Women on the Net* project. Based in Rome.

Women's Environment and Development Organization: **www.wedo.org**
Gives updates on WEDO's many national and international campaigns concerning women. Based in New York.

Women's Net: **www.womensnet.org.za**
A vibrant and innovative networking support programme designed to enable South African women to use the internet to find the people, issues, resources and tools needed for women's social action.

18

The Internet and Democracy

Stephen Lax

Prominent among the many and varied claims about the social potential of the internet is that it will enhance the democratic process. At a time when both interest and participation in politics are perceived to be in decline, commentators across the world are suggesting that new information and communication technologies (ICTs) can link both government and governed. Others suggest that they could promote debate and discussion among the electorate. For the British Government, this is part of the 'modernization' of a society in which, we are told, ideas of class, interventionism and regulation are old-fashioned. Now, knowledge is the new 'capital' to be accumulated and information becomes the key commodity for exchange.

Certainly ICTs enable novel, 'democratic' practices to take place: people can use the internet to access government documents or to visit campaigning organizations; groups of people can engage in discussions through e-mail networks. But to draw the conclusion that this means society at large will become more democratic is questionable. Will barriers to access to these technologies mean that participation is confined to a privileged few? If information provision is central to a better-informed electorate, should we be concerned about the quality or veracity of that information? More fundamentally, what are the reasons for supposing that provision of information and access to new (though not necessarily novel) communication channels are any more likely to engage electors and to ensure that more of the people will be able to exert political influence?

The claims

The Labour Party in Britain has argued (1995: 17) that 'in a world where, increasingly, knowledge is the source of power . . . technology can empower and free individuals and enrich their communication with the state'. Its spokesperson argued that 'The electronic revolution could significantly alter the effectiveness of UK democracy by ensuring that ordinary people could constantly access information and input their views using new technology' (Allen, 1995). Its plans for devolution of political power to Scotland and Wales included full use of ICTs

18.1 Tony Blair smoulders on the UK Labour Party's website.

with videoconferencing between constituents and representatives, and instant opinion polling in what would be a 'laboratory for democracy' (Arlidge, 1997).

Behind the rhetoric, for governments the democratic role of ICTs lies in making democracy more efficient, by offering easier public access to government documents and by allowing more direct communication between representatives and constituents. Further, electronic processing and exchange of some of the functions of government – for example, tax returns and welfare claims – should allow more responsive delivery of services as well as creating cost savings (Taylor *et al.*, 1996). Certainly examples exist of attempts to deliver services through ICTs, but these remain small in scale or simply experimental, and so there remains little evidence of their effectiveness in either delivering the service or saving money. The more worthy intention expressed above of a more direct say for the electorate in decision-making by the deployment of new technologies, is still less developed. Coleman (1999: 18) sees the interests of the British Government in particular as being economic rather than political, 'efficient government' meaning cheaper government, rather than the involvement of more of the people.

Governments are not alone in arguing the case for the democratic potential of ICTs. Others argue that the new ICTs offer more than the efficient parliamentary democracy described above. Falling numbers of voters taking part in elections and declining attendances at fewer political meetings are cited as evidence of a deepening disenchantment with the traditional political processes. If people are to engage with politics and become active citizens, some new means of conducting the political process must be developed, and this can be achieved through new technologies. According to *Wired* magazine's Kevin Kelly (1995), 'the internet revives Thomas Jefferson's 200-year-old dream of thinking individuals self-actualizing a democracy'. The parallel developments of declining involvement in 'traditional' political processes and the growth of political groups separate from the state – in other words pressure groups and single-issue campaigns – have led to debate about ICTs focusing on this 'other politics'. The discussion here will consider two different but overlapping perspectives on ICT use. The first welcomes the new technologies as enabling pressure groups and campaigners more effectively to organize and publicize themselves, to recruit new members, and to co-ordinate activities and campaigns. The second view sees the technology as making possible a political forum where debate can flourish, consensus be achieved and policies be put forward. Clearly there is a continuum between these two possibilities, but the different perspectives suggest particular assumptions about the nature of politics and democracy today.

The technology of democracy?

One use of technology for democracy is to deliver information, from governments and from other organizations. This one-way information flow can be delivered over a variety of channels – print media (newspapers and mailshots), broadcasting technologies (radio and television) or data communication networks such as teletext or videotext. However, the internet is the new medium which has re-energized the debate about technology and democracy.

The internet serves as both a one-way and a two-way network. Much of its use is for people to access documents and other information (text, audio and video) in ways which are, in concept, little more than sophisticated developments of the use of earlier technologies. Certainly, search engines and Web links allow easier navigation than, say, teletext or videotext searching, and the rapid development of coding techniques enables a variety of media forms and large quantities of data to be delivered. Even so, much of this information is in some way 'official' in nature – for example, from government departments, or commercial or other established organizations – and so it is also obtainable by means other than the internet (albeit often less easily). The 'unofficial' material on the internet includes personal Web pages and small organizations' websites, and this is the sort of information that is unlikely to be found on news-stands, and is also not likely to make its way on to a radio or TV channel or into newspaper columns. The falling costs of computer technology and internet access, and simpler authoring software, mean that it is almost as easy for a solitary individual or tiny group to put their aims and thoughts on the World Wide Web as it is for corporate or state giants. It is also just as easy *in principle* for someone anywhere in the world to look at those ideas as to seek the views of News Corporation or CNN, for instance.

If the provision of more information from a greater variety of sources were all that were required for an enhanced democracy, then this would indeed represent a democratizing technology (as would satellite and cable television). Certainly greater availability of information is a prerequisite for more democracy (though it helps to know where it has come from) and early uses of computer networks, by groups such as Public Data Access, aimed to make public information more freely available (Downing, 1989). However, mere expansion of the quantity or range of information is not enough. The fact that more information is *available* does not mean that access to it is straightforward. Finding particular ideas or pages remains a rather hit-or-miss affair unless the Web address is known (often learnt from other, conventional media), and unknown pages are often reached by links from more familiar sites or by judicious (or fortuitous) use of search engines. So access to minority views relies strongly on being linked from more popular sites or working their way up search engine hierarchies – the playing field that is the World Wide Web is far from level.

If more information of itself does not mean more democracy, where else should we look? The earliest uses of computer networks were for the exchange of e-mail messages. This remains a relatively low-tech application; it is text-based, requiring little bandwidth, and is thus fast and reasonably cheap. The widespread adoption of the standard internet protocol (TCP/IP) in the 1980s meant that rapidly growing numbers of people had access to international e-mail. (Prior to this common protocol, e-mail traffic was constrained within individual networks which could only interconnect with difficulty.) Informal e-mail groups became established, often based on common professional interests (in the universities and research institutes where networking technologies first developed) but organized across nations. They would circulate messages among the whole group rather than to individuals, and 'bulletin boards' allowed the posting of notices, accessible by any group member at any time. Commercial access to these networking technologies and increasing ownership of home computers allowed online information services such as CompuServe, beginning in 1979, to extend this facility into the domestic sphere. Similar groups evolved within these networks, and when in the early 1990s online services began to allow full internet access, e-mail groups expanded rapidly in number (there are now thousands covering every conceivable subject). It is reasonably straightforward to set up e-mail lists and newsgroups (which are similar, though newsgroups tend to be more public or open) and some internet organizations provide this service free. Messages are usually archived and so can be reviewed if desired. Since the circulation takes place via e-mail, message downloading does not necessarily require high-speed data links, so is accessible to anyone with quite modest technology linked to the internet. The claim for their democratic potential is that they represent a new 'public sphere' where deliberation can take place between all citizens on an even footing, without intervention from state or corporate interests.[1]

The use of telephone lines for access to the internet immediately establishes global coverage, and technological developments of the telephone network – for example, asymmetric digital subscriber line (ADSL) or integrated services digital network links (ISDN) – mean that higher data speeds will become more accessible at lower costs to both fixed and mobile equipment. Delivery of audio and video material of decent quality will undoubtedly become possible, and two-way video-conferencing more user-friendly. These are some of the technological developments that are exciting those who argue for the internet's democratic potential.

The internet and campaigning organizations

For campaigning organizations, the use of the internet builds upon existing structures. The environmental movement, for example, is well established throughout the world. Some organizations, like Greenpeace, have long had an international profile while others, such as Friends of the Earth, were and remain national organizations (although they may have links with sibling organizations in other countries). These organizations were quick to exploit ICTs both for organizational purposes and, as the number of computers with internet connection grew, for publicity and information delivery. Their Web pages are full of information about current campaigns, with documentation (for example, petitions or letters to MPs) available for download, online membership forms, contact details and, often, links to other organizations. In this way the Web pages function as a newsletter or magazine that might otherwise be sent only to members.

For other groups, the internet plays a more central role. In more loosely structured campaigns, such as anti-road protests or 'critical mass' cycle rides, the websites serve as detailed information points – for example, giving the location and time of activities. Lack of funds might prohibit a properly organized mail-shot to supporters, so the Web sits alongside publicity in other limited

18.2 Graffiti (on David Gauntlett's street) in Leeds, UK, promoting the June 18th anarchist website.

castellano : deutsch : francais : italiano : nederlands : russkoe

:june 18 1999

An International day of action, protest and carnival aimed at the heart of the global economy.

The latest J18 bulletin - what's happening and where. Uploaded 6/6/99

"Support Press Freedom" - J18 reporting 'on the day'

Check out the detailed online London map and book on the inner workings of the Square Mile

The Intercontinental Caravan The official G8 summit site

"we are conscious of the devastating capability of transnational capital but we are also conscious of the creative capacity of imagination and freedom. That's why we will protest in force but we will also celebrate with joy, the joy of making possible human contact, warmth, art and life."

Club de los Intelectuales Podridos, Colombia
Taking action on June 18

me
ntacts
sources
lated news
dio
porting

4 DAYS TO GO!!

PRESS
Please Read

18.3 The 'Carnival Against Capitalism' website.

circulation magazines and newsletters as a key means of organization. The 'June 18th' protests in cities around the world to coincide with the 1999 G8 summit on world poverty were publicized on the Web with details of activities and contact phone numbers. Dubbed the 'Carnival Against Capitalism', London's protest achieved significant media coverage after protesters and police clashed in the city's financial district (thereby achieving far greater visibility than it otherwise would have done). The *Guardian* even reported that the demonstration was entirely dependent on the Web (Dodson, 1999). This is clearly untrue. It is not credible to imagine that such a protest could not have happened without the use of the Web. The full range of other, 'conventional' means of organizing protests were used: posters, leaflets, telephone, word of mouth, e-mail of course, and even 'www.j18.org' graffiti which appeared in cities prior to the event (see Figure 18.2). No doubt a number of protesters did turn up through having seen notices on the website, but most will have visited that site after being alerted through one of these other mechanisms.

Here, the internet works alongside other technologies as a useful means of organizing campaigns: e-mail for contact with and document delivery to activists, Web pages for publicity and advertisement. Other technologies play a similar role. Keck and Sikkink (1998) rank cheap and reliable transport (principally air travel) equally significantly as ICT developments in their discussion of transnational campaigns. Undercurrents uses miniature video cameras to record protests and to document campaigns for distribution by video cassette. To argue that any particular technology uniquely constitutes a force for democracy would be mistaken; the role of new technologies is a complex one. Two examples illustrate this.

1. In June 1999, the City of London police went to the courts to secure access to all video footage of the Carnival Against Capitalism shot by any journalist in order to identify protesters. It is reassuring that they failed in their quest, but the irony is that a 'democratizing' video technology almost had the opposite effect.

2. At the outbreak of NATO bombing of the former Yugoslavia in March 1999, the independent Belgrade radio station B92, which had long been overt in its opposition to the Serbian Government, was taken off air by the authorities, who took over its transmission frequency. It began broadcasting instead over the internet. Its programmes (and its plight) reached journalists and human rights organizations through its website, and the closure was widely reported in the traditional media. Other sympathetic radio stations carried its programming. Ten days later, state authorities went further and took over the studios, preventing any further internet transmissions.

The technology did not simply subvert the power of state mechanisms such as the police and judiciary. Nevertheless, the internet can be an alternative information channel: during the same war, a number of websites carried eye-witness accounts of the NATO bombing, accounts largely unreported by western media (see Taylor's chapter in this volume).

In recognition of the potential value of the internet to campaigning groups, a number of organizations have set out to promote the use of ICTs among campaigning and political groups by providing advice, technical support and internet access. GreenNet describes itself as seeking to promote electronic networking for groups involved in human rights, environmental activism and sustainable development, and to provide a platform for lobbying on ICT issues such as equitable access and plurality of language. A founder member of the Alliance for Progressive Communications, an international umbrella for organizations promoting similar services, GreenNet is funded by a variety of charitable foundations and could be described as a clearing house for progressive groups. The Labour Telematics Centre does much the same for trades unions and related organizations and, funded by the Workers Education Association, it conducts research on the educational and organizational potential of ICTs (Herman and Holly, 2000). These sites, therefore, act more as the starting point rather than the focus of political activism.

Established campaigning groups can use ICTs to great benefit for their internal organizational functions, in the same way that most businesses and public organizations use e-mail and intranets. The emergence of GreenNet and similar groups is testimony to the importance of these technologies as a relatively low-cost means of information exchange. There is less evidence, however, to suggest that new ICTs offer unique advantages for campaigning purposes over other methods and technologies, or that they are spawning mass protest movements. Traditional campaigning techniques such as media coverage (Jordan, 1998), mailshots and political lobbying continue, and 'old' technologies such as telephones and fax machines are, equally, more important than ever before to the running of an effective campaign.

The internet and the public sphere

An approach which at first appears rather more radical conceives of electronic networks as forums for the deliberation of political ideas and policies. This is not a new idea: 'teledemocracy' experiments include the Ohio QUBE experiments of the 1970s, in which cable television subscribers could use a push-button keypad to vote on questions posed on the television screen (Arterton, 1987; Elshtain, 1982). The current conception would exploit the true interactivity of e-mail groups to allow debate, rather than mere electronic voting on questions posed by someone else. The idea is that e-mail discussion groups open up access and draw in all kinds of people: 'the shy, the disabled, and carers . . . who are socially disadvantaged, obliged to stay at home or otherwise have little voice' (Tsagarousianou *et al.*, 1998: 6). Discussion would lead to opinion formation or to consensus on political issues, thereby involving the electors in decisions that are currently left to elected political representatives. Some proclaim these new forums as replacing the now outmoded town hall or trades union meetings.

Opinion varies as to the degree to which these forums should determine outcomes: at one extreme, electronic technologies could be provided cheaply enough to allow almost every political decision to be put to the vote; the far more common view, however, envisages retaining a representative democratic structure of some sort, using technology to enable representatives to gauge the electorate's views more accurately.

In a sense the prototype for this forum already exists in the many newsgroups set up to discuss political issues. Wilhelm (1998) studied a number of political newsgroups in an attempt to establish how effective they might be in promoting deliberation or consensus-building. He suggests that, while there certainly was a sense of discussion on most groups – that is, members would respond to one another in their postings – much of this was to provide opinion rather than solve problems or seek consensus. There was no evidence of cultivation or development of 'public opinion'. He concluded that much of the participation was simply for the purposes of ordinary pleasurable conversation. Of course, the study is flawed to the extent that these newsgroups were never intended to formulate policy or establish consensus, and in a forum which was established in the knowledge that its deliberations would result in some consequence, the level of discussion might well be different. Nevertheless, Wilhelm's study highlights some important ways in which electronic debate differs from face-to-face discussion, and he rejects the idea of the internet as public sphere.

There are, however, a number of examples of networks which have been established precisely in order to deliberate policy and develop consensus. These civic or community networks often link up a 'community' which is already in some way established, most commonly on a geographical basis. Among the most familiar are Amsterdam's *Digital City* and the *PEN* network in Santa Monica, California (see Tsagarousianou *et al.*, 1998). Others seek to generate debate around specific issues rather than being geographically connected. The UK's Citizens Online Democracy (*UKCOD*) has hosted a number of e-mail forums on issues such as transport policy, European monetary union and the Constitution. While these initiatives are largely experimental, there is little evidence that any have either involved a substantial cross-section of the community they purport to represent, or had any significant effect on policy. Many appear to be short-lived, with a flurry of electronic activity for a while before falling out of favour with participants.

This replicates the findings of Arterton in his study of numerous US projects. He argued that participation declined after the novelty factor began to wane and, significantly, the rate of that decline was greater the further that participation was from actual policy influence (1987: 148). Brants *et al.* (1996: 239) report of the Amsterdam initiatives that 'the [pressure groups and citizens] were also dissatisfied with the lack of follow-up in terms of political consequences'. Coleman (1999: 21) optimistically viewed the *UKCOD* forum on 'Freedom of Information' as 'an unprecedented opportunity for members of the public . . . to submit comments on the proposed legislation and . . . receive online responses from the minister with responsibility for the White Paper'. However, the Bill that subsequently emerged was strongly criticized (in, for example, *The Economist*, 1999b) as falling far short of expectations.

Almost all of these projects have been initiated by a group of 'concerned' individuals rather than as a response to an identified public demand. Arterton (1987: 199) comments on 'elites controlling the agenda' in the 1980s US projects. In so far as they seek merely to gauge opinion which may (or may not) influence politicians, these projects are actually very conservative in aim. While recognizing that existing democratic practices are flawed, there is no attempt to take away power from politicians and truly place it in the hands of the people; thus the electorate might simply become still more alienated. Coleman (1999: 21) alerts us to the dangers of mistaking public relations exercises for genuine attempts at public consultation, and without an explicit link to decision-making, participation in electronic consultation is likely to remain low. Budge (1996) argues that new technologies do for the first time permit deliberation and genuine decision-making to be left to electors. His version of a 'mediated' direct democracy is more sophisticated than crude electronic voting on every issue, retaining a role for political parties and other intermediaries. However, the key question of what mechanism can ensure that those decisions are indeed binding is not answered.

Access to technology

That access to ICTs is uneven is self-evident, but it is important to emphasize some of the issues. The demographics of internet access are widely available: the 'average' internet user is male, well educated, and wealthy. Data from the 'futura.com' project at the University of Leeds suggest that, in mid-1999, around 36 per cent of UK households had a computer, and although another 16 per cent claimed they would like a computer, they had no plans to get one (Svennevig *et al.*, 1999; Svennevig and Morrison, 2000). However, one in three adults (34 per cent) were not interested in having a computer at home. A total of 17 per cent had internet access at home, while 68 per cent of respondents were either not interested or had no plans to get it. Thus one in two people did not intend to get a home computer in the foreseeable future, and more than two out of three had no plans for internet access. At a time when the internet is the subject of much promotion by both government and business, this figure may represent a lack of enthusiasm that proves resistant to persuasion. (For the latest internet demographics, see the sites listed at www.newmediastudies.com/stats.htm.)

Other routes to internet access, such as through cable television, appear no more likely to succeed: 87 per cent had no plans or were not interested in cable television itself, while 98 per cent rejected the idea of internet access through cable television. It might be argued that until such systems have been demonstrated, then demand is bound to be low (the 'early adopter' problem, where take-up of any new technology is slow to begin with, but picks up once a few people have tried it out and awareness begins to rise). But this would not explain the low take-up of home computers, which are now established enough for there to be a large second-hand market in machines that will fulfil most household computing needs. The emergence of free internet services also removes one of the main cost barriers to internet access for computer owners (the remaining one in many countries being the cost of phone calls). Thus while the technology is still expensive for many, it is now less so, and could more easily be purchased if there appeared to be a good reason to do so. Currently, such a reason does not apparently exist. Cable television systems have also been around in the UK long enough for them no longer to be the preserve of the early adopters, yet figures show that the penetration rate (the percentage of those to whom cable is available who actually subscribe) is almost static, increasing only slowly from 22 per cent in 1993 to 24 per cent in 1999.[2]

Thus while cost remains a barrier for some households (just as it does for the telephone, equally an important democratizing technology), a significant limitation to the democratic potential of the internet must be the lack of interest or appeal to electors. Providing networked terminals in public places such as libraries, schools and community centres is not likely to work if there is little perceived need to use them, or, more importantly, a lack of interest in developing the skills required to use them.

Further, the demographic profile of those who do not have access to (or interest in) these technologies – predominantly female, poorly educated and in lower social classes (C2/D/E) – matches those who are already unlikely to participate politically, according to Parry *et al.* (1992). They suggest that women, the working classes (as they put it) and those with few if any educational qualifications are more likely to limit their political activity to occasional voting or complete inactivity. Conversely, the groups most likely to participate in political activity are the wealthy, male, well educated, and members of the 'salaried class' (1992: 232–34). These are, of course, the characteristics shared by those most likely to own and use new communications technologies like the internet. So any argument that technology might aid democratic participation must acknowledge the likelihood that, first and foremost, it is assisting those who already participate. Consideration of the democratizing potential of ICTs must therefore look beyond the technology and examine access to the democratic process itself.

Democracy without technology

It is easy to understand why new technologies are held up as solutions to the 'problem' of political apathy or alienation. Voting in elections is declining in Europe and the USA, and membership of political parties continues to fall. Proposed remedies include citizens' juries (Delap, 1998; McLaverty, 1998), citizenship lessons in schools (Cassidy, 1999) and, of course, new technology. The reasoning for the inclusion of technology ranges from the near-deterministic (for example, Toffler, 1980; Rheingold, 1994; Poster, 1997; Mulgan, 1997), in which case the mere existence of ICTs is sufficient remedy (and the only problem then is ensuring equitable access), to the more realistic, where the market is recognized as an inadequate mechanism for information provision, and so requires regulation by government (Percy-Smith, 1996; Wheeler, 1998). To a greater or lesser degree, however, all these arguments suggest that the principal fault with the democratic process, an imbalance of power between electors and political and corporate institutions, can be rectified by access to better information and argument. Media and communications research has very successfully demonstrated the ways in which political information and debate is manipulated in the interests of the powerful. Yet the problem with democracy is not, and has never been, a deficiency in the quality or quantity of information or debate.

The 'knowledge is power' equation is one that fits neatly into a view of a society in which information is king. The UK Chancellor of the Exchequer has written that 'the defining characteristic of economy is less an individual's ability to gain access to capital and far more his or her ability to gain access to knowledge' (Brown, 1996). However, as Hirschkop puts it (1998: 214) 'those who rule do not rule because they know more'. The problem is a lack of political accountability. If electors have little control over decision-making once they have voted their politicians into government, they are unlikely to get very excited about the formal political process. Without some means of ensuring that collective decisions will result in political action, there is no reason to imagine that electors are any more likely to participate in political debate on computer networks than they are currently to vote or write to their representatives – fewer than one in ten UK electors writes to his or her MP (Parry *et al.*, 1992: 423), and there is, of course, far greater access to the 'technology' of letter writing (although it should be remembered that illiteracy remains significant, though under-discussed, in countries like the United Kingdom where one in five are deemed to have poor levels of literacy (Office of National Statistics, 1997; Bynner, 1997).

There is little question that corporations have more power and influence over governments than individual electors. That is the reason for the formation and continued existence of trades unions and pressure groups, and suggests that, far from there existing a new form of society with a corresponding need for a new form of democracy, the need for political struggle in all its forms continues. Strikes, demonstrations, lobbies of parliament and so on have not disappeared; such methods continue to replace dictatorships with more democratic societies (Indonesia being the most recent example at the time of writing). In these processes, communications technologies play an important role in organization and information dissemination, but of course the same technologies are used by both sides. How the quest for political power proceeds is dependent on a far greater number of forces than the use of the latest technologies.

So the arguments that the internet is an inherently democratic technology or, more cautiously, that it can be used in ways that enhance democracy, are flawed, and amount to little more than a technical fix to an old political problem. It is tempting to believe in the rhetoric, and there are none more willing to repeat it than governments seeking legitimacy and hoping to remain in office. Buoyed up by the discourse of a new information society, the techno-democracy offers a comfortable route to a more peaceful, more equitable future. But to believe in this means accepting that words and ideas alone are sufficient to bring about fundamental change. If that were the case, then certainly the internet (and a few broadcasting technologies) would be all that were needed. But intellectual activity alone does not redress democratic imbalances. The Carnival Against Capitalism, like so many examples before it, showed that when people take to the streets the real sources of power (the state, judiciary and big business in this case) are challenged.

The internet remains a valuable resource in attempts to achieve greater democracy, as are the telephone, fax machine, video camera and the printing press, and any organization is likely to benefit from using it. It allows more rapid organization and communication, and it may permit limited deliberation. In so doing it could draw some people into political activity. But while the internet remains in the hands of the relatively privileged minority who are already more inclined to participate, it is doubtful that it will induce a substantial number of new people. To create a more democratic society, political activity must amount to more than exchange of ideas and information and, beyond better organizing the already active, the internet's role in nurturing a more democratic, participatory society is likely to remain a minor one.

Notes

1. 'Chat' technology, which involves a number of people simultaneously connecting to the same server and engaging in real-time dialogue, has been discussed more for its novelty and role playing than for any democratic potential. It certainly offers no more, and probably less, scope for political participation than newsgroups, and so does not merit separate treatment in this discussion.
2. Figures from Independent Television Commission data.

USEFUL WEBSITES

Alliance for Progressive Communications: **www.apc.org**
Umbrella organization for promotion of electronic networking for environmental, human rights, development and peace groups.

Campaign for Freedom of Information: **www.cfoi.org.uk**
Campaigns against unnecessary state and corporate secrecy and for a Freedom of Information Act.

Campaign for Press and Broadcasting Freedom:
www.cpbf.demon.co.uk
Campaigns for media reform and to promote policies for a diverse, democratic and accountable media. It works principally with media trades unions.

GreenNet: **www.gn.apc.org**
UK-based founder member of Alliance for Progressive Communications (see above) which shares the same aims. GreenNet has over 300 group and individual members.

Labour Telematics Centre: **www.labourtel.org.uk**
Supports and encourages trades unions and labour movement organizations in gaining access to ICTs. It is also concerned with the impact of new ICTs on the labour process, conditions of employment and the nature of work itself.

UK Citizens Online Democracy: **www.democracy.org.uk**
Hosts a number of e-mail discussions ('forums') on various UK political issues, e.g. the Constitution, and Freedom of Information.

19 // Community Development in the Cybersociety of the Future

Howard Rheingold

The quality of community in tomorrow's wired world is an important concern. It is not, however, the first question we need to ask. The prefix 'cyber', from the Greek word for 'steersman', implies that cybersociety will be steered in some manner. The first question to ask is: Who will be doing the steering?

Decades before computers existed, George Orwell and Aldous Huxley wrote about future dystopias where society is commanded by an elite who use advanced communication tools to control the population. The malevolent dictator Big Brother and the paternalistic dictator Mustapha Mond used technologies of surveillance and persuasion to steer the societies of *1984* and *Brave New World*. E.M. Forster, also writing years before digital technology emerged, wrote a novella, *The Machine Stops*, that painted a future society steered by the machines themselves.

Today's world is a combination of all three visions, with a surprisingly democratic twist. The Orwellian portion is the invasion and commodification of privacy, aided and abetted by digital information gathering and surveillance tools. The Huxley portion is the disinfotainment machinery that sells experiences, beliefs, issues and candidates to a world that willingly pays for the illusion of information in the guise of entertainment. The Forster part is the globalized economy, where liquid electronic capital has become detached from humanly recognizable goods and services.

The global economy depends upon a rapidly self-innovating technological infrastructure. Superheated economic competition requires the biggest players to concentrate massive resources on technology development. For these reasons, the only thing we can know with any degree of certainty about tomorrow's world is that technologies will be more powerful than they are today. And communication technologies, because of their ability to influence human perceptions and beliefs as well as their power to command and control automatic machinery, will continue to grow more powerful and persuasive, if not more true, authentic and humane.

The democratic twist is that more people today have more to say about how their world is steered than at any other time in history. Structurally, the internet has inverted the few-to-many architecture of the broadcast age, in which a small number of people were able to influence and shape the perceptions and beliefs of entire nations. In the many-to-many environment of the net, every desktop is a printing press, a broadcasting station and place of assembly. Mass media will continue to exist and so will journalism, but these institutions will no longer monopolize attention and access to the attention of others.

It is not yet clear how this democratization of publishing power will translate into political change. The critical uncertainties today are whether the citizenry will learn to use the new tools to strengthen the public sphere and whether citizens are going to be any match for the concentrations of money, technology and power that are emerging in the internet era.

First, I want briefly to outline how I came to know and care about the kind of world we are building when we use the internet as a communication medium. Then I want to discuss two fundamental questions we must address in order to build humane and sustainable communities in the future. The first question refers to the public sphere – how will new media affect the free and open discourse that forms the bedrock of democracy? The second question is about the role of news media – what place does traditional journalism play in a world where the power to publish and communicate is radically diffused and disintermediated?

I am still hopeful that informed and committed people can influence the shape of tomorrow's cybersociety in a positive manner, although it has become increasingly clear that democratic outcomes won't emerge automatically. A humane and sustainable cybersociety will only come about if it is deliberately understood, discussed and planned now – by a larger proportion of the population and not just big business, media, or policy elites.

Intelligent and democratic leadership is desperately needed at this historical moment, while the situation is still somewhat fluid. Some 10 years from now the uncertainties will have resolved into one kind of power or another.

How I fell into cyberspace and what I found there

As a freelance writer, I spent over a decade in solitary confinement, labouring over a typewriter, before the prospect of word-processing lured me into the world of personal computers. When I bought a US$500, 1200-baud modem in 1983, I discovered a world of conversation online as well, through the rich ecology of the thousands of PC bulletin board systems (BBSs) that ran off single telephone lines in people's bedrooms. At the same time, I was researching the origins of personal computers and computer-mediated communications.

In 1985, I joined the electronic conferencing system, the WELL, and first started thinking about the social aspects of online discourse when the WELL's parenting conference formed an online support group for our friend Phil, whose son had been diagnosed with leukaemia. Over the years, Phil's friends contributed a stream of emotional support, and over US$30,000. Anyone who declares that the most important elements of community are impossible online needs to talk to Phil and his family, or the tens of thousands of people like them, for whom the net has been a lifeline.

In the 15 years since I joined the WELL, I've contributed to dozens of such fundraising and support activities. I've sat by the bedside of a dying, lonely woman, who would have died alone if it had not been for people she had previ-

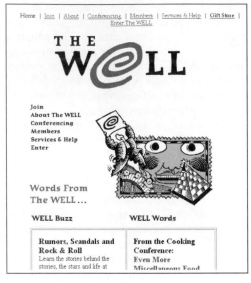

Home | Join | About | Conferencing | Members | Services & Help | Gift Store |
Enter The WELL

THE
W@LL

Join
About The WELL
Conferencing
Members
Services & Help
Enter

Words From
The WELL...

WELL Buzz   WELL Words

Rumors, Scandals and   From the Cooking
Rock & Roll   Conference:
Learn the stories behind the Even More
stories, the stars and life at Miscellaneous Food

19.1 The WELL today.

ously known only as words on a screen. I've danced at four weddings of people who met online. I've attended four funerals and spoken at two of them. In 1988, concerned about the mass-media image of computer BBSs as cults for antisocial adolescent males with bad complexions, I wrote an article for *Whole Earth Review* about 'virtual communities'. I knew from direct experience that people can reach through those computer screens and touch each others' lives.

I had not travelled a great deal before I started the research for my book on the subject, but virtual communities, and the people I've met through them, have led me around the world a dozen times and more. I shared lunch with 60 young Web designers in Stockholm, who had exchanged hundreds of messages with one another each day via an electronic mailing list, but who had not met in person and en masse until that luncheon. I spent the night with a Buddhist monk in Shigaraki, Japan, who ran a computer community for people in the Lake Biwa region. People I had previously only known online let me stay in their homes when I visited Sydney and Adelaide, Tokyo and Amsterdam, Paris and Vancouver. I've visited chatters, BBSers, MUDers, mailing listers, in Australia, England, Finland, France, Germany, Holland, Japan, Sweden and Switzerland. I received so much e-mail from people who wanted to talk about virtual communities that I started a virtual community for those discussions.

A few years ago, I crossed the line from participant observer into a more active role: I became a compulsive instigator of virtual communities. I created a Usenet newsgroup, sci.virtual-worlds, that is still used by VR researchers. Then came The River, a virtual community that is a California Cooperative Corporation, in which participants each have the opportunity to buy one share of ownership and have one vote in the governance of the operation. In 1994 I was the executive editor of *HotWired*, the first commercial webzine. We used a primitive Web-based conferencing system, one of the first. In 1996, I founded *Electric Minds*, a webzine with an integrated webconferencing and chat system.

In 1997, I sold *Electric Minds* and created *Brainstorms*, a private virtual community. I also started one for alumni of my college, one for a service organization fighting blindness in Asia, and am creating a national network of regional virtual communities that are linked to the geographic communities of cable-modem users.

It would be wrong to conclude that I am an uncritical enthusiast of virtual communities. Like all technologies, this medium has its shadow side, and there are ways to abuse it. Right now, the most publicized form of abuse is the fashionable illusion that there are fortunes to be made in virtual community building.

Lately, vague talk of 'community' has become fashionable among internet entrepreneurs and financiers. I am sceptical, based on my own experiences growing virtual communities, that more than a few will make real money in the virtual community business. It's too difficult to aggregate millions of people, and keep them aggregated, and too easy for people to roll their own online communities.

John Hagel and Arthur Armstrong, two McKinsey consultants, published a book in 1997 called *Net.Gain* which purports to show that hundreds of millions of dollars are to be made in aggregating virtual communities. Although I don't doubt that a dozen of the largest players will make advertising and e-commerce profits from the activities of people using virtual communities, I don't believe that online community is going to succeed as a profit-making industry for very many entrepreneurs.

The greatest value of virtual community remains in its self-organizational aspects. Any group of Alzheimer's care-givers, breast cancer patients, parents of learning-disabled children, scholars, horse breeders – any affinity group that has a need or desire to communicate – can start an e-mail discussion group, a chatroom, or a Web forum. Using internet social tools is a literacy, not a commodity. The greatest products of the printing press had little to do with paper and ink, but more to do with the powers of a literate population. The greatest impact of virtual communities will not come from advertising revenues for online chatrooms, but from the new forms of culture that will emerge from virtual communities.

For commercial organizations that are truly committed to broadening their communications with their customers, subscribers, suppliers, value-added retailers, users or others that constitute the company's 'community', well-designed message boards and chatrooms can prove valuable. But they will only work in this respect if they are regarded as a cost of doing business, an aspect of marketing, support and/or customer relations, and not as a profit centre. If you squeeze your community to make a profit at the same time as you are trying to coax it into taking its first breath, you will simply kill your enterprise. Unlike other aspects of the internet it takes months, even years, to grow valuable and sustainable virtual communities.

Over the years, I've learned that virtual communities are not the norm, but the exception; that they don't grow automatically but must be nurtured. Any groups that are thinking about adding chatrooms or message boards to their Web pages, expecting community to blossom without much forethought, design, or commitment of ongoing resources, is headed for failure.

In order to succeed, a virtual community has to have an affinity – the answer to the question: What would draw these people together? It has to present a user interface that doesn't baffle the newcomer, but gives a range of options to the experienced user. Building a social space online does not guarantee that people will inhabit it. It has to have a social infrastructure, including simple written agreements to a social contract governing online behaviour and sanctions for transgression. It needs skilled human facilitation. And

19.2 A painting by Howard Rheingold, possibly influenced by years of virtual community living. Or not. See www.rheingold.com for more.

there must be some plan for bringing a continuing stream of newcomers into the community.

The social side of the net has its shadow side, and it isn't hard to find. I've seen that the relative anonymity of the medium, where nobody can see your face or hear your voice, has a disinhibiting function that cuts both ways – people who might not ordinarily be heard in oral discourse can contribute meaningfully, and people who might not ordinarily be rude to one's face can become frighteningly abusive online. As the net has grown, the original norms of netiquette and collaborative, co-operative, maintenance of an information commons that enriches everyone have been assaulted by waves of clueless newbies and sociopaths, spammers, charlatans and loudmouths. Maintaining civility in the midst of the very conflicts we must solve together as citizens isn't easy.

The net is the world's greatest source of information, misinformation and disinformation, community and character assassination, and you have very little but your own wits to help you sort out the valid from the bogus.

There is no single formula for success in virtual community building, but there are several clear pitfalls, any one of which can cause the effort to fail. In order for a virtual community to succeed, the software must have a usable human interface, something which was not available until relatively recently. Unfortunately, many virtual community organizers don't know better, or are sold on something by their investors, and use older paradigms for online communication, which drives away those who have something to communicate but are not compelled to spend their time fiddling with technology. Another necessity for success is a clearly stated policy regarding online behaviour that all participants must agree to. Having such a policy won't guarantee success, but not having such a policy probably guarantees failure.

Give people sensible rules and most of them will be very happy with that. Some communities will have very loose rules, some will be far more formal and controlled; the most important point of the exercise is that every participant agrees to a clear written statement of the rules before joining. People sometimes want to make up their own rules. If a subgroup wants a community with different rules, then it should formulate and agree upon those roles and roll its own listserv, webconference, or IRC channel. A warning: 'policy thrashing' over meta-issues such as how to elect the people who make the rules can swallow up other forms of discourse. Face-to-face meetings are still far superior to online discussion for resolving conflicts and coming to agreement where consensus is not clear.

Most importantly, people who have had experience in dealing with online discourse need to participate, moderate and host. Facilitating convivial and useful online discourse is a skill, and one that is best learned through direct experience. Because behaviour online tends to degenerate in the absence of conversational cues such as tone of voice, facial expression, or body language, it is necessary for experienced users to model the behaviour that the medium requires in order to maintain civility. Without a cadre of experienced interlocutors to help point out the pitfalls and the preferred paths, online populations are doomed to fall into the same cycles of flame, thrash, mindless chatter and eventual dissolution.

The social and informational treasures of cyberspace are what drew me into the world of virtual communities, but when I began to study the significance of these new media on our culture, I realized that the most important questions had to do with the political implications of global 'many-to-many' media. Who would gain wealth and power? Who would lose?

The internet and the public sphere

The public sphere is where people, through their communications, become citizens. The printing press did not cause democracy, but it made a literate population possible, and literate populations, who are free to communicate among one another, came up with the idea that they could govern themselves. Radio and television each had effects on the public sphere. The internet will have an effect. But we won't know what it is for a few more years.

Will the internet strengthen civic life, community and democracy, or will it weaken them? Failure to make the importance of this question clear to the public has been a shameful episode in the history of journalism. As one of the people who gets called for quotes on a daily basis, I can tell you that I've been talking about this issue for years, but all that ends up on the air or in print is something about porn or hackers or bomb recipes on the internet. How do we introduce this truly important matter to popular discourse?

'The public sphere' is the what German political philosopher Jurgen Habermas called that part of public life where ordinary people exchange information and opinions regarding potholes on Main Street and international politics. Habermas focused on the media – pamphlets, debates in coffee houses and tea houses, committees of correspondence – that incubated democratic revolutions in the eighteenth century. Habermas (1991: 398) wrote:

> By 'public sphere', we mean first of all a domain of our social life in which such a thing as public opinion can be formed. Access to the public sphere is open in principle to all citizens. A portion of the public sphere is constituted in every conversation in which private persons come together to form a public. They are then acting neither as business or professional people conducting their private affairs, nor as legal consociates subject to the legal regulations of a state bureaucracy and obligated to obedience. Citizens act as a public when they deal with matters of general interest without being subject to coercion; thus with the guarantee that they may assemble and unite freely, and express and publicize their opinions freely.

Because the public sphere depends on free communication and discussion of ideas, clearly this vital market-place for political ideas can be powerfully influenced by changes in communications technology. Again, according to Habermas:

> When the public is large, this kind of communication requires certain means of dissemination and influence; today, newspapers and periodicals, radio and television are the media of the public sphere. ... The term 'public opinion' refers to the functions of criticism and control or organized state authority that the public exercises informally, as well as formally during periodic elections.

The sophisticated and wholesale manufacture of public opinion, and the domination of popular media by electronic spectacles, had damaged the public sphere just as industrial pollution has damaged the biosphere. I believe the foundations of democracy have been eroded, for the reasons Neil Postman cited in *Amusing Ourselves to Death* (1987): the immense power of television as a broadcaster of emotion-laden images, combined with the ownership of more and more news media by fewer and fewer global entertainment conglomerates, has reduced much public discourse, including discussions of vital issues, to soundbites and images.

Opinion-shaping techniques originated in the print era, but truly grew into their present degree of power during the era of broadcast media. Now that the internet has turned every desktop computer into a potential global printing press, multimedia broadcasting station and place of assembly – what will change? Will citizen communications via the internet be commodified, co-opted or shaped? Have citizen forums been neutralized already, or were they never a threat to centralized control of public opinion? Are many-to-many media less easily manipulable than mass media, or does the manipulation simply come in a different form? Which way can the internet go? When the present turbulence clears, who will have more power because of the internet? Is there a concrete way of preserving a universally accessible public area in a rapidly privatizing internet?

There is a role for the skills learned in the 'traditional' mass media here. If ever there was a time for good journalists and civic-minded editors and producers to help us ask these questions, it's now.

The role of journalism in cybersociety

I believe that the first role for journalists and news organizations today is to try to maintain some kind of gold standard for truth-seeking in an environment where everyone is an eyewitness, Matt Drudge (www.drudgereport.com) can send the cream of American journalists to root in the mud like hogs, talk radio is a haven for protected but socially corrosive hate-speech, and tabloid television is a big money-maker.

The news organization of the future might not need printing presses or broadcasting stations, but I can guarantee that the more varied and untrustworthy the information on the internet becomes, the more valuable will be a network of educated and experienced professionals, who know how to cultivate and qualify sources, to second- and third-source stories, to verify and corroborate reports, to simplify complexities without dumbing them down, to find the human story without peddling human suffering.

The other important role news organizations ought to play in the age of many-to-many media is the role of active host and participant in community-building. Establishing a dialogue with readers and viewers that extends beyond 'letters to the editor' is a start. A few traditional news organizations, like the *San Francisco Examiner*, with its *SF Gate* (www.sfgate.com), have been experimenting for years, with some modest success, in the area of online communities for subscribers. There is a more pointedly specific movement afoot, however: the movement for 'civic journalism'. I believe that the practices and beliefs underlying civic journalism flow naturally from the concerns about the public sphere that I have outlined.

The Pew Center for Civic Journalism defines Civic Journalism this way:

> Civic journalism is both a philosophy and a set of values supported by some evolving techniques to reflect both of those in your journalism. At its heart is a belief that journalism has an obligation to public life – an obligation that goes beyond just telling the news or unloading lots of facts. The way we do our journalism affects the way public life goes. Journalism can help empower a community or it can help disable it.

Fortunately, a number of pioneers have already performed concrete experiments, so those organizations today that are interested in civic journalism can look to the case histories cited on the Pew Center website and other online sources. One of many such resources is a collection of case histories. In the introduction to *Adventures in Civic Journalism*, Jan Schaffer, Executive Director of the Pew Center wrote:

What these projects have in common is that they did not stop at simply unloading a lot of information on their readers and considering the job done. That was only the start. They moved on to build some roles for their intended audience as active participants in solving the problem. They gave readers entry points for having a voice and for taking responsibility – and the readers came aboard and shouldered some stake in the outcome.

In Portland, Maine, it meant giving ordinary citizens direct access to question candidates in a presidential election year, only to see that blossom into a desire by those citizens to stick together and to do more.

In Binghamton, New York, it meant inviting teams of citizens to figure out ways to resuscitate a severely depressed local economy.

In Springfield, Missouri, civic journalism took to the streets to chronicle a rising tide of juvenile crime and found the community rallying at a 'Good Community Fair'.

In St Paul, Minnesota, the journalists built on their coverage of safety and intergenerational issues to help citizens grapple with the issues of poverty in the context of welfare reform.

And in Peoria, Illinois, a new generation of leaders rose from the community after journalists examined the societal changes that led to a leadership decline.

Taken together, the experiences shared in these case studies amount to a blueprint for journalists interested in energizing their coverage and bringing about change in their community.

Forgive the America-centric examples. I mean only to point towards some concrete experiments. I believe that well-thought-out and well-run virtual communities can play an important role, along with civic-minded journalism, and face-to-face community-building, in the creation of a cybersociety we would be proud to hand on to our children. I want to close with a suggestion. You can amplify your efforts to build authentic community and online forums that serve a commercial, educational, or civic purpose by communicating regularly with one another about best practices and common obstacles. Is it too radical to propose that a group of community-builders ought to consider building their own community, online and face to face?

Note

This is a revised version of a talk given at the BBC Online Communities Conference, held in London in June 1999. Howard Rheingold and David Gauntlett thank BBC Online for granting permission for the text to be used here.

USEFUL WEBSITES

Howard Rheingold: **www.rheingold.com**
The books *Tools for Thought* and *The Virtual Community* are both available here in full-text, hyperlinked versions, alongside other articles and resources on virtual communities.

Habermas links: **www.helsinki.fi/~amkauppi/hablinks.html**
An annotated, up-to-date set of links, leading to useful articles about Habermas and the public sphere.

Democracies Online: **www.e-democracy.org/do**
Promoting online civic participation and democracy efforts around the world through information exchange, experience sharing, outreach and education.

Philosophy and Civil Society – Inventing Postmodern Civic Culture: **www.civsoc.com**
Site by Tom Bridges devoted to the philosophical examination of civil society and civic culture, and 'the contemporary crisis of liberal democratic civic culture in the postmodern period'.

Pew Center for Civic Journalism: **www.pewcenter.org**
The Pew Center is an incubator for civic journalism experiments that enable news organizations to create and refine better ways of reporting the news to re-engage people in public life. See its 'Case Histories in Civic Journalism' at www.pewcenter.org/doingcj/pubs/stop.

20

The Indian Diaspora in the USA and Around the Web

Madhavi Mallapragada

Editor's note

This chapter concerns internet use by the Indian diaspora in the USA, whereas the subsequent chapter is about Cherokee Indians and the net. Therefore, as you will appreciate, the Indians referred to in the chapter below are members of families who have come from India to the USA since the start of the twentieth century, whereas the 'Indians' discussed in the next chapter are Native Americans – not from India at all.

In this chapter I examine the role and place of internet technology, especially the World Wide Web, in the lives of the Indian diaspora in the United States of America. While the task of listing and discussing the range and variety of issues that emerge and circulate in these 'digital diasporas' is outside the scope of this chapter, the next few pages will offer the reader a sense of how this technology is being used by a populace that is faced with the task of negotiating everyday life in the immigrant space. To that end, I will first offer a brief overview of the Indian diaspora in the United States; second, give a sense of the range and nature of information and discussion that is integral to the interlinked 'diasporic' websites; and third, offer a summary of the interrelationship between this technology and the experience of the Indian diaspora in the USA. Lastly, I will argue that given the nature of the technology and its place in the everyday practices of the Indian diaspora, the World Wide Web is changing the way diasporic or immigrant lives are experienced. In other words, the case study of the Indian diaspora in the USA is a fascinating example of the interface between technology and culture. I argue that the internet, especially the Web, is being utilized by the Indian diaspora (and arguably, by a host of other 'marginal' cultures) to meet important social and cultural needs. Given the overwhelming contribution of Indian immigrants to the hi-tech industry based primarily in Silicon Valley, it is no surprise that the internet is the medium used for forging business ties and networking among professionals. While this is an important aspect of the immigrant culture, I choose to focus on the 'cultural work' that is at 'play' in the dissemination of ideas and information on the Web.

An overview of the Indian diaspora in the USA

The first Indian immigration wave to the USA is believed to have taken place between 1907–14; however it is only since 1965, when the Immigration and Nationality Act was amended to emphasize the family unification system, that there has been a steady increase in the immigration of Indians to the USA (Mogelonsky, 1995). The present population estimate stands at around 1.3 million Indians (Levins, 1999). While in the late 1950s and 1960s the immigrants were primarily highly educated doctors and engineers, there have been significant changes since. In the 1980s and, more significantly, the 1990s, the character of the Indian diaspora has become very diverse along class, educational, income and social citizenry lines. The diaspora includes the first- and second-generation Indian-American, the H-I visa worker, the worker's spouse on a dependent visa status, visiting relatives of the immigrants, the visiting scholar, the tech expert who juggles a life in New York with a life in Mumbai, and the steady stream of students. This shift in the character of immigrant patterns to the USA can be attributed to a number of reasons, primarily the demands of the global economy, the explosion of the computer software industry, the ever-increasing demand for techno-savvy professionals, the global circulation of ideas and cultural products and, last but not least, the rapid advances in, and proliferation of, communication technologies (see Appadurai, 1996; Cohen, 1996).

Digital diasporas: community and culture on the Web

The term 'diaspora', initially used to refer to the migration of the Jewish people, evokes the notion of loss of homeland, dispersal and the rebuilding of lives in 'alien' cultures. Given the contemporary context, where the migration of people is characterized by numerous impulses, the term begs for theoretical revision. Nevertheless, the play of nostalgia and memory in *experiencing* home, and *recreating* home in the host culture, is broadly symptomatic of diasporic cultures (see Naficy, 1993). The Indian diaspora is no exception, tellingly evidenced in the elaborate system of social, cultural, religious and professional organizations, all of which coalesce around ideas of commonality of origins and present lives, shared culture and heritage, and common goals and desires. India is an extremely diverse society and, naturally, this diversity is reproduced in the diaspora. However, while commonality and a corresponding difference from 'others' can hence be forged along multiple axes – such as national, regional, religious, caste, gender, occupational and other identities – there is a constant struggle given the fact that most of us inhabit many identities.

For instance, I as an Indian, Telugu-speaking Hindu female graduate student, have something in common with people who are Indian but not Telugu speaking, non-Indian but Telugu-speaking, Hindu but not female, female but not graduate student and so on. The point here is that it is the same struggle over identities, forging commonalities and maintaining difference, preserving home and reinventing it to suit one's altered lives that is reproduced on the Web (see Jones, 1995b; Mitra, 1997; Morley and Robins, 1995). One needs to remember that the Web does not exist in an isolated space. It exists in a social world where Indian restaurants, theatres showing Indian films, cultural and other organizations for Indian-Americans, ethnic media such as newspapers, satellite channels from India, television programmes made in the USA for the Indian community, and the like, share the space with their 'American' counterparts. (Usage of 'Indian' and 'American' is oversimplified here, to make a broader point.)

One can broadly categorize the Web pages and sites pertaining to the Indian diaspora into the personal Web page and the commercial or institutional site. Personal Web pages are the homepages of individual users of the Web (see Cheung in this volume). In a number of instances, the use of the personal home page is restricted to being an online résumé, wherein one finds little else except educational and work-related information. It can be assumed that the primary audience for such a page is meant to be potential recruiting organizations. On the other hand there are those that operate as multi-mediated expressions of the self. The *DesiWeb* site (www.ccnet.com/~venkatr/desiweb.html), maintained by Venkat Pullela, is a collection of links to Indian homepages. 'Desi' in Hindi refers to someone who belongs to 'desh' (country), and is used in the diaspora to refer to Indians. An examination of the pages linked to from this site reveals that the personal homepage is a mix of personal details such as interests, family albums, educational background, friends and so on, plus lists of links or sites of interest. The latter can be interesting in that they often reveal the specific identities that the person in question privileges. For instance, a Telugu-speaking person might add links to a map of Andhra Pradesh whose natives speak the Telugu language, links to the film industry occasionally referred to as 'Tollywood', or links to the Telugu Association of North America, which is a cultural organization that aims '. . . to preserve and propagate the Telugu cultural heritage and maintain the identity of people of Telugu origin and to provide a forum for Telugu literary, cultural, educational, social, and charitable interactions among its members' (www.tana.org).

These links pages show how 'specific' one's construction of the idea of the community can be, the community that one belongs to and addresses. The inclusion of personal memorabilia in conjunction with selected sites of interest is interesting in that, first, a medium that allows for anonymity to a certain degree, is deliberately used to construct and circulate personal histories and memories; second, it offers an avenue for the immigrant to 'imagine' community. In my usage of 'imagined community', I invoke the definition by Benedict Anderson, who states that the idea of the nation is imagined around a set of shared practices and goals. The term 'imagined' is used 'because the members of even the smallest nation will never know most of their fellow-members, meet them, or even hear of them, yet in the minds of each lives the image of their communion' (Anderson, 1991: 6). And this process of re-inventing the community in the digital diaspora is symptomatic of the need to forge cultural and social alliances that create a sense of identity; a point made by Howard Rheingold (1993) who states that 'virtual communities . . . are in part a response to the hunger for community that has followed the disintegration of traditional communities around the world'.

As for the commercial or institutional sites that are part of the virtual Indian diaspora, one could include the numerous sites that are online versions of print and other media, both from India and the USA; sites that give restricted access to their product be it a magazine or a newspaper; sites that could be categorized as institutional, including commercial and not-for-profit organizations as well as government institutions; and, among others, sites that serve as information

networks in that they contain links to numerous websites, forums, chatrooms, newsgroups, search engines etc. For instance, the website for the *IndiaWorld* network (www.indiaworld.co.in), which is arguably India's largest internet family, contains sections such as finance, astrology, business, news, cricket, investing, cooking, the internet in India, Asian news, travelogue and 'matrimonials'. The page is also significant for its use of advertising space. Most prominent in the advertising segment are those for phone cards that offer competitive prices for calls made from the USA to India, for sending cards and gifts to family and friends in India,

20.1 The *IndiaWorld* website: 'India's largest internet family'.

and for Web hosting, internet banking and shopping online.

It is significant that though the network is maintained by a media group based in India, its advertising is also geared to Indians abroad and in the case of the phone card advertisements only to Indians in the USA. Correspondingly, the website for *Indians Abroad Online: Empowering the Community* (www.iaol.com), is geared specifically to the Indian community in the USA with the vision of using technology to help build a stronger community. In the section entitled 'community', one can access the homepages of the various Indo-American communities that function within the USA, for example the American Association of Physicians of Indian Origin (AAPI), or the Association for India's Development (AID), or Rajasthali: Asian Indians from Rajasthan. In the latter, the identities that are enmeshed in the title are that of a regional origin in India (Rajasthan) and that of an ethnic minority in the USA (Asian-Indian). However, what is interesting in the 'production' of identity in a diasporic space is the 'reinventing' of one's national identity (from India) as an ethnic minority identity (Asian-Indian), totally erasing the fact that the culture, cuisine and customs of a person from the state of Rajasthan are very different from that of the state of Kerala. In other words, 'ethnic selves' are very different from identities *within* India (see Radhakrishnan, 1994).

While the past operates to create a sense of community, the present also allows for the regrouping of people around some commonality, as in the case, for example, of the website www.bayareaindian.com, whose primary audience is the Indian community that lives in the San Francisco Bay Area. The website claims to bring 'Indians closer one click at a time'. The website in many ways operates as a bulletin board for the community, by providing information about the week's movie releases, the best restaurants in the area and the like. While this site is an instance of Indians attempting to draw very specific notions of community that involve sharing the same physical space and time, the way traditional communities were to a great extent imagined, the example of www.saivasiddhanta.com is quite the opposite. Maintained by the monks of the Saiva Siddhanta Theological Seminary at Kauai's Hindu Monastery on the island of Kauai in the Hawaiian islands, the website is an online Hindu centre and

20.2 The Saiva Siddhanta Hinduism resources.

contains information about Hindu texts, the basics of the philosophy and a link to Hindu resources online at www.hindu.org. Among the online resources are listings of the various temples in and outside India. An interesting feature of this segment is the manner in which the online version attempts to recreate the experience of actually visiting a temple. For instance, a click on www.vaishnodevi.com/darshan.htm (not the official site) allows one to access a close-up image of one of the inner precincts of one of the most popular shrines in North India. To complete the experience, one can chant the online hymns and listen to the bhajans in streaming RealAudio format.

Another significant part of Indian diasporic internet communication is the interaction and debate generated in the discussion forums and chatrooms. While a number of chatrooms involve lighthearted conversations with fellow members, often bordering on the flirtatious, the discussion forums tend to be moderated arenas for the more heated struggle over cultural and political agendas. Not only is the content of such a discussion forum a rich site for the examination of the cultural politics of its members, but the very categories that make up the forum are illuminating. For instance, if one were to access the discussion forum page of the website www.indolink.com, one would see the first three forums, entitled India, USA and Canada. Considering the context, we know that they must allude to Indian communities based in these countries, although splitting up the discussions in this way is not unproblematic. The other categories include Consumer Affairs, Immigration, Women's Corner (!), Cricket, Arts and Culture, Youth Chat, Parenting, Bollywood, Tamil Cinema, Silicon Valley and Mumbai. The site is primarily geared towards addressing the needs of the Indians in the USA. Despite its claim to link Indians worldwide, the site clearly creates its own system of inclusions and exclusions, evidenced in the special category for Indians in Silicon Valley, or the inclusion of Tamil Cinema to the exclusion of all other regional cinema in India.

This system of inclusion and exclusion is also evident in the debates and conversations that occur on the forums. For example, in the Parenting Forum, a person enquired about means to make one's children understand Indian culture in interesting ways (the initial discussion revolved around Hindi film and Indian culture). In response, one discussion member suggested, 'Actually, as a matter of fact there are a number of ways to make them understand our Indian culture. You can take them to a Hindu temple . . .' (www.indolink.com/Forum/Parents, 22 November 1998). This is an instance of the manner in which, all too often, discussions about Indian culture tend to conflate Hinduism with Indian culture to the exclusion of everything else, and weave notions of 'authentic' and 'true' identity around it. Another instance is an advertisement on the main page of www.indolink.com for a free video on 'Indian heritage' where two images constantly alternate as cues for Indian-ness, those of the Hindu Gods Krishna and Ganesha. What is relevant here is the subtle system of inclusion (the Hindu diaspora) and exclusion (the non-Hindu diaspora) that defines the community. And given the fact that the Indian diaspora is largely a Hindu diaspora, it points to the underpinnings of power in the circulation of culture (see Mukta, 1995).

Finally, a feature of the Web that is a very dynamic part of the process of creating 'community' is made up of the matrimonial sections that appear on several websites. A survey of the matrimonial databases of a few sites suggests that the Web has grown to be not just a popular but also a socially legitimate venue for the search for eligible life partners. One need only type in some keywords and the electronic matchmaker delivers a partner based on specifications such as age, caste, regional and linguistic affiliation, and in some instances even height! The matrimonials are a telling instance of the ways in which cybertechnology is being utilized to retain traditional notions of community and in-group membership.

'Indians abroad online': negotiating identities in diaspora

In this section, I summarize some of the significant issues that emerge in the context of the Indian diaspora and the Web. The first concerns the technology and the nature of the technology. Not only is the internet economy booming, but Indians are also especially invested in it, in particular as internet entrepreneurs. I argue that the technology of the internet is being utilized to meet the cultural needs of the immigrant Indian. The second issue concerns the nature of the diasporic experience that involves the constant tension between maintaining a very distinct 'immigrant' identity and acculturating oneself to the host culture. This tension is evident in the make-up of the Web pages and links, and in the discussions between the members of a given forum. Especially relevant in this context are the debates surrounding 'culture', 'tradition' and identity. There are many instances when a more recent immigrant (also referred to, not entirely flatteringly, as an FOB – 'fresh off the boat') claims greater access to the 'authentic' experience of things Indian, be that culture or religion, in the process denying the second-generation Indian-American's experience or reinvention of the Indian self in the American context as authentic. (The latter are sometimes also called ABCD, or American Born Confused Desi.)

The significance of debates of this nature is not in their nuanced understandings of how culture operates, but rather in the fact that 'culture' is the site of constant struggle (see Hall, 1980). It also reflects the point that identities are constantly in process and need to be constantly 'imagined'. The Web allows for the continual 'imagining' of identity in very immediate and quotidian ways, through: for instance, reading the latest headlines from India's major newspapers, debating the political scene in India, discussing Indo-American relations on immigration and visas, responding to a posting on a recent music concert in Chicago, sharing a recipe for a particular dish, gushing over the latest Bollywood film, or berating the histrionics of a particular actor. It is these shared practices that enable the diaspora to create and critique its idea of community.

While I do not wish to suggest that the Web has transformed the life of every Indian immigrant in the USA, it is reasonable to conclude that cybercommunication is reframing the Indian immigrants' experience of migration, relations with home and the rest of the diaspora around the globe.

Conclusion

In this chapter I have argued that the World Wide Web has emerged as one of the most significant cultural phenomena of recent times. In the context of the

Indian diaspora in the United States, I contend that it enables the continuous production of a cultural identity that is indicative of their complex lives as immigrants. The Web offers the immigrant populace a space where, unlike in a more traditional medium, such as mainstream television, the immigrant can feel at home.

USEFUL WEBSITES

123India: **India's premier portal: www.123india.com**
One of the most extensive India-related information servers, the site contains links to news, business, entertainment, media, government, arts and culture, and more.

IndiaWorld: **India's largest internet family: www.indiaworld.co.in**
An India-related network of websites, this contains links to leading newspapers across the Web, world cricket, investing, Indian history, Indian cuisine and the internet in India as well as online shopping and gift houses.

Indolink: **Linking Indians Worldwide!: www.indolink.com**
A US-centric site that contains sections on living, entertainment, business, news, sports, family, Indian communities in Sweden and Canada, immigration and embassy-related offices, and a very popular discussion forum.

Internet India: **www.internetindia.com**
This site claims to be an 'online expression and integration of India and Indians'. Contains sections on business, culture, travel and health, as well as features on Indian art and music and an exchange board for discussing India-related business opportunities.

Rediff On The Net: **www.rediff.com/rediffus.htm**
A US-centric site that contains sections on India-related news and entertainment, Indo-US-related news and cultural calendar, business, shopping, technology news and various chat forums.

Indians Abroad On-Line: Empowering The Community:
www.iaol.com
This site contains a directory that is arguably the largest Indian database on the Web; besides that it features sections on news divided into categories such as India regional and national, Indians abroad, India's neighbours, international news, chat forums and matrimonials, plus community links such as information on desi parties in the USA, Indian organizations, and sections for women and second-generation Indian immigrants.

21

The Cherokee Indians and the Internet

Ellen L. Arnold and Darcy C. Plymire

Current use of the internet by the Cherokee Indians reflects many aspects of the historical situation of the Cherokees since the early 1800s. The Cherokee people, who called themselves *Ani`-Yun`wiya*, or the 'Principal People', originally occupied approximately 135,000 square miles in parts of what are now eight south-eastern states. By the early 1800s, their territory had been drastically reduced through treaties and other actions by the US Government. One of the so-called Five Civilized Tribes of the Southeast, the Cherokees were quick to adopt many of the ways of the Europeans. In 1821, Sequoyah created the Cherokee Syllabary, which enabled their language to be written, and the Cherokee people quickly gained a greater degree of literacy than their Euro-American contemporaries. They drafted their own constitution, published the first Indian newspaper (the *Cherokee Phoenix*), and established the town of New Echota in Georgia, which served as both a seat of government and an economic centre for a thriving independent nation.

Under pressure from Euro-American settlers seeking gold and land, the US Congress made plans to remove the Cherokee people from their land. Progressive Cherokees, proponents of Americanization, fought in the American courts to force the US Government to honour its treaties with the Cherokee Nation, arguing its sovereign status. Many traditionals opposed assimilation into American society, yet the Cherokee Memorials – eloquent documents arguing against removal – demonstrated that even the progressive leaders who drafted them wished to preserve a distinct cultural identity as well as their newly acquired status as 'civilized'. When the Cherokees lost their battle in the courts, 16,000 of them were forced by the US Army to relocate 1000 miles to the west to Indian Territory. On this infamous Trail of Tears, called *Nunadautsun't* ('the trail where we cried') in the Cherokee language, more than 4000 Cherokees died.

Several hundred Cherokee people, mostly traditionals, remained in the east, hiding from settlers and soldiers. Eventually they re-established themselves and, in 1848, were formally recognized by the US Government as the Eastern Band of Cherokee Indians. The Eastern Band now numbers about 12,000 enrolled members, the majority of whom live on the Qualla Boundary in western North Carolina, a 56,000-acre-square portion of their original homeland which has its seat in the town of Cherokee. This land, purchased by Will Thomas, the adopted White son of a Cherokee leader, and presented to the Cherokees in the late nineteenth century, is now held in trust for the Cherokee people by the US Government and is administered as a reservation. Like other reservations, Qualla Boundary has a complex status as a semi-sovereign nation, exempt from the jurisdiction of state governments in most matters, yet subject to a great deal of control by federal government. The Western Band of Cherokees, known officially as the Cherokee Nation of Oklahoma, now occupies a jurisdictional service area of 4,480,000 square acres with a capital at Tahlequah, and has 170,000 enrolled members. Together Cherokees form one of the two largest tribal groups in the USA.

The question of assimilation remains relevant to Cherokee Indians today. The construction and use of the official websites of the Eastern Band (www. Cherokee-nc.com) and the Cherokee Nation of Oklahoma (www.Cherokee.org) reflect many elements of the historical relationship of the Cherokee Nation to the nation and government of the USA. The Oklahoma site primarily serves its community by providing links to human services, political news and organizations, and cultural and historical information. The Eastern Band site provides access to cultural and historical information as well, but because of its proximity to the popular Smoky Mountains National Park and the Blue Ridge Parkway, the Eastern Band has also been able to use its website to help build a thriving tourist economy. Observing the websites as outsiders, we suggest that they are skilfully designed aspects of increasingly successful political and economic efforts to use the dominant paradigm and its technologies to protect and preserve the unique cultural heritage and identity of the Cherokee people, and at the same time to expand the nation's control over its own affairs and its influence on American culture.

The debates

Cherokee use of the internet must be considered in the light of wider debates about whether computer technology and the internet medium help to preserve or tend to destroy indigenous cultures and traditions. Mark Trahant (1996), a professional scholar and member of the Shoshone-Bannock tribe of Idaho, speculates that the internet might be a medium particularly well suited to teaching in Indian communities, because it is more like traditional oral and pictographic forms of communication than are the typical written forms of the dominant culture. The imagery and fluidity of the Web, like pictographs, allows the user to enter where they like and continue in whatever direction they choose; like the story-telling tradition, in which both teller and audience participate in the exchange of stories and their meaning, the Web undermines both the power of the individual author and the presumed linearity of history. The stories told on the Web, like the stories told in pictographs or oral narration, change according to the teller, listener or user.

According to Trahant, internet use by Native Americans is on the rise. He speculates that growing use of the internet by tribal groups will have several beneficial consequences. Since the medium requires less capital outlay than does print media, Native groups might get their perspectives on political and social issues into circulation more easily. Second, tribes might use the sites to teach language and history, as do the Navajos and the Cherokees. Third, Trahant states that 'one of the oldest battles in the Native American press is over who controls information' (19). Print media may give tribal governments or federal agencies the power of censorship, while the internet grants individuals a greater voice. Finally, individuals might use the net to communicate with one another, through newsgroups and e-mail discussion lists, to build the bonds of community across time and space.

Trahant's high hopes for the new medium mirror the utopian tenor of much mainstream scholarship on the internet. For example, Paul Levinson (1997) contends that 'telecommunication of text via computer is ... a revolution in writing or authorship' (126), since anyone with access to a computer and modem is potentially an author, publisher and distributor of texts. Though the cost of personal computers may still be high for many individuals or groups, the technology is far more accessible than is the publishing industry. That accessibility virtually eliminates gatekeepers, such as editors and publishers, and allows a far greater diversity of ideas to enter circulation. Based on these characteristics of the internet, many have come to view the medium as a virtual democratic utopia. We agree that the implications of online publishing do seem to have revolutionary potential. If Michel Foucault (1980) is correct in stating that the producers of knowledge have power over those who are the subjects of knowledge, then the established media will typically produce relationships of power that privilege those who already hold positions of social power in capitalist societies. The internet, which opens the publishing field to groups who lack capital and power, can in theory allow marginalized individuals and groups to produce their own knowledge, put it into circulation and, as a result, gain a greater measure of social power.

In addition, proponents such as Sherry Turkle (1997), claim that 'on the Internet ... people [may] recast their identity in terms of multiple windows and parallel lives' (72). Theoretically, one may produce an online identity that does not correspond to one's real-life race, class or gender, or one may produce multiple identities, all of which may be in circulation concurrently. This may make the internet a particularly effective medium for negotiating the complex, and often conflicting, demands of both American and tribal cultural identities. According to the cybertopian worldview, 'the Internet deemphasizes hierarchical political associations, degrading gender roles and ethnic designations, and rigid categories of class relationships found in traditional, visually based and geographically bound communities' (Ebo, 1998: 3). Communities online, therefore, have the potential to create meaningful social groups that do not merely reproduce inequalities among real-life social groups. If that is the case, then the medium might be a force for building more egalitarian communities by breaking down race, gender and class barriers.

The idea of virtual community has been subjected to necessary scrutiny, however. Laura Gurak (1997) argues that while online aggregations are not the same as communities bounded by time and place, the internet can foster rhetorical communities united by a common ethos. Others, like Shawn Wilbur (1997) are more sceptical. He contends that, at worst, virtual community is 'the illusion of a community where there are no real people and no real communication' (14). Likewise, Derek Foster (1997) asserts that the medium 'allows each individual user an equal voice, or at least an equal opportunity to speak' (23). Yet, he wonders if the ease of communication in cyberspace actually translates into a sense of community – 'a set of voluntary, social and reciprocal relations that are bound together by an immutable "we-feeling"' (25).

For Indians, many objections are more specifically cultural. *New York Times* writer Elizabeth Cohen (1997) summarizes the concerns of Native spokespeople she interviewed that 'websites may not always represent the people and tribes they say they do, and that certain sacred and guarded cultural knowledge could be misunderstood or misused if it ends up on the Web' (2); she especially decries '"cyber-shamans" [who] feign tribal affiliation to sell various so-called native goods and services' (3). Lakota scholar Craig Howe (1999) maintains that, because land and geographic location are fundamental to specific tribal identities, 'the pervasive universalism and individualism of the World Wide Web is antithetical to the particular localities, societies, moralities, and experiences that constitute tribalism' (7). Or, as Dakota/Salish novelist Philip Red Eagle (1999) put it in an online discussion of the subject, 'Community is about responsibility to a specific group of people who practice culture with one another.' Jerry Mander (1991), a non-Native writer, insists that the computer destroys ways of thinking and acting that are fundamental to oral cultures, and inculcates values counter to Indian traditions. Because computers rely on an information exchange model of communication, they contribute to a worldview that reduces the natural world to resources to be managed and controlled, at the expense of an embodied interrelationship with the world that is characteristic of traditional indigenous lifeways.

The internet also may reproduce rather than challenge social inequalities. Though users cannot see each other, they may not have abandoned all judgements on the basis of race, class, gender and ethnicity. If members of socially marginalized groups appear equal on the internet, it may simply be that they can successfully masquerade as white and/or male. Second, while individuals and minority groups may more easily 'publish' on the internet, readership is limited at best. Thus knowledge and ideas that challenge the status quo may remain marginalized. Third, access to the internet is not equally distributed along lines of race, class, gender and ethnicity. Demographic statistics show that the majority of internet users are college educated, affluent, white and male (though the balances are slowly changing — see www.newmediastudies.com/stats.htm). Thus the democratic potential of the internet has hardly been realized.

Wolf (1998) notes that studies she surveyed on internet usage by minority groups make no note of use by Native Americans. As in many other disciplines, research and critical attention to Indian use of the internet is ghettoized, limited primarily to studies specifically about Native Americans; such a practice reproduces what many have called 'the vanishing Indian syndrome' by implying that Indians no longer exist as a vital and influential part of the American population. In addition, start-up costs of internet use (i.e. a computer and a modem) are still prohibitively high for many Native Americans. Native Americans remain the poorest minority in the USA, and many do not even

21.1 Online news at *Indian Country Today*, one of many Native American Internet resources.

have access to the telephone service (Yawakie, 1997). Yet, internet sites for and about Indians abound. An Indian Circle webring (www.indiancircle.com) provided by the Western Band site lists the more than 550 federally recognized Indian tribes of the continental USA and Alaska, 100 of whom have active websites. Searching for 'Cherokee Indians' in a search engine such as AltaVista yields thousands of pages.

The websites

The sheer number of sites pertaining to Cherokee Indians makes a general survey impractical, so we chose to limit our study to the official homepages of the Eastern and Western Bands. Both homepages are works in progress; while we were studying them, design and content changed, and we assume that those changes will continue. In addition, there are many 'unofficial' sites for and about the Cherokees. Many of them are interesting and informative, but some appropriate the trappings of Cherokee identity while spreading unreliable information. Thus our study does not represent a comprehensive survey of information on the Cherokees.

Both homepages are produced by outside organizations under the direction of tribal members, but the two pages offer striking contrasts. The Oklahoma page (www.cherokee.org) is designed primarily for Cherokee users and sympathetic outsiders. Entitled 'The Official Site of the Cherokee Nation', it offers access to tribal government pages with links to educational and human services, information on community development, finance and genealogy, as well as news, politics, culture and history. News comes in the form of press releases issued by tribal government and items from current and past issues of the *Cherokee Advocate,* the modern descendant of the *Cherokee Phoenix.* The Western Band offers links to sites as diverse as the Alpha Bet Jewish Day School and the Department of the Interior but, surprisingly, this Cherokee Nation homepage does not mention the Eastern Band.

The Eastern Band's homepage, called simply *Cherokee* (www.cherokee-nc.com), with a line at the bottom of the page identifying it as 'The official homepage of the Cherokee Nation', links the user directly to information on tourism and gaming (casino gambling) on the Cherokee Reservation and in the Great Smoky Mountains National Park. Attractions on the reservation mirror those in the surrounding park – fishing, hiking and camping – but the town of Cherokee also offers visitors shopping, museums and a chance to gamble at Harrah's Cherokee Casino. Like the Western Band, the Eastern Cherokee site provides a link to press releases, but those documents, too, offer a contrast.

Whereas the Western Cherokees' press releases provide information on politics and current events, the Eastern Band's press releases inform the reader about coming attractions. While the Western Band homepage makes no mention of the Eastern Band, the Eastern Band site now links to the Western Band, although for a number of years it did not, reflecting the geographical and historical division of the nation. However, the addition of this link in late 1999 suggests that the Web may indeed have the potential to bring these two communities closer together.

The contrast between the press releases raises an interesting point about the internet and freedom of the press. Trahant (1996) argues that the internet can help Indians avoid censorship by corrupt tribal governments. Recent press releases from Oklahoma reveal that the tribal government in Tahlequah is in disarray. Information on corruption at the highest levels of government is freely available on the internet through the tribe's own newspapers. On the other hand, the North Carolina press releases are prosaic, and no part of this site offers the exchange of hard news or information on politics. The site functions, in effect, as an agent of impression management. The primarily non-Native visitors to the *Cherokee-NC* site will see a limited view of the Cherokee people and their community.

Tribal member Dave Redman, who created the North Carolina website in 1997, confirms that this homepage is intended for use by tourists, and that tourists are indeed the primary users (personal communication, 1999). Its goal is to expand tourism and advance economic growth on the reservation. Gaming is the lynchpin of the Cherokees' development strategy, as it has been on other reservations. Like other tribes, many Cherokees view gaming as 'simply a profitable business, upon which economically dormant Indian nations can regain long lost territory, cultural prerogatives and community structures built on respect' (Johnson, 1995: 18). Capital acquisition, however, is not an end in itself for the Cherokee Nation in North Carolina. The proceeds of gaming are reinvested in the community. Projects funded by gaming revenues include a new youth centre, which provides access to computers and the internet, and a community computer centre. Other beneficiaries include a new Cultural Resources Division, a newly redesigned museum, a language preservation programme (which records native speakers of Cherokee language on CD-Rom) and the Cherokee school system. A link from the Eastern Band's homepage brings the user to a Cherokee elementary school site and the homepages of Cherokee fifth graders. Each child's page contains his or her picture, their name in Cherokee and a short autobiographical description.

The elementary school homepage is interesting on several levels. The children's homepages might be viewed as a marketing ploy. If the Cherokee use their Web pages to sell themselves to tourists, then why not use the words and faces of their children to enhance the appeal? Yet there seems to be much more to the school pages than marketing. The Nation's homepage and most of the pages to which it is linked consist of text with a few pictures. They offer convenient access to information that could be provided in brochures and other print formats. The elementary school's homepage is far more complex, a multimedia page with exciting graphics, moving pictures and sound. For example, a visitor can click on a 'culture' option to hear a Native story-teller recite Cherokee legends in English with Cherokee translations.

The elementary school homepage reflects a process of building physical relationships among Cherokee children and the elders of the community through a restoration of the story-telling tradition and the Cherokee language. Thus links are reforged between children who are just beginning to learn the language and their few remaining elders for whom Cherokee is their first language, a connection broken by decades of Indian boarding school experience which forbade the use of Native languages. At the same time, parents and extended family are drawn to take advantage of internet access at the local public library and the planned community computer centre in order to experience the results of the children's efforts. The oral tradition and language translation reproduced on the internet thus becomes a mode of translation between Cherokee and English, and a translation across the generations – a literal re-linking of community members who have been separated by the destruction of their language and culture, and by the introduction of outside educational models.

The elementary school's homepage may also be viewed as a symbol of the Eastern Band's commitment to education and technology as tools for self-determination. The fifth-grade students were not merely learning skills for success in education or work when they created their Web pages. They were learning skills that will ultimately allow the Cherokee to be less reliant on outside businesses and organizations to develop their technological capacities. And, as Trahant points out, 'images are likely to evolve into the Internet's most powerful element', and Indians have an opportunity to be at 'the cutting edge' of this new technology (1996: 18). The Eastern Band website and its links also both reflect and contribute to increasingly successful efforts by Cherokee leaders to recover and retain profitable participation in the capitalist economy of the larger nation. Profits are not only channelled into community services and cultural preservation, they have also expanded the actual land base of the community by funding the purchase of an ancient burial site, and they support business ventures such as the Nation's new bottled water industry and small business loans. Redman hopes the website will increasingly be used to link to websites for local businesses.

Thus the Eastern Band website actively alters the way Qualla interfaces with surrounding cultures. The website draws non-Natives from around the world (Redman reports that a large percentage of site visitors are German, French, Japanese and of other nationalities) to contribute to economic recovery and cultural preservation. The website creates a balance of welcome and invitation with subtle suggestions of responsibility. The site design encourages visitors to recognize connections between historical removal and destruction, and the current living situations of real people, and thus potentially to perceive their consumption of Cherokee attractions and products as participation in recovery. The site also clearly builds connections with other indigenous peoples, not only by creating links to resources, like the *NativeWeb* link (www.nativeweb.org) available on the genealogy pages, but also by connecting groups and individuals. On the day of our last conversation (October 1999), Dave Redman reported that he had just received a request from a child of a tribal group in Scandinavia for a penpal in Cherokee.

Conclusion

In our examination of the two websites, we attempted to address the question: Does use of this potent western technology necessarily lead to the degeneration of Native groups, or can Indians use the medium to further the goal of 'reindigenization' – the process of strengthening tribal ties while asserting sovereign rights and fostering self-determination? We conclude from our study that tribal websites can be powerful agents for community development and cultural continuity within change. The Cherokee Nation of Oklahoma site offers the possibility of developing a sense of community by linking people to services and organizations, and to each other through free e-mail accounts and discussion lists; both bands' sites literally enlarge community by providing information about genealogy and enrolment that will help people with Cherokee ancestry become members of the tribe, while screening out non-Native wannabes or those merely interested in gaming profits. While the internet may not have yet 'earned the name Great Equalizer' (Wolf, 1998: 18), the Eastern Band website in particular suggests that some communities are already realizing the internet's potential for democratic and material equalization. For the Eastern Band, the internet helps to control access by the dominant culture to Cherokee culture and its representations; it also appears to be a significant part of a stunning recovery of its success in the early 1800s as a thriving community in the intersections of Euro-American and tribal cultures.

USEFUL WEBSITES

Cherokee (Eastern Band): **www.cherokee-nc.com**
The official site of the Cherokee Nation (Western Band): www.cherokee.org.
The sites discussed in this chapter.

NativeWeb: **www.nativeweb.org**
Resources for indigenous cultures around the world.

The Cherokee Messenger: **http://www.powersource.com/cherokee**
Produced by the Cherokee Cultural Society of Houston.

First Nations site index: **www.dickshovel.com**
Lists many internet Native American resources.

Indian Country Today: **www.indiancountry.com**
Website of America's largest Indian newspaper, offering news, archives,
editorial features and more.

Virtual Library – American Indians:
www.hanksville.org/NAresources
An index of Native American resources on the internet.

NativeNet: **http://cs.fdl.cc.mn.us/natnet/index.html**
Website dedicated to 'protecting and defending Mother Earth and the rights
of indigenous people worldwide'.

22

The World Wide Web goes to War, Kosovo 1999

Philip M. Taylor

Despite similarities with previous conflicts, every war has its own unique characteristics. As far as military-media relations are concerned, Korea was, strictly speaking, the first television war, Vietnam the first colour television war, and the Gulf War of 1991 the first 'real-time' television war. During the course of the twentieth century, the presence of the mass media observing fighting forces has heightened the level of public scrutiny towards conflicts that were hitherto confined largely to those combatants taking part in them. In this respect, Vietnam is often cited as the exception to the norm of media support for 'our boys' in 'our wars' in that the media stand accused of alienating US public support for the war in South-east Asia by showing, for the first time, the graphic 'realities' of modern warfare.

In the transition from 'total war' to 'television war', one consequence of this is that civilian (and, in countries like the USA, military) casualties have become increasingly unacceptable to a watching global television audience, with a corresponding growth in 'smart' weapons technology in an attempt to minimize them. And, as the Gulf War demonstrated, the military were even prepared to place cameras on those weapons to demonstrate to the watching audience that everything was being done to minimize 'collateral damage' in a new era of 'clean warfare'.

At the military-media interface, democratic publics have traditionally relied on the professional journalist to serve their 'right to know' about the nation's performance on the battlefield and to 'tell them the truth'. This 'spectacle of war' or 'media war' has been likened to mere voyeurism for a global live television audience watching from a safe distance, with all the accompanying problems associated with image-reality gaps, censorship and propaganda.[1] However, new communications technologies – such as the fax machine, the mobile phone and the video palmcorder – have greatly increased potential for voyeuristic access to the fighting areas. Moreover, these personal media have widened greatly the levels of non-journalistic participation in the process of disseminating news of conflicts from the battlefield that helps to shape popular views about them. The internet, as a genuinely interactive medium, is the apogee of this development. 'For the first time anyone on the Internet can receive a flow of combatant news, comment and pictures – and, for those with right equipment, audio-visual programmes and news conferences.'[2] But the real point is that anyone with such equipment could also *transmit* their news, comment and pictures to a global audience, bypassing the traditional mass media. And although many still regard internet access as a passive activity, the Serbs at least did not see it as such.

In October 1999, General Shelton admitted for the first time that NATO had conducted 'information warfare' against Serbia. Further details will no doubt emerge in due course but this was a surprising admission in the light of how badly NATO performed in the first internet war. What we do know is that 'information warfare', or 'information operations' as it is now more commonly being described, is gradually penetrating the military planning process in advanced information societies. Essentially, this is a new concept of warfighting against new types of adversaries in new forms of battlefields (or battle 'spaces') that forms part of the so-called Revolution in Military Affairs (RMA). It requires the application of new technologies, especially new communications technologies, to improve military 'command and control' capabilities in defeating an enemy by 'smart' applications, intelligent systems such as computers and satellites, and by applying other advanced technological assets. It is all the more surprising, therefore, that the main protagonists of such theorizing did not practice what they preached.

Much nonsense has been written about information warfare and especially about one of its central 'tools', the internet. This should come as no surprise to anyone who appreciates that it has always been thus, not only with emerging military strategies but also with all-new emerging communications technologies, until they gain widespread acceptance and bed down to normal commonplace usage. Neither the internet itself nor 'information operations' have yet to reach that status in most countries. In Serbia, it was estimated that a maximum of 50,000 of its ten million population had access to the internet, with less than a thousand in Kosovo itself.[3] During the conflict with NATO, television remained the main source of information for 60 per cent of Serbs, followed by newspapers, word of mouth and radio. Four in ten Serbs listened to foreign radio stations (with Radio Free Europe being the most popular) and slightly less foreign television. Only one in ten Serbs used the internet 'frequently' (2 per cent) or 'sometimes' (7 per cent) for information, but over half of the 'sometimes' users believed that the information they gained was inaccurate. In the first post-conflict survey of Serb media usage, the internet – in terms of usage and credibility – was remarkably placed above NATO television (deployed by flying TV platforms known as the Commando Solo) but actually below the 104 million NATO leaflets that were dropped over the country.[4]

In due course the internet may gain widespread levels of Serbian public acceptance similar to those, for example, in the United States. In 1999, however, most people continued to rely upon traditional mass media as their principal source of information about what was going on in the world around them. Internet users remained an elite, albeit a sizeable one, confined largely to specific educational and economic circles. Yet this elite was highly influential. It consisted of opinion-makers, people who were in a position to influence much larger numbers of people, and the very type of people who would want to get the story behind the story, for which the internet is an invaluable tool. As such, this was a significant target audience for anyone battling for access to hearts and minds about the rights and wrongs on any given issue. The Serbs realized this, but NATO didn't.

It is axiomatic of both the internet and of emerging information warfare thinking that, with comparatively limited resources, a widespread global impact is possible. The Kosovo Liberation Army certainly recognized this by its establishment of a website long before the conflict with NATO began. Nor were they the first to recognize the potential of the internet for political and global communications. Much has already been written about the Zapatistas' use of the Web from 1995 to promote their cause against the Mexican Government over the Chiapas dispute. The Tamil Internet Black Tigers launched simultaneous e-mail attacks on 18 Sri Lankan embassies and were even able to disrupt electrical power supplies into Columbo. We have also seen how electronic information flows increased outside awareness of what was happening in Bosnia, Zaire and Indonesia. From the moment the Web became visible in 1992 as the user-friendly 'front-page' of the internet, pressure groups and non-governmental organizations have begun to seize upon the technology as an ideal instrument of 'electronic democracy' and of lobbying for a wide variety of causes. Indeed, even in the so-called 'first information war' in the Gulf in 1991, e-mail was added to the arsenal of information weaponry as a means of communicating with the enemy.

The Serbs were also quick to realize just how far this technology had developed since then, or indeed even since the end of the Bosnian conflict in 1995. As a result, they were frequently able to place NATO on the defensive as its spokesmen proclaimed the 1999 conflict to be in a 'humanitarian' cause. And because the Serbs controlled the media in Kosovo itself, from where it was too dangerous, once the bombing started, for most western correspondents to report in a consistent way, the Kosovo Albanians also seized upon the technology to proclaim their experience to the outside world. In addition to the KLA's own site, the self-proclaimed Kosovo Government in exile ran its own site from Geneva. When the Serbs closed down the independent radio station B92 it merely moved to a different location in cyberspace, based in Holland, and continued its protests.[5]

The Kosovo conflict was unusual in that it created higher levels of uncertainty among the 'chattering classes' about the moral and legal justifications of NATO's bombing campaign. It will take much more research before any correlation can be made between these slightly higher than normal levels of ambiguity among members of this elite audience and their usage of and access to the internet. With only the thinnest legal backing, and arguably an actual violation of both the UN's and NATO's charters, NATO governments justified the campaign largely in moral terms, as a humanitarian mission to rescue the Kosovans from genocide. With Britain at the forefront of the information campaign, the war was framed in terms of the British Labour Government's so-called 'ethical foreign policy'. Whereas the majority of people backed their government's war effort and accepted it as a 'just war', and had the television images of fleeing refugees to reinforce their support for it, the kind of people who used the internet for accessing information behind the journalistic gatekeeping of news stories may not have been quite so sure. It was these very voices of dissent, absent from the traditional media coverage of the war, that seized upon the internet as a medium of transmitting their reservations around the world.

The Serbs certainly demonstrated an understanding of all this by devoting considerable resources to internet communication during the Kosovo conflict. They saw the World Wide Web as a unique instrument for waging their own 'information warfare' against NATO countries and for getting their message across to global elite, if not public, opinion while refuting or challenging the arguments of their adversaries. Indeed, from the moment the NATO bombing commenced on 24 March 1999, and as it extended into targeting Serbia's military-civil infrastructure, including Serbian television and radio transmitters and stations, it was perhaps their only weapon of retaliation.

⦿ **22.1** The relatively similar sites of the Serbian Information Ministry and NATO.

The novelty of this campaign needs to be analysed in two strands: first, in the area of what has traditionally been labelled psychological warfare fought on a tactical level; and, second, in a more strategic sense of the wider information war. The problem with trying to analyse traditional warfighting with the internet as part of the equation immediately becomes apparent. In cyberspace, it is not really appropriate to talk in traditional terms about battle 'fields', nor can one really distinguish between tactical and strategic battle 'spaces'. Moreover, the internet as an interactive medium of communications by individuals with access to it – and electricity – redefines not just the way information flows within and beyond an area of conflict but also 'demassifies' the traditional monopolistic role of journalists as observers of other people's misery. When one adds to this that the nature of conflict in the post-Cold War era has increasingly blurred the distinction between soldier and civilian, especially in conflicts that involve 'ethnic cleansing' (such as Bosnia, Rwanda and Kosovo), we also need to rethink our traditional concepts of 'the enemy' and 'enemy soldiers'.

Traditional methods of reaching enemy soldiers and civilians with targeted information and messages – psychological warfare – continued to be used in 1999, as epitomized by the millions of leaflets that were dropped by NATO over Serbia and Kosovo during the conflict.[6] Other traditional media, such as broadcasting, were also employed, not just at the strategic level but through such international radio services as the Voice of America, the BBC World Service and Radio Free Kosovo. The growth of commercial satellite television also meant that Serbs with satellite dishes could watch CNN, Sky News and BBC World. Radio and television signals at the tactical level were supplemented by Commando Solo, a converted EC 130 airborne television and radio platform operated by the United States out of Hungarian air bases. Commando Solo broadcasts identified themselves as 'Allied Voice Radio and Television', with programming provided by the Serbian service of Radio Free Europe. However, the only true communication innovations in the Kosovo conflict were accessible mobile telephones and internet access. Hence Serb citizens in Belgrade or Novi Sad could call phone-in shows such as the BBC's *Radio Five Live* and air their views to a British audience without any censorship, or ordinary Serb citizens could send e-mails to NATO to appeal for the bombing to stop.

A key element of information warfare is information denial to the enemy. When NATO attacked the Serbian state television service (RTS), it may have caused worldwide outrage (mainly, it has to be said, on the part of journalists) but it was militarily logical in the attempt to gain command and control over the information flow both to and inside Serbia. Besides, argued NATO spokesman Jamie Shea, 'RTS is not media. It's full of government employees who are paid to produce propaganda and lies. To call it media is totally misleading. And therefore we see that as a military target. It is the same thing as a military propa-

ganda machine integrated into the armed forces. We would never target legitimate, free media.'[7] But what about new media, since the very point of cyberspace
is that it is everywhere there is a computer with which to access it. Certainly,
the closely integrated Soviet-style civic-military infrastructure of the Serbian
state meant that power installations were also deemed 'legitimate targets' and
this frequently meant that electricity supplies and telephone services that used
copper-wire technology were badly affected by the bombing. But still the
messages and e-mail continued to flow, reiterating the core Serbian official propaganda themes emphasizing the illegitimacy of the NATO=Nazi 'aggression' and
the unanimity of the Serbian people united in support of the Milosevic Government. We may never know how far the latter was true or, indeed, if it was, how
far this was actually caused by the NATO bombing in the first place.

The experience of the Blitz in 1940, or of Hanoi in 1969, would certainly
seem to suggest that bombing consolidates rather than shatters morale. Because
mass bombing fails to discriminate between ruler and ruled, there is a unifying
consequence that cloaks itself in nationalistic slogans. Even though 'smart
weaponry', in the form of cruise missiles and laser-guided bombs, was used extensively in the bombing of Serbia, when a bridge, power station, railway station or
TV station is targeted it invariably affects civilians. Incidents where civilians
were 'accidentally' killed added to the sense of outrage. Many Serbs therefore
found the internet to be a useful method of letting their anger at NATO's 'fascist
aggression' be known. The reasons for that aggression, namely the ethnic cleansing of Kosovo, were largely absent from official Serb media outlets. When foreign
satellite stations began showing pictures of fleeing refugees on the Albanian and
Macedonian borders, it was explained away by claiming that they were fleeing
NATO air raids rather than Serb genocide. As one media analyst observed, 'the
ability for each side to create its own reality is almost unlimited'.[8] Yet, as another
observed, 'the laptop, the modem, the cell phone and the satellite are making it
hard for either side to have a complete control over the manufacture of wartime
reality'.[9]

In the 'fog of war', was the internet able to bring any clarity? The answer
is probably not, given the dominance of the polarized propaganda themes disseminated by both sides and reflected in the traditional media that most people still
relied on for their information. Many internet sites merely reflected those
themes. However, what the internet user was able to do was to debate the
issues.[10] Many university campuses hosted sites designed to do precisely this and
to exchange information that was not freely available in the traditional media.
Or at least, it was not readily available in one media outlet. The ability to search
the internet for information from numerous sources, including online newspaper
and television sites, greatly increased the opportunity to accumulate a broad
spectrum of news and information – as well as opinions – from one's desktop.
But whether this helped anyone understand better what was actually going on
in Kosovo is highly unlikely. After all, despite the proliferation of atrocity stories
about Serbian 'ethnic cleansing', it was only when the bombing stopped and
NATO troops entered the region that undisputed evidence could be gathered. And
the presence of individuals, as distinct from traditional journalists, cybercasting
their individual views directly and without mediation to the internet audience
may merely have created more confusion than clarity.

Despite the efforts of cyber-Serbia through such sites as *Serbian Ministry of
Information*, Serb physical control of Kosovo enabled them to limit the damage
caused by cyber-Kosovo. For example, before the bombing began, the *Daily Times
(Koha Ditore)* in Pristina was refused access to a recently completed fibre link to

Belgrade that would have enabled it to become an internet service provider.[11] But how did the Serbs perform against NATO in this cyberwarfare? Preliminary research suggests that they did better than expected. Of course, one reason for this was that most of NATO's 19 member countries enjoyed more sophisticated computerized networks for the Serbs to infiltrate or disrupt. Yugoslavia's own internet infrastructure was pretty limited, but if NATO had decided to target it, it would merely have opened up new routes for cyber counter-attacks. 'We have lots more to lose than they do if we go down that route,' claimed one expert.[12] This did not, of course, prevent Serb attacks on NATO's own homepage or anti-NATO hackers disrupting the website of the White House.[13] One individual in Belgrade was able to cause considerable damage by e-mailing 2000 messages a day, some containing the Melissa and more pernicious Papa macro-viruses, to NATO's website using a 'ping' bombardment strategy to cause line saturation.[14] The website of the British Ministry of Defence, which translated its website into Serbian to counter Belgrade censorship, at once stage was receiving 150,000 hits per day, 1400 of which were from inside Yugoslavia.[15] But it would appear that NATO itself, for all its obsession with information warfare/operations, was caught on the hop and singularly and collectively failed to use the internet as an effective weapon of war. Its own internet site reflected traditional democratic propaganda methods of providing 'straight news and information' as part of a 'strategy of truth'. Of course, it was NATO's truth not Serbia's, and while NATO press conferences (not always successfully) fell into a traditional pattern of attempting to establish the most credible truth about what was happening, they missed a trick on the internet where the Serbs attempted to undermine everything NATO claimed with their own counter-claims, debates and even disinformation.

The Serb infowar nerve centre was based on the 13th floor of the Beogradjanka building where volunteers – mainly students – linked with more than 1000 other computer volunteers at six other centres in Belgrade. Day and night, they debated in chatrooms, translated articles into English and linked with other anti-NATO groups and individuals worldwide. They were led by 'Captain' Dragan Vasiljkovic, who ran unsuccessfully against President Milosovic in 1992. This 44-year-old former paramilitary veteran of Croatia and Bosnia redirected the funds he had set up for Serbian veterans into the psychological warfare computer centre.[16] 'We are all targets' was the principal slogan deployed to show the outside world that the Serb people were united behind their government under the rain of NATO bombs.

For its 'psychological warfare' against Serbia, NATO appears to have confined itself to traditional 'tactical' methods – leaflets, radio and television – deployed largely on the ground in Kosovo and Serbia. Whether they will be able to do this in future is highly unlikely in light of the experience of the Kosovo conflict. There is no such thing as tactical information on the internet. Yet this is precisely the area that information-age governments need to address. For example, in the United States, US armed forces or government agencies such as the US Information Service are expressly forbidden to conduct 'propaganda' and 'psychological warfare' on US soil. For this reason, defined by the Smith Mundt Act, a US citizen accessing the Voice of America site will find a much more limited service than his or her European or Asian counterpart. If NATO's US-led campaign against the Serbs was to utilize the internet in its information warfare campaign over Kosovo, it would have violated these traditions quite simply because US citizens would have been able to access the messages contained in that campaign. As a result, no military planner has as yet been able to resolve the geographical problems of the internet's actual or physical location in cyber 'space'.

Moreover, there was another unresolved issue, namely how reliable is the internet? Further evidence of the breaking of the previous monopoly of the war correspondent to report from the front came in the form of messages from people whose homes had been bombed, or from monks at a Serbian monastery near the Albanian border, all contained in e-mails from addresses ending in '.yu' (Yugoslavia). The difficulty, of course, was in checking authenticity – both of the senders and of the information itself. And whereas it can be argued that one has the same difficulty with reporters and newspapers, the point is that the *profession* of journalism has a tradition of values and responsibilities to such issues as 'the truth' that simply does not, as yet, exist on the Web. Thanks to the internet, therefore, the fog of war in Kosovo merely got thicker. For the Serbs, and accordingly for the 19 NATO countries they faced, the Kosovo conflict was to the internet what the Korean war was to television. NATO's performance was such that it will need to ensure that its next conflict, if there is one, does not become another Vietnam.

Notes

1. For a discussion of these issues, see Philip M. Taylor, *Global Communications, International Affairs and the Media since 1945* (London, Routledge, 1997).
2. 'Internet surfers join web war', *The Sunday Times*, 28 March 1999.
3. Preston Mendenhal of MSNBC, 'Kosovo: the wired war', on ZDNET (www.zdnet.com), 7 August 1998.
4. USIA Opinion Analysis, 'State-Run Stations Remain Trusted Source for Serbs', 16 September 1999 (US Information Agency, Washington). This survey conducted by a market research firm in Serbia (excluding Kosovo) for USIA was based on face-to-face interviews with 1103 Serb adults between 26 August and 1 September 1999.
5. http://helpB92.xs4all.nl.
6. 'NATO leaflets warn Serb troops of "certain death"', CNN Interactive (www.cnn.com), 26 April 1999; Greg Seigle, 'Alliance plays the psychological game into Yugoslav airspace', Jane's Information Group (http://jdw.janes.com) 26 April 1999.
7. 'Off the Air: Are NATO air strikes against Yugoslav media outlets justified?', Global Reporting Network Publications (www.nyu.edu/globalbeat), 4 May 1999.
8. Kathleen Hall Jamieson, cited in Frank Bruni, 'Two dueling views of reality vying on the airwaves', reproduced from *The New York Times* on the Reagan Information Exchange (www.reagan.com) 19 April 1999-09-19.
9. Mackenzie Wark, 'Yugoslavia: Air war leads us astray', in *The Australian*, (reproduced on www.infowar.com) 31 March 1999.
10. A good example of this was the piece written by Tomas Jovanovic entitled 'America wages propaganda war concerning Kosovo conflict' on UCLA's site on 12 April 1999 (www.dailybruin.ucla.edu).
11. Preston Mendenhal of MSNBC, 'Kosovo: the wired war', on ZDNET (www.zdnet.com), 7 August 1998.
12. Frank Cillufo, director of the information warfare taskforce at the Centre for Strategic and International Studies at Washington DC, cited in 'Infowarfare part of NATO's arsenal?', on ZDNET (www.zdnet.com) 26 March 1999.
13. Reuters, 'NATO confirms site hack, e-mail jam', on ZDNET, 31 March 1999.
14. Associated Press, 'Serb hackers disrupt NATO e-mail', on the *Las Vegas Sun* site (www.lasvegassun.com), 31 March 1999.
15. Rebecca Allison (PA News), 'Belgrade hackers bombard NATO website' (www.infowar.com) 31 March 1999. We should note that number of 'hits' does not always mean 'number of viewers', since the typical method of counting hits merely describes the number of files (including graphics, logos, bits of frames) served by the host. The actual number of visitors may be only 10 per cent of the number of hits.
16. Michael Satchell, 'Captain Dragan's Serbian Cybercorps', World Report, 10 May 1999 (US News Online at www.usnews.com).

USEFUL WEBSITES

NATO: **www.nato.int**
NATO's official site, complete with archives and details on the ongoing situation with KFOR.

Serbian Information Ministry: **www.serbia-info.com**
The official site of the Serbian Information Ministry – in English, so you need to ask yourself why.

Institute for War and Peace Reporting: **www.iwpr.net**
An invaluable site for monitoring media developments in the Balkans area as a whole.

BBC News:
http://news.bbc.co.uk/hi/english/special_report/1998/kosovo
The BBC Online archive about the crisis.

23

New Ways to Break the Law: Cybercrime and the Politics of Hacking

Douglas Thomas

As cyberspace becomes an increasingly central part of everyday life, it opens new opportunities and presents new challenges to our senses of security and community. In particular, issues of online behaviour involving the law are an important consideration as cyberspace comes to play an increasingly central role in communication, commerce, and the sharing of data and information. Traditionally the law has been able to identify and control social behaviours with threats of surveillance and punishment. Virtual crime, or 'cybercrime', presents a new set of challenges, however. Unlike crimes in the physical world, crimes committed online are difficult to monitor and divorced from the body. Crimes such as trespassing are called into question when there is no actual physical area being trespassed upon, and no physical body performing the trespass.

This chapter examines the subculture of computer hackers in an effort to better understand how issues of cybercrime and community can be critically examined. Hackers, as a subculture, have been at the forefront of such challenges and explorations, often confounding the structure and nature of law, and in the process using various forms of transgression to form new communities, both online and in the real world. In analysing this subculture, I examine representations of hackers, both through culture and their own self-image, provide a brief history of hackers and hacking, detail several ways in which hackers have invented 'new ways to break the law', and, finally, explore the political debates surrounding hackers and hacker culture.

Who are hackers?

The popular media has undoubtedly played a major role in how the public views the image of the hacker. Films such as *WarGames, Hackers* and *The Net*, have shown us an array of kids who find themselves in over their heads, struggling to save themselves (and often the world) from destruction. In books, and the mass

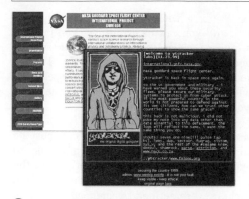

● **23.1** NASA's Goddard Space Flight Center website, before (left) and after (right) it was hacked in November 1999. 'Please secure our military systems to protect us from cyber attack' the helpful new page asks politely.

media, hackers are often framed in terms of their crimes, from the most trivial to the grandiose.[1] These films preach to us the dangers of technology and warn us of its ability to threaten our existence (*WarGames*), cause ecological disaster (*Hackers*) and destroy our identities (*The Net*). The books give us tales of international espionage, gang warfare, and threats to national security. As one might expect, the realities of hacking are somewhat less grandiose, most likely involving free phone calls, rearranged Web pages, and pranks.

Hackers, as a rule, are boys – predominately white, suburban boys – who are generally between the ages of 14 and 20. The 'grand old men' of the scene are often in their twenties. Hacker culture exemplifies what Anthony Rotundo (1998) has described as 'boy culture', that moment of adolescence characterized by the testing of the boundaries of adult authority and the expression of independence. Accordingly, it is not surprising to see hackers and hacker culture as a resistant subculture that challenges mainstream culture and expresses itself through oppositional codes and by challenging adult, primarily male, authority.

While the popular image of hackers as 'criminals' is widespread, the types of crime they usually commit are relatively benign. There are two unspoken rules of hacker culture: first, never act maliciously (acts that damage or destroy data); second, never hack for financial gain. These rules are born from a recognition that is part practical (damage and financial gain will get you arrested) and part ethical (hackers claim that their exploits are for exploration and knowledge, not to cause problems or make money). To most hackers, damaging a system or getting paid to hack would be like visiting a museum in order to destroy paintings or sell them to the highest bidder. On a more practical level, they are also the primary offences for which hackers are arrested.

Stories that involve damage or financial gain are also those most frequently reported in the mainstream press. As a result, the primary image of the hacker in the popular imagination is that of the criminal. Extreme cases, such as that of Kevin Lee Poulsen, a hacker accused of espionage (charges that were eventually dropped), make for sensational news items and grab public attention. Therefore most public perception of who hackers are and what they do is shrouded in a cloak of mystery and criminality. Hackers, however, see themselves as upholding a staunch ethic, functioning as watchdogs against industry abuses and as pioneers, exploring the frontiers of the digital age. While the popular press and media construct hackers as criminals, hackers see themselves quite differently. As Loyd Blankenship (1985) wrote in 'The conscience of a hacker' (often cited as 'The hacker manifesto'):[2]

> We make use of a service already existing without paying for what could be dirt-cheap if it wasn't run by profiteering gluttons, and you call us criminals. We explore . . . and you call us criminals. We seek after knowl-

edge . . . and you call us criminals. We exist without skin color, without nationality, without religious bias . . . and you call us criminals. You build atomic bombs, you wage wars, you murder, cheat, and lie to us and try to make us believe it's for our own good, yet we're the criminals. Yes, I am a criminal. My crime is that of curiosity. My crime is that of judging people by what they say and think, not what they look like. My crime is that of outsmarting you, something that you will never forgive me for.

This contrast between media images and hackers' self-perceptions, can best be understood by examining the historical and political contexts that gave rise to hackers and hacking. Hackers' self-image can be traced back to the origins of the movement, starting with students at major research universities in the 1950s and 1960s. As Steven Levy defined them, hackers were defined by their adherence to an ethic, a code of beliefs that was predicated on access to computers, freedom of information, the mistrust of authority, judgement of others based on skill and performance, and the belief that computers could be used for constructive social change (Levy, 1984: 39–50). This first generation of hackers often had to resort to unusual means to solve problems, and were fond of practical jokes and pranks. Thus, the history of hackers and hacking is invariably connected to the ethics and traditions of that first generation.

A brief history of hacking: old school and new school

Hackers are often divided into two groups: 'old school' hackers and 'new school' hackers. The old school refers to the hackers of the 1960s and 1970s who are generally credited with the birth of the computer revolution, and subscribed to an ethic of 'free access to technology' and a free and open exchange of information. These hackers are the 'ancestors' of the new school hackers, the hackers of the 1980s and 1990s, generally stereotyped as 'hi-tech hoodlums' or computer terrorists. Historically, however, the two groups are linked in a number of ways, not the least of which is the fact that the hackers of the 1980s and 1990s have taken up the old school ethic, demanding free access to information. Further problematizing the dichotomy is the fact that many old school hackers have become Silicon Valley industry giants and, to the new school hackers' mind-set, have become rich by betraying their own principles of openness, freedom and exchange. Accordingly, the new school hackers see themselves as upholding the old school ethic and find themselves in conflict with many 'old schoolers' now turned corporate.

In the 1980s, hackers entered the public imagination in the form of David Lightman, the protagonist from the hacker thriller *WarGames* (1983), who would inspire a whole generation of youths to become hackers, and later, in 1988, in the form of Robert Morris, an old school hacker who unleashed the internet worm (a self-replicating virus), bringing the entire network to a standstill. These two figures would have significant influence in shaping hacker culture and in popular media representations of it. In the wake of these public spectacles would emerge the new school, a generation of youths who would be positioned both as heroes (like Lightman in *WarGames*) and villains (like Morris) and who would find little or no institutional or government support as the old school had two decades earlier.

The new school emerged in an atmosphere of ambivalence, where hacking and hackers had been seen and celebrated as both the origins of the new comput-

23.2 *2600: The Hacker Quarterly*, the new school's magazine of hacking tips and debates.

erized world and as the greatest threat to it. New school hackers responded by constituting a culture around questions of technology, to better understand cultural attitudes towards technology and their own relationship to it.

The old school of hacking is perhaps best known for one of its basic tenets: 'information wants to be free'. It seems odd, then, that the new school of hackers, who follow many of the traditions of their older predecessors would be so staunchly supportive of something like cryptography. Cryptography is, essentially, the study of secrets – how to secure information and prevent others from seeing what you would like to keep secret. Such a principle appears to violate what Steven Levy described as the 'hacker ethic' in his 1984 book *Hackers: Heroes of the Computer Revolution*. But that was 1984, and hacking isn't what it used to be.

When one speaks of hackers, then, one is *either* referring to the valorized heroes who made personal computing a reality, or one is talking about the new generation of kids who break into computer systems, alter Web pages, or shut down systems with DoS (Denial of Service) attacks. As outlined above, these two types of hacker divide roughly into two groups: the 'old school' and the 'new school'.

On the surface, there appear to be tremendous differences between old school and new school hackers. Old school hackers were students at MIT, Harvard and Cornell in the 1950s, 1960s and 1970s, and were members of computer hobby clubs. New school hackers are kids of the 1980s and 1990s, raised on *WarGames, Hackers* and *The Net*. The differences between the two groups are, apparently, pronounced: old school hackers were the founders of many of the start-up companies that made the computer revolution possible; new school hackers were the founders of hacker groups such as the Legion of Doom and Masters of Deception, and would endure visits from the Secret Service and the FBI, and spend time in jail. But just below that surface, the line between the two begins to blur. Hacking hasn't changed all that much, but the context in which it occurs most definitely has.

The story of the Apple computer is often cited as one of the great old school hacker 'success stories'. Steve Wozniak and Steve Jobs still get a lot of mileage out of the story of how they built and sold 'blue boxes' (devices that enabled one to make free long-distance phone calls) in their Berkeley dorms. Old school hackers, like Wozniak and Jobs, were adventurers, explorers and innovators. When old school hackers ran into a problem, they 'hacked' their way around it. The result, usually a elegant piece of computer code or a new hardware device or configuration, would be proof of their status. These hackers were idealists of the first order, preaching their gospel – 'information wants to be free'. They were also naive. The fact that DARPA (the Department of Defense's Advanced Research Projects Agency) funded almost all of their research (including the internet) and that such research would go towards making better bombs, missiles and guidance systems during the Vietnam War, for example, is usually excised from the nostalgic account.

If you ask almost any of these old school hackers about the hackers of today, their first response will be this: 'These kids today, they're not hackers. They break into systems, copy software, break copy protection, and generally violate the principles that inspired the hacker ethic of the 60s and 70s.' And, on the surface, they are right. But if we compare the two contexts – the 50s, 60s and 70s with the 80s and 90s – two things becomes clear: first, the context that enabled these old school hackers to experiment and innovate no longer exists; second, the loss of that environment is the direct result of those old school hackers violating their own most deeply held principles. In short, the old school went corporate. The first thing Jobs and Wozniak did, for example, was make the Apple proprietary (which may well lead to Apple's ultimate demise). They took the hacker ethic, 'information wants to be free' and turned it on its head. Others followed suit. The only person not to sell out was Bill Gates – he was corporate from the very beginning. Information wants to be free, but old school hackers wanted to be rich.

The 'new school' emerged in the wake of the incorporation and commodification of the computer (the PC in particular). New schoolers had tools that the old school never did, namely the PC, but no place to go and no government grants to build networks. They did, however, have modems, which opened up a whole new world of networked communication. The new school hackers didn't have to own any big machines to explore them, they just had to find them, connect to them and play. Innovation gave way to curiosity. But in most cases, exploration was met with obstacles. These hackers grew up in a world where the creed 'information wants to be free' didn't make much sense. That battle had been fought and lost; and it had been lost (or perhaps more appropriately 'surrendered') by the people that started it in the first place, the old school hackers. Hacking had given way to corporate secrets. Where the old school had lived in a world that threatened to become secret, new school hackers grew up in a world that *was* full of secrets: PIN numbers, house alarm codes, phone access codes, voicemail codes, passwords, credit card numbers and the like.

In a world in which secrets govern everything from financial transactions to reading e-mail to defining one's identity, secrecy becomes a way of life. Secrecy is power – government power, bank power, police power. But secrets can be broken or revealed, rendering them worthless. Power can be maintained through the creation of secrets and, therefore, can be stripped away in the revelation of secrets. Accordingly, for the new school hackers, there are dual concerns: breaking secrets and keeping secrets. If you are going to be a hacker, you had better know how to do both. There is an irony at work here, and new school hackers will be the first to admit it – you need to keep your secrets safe (especially your identity) if you are going to be successful at breaking others'. If it is true that the battle for freedom of information has been fought and lost, then the new school hackers are truly following in their predecessor's footsteps. If information still wants to be free, then it is the new school hackers who will liberate it. What the old school hackers don't see, and don't understand, is that the ideals they one preached are still alive and well in the next generation.

What cryptography and security are about today is keeping secrets safe in a climate where privacy and security are threatened on a daily basis, and software and systems that don't take security seriously are prime targets for hackers to make this point clear. The hackers of today are no more malicious, deviant, or criminal that their counterparts of 20 and 30 years ago. In fact, they share the same curiosity and desire to learn that inspired a revolution. The difference is that new school hackers have to live in the world that the old school made for them and, more often than not, they have to hack their way out of it.

New digital crime

New school hackers have invented a set of new crimes for the digital age and law enforcement has been slow to respond. One of the primary problems of identifying hackers' crimes is that they happen for the most part in a virtual space, a space which the law itself has trouble understanding. As a result, when hackers are arrested and charged with crimes, they rarely find themselves charged with violating newer laws specifically designed to combat cybercrime (such as electronic trespassing). Instead, hackers are most frequently hit with serious charges of conventional fraud.

Even as the law has difficulty dealing with them, hackers are continually inventing new ways to break the law. These crimes, often categorized as fraud, fall into three categories: social engineering, getting root and hacktivism.

'Social engineering', as hackers refer to it, is the process of obtaining information through interacting with people, often posing as a helpless neophyte or computer expert. The idea behind social engineering is that hackers can gain knowledge and learn secrets by taking advantage of social relationships of trust and by exploiting a common discomfort that many people feel with technology. A common social engineering trick, for example, is to pose as a computer security expert, telling an unsuspecting user that their computer account is in jeopardy. In order to 'test' the account, the hacker will ask the user for his or her account information and password. The more urgent the hacker can make the request seem, the more pressure he or she can generate on the unsuspecting user. The result is that by posing as someone with expertise or power, hackers can gain incredible amounts of information simply by asking for it.

The success of social engineering attacks rests on two related issues. First, that small, but vital, pieces of information are major gatekeepers to access. For example, the only way that computers are able to validate a user's identity is through secrecy. The very concept of a password is based on a shared secret. The computer asks the user 'what is your password?', and the user's ability to answer that question – to, in effect, share that secret with the computer – is the only way in which it can validate the user's identity. Unlike the physical world, where we have bodies, sights, and sounds to confirm information, the computer relies exclusively on secrecy and information to validate identity. As a result, knowing and sharing a secret is performing an identity. The second reason that social engineering attacks succeed is based on a general sense of discomfort with computers. According to one computer hacker, 'if you ask a person if they are having trouble with their computer, 95 per cent of the time they will say yes, even if there is nothing wrong'. This sense of discomfort makes users less careful with information such as passwords. To complicate matters, many systems force users to choose passwords that are difficult for hackers to guess, with unintended consequences. While such programs do result in more secure passwords, they also make them more difficult to remember and use and many users end up writing them down, often in obvious places for easy access. In a surprising number of cases, a routine tour of a company office will reveal a number of Post-it® notes stuck to monitors with user names and passwords in plain sight.

To the hacker, information is access. Even things like company phone books, carelessly discarded in the waste bin, can be a treasure-trove of information, allowing a hacker to impersonate anyone in the organization, complete with title, phone number and office information. A discarded memo may provide a cover story for a phone call to a secretary: 'I needed to get into Sarah's account for the X11 project. She left me the password, but I can't seem to find it. You wouldn't happen to know it would you?'

Social engineering in many ways defies the representation of the hacker as a 'hi-tech' wizard. It is, however, far and away the most common means of access to information and hackers rely on it extensively. As one hacker commented, 'Sure I could spend 3 days straight trying to break in, but why waste the time?' With one phone call, a hacker can get the same information and pursue more interesting areas of exploration.

Once a hacker is inside, the goal of hacking changes. On every system there is a privileged account, usually referred to as the 'root' account. This account gives the hackers complete control over the system, the ability to read (and alter) files and even to shut down the system should he or she choose to do so. Apart from exercising a degree of control over the system, root access allows the hacker to do something else – cover his or her tracks. By becoming the root user, the hacker can erase any log or trace of his or her presence on the system, making it appear as if he or she had never gained access at all. Doing so greatly reduces the risk of getting caught and allows the hacker to continue his or her explorations from a new starting point, so even if they are traced back to their point of origin, there is still a buffer between the hacker and the place from which they are hacking.

Root access also allows a hacker to take advantage of other system flaws in order to create trojan horses or backdoors in the system. In the event that the hacker is discovered and shut out of the system, these programs can leave other entrances that will allow the hacker back in at will. Root access, then, provides a large degree of control over the system and is the ultimate end point for exploration.

Apart from exploration, there has been a new set of activities which hackers have taken up under the banner of 'hacktivism'. Hacktivism is the idea that computer hacking can be applied to activist goals and produce social and political change in the world. Often done as a form of protest, hackers frequently break into computer Web servers and rearrange Web pages to display social or political messages. Those messages have ranged in scope from attacks on a furrier's website where the page was replaced with an anti-fur message and images of animals in traps, to defacement of political party Web pages in the UK, to calls for the liberation of East Timor. In 1998, the website for the *New York Times* was hacked in protest at the imprisonment of computer hacker Kevin Mitnick. Some 3 years earlier, Mitnick had been arrested in North Carolina, where *NYT* reporter John Markoff had been part of the investi-

23.3 Indonesia's Foreign Affairs website, as it is normally (left) and after being hacked by protesters seeking freedom for East Timor in 1996 (right).

gation and had written extensively about the pursuit of Mitnick. The *Times* was forced to shut down its website for nearly 8 hours over the weekend that the Starr report was released and when traffic was anticipated to be at an all-time high.

The hack of the *NYT* website was the first instance where a major media website lost revenue as a result of a hack which claimed that its coverage had been unfair (the hacked website accused Markoff of unethical and criminal behaviour in the apprehension of Mitnick). Mitnick's case further served to radicalize an entire generation of hackers, prompting them to protest publicly against his arrest and prosecution, through means both legal and illegal. Hackers created a 'Free Kevin' movement which included media interviews, a public awareness campaign and several high-profile events, one of which included a plane skywriting 'Free Kevin' over one of the protests. To understand the importance of hacktivism, we must return to the split between the 'old school' and the 'new school'.

The politics of hacking

Over the past few years there has been a decided shift in the way hackers think about the world. Born from an idealistic model of personal, individual achievement, the very idea of hacking has always been a singular and isolated phenomenon. In the early days, hackers rarely worked in groups or teams, preferring to 'hand off' programming solutions to one another in the process of what they called 'bumming code'. Each time a program was handed off, it would be improved slightly and then passed along to the next hacker, and so on. Hackers of the 1980s and 1990s, who began to form loosely knit groups such as the Cult of the Dead Cow, the Legion of Doom and Masters of Deception, practised a similar ethic: hackers would learn from one another, but generally the understanding was 'everyone for themselves' – especially whenever someone got arrested!

That ethic, which began with the hackers of the 1960s and 1970s, is beginning to dissolve in the face of politics. Old school hackers are often disgusted by the antics of their progeny. Indeed, many old timers insist that the hackers of today are unworthy of the moniker 'hacker' and prefer to terminologically reduce them, calling them 'crackers' instead – the idea being that 'crackers' are petty crooks, as opposed to 'hackers', who see themselves as more sophisticated explorers. That distinction denies too much history, too many connections, and is often nothing more than a nostalgic, and very convenient, revision of their own histories. The earliest hackers did most of the things for which they criticize today's hackers. They stole (the Homebrew Computer Club was famous for pirating code); they regularly engaged in telephone fraud and used all sorts of hacks to avoid paying for things (best represented by the hacker journal *TAP*, which taught people how to steal everything from phone service to electrical power); and they had no problem with breaking and entering or hacking a system if it meant more time on the mainframe (see Sterling, 1992). They also tended to forget a lot of things. Who paid for all those computers at Harvard, Cornell and MIT? Who funded ARPAnet? Could it be the same folks who were busily napalming indigenous persons halfway around the globe? And why were those computer labs such a potential target for anti-war protesters in the 1960s that they needed bullet-proof Plexiglas to shield them? The old school history is not as simple as it sometimes appears. Yes, they were the geniuses who gave us the first PCs, but along the way they tended to be implicated in a lot of nasty business, to most of which they were all too willing to turn a blind eye.

I don't mean to suggest that old school hackers were not hackers, only that they weren't all that different from the new schoolers they like to brand 'criminals', 'crackers' and the like. Where the old school seems to come off as (at best) forgetful, the new school has shown a new kind of commitment, something that is virtually unthinkable to the hackers of yesteryear. The hackers of the late 1990s are becoming *political*. There is a new move to group action, political involvement and intervention.

Recently, seven members of the Boston hacker collective, the L0pht, testified on Capitol Hill before the Senate Governmental Affairs Committee. As fellow hacker Peter the Great described it in his write-up of the testimony:

> Mudge gave a short, elegant statement which set the tone for the rest of the day's talks. He expressed his hope for an end to the mutual animosity that has long existed between the hacker community and the government and his sincere desire that the ensuing dialogue would pave the way towards civility and further collaboration between the two sides. This was a beautiful moment. It was as if a firm hand of friendship was being extended from the hacker community to the senate. I was moved, truly.

This is a gesture that would have been virtually unthinkable only a few years ago.

Even more dramatic is the fact that the hacker collective Cult of the Dead Cow has a *policy on China*. In part, that policy was used in its justification for the release of Back Orifice, a computer security program that exploits vulnerabilities in Windows 95 and 98 operating systems. According to the cDc, Microsoft's decision to choose profit over human rights in supporting trade with China implicates it in the politics of oppression. The cDc has been working to support a group of Chinese dissidents, the Hong Kong Blondes, who are learning to use encryption and hacking techniques to stage interventions in Chinese Governmental affairs to protest Chinese human rights violations.

Most recently, in the USA, hackers have begun to band together in an effort to raise public awareness about the imprisonment of Kevin Mitnick, the aforementioned hacker facing a 25-count federal indictment who has been incarcerated without a hearing and has had the evidence to be brought against him withheld from discovery. In response to Miramax's decision to film Mitnick's story, hackers have banded together, launching a full-scale protest (among other things) in front of Miramax's offices in New York. The campaign also includes letter-writing initiatives, the distribution of 'FREE KEVIN' bumper stickers, websites, T-shirts, and even an online ribbon campaign.

23.4 One of several websites supporting hacker Kevin Mitnick (www.freekevin.com).

Computers have begun to affect us in undeniably political ways. The globalization of technology, coupled with the power that the computer industry wields, makes the hacking of today an essentially political act. Some of the effects can be seen in the highly politicized trial of Kevin Mitnick and in the efforts to pass the WIPO treaty, US legislation that makes hacking (even legal experimentation) a criminal act.

The differences between old school and new school hackers are not as great as they might appear or as they are often made out to be. If there are differences, they reside in the fact that hackers today are stepping up and taking a kind of political responsibility that was altogether alien to their predecessors.

The future of hacking goes hand in hand with the future of technology. Today's hackers share not only a common ancestry with the 'old school' hackers, but also a common set of values and ideas. What has changed is the context in which hackers perform. The distinction made between the old school and the new school of hackers overlooks the many similarities between these two groups, not the least of which is the desire to see new uses for technology that help raise awareness of both the problems and possibilities that such technology presents.

Notes

1. See, for example, Paul Mungo and Bryan Clough, *Approaching Zero: The Extraordinary World of Hackers, Phreakers, Virus Writers, and Keyboard Criminals*, New York: Random House, 1992; Katie Hafner and John Markoff, *Cyberpunk: Outlaws and Hackers on the Computer Frontier*, New York: Simon & Schuster, 1991; Clifford Stoll, *The Cuckoo's Egg*, New York: Simon & Schuster, 1989; Jonathan Littman, *The Watchman: The Twisted Life and Crimes of Serial Hacker Kevin Poulsen*, Boston: Little, Brown & Company, 1997; Jonathan Littman, *The Fugitive Game*, Boston: Little, Brown & Company, 1996.
2. This essay, originally published in the hacker underground journal *Phrack* has taken on a life of its own, often cited now as 'The hacker manifesto', it has appeared on countless websites and T-shirts, and has even made an appearance in the MGM film *Hackers*.

USEFUL WEBSITES

Hackers.com: **www.hackers.com**
Glossy site with lots of hacking news and resources.

2600: www.2600.com
Website of the hackers' magazine, with news, resources, and an archive of hacked sites.

Hacker News Network: **www.hackernews.com**
Smart site delivering 'the real news from the computer underground for the computer underground . . . without the biases of the mainstream media'.

The Linux Documentation Project: **www.linuxdoc.org**
Masses of information about Linux, the successful, freely distributed operating system loved, and indeed built, by hackers.

24

The Future: Faster, Smaller, More, More, More

David Gauntlett

'The future belongs to those who believe in the beauty of their dreams,' said Eleanor Roosevelt. Winston Churchill was similarly optimistic: 'The empires of the future are the empires of the mind,' he said. It's far from predictable, though. 'You can never plan the future by the past,' warned Edmund Burke. I know all this, of course, because I just spent three minutes at www.quoteland.com, a free online database of quotes.

A more worrying portent of the future is that, before that, I tried 'www.quotation.com', but it wanted to quote me a price for something. Then I guessed that 'www.quotations.com' might be a website offering me some literary words of wisdom. And it would – for two dollars per set. Internet cynics would say that these were clear indications that the Web – once thought of as a free and democratic global resource – is being gobbled up by the corporate and the greedy. As Quoteland.com tells me that Paul Valery has observed: 'The future isn't what it used to be.'

The future, of course, is notoriously difficult to predict. People will come up with some great – and some less than great – ideas which will change how we do things. We don't know what they are yet. Nevertheless, we can be reasonably sure that the internet and the Web will develop in certain ways. Technology experts are always making predictions about the future of the internet, and a bunch of the most likely ones are summarized below. A primary source for this was a survey of internet industry leaders and experts, on the future of the net, published in American business magazine *Worth* (November 1999), as well as the predictions made in other technology magazines and newspapers as we entered 2000. By the time you read this, you may want to consult such sources as well, to see what's happened since we sent this book to the printers: the invention of internet-enabled puppies, probably, and an umbrella that downloads weather forecasts.

What happens next?

All aboard

More and more people will use the internet, and it will become as common as television is now (perhaps because it will merge with TV anyway).

However: at the start of the twenty-first century, the internet reached 200 million people (see the panel near start of Chapter 17). But that is less than 4 per cent of the world's population. Half of the people in the world don't even have access to a telephone. So we need to keep the idea that 'everybody is using the internet' in perspective. Nevertheless, the point that the internet will become even more ubiquitous in developed countries is almost certainly true.

Instant everything

Bandwidth will increase (and the size of information files may decrease) so that downloading everything will become faster. Much, much faster. You won't have to wait for anything, so you won't so much perceive it as 'fast' but 'instant'. Click a Web link and the new page will appear, with graphics, sound and video, straight away. High-resolution movies will also soon burst instantly into your home (see 'integration of TV with the internet' below).

However: a divide may develop between those with super-fast internet connections and those with slowish ones, leading to a two-tier (or multi-tier) internet. And people who do not live in big western cities may not be able to get access to the fast connections. Meanwhile, super-fast delivery of content will mean that we are exposed to even more cheeky advertising, such as full-screen ads popping up for a few seconds before you get to the page you actually want.

The internet vanishes

At the moment, we usually access the internet by sitting down at a computer. Everybody knows that's where the internet is: at a computer terminal. But it is predicted that the internet will 'disappear' into a multitude of devices. It is becoming integrated into some of these already, such as mobile phones and video game consoles. But it will also be connected to other household appliances, walls, cars, security systems, watches, clothes, and other everyday items. This means it will be more, not less, prevalent in everyday life.

However: accessing the Web via a rectangular screen, about the size of a magazine, is highly satisfactory. A keyboard is often also required; speech recognition, or pure point-and-click, may partly replace this, but many people find typing to be their preferred method of composing text. So we may still prefer to browse the Web on gadgets that are similar to today's best laptops, except much lighter and thinner. Or devices like those electronic clipboard things that the captain would have to fiddle with most weeks on *Star Trek*.

Vanishing wires, missing gadgets

Cheap wireless communications will mean that all of the devices in your home or workplace will communicate with each other using radio waves. (A central computer will still have a good old cable to the internet, however.) The devices will get smaller and smaller, until people complain that they are much too fiddly, and then they will get a bit bigger again.

However: whether the gadgets are tiny or merely small, you will still probably lose them down the back of the sofa. Life isn't going to change *that* much.

Instant-on and always-on

At present, when I want to access the Web at home, I switch on my computer. Some 3 minutes later, after it has kick-started Windows, checked itself for viruses, polished its disk space and cleaned its teeth, it is ready to receive my first instructions. I click on my internet connection and wait for

24.1 Devices of the future. Tiny things. You will lose them.

another minute whilst my modem asks my ISP how it is feeling and whether it wants to go to the pictures. If I am still awake, I can then crawl around the internet.

Soon, the 'on' switch will have a machine running straight away ('instant-on'), a luxury already enjoyed by users of the Apple iMac. Internet connections will also be permanent ('always-on'), so that home users will not have to wait to go online, as a majority have to at the moment.

However: once again, there will be internet users who cannot afford, or gain access to, these innovations and will have to rely on the old technologies. Meanwhile educators will argue that having to read a newspaper while your computer powered up was an educational benefit which should be restored to all computers with the installation of pointless delay circuits.

Integration of TV with the internet

Fast net connections will mean that high-quality TV pictures can be streamed into your home. You may have noticed that this has been happening for decades via technologies called 'television' and 'video', of course, which often makes the computer experts who get very excited about their innovative 'full-screen video' (see, for example, www.theonion.com/onion3308/ realtimetv.html) appear rather silly. But with TV programmes and movies available from the internet, the user would have total choice over what to watch, and when, from a potentially massive range of options.

However: viewers would have to pay for this privilege, or have their viewing interrupted by adverts. But we are used to that already.

Integration of the internet with everything else

The implication of 'The internet vanishes' (see above) is that all of the electrical devices and appliances in a home or organization will be connected to the net. Your computer would be able to get your washing machine, heating and lighting to do exactly what you wanted at certain times of day. You would be able to monitor what was going on at home from your computer at work, or from your mobile phone. And then your robot vacuum cleaner might declare war on your neighbour because it didn't like what she wrote about *Buffy the Vampire Slayer* on her website, and your sandwich toaster would make a bid for world domination using the knowledge of money markets it had absorbed from the net. (Not really: appliances would only send and receive limited operating signals, and wouldn't all offer you Web access, let alone study Web content themselves.)

However: this sounds, at the moment, like a non-essential luxury for lazy (or busy) rich people. Switch on your own damn washing machine. Also, this will only be convenient when houses are routinely designed with a built-in internet infrastructure.

Ubiquitous internet means ubiquitous e-commerce

Commercial adverts, logos and messages will continue to proliferate on the Web. The internet gives companies more opportunities to sell things, but at the same time gives them very stiff competition from other businesses which no longer have to be geographically close in order to compete. More products will be tailored to individual orders and constructed on demand. We may have to start making 'micropayments' to useful commercial Web services, like news and information sites, in order to read their content. Companies will continue to think of ways to succeed in the battle for the attention of Web users. They will also create a more 'personalized' experience by developing ever-more sophisticated ways of 'learning from' your browsing habits and personal data (spying on you in order to present you with carefully targeted commercial junk, in other words).

However: people may resist some of this commercialization of the Web. But in many areas they won't really have a choice.

Political and cultural change

The internet will help activists, lobbyists and pressure groups to organize their activities more effectively. Regular online voting might mean that more people would become interested in issues and engaged by the political process. Or online voting might suffer from enormous reliability and security problems, and be a disaster.

Information about culture and politics can be shared much more easily over the internet, and the Web offers great distribution opportunities to the creative arts. Art and culture designed purely for the internet will continue to grow. Information warfare will replace military might, except when dealing with rogue states and amateur terrorists. Artists may borrow ideas from the information warfare experts and orchestrate powerful attacks on established culture. (I don't know what that last one means, though.)

However: people who are already interested in politics, or in arts and culture, may become even more engaged and interested in these areas because of the internet. But what about all the other people? Their attention may have been grabbed and disconnected from the rest of the internet by the online shopping malls. And, as for information warfare, if all sides become equally good at it, then the numbers of people willing to shoot at and bomb each other will not decline.

More of everything

If more and more people join the Web-using community, then more and more people will want to create their own websites. Some academic Web experts feel (as we saw in Chapter 1 of this book) that the commercial presences on the Web are suffocating the non-commercial and personal ones. There is certainly an enormous need for us to be concerned about this, and to fight against it. But to assume that companies have already taken over the Web seems a boringly obvious pessimistic view, and it's not really true. Hopefully, having a website will come to seem even more everyday and normal for everybody. The tools for creating websites will (hopefully) become even more simple and intuitive, increasing the likelihood of mass participation. It's a great medium for self-expression and for learning about things.

However: businesses are powerful, and they want people to be reading a small range of commercial sites on the Web (ideally, all ones owned by themselves), not writing their *own* interesting and creative sites. Hopefully these corporations will not win. The two can live quite happily, side by side, on the Web.

In conclusion

In the longer term, of course, nobody really knows what's going to happen. An article in the UK's *Independent* newspaper (December 1999) says that, by 2050, online voting will replace governments, and robots will do most of the routine manual jobs, and everybody will be more free and more rich than they are now (Gulker, 1999). But what about all the unemployed workers and politicians? (They may have to find work in PR companies telling us how to vote and which robot to buy). If we turn to the cinema, the only thing that movies about the future can agree on is hover-cars and talking computers, neither of which we can't live without, and they normally go wrong anyway, even in the films. Forget it.

The one thing that makes new media truly exciting is *participation*. If internet technologies continue to help people express themselves, share ideas, communicate with others and, in doing so, help one another, that will be welcome. If new media becomes like television, where a small number of well-resourced people produce content for it, and most people merely view it, that will be profoundly disappointing, even if the content is varied and useful. There will be an ongoing tension between those who want to turn the Web into a corporate-controlled business and entertainment park, and those who say that, whilst businesses can have their place, we must preserve the unique participatory nature of all new media developments.

If any one source says that it wants to provide all of the Web content you will ever need, be extremely wary. Those childhood fairy tales, which warned of evil witches tempting nice people to their downfall with attractive promises, weren't mere light entertainment. Which would you prefer to see: a playground where children play creatively with each other, or a playground where the children can only sit in rows and watch a colourful circus . . . forever?

No one controls the Web at the moment, and no one should *want* to. Stake your claim in the future now by making your own website and attracting visitors. Remember to make it *about* something, or fill it with unquantifiably beautiful artistic riches (but making a website that's *about* something is easier). Website technologies and styles may change, but at least you'll have a foot in the door. That's the same door some big businesses may try to jam closed when you're not looking. So be vigilant. But most of all: be creative.

Glossary

This glossary of technical terms – plus a few people, acronyms, programs and companies – was compiled by David Gauntlett and David Silver.

Acrobat, Adobe – Software that runs on different platforms (computers with divergent operating systems), allowing documents to be viewed exactly as originally intended, complete with layout and graphics. Used on the Web by people who insist on having total control over document formatting, or who can't be bothered to convert the documents into Web pages, which would often be preferable. The Acrobat viewer is free; Adobe makes its money by charging for the software which converts documents into Acrobat files.

ADSL – Asymmetrical Digital Subscriber Line, an extremely fast way of sending data down standard copper phone lines.

Andreessen, Marc (1972–) – Whilst a student at the National Center for Supercomputing Applications (NCSA) at the University of Illinois, Andreessen produced, with staff member Eric Bina, the first Web browser with a graphical point-and-click interface (like Apple and Windows operating systems), called *Mosaic*. This popular early browser, first distributed free over the internet in February 1993, really kick-started interest in the Web. In 1994, Andreessen and Jim Clark launched Netscape Communications Corporation, and Netscape dominated the browser market for around four years, although Microsoft later succeeded in its late-starting bid to seize power in this area.

AOL – The leading commercial online service that serves as an entry point to the internet for over 20 million users. (A merger in January 2000 saw the company become AOL Time Warner). As a result of its user-friendly interface and wall-to-wall marketing, AOL attracts countless network newcomers which, in turn, attracts widespread hostility from internet old-timers towards 'AOL newbies'.

ARPANET – An experimental computer network created by the United States military during the Cold War. Established in 1969 by the Advanced Research Projects Administration (ARPA) to support military research and nuclear attack-proof communication, ARPANET stands as the original ancestor of the internet.

Attachment – A file (such as a document, spreadsheet, or graphic) sent 'attached' to an e-mail message.

Banner advert – Long, thin advert appearing on a Web page. ('Banner ads' may also refer to online adverts generally, regardless of their shape.) Many sites make some money by selling banner advert space. Banner ads are often animated and they are considered annoying by many. Some ads even include little games in a bid to get the user to click through to the advertiser's website.

BBS – Short for bulletin board system, a BBS is an open computer system which members can dial into (via a phone) in order to send e-mail, join discussion groups and download files. Around since the 1970s, BBSs were originally locally based but now often provide access to a broad spectrum of internet applications, including e-mail, telnet and FTP.

Berners-Lee, Tim (1955–) – Invented the World Wide Web during 1990-91, whilst working at CERN, the European Particle Physics Laboratory in Geneva (see Chapter 1). In 1994 he later established the World Wide Web Consortium (W3C) to oversee the Web's development and to recommend universal standards. His book, *Weaving the Web* (1999), gives a valuable account of the development of the Web, and his original ideas and intentions for it.

Bookmark – A routine perfected by Netscape Navigator which allows Web surfers to save a URL to a site or page that he or she has already visited, and revisit the site at a later point in time. In Microsoft's Internet Explorer browser, these are called 'Favorites'.

Browser – Software for viewing and travelling around the Web, such as Netscape Navigator and Microsoft's Internet Explorer.

Bug – Computerese for a software error or programming glitch which causes the computer to malfunction or crash. Bugs are always around, seldom liked and never entirely eliminated.

Cache – A small, fast area of computer memory used to hold recently accessed data. Most often applied to Web browsers' cache, memory spaces used to hold recently visited websites.

Cascading Style Sheet (CSS) – An extension to HTML which allows styles (colour, font style and font size, for example) to be specified for certain elements of a hypertext document. CSSs are especially useful when preparing many, slightly different HTML pages.

CD-Rom – a compact disc used with a computer (as opposed to a stereo) which holds large amounts of digital information. Until recently, CD-Roms stored information which users could only access. Today, with the proper software and hardware, users can access and alter the information. Compared to the now old-fashioned looking floppy disks, the silver CD-Roms look reasonably cool.

CGI – Common Gateway Interface (CGI) scripts are computer programs that are placed on Web servers, and allow Web pages to process data entered by the user.

Chat – A form of online communication which allows users to have conversations in real time. When participating in a chat discussion, users' messages instantaneously appear on another user's computer monitor or, while in a chatroom, on the screens of multiple users.

Compression – Files can be compressed (in various ways) so that they can be downloaded more quickly. For example, 'red dot, red dot, red dot, red dot, red dot, red dot, red dot, red dot' is the standard long-winded way in which a computer would describe a graphic which, when displayed, looks like a red line. But it could just say '9 red dots'. That's compression.

Cookie – A bit of information, such as a reference number, saved on a Web user's hard disk drive by a website, so that the site can 'remember' information about that particular user. These cookies are saved in one cookies file, which is a simple text file which cannot, in itself, do any harm. Cookies only enable websites to recall information the user has given to them; they do not send information like your name or e-mail address to a website of their own accord.

Cracker – A hacker who causes damage to systems, or uses stolen data for illegal means. Some hackers like this term to be used, to differentiate 'bad' hackers (crackers) from ordinary hackers, who (in this use of two terms) just enjoy trying to access supposedly secure systems, but don't do any harm.

Cybercafe – A cafe offering internet access. These range, like all cafes, from the very stylish to the very smelly. At the moment, cybercafes look like cafes with a load of computers on the tables. In the future, we are told, internet access will be offered by things like coffee cups anyway, which will save a lot of space.

Cyberpunk – A sub-genre of science fiction inspired largely by William Gibson's 1982 novel *Neuromancer* and characterized by futuristic computer network-based societies. Recently, the term cyberpunk has been (incorrectly) co-opted to refer to any cultural phenomenon involving digital technology and tight black leather.

Cybersex – Often called 'tinysex' or 'one handed surfing', cybersex refers to sexual activity or arousal which takes place within computer-mediated environments such as MUDs, chatrooms and e-mail.

Cyberspace – A more mainstream and literary term for the internet, cyberspace refers to the conceptual space where computer networking hardware, network software and users converge. The term was originally coined by William Gibson in his 1982 novel *Neuromancer*.

Cybersquatting – The practice of buying domain names with the intention of selling them on, subsequently, to companies that are willing to pay lots of money to have them. In the mid-1990s, enterprising people would buy up '.com' domain names which just happened to be those of well-known companies, knowing that, soon, those companies would be willing to spend a lot of money buying rights to their brand's domain. Others just bought names like 'toothpaste.com' knowing that someone would be bound to want to pay lots of money for them soon. Some legal precedents have now made the purchase of domain names which are the same as existing well-known trademarks illegal (in some countries).

Default – The original arrangement of something – the 'factory setting'.

Digital – A description of data that is stored or transmitted as a sequence of discrete symbols from a finite set, most commonly as binary data (zeroes and ones) represented by electronic or electromagnetic signals. The less precise form of data that preceded digital was analogue. CD-Roms are to vinyl records as digital is to analogue.

Digital camera – Digital cameras take photographs like normal cameras but save them in digital form (as JPEG or GIF files, for example), thereby allowing fast and easy transfer to the Web.

Digital versatile disc or digital video disc (DVD) – A high-density compact disc used for storing large amounts of data, especially high-resolution audio-visual material. Currently, DVDs provide over seven times the storage capacity of CD-Roms and are often used to store and trade pirated versions of films and television shows. Commercial DVD releases of movies contain a host of bonus features, such as interviews and 'making of' films, except for those designed towards the end of the week, when the makers can't be bothered.

Domain – The location of a website, ending in a suffix such as '.com' (for commercial sites), '.org' (non-profit organizations), '.edu' (education), '.gov' (government), '.net' (internet-related), or regionally specific variants such as '.co.uk' (UK company), '.ac.uk' (UK higher education), '.gouv.fr' (French government). A domain may contain several websites at different addresses within it; it's the very broadest description of where a site resides. (*Geocities.com*, for example, gives a home to millions of sites.) A domain name doesn't *necessarily* lead to a website, as they can be bought and then not used, or used only for e-mail. (See also **Cybersquatting**.)

Domain Name Server (DNS) – A server on the internet which matches domain names to IP addresses, telling computers where to look for requested pages or files.

Dreamweaver – Popular and effective Web page-making and website-managing software, produced by Macromedia. Takes a **WYSIWYG** approach (see below) but is particularly appreciated by website authors because it doesn't mess up your HTML. (Other programs are more arrogant and sometimes rewrite the code – often in a way that the user does not appreciate.)

E-commerce – Electronic commerce: money-making business on the internet.

E-mail – Messages sent via the internet from one user to another. As new internet applications come and go, e-mail remains the most simple and most cherished use of the net.

FAQs – See **Frequently Asked Questions**.

File – A collection of information (a graphic, a software program, an e-mail, for example) recognized and treated as a single unit by a computer.

Flame – An abusive e-mail, usually sent to someone who has made an ignorant, offensive or commercial contribution to an e-mail or newsgroup discussion.

Flash – Vector-based graphics and animation format (see **Vector-based graphics**) developed by Macromedia, popular on the Web because it can deliver attractive websites – with interactive graphics and sound – with small file sizes.

Freeware – Software distributed for free, with no restrictions, over the internet (or by other means).

Frequently Asked Questions (FAQs) – Common form of Web page which provides answers to those questions frequently sent to the website.

FTP – Short for file-transfer protocol, FTP refers to (a) a method of transferring one or more files from one computer to another on a network or phone line, and (b) an application program that moves files across the internet using the file-transfer protocol.

Gates, Bill (1955–) – Chief Executive of Microsoft from 1975 to January 2000, when he became Chairman and Chief Software Architect (Steve Ballmer is the new Chief Executive). Extremely rich, obviously. Not popular amongst internet people, who often feel that Microsoft has tried to turn the universal internet into Microsoft Internet™.

GIF – A graphics file common on the Web, which uses a palette with a limited number of colours to keep its file size down.

Gopher – A menu-driven program developed at the University of Minnesota which helps users explore, locate and retrieve information on the internet. Gopher organizes all information via a series of hierarchical menus. Actually, lots and lots of menus. Happily, the World Wide Web has basically replaced it.

Hacking – Gaining access to supposedly secure computer systems without the consent of the system's owners.

Hard copy – The printout, on paper, of data (such as a website).

Hard disk – Often referred to as a hard drive, a hard disk is a magnetic disk mounted permanently in a computer's central processing unit, or CPU. Hard disks are used to store data, primarily permanent operating applications and temporary files.

Hits – Often taken to mean the number of visitors to a Web page or site: people say 'My site received a million hits last month' and assume this means that a million people visited the site. But it doesn't. The number of hits is the number of requests for files made to the Web server. An average Web page is made up of one HTML file and several graphics files (containing logos, pictures, buttons, bars and so on). So loading one Web page might notch up 10 hits, for example. And then the same visitor might look at other pages, easily generating 50 or 100 hits. So 'a million hits' would never mean a million visitors; it would more likely represent, say, 50,000 visitors, although the percentage of actual visitors (compared to number of hits) will vary from site to site. (Note: To confuse matters further, sometimes people say they had 'a thousand hits' when they actually know that they had a thousand visitors, but they think that 'hits' is a more trendy word for that, which it isn't.)

HTML – Hypertext Markup Language, simple computer language which most Web pages are written in, devised by Tim Berners-Lee. An HTML Web page is a text document with added HTML tags; these tags, in <angular brackets>, tell the browser how to arrange and format the text, where to add graphics, where links are and so on.

HTTP – Hypertext Transfer Protocol, devised by Tim Berners-Lee as a fast, universal protocol for passing files around the internet, particularly suited to the hypertext system on the Web.

Hyperlink – On a Web page, a hyperlink (or simply 'link') is text or a graphic which the user clicks on in order to proceed or move to a related page.

Hypertext – Text which includes links or shortcuts to other documents, allowing the reader to jump easily from one text to related texts, and consequently from one idea to another, in a multi-linear, non-sequential manner. Originally coined by Ted Nelson in 1965, hypertext serves as the organizational foundation for the World Wide Web.

Internet – A worldwide network of networks which connects computers around the world. First incarnated as the ARPANET in 1969, the internet has transformed from an internal military network, to an academic research net, to the current communication and commercial internet of today. It supports services such as e-mail, the World Wide Web, file transfer and Internet Relay Chat. The internet is commonly referred to as 'the net', 'cyberspace' and 'the information superhighway'. It's also what all the commotion is about.

Internet Explorer – Web browser, produced by Microsoft from 1996, and given away free (and bundled or 'integrated' with Windows) in order to compete with Netscape Navigator. Despite being shunned by those opposed to Microsoft's dominance of the software market, IE had become the most-used browser by 1998.

Internet Service Provider (ISP) – Company or organization providing access to the internet. When a home internet user goes online, their computer phones their ISP (via a modem), which provides a gateway to the internet.

Intranet – A network used for internal communications within an organization.

ISDN – Short for Integrated Services Digital Network, ISDN is a set of communications standards offered by telephone carriers which provides users with extremely fast internet connections. ISDN allows a single wire or optical fibre to carry voice, digital network services and video, and is believed by many to be the network which will ultimately replace the telephone system.

ISP – See **Internet Service Provider**.

Java – A programming language created by Sun Microsystems and featured on many websites. As a platform-independent language, Java programs can be run on any computer, either as a free-standing application or as an applet placed on a Web page. While Java has served to increase Web interactivity and expand multimedia, it is scorned by others for increasing download time and fostering a more commercially focused World Wide Web.

JPEG – A compressed graphics file common on the Web, which can contain up to 16 million colours and so is used for 'photographic'-type images.

Killer application – Software (or more broadly, an idea) that is so appealing to users that they will change their computer (i.e. buy a new one) in order to be able to use it. The World Wide Web was the 'killer app' that made the internet sufficiently desirable that people would go out of their way to get the equipment to access it.

Linux – A platform-independent operating system created by Linus Torvalds and friends starting about 1990. Unlike other operating systems, such as Windows 98, Linux can be downloaded and distributed for free. For this reason, many consider Linux to be the most worthy threat to Microsoft's computing hegemony. Assembled collaboratively by literally thousands of users, Linux is often referred to as the world's greatest hacker project in history.

Listservs – Often (technically incorrectly) called mailing lists, listservs refer to (a) the software that makes possible automated mailing list distribution systems and (b) the online communities that arise from such lists. Listservs can be either moderated or unmoderated and differ from mailing lists due to their automated means of subscribing and unsubscribing.

Microsoft – Founded in 1975 by Bill Gates and Paul Allen, Microsoft is the world's largest supplier of operating systems and other software for personal computers. Some of its software products include MS-DOS, Microsoft Windows, Windows NT and, most recently, Microsoft Internet Explorer. Due to their heavy-handedly aggressive marketing tactics, many net-heads actively and enthusiastically hate Microsoft.

Modem – A device that enables a computer to send and receive information over a telephone line.

MOO – A type of **MUD**, MOO is short for Multi-User Domain, Object-Oriented and differs from MUDs by allowing users to interact with programmable objects. In keeping with MUDs, these objects are usually dungeons, dragons and whips.

Mosaic – Popular early Web browser. See **Andreessen**, above, who co-wrote it.

MP3 – Popular format of audio files which provide good-quality digital sound but take up (relatively) few kilobytes. MP3s are therefore popular on the internet, because you can download good-quality music quite quickly.

MUD – Short for Multi-User Domain or Multi-User Dungeon, MUDs are online role-playing environments. MUDs occur in text mode – similar to a chatroom – where players assume a spectrum of identities and explore a range of environments, often based on fantasy fiction or sexual situations.

Netscape – See **Andreessen**, above, who founded this company.

Netscape Communicator – Suite of software including Navigator (Web browser), Messenger (e-mail program) and Composer (for producing Web pages), plus other features.

Netscape Navigator – Web browser, launched in 1994 by Marc Andreessen (see above), who had written the first popular browser, Mosaic.

New media – Term which embraces all of the 'new' forms of electronic media – newer than TV and radio, that is – such as multimedia CD-Roms, the internet, and video games. Sometimes it is taken to mean 'the Web' although it is really a broader term.

Newbie – Someone new to the internet. Newbies are sometimes sneered at by established internet users, such as long-standing members of e-mail discussion lists (listservs) who tend to be annoyed when a 'newbie' joins and starts posting 'ignorant' questions.

Newsgroups – A public online space where messages are posted for public consumption and response. The most available distribution of newsgroups is Usenet, which contains thousands of newsgroups devoted to all kinds of (diverse and perverse) topics. Often referred to as the original public sphere of cyberspace, newsgroups are currently over-run by **spam**.

Plug-in – An extra bit of software which has to be added to a browser before a certain type of file can be viewed. For example, Flash animations cannot be seen unless one has the Flash plug-in. Recent browsers come with a number of the most common plug-ins pre-installed.

Portal – A website which aspires to be your primary point of contact with the Web, usually offering a bundle of news, search facilities, free e-mail, chat areas and other gimmicks. Examples include Yahoo!, Netscape Netcenter, BBC and Handbag.

Program – Used as a noun to describe a series of instructions that tell a computer what to do, or as a verb to describe the act of creating or revising a program.

QuickTime – Refers to both a standard and an application used by Apple computers for integrating full-motion video and digitized sound into programs and websites.

RealAudio – A browser plug-in used for playing real-time audio over the Web. On a standard slowish modem connection, RealAudio can sound a bit like a radio underwater.

RealVideo – A browser plug-in for playing real-time video over the Web. On a standard slowish modem connection, RealVideo can look like a jerky, blocky computer game from the land that time forgot.

Scanner – Machine that scans an image, such as a photograph or newspaper article, and turns it into a file which can be displayed and manipulated on a computer.

Search engine – Search facility based on a database of as much of the Web's content as possible, compiled by electronic 'spiders' or 'robots' which roam around the internet cataloguing content. (Therefore search engines are different to directories, such as Yahoo!, which are more selective and are compiled by humans.) Examples include AltaVista, Excite! and Google.

Server – A computer or set of computers that provides client stations with access to files and printers as shared resources to a computer network. The most common servers are Web servers which send out Web pages, mail servers which deliver e-mail, list servers which administer mailing lists, and FTP servers which hold FTP sites and deliver files to users who request them.

Shareware – Software which is usually free initially, but may ask you to register the product and pay its creator after a certain trial period, or which might ask you to make a voluntary payment if you like the software and use it regularly. Shareware is often distributed over the internet.

Shockwave – A more complex, programmable variation of Flash (see above) which can be used to produce interactive games, multimedia presentations, or other applications, which run from websites. Macromedia's Director software is needed to produce Shockwave content.

Site – See **Website**.

Spam – Junk e-mail, sent to several people at once. Any e-mail that is not written for your personal attention can be seen as spam. E-mail advertising or promoting something is spam; chain letters and virus hoaxes are also regarded as spam by most sane people.

Style sheet - Often referred to as a template, a style sheet is a file or form which defines the layout of a document. Most commonly found in website production, word-processing, and desktop publishing, style sheets are useful in that they give designers the ability to use the same style sheet for many documents.

Surfing – Popular term for wandering around the Web, like 'channel surfing' television, and therefore a regrettable term since it positions the Web user as rather passive.

Torvalds, Linus (1970–) – Created the first version of **Linux**, a one-time experimental version of the UNIX operating system whilst a student at Helsinki University. A hero among net-heads and the antithesis to **Bill Gates**, Torvalds worked with thousands of programmers to alter, tweak and perfect Linux and to keep it free of charge.

UNIX – The operating system upon which the Internet was developed. UNIX was developed in the late 1960s/early 1970s as a joint venture between General Electric, AT&T Bell Laboratories, and MIT. Later, UNIX grew with support from the University of California, Berkeley and other universities. There are several free versions of UNIX, including **Linux** and FreeBSD. Among many, knowledge of Unix is the bar that separates technical net-heads from **newbies**.

URL – Uniform Resource Locator: the address beginning 'http://' (see **Hypertext Transfer Protocol**), which can point to a file on a Web server anywhere in the world. Some people call this URI, for Universal Resource Indicator (suggesting that the same address will always point to the same file in the same place), as preferred by Tim Berners-Lee, but most people ignore that.

Usenet – Originally implemented in 1979-80 by Steve Bellovin, Jim Ellis, Tom Truscott and Steve Daniel at Duke University, Usenet continues to be the largest worldwide collection of newsgroups. While not part of the internet, Usenet can be reached through most Internet service providers and provides over 10,000 public forums on practically every topic under the sun. Really. The names of newsgroups are comprised of a string of words separated by dots, such as 'rec.sport.sumo' or 'alt.barney.dinosaur.die.die.die'.

Vector-based graphics – A graphics or animation system which can deliver complex or large graphics but small file sizes, by describing the shape and position of elements, rather than describing them pixel-by-pixel (as conventional graphics formats do). Vector-based graphics can be scaled up or down but always retain a smooth appearance, because instead of explaining the layout of square pixels, the format is saying, for example, 'draw a curve from the centre of the shape to the top-left corner'.

Virtual – A commonly used adjective which refers to anything remotely related the internet. Online discussions become virtual communities; online environments become virtual realities; and a dodgy e-mail describing what one user would do to another in which way and how often becomes virtual sex.

Web – The World Wide Web. According to its inventor, **Tim Berners-Lee**, Web should be written with a capital 'W' when used as abbreviation of World Wide Web.

Webmaster – Grandiose (and arguably sexist) term meaning the person responsible for creating or maintaining a website.

Web page – One page of the Web. Usually an '.htm' or '.html' file, which then may call for various graphics or multimedia files to complete its appearance on a user's screen. Normally a web page is part of a website.

Website – A group of related Web pages, produced by one person, group or organization, which are closely interlinked. For example, the website www.newmediastudies.com contains several Web pages about new media.

Webzine – Written, edited, and designed by individuals, collectives, or corporations, webzines are zines that exist on the Web. Some are electronic versions of existing print magazines, but the 'true' webzine exists solely in cyberspace.

Webzines originated as online public spheres for disgruntled, sarcastic teens and were products of love, unregulated ego, and/or a serious need to get a life. Recently, however, the term webzine has also become synonymous with the online version of a traditional, corporate magazine.

WELL, the – Short for the Whole Earth 'Lectronic Link, the WELL is a commercial online community which was established in 1985 to serve San Francisco's Bay Area. Currently international in scope, the WELL is perhaps the most well-known virtual community in the world, a result no doubt of its devoted subscribers and of Howard Rheingold's seminal work *The Virtual Community*.

Wired **(magazine)** – Originally established in 1993 by Louis Rossetto to cover impending digital culture, *Wired* has become a mainstream mouthpiece for the new digital economy, with an occasional libertarian nod towards the more social and political ramifications of the Information Age. Glossy, full of ads and overflowing with self-importance, *Wired* represents all the unfulfilled promises of cyberspace.

World Wide Web (WWW) – A global web of interconnected pages which (ideally) can be read by any computer with a Web browser and internet connection. More technically and specifically, the WWW is the global web of interlinked files which can be located using the HTTP protocol.

WWW – See **World Wide Web**.

WYSIWYG – An abbreviation for What You See Is What You Get, and pronounced 'wizzywig'. In Web terms, WYSIWYG programs allow website designers to design Web pages on screen. The software displays what the page will actually look like when viewed in a browser – as opposed to showing a screenful of HTML code.

Yahoo! – Popular directory of websites (www.yahoo.com), compiled by actual humans. People with websites have to fill in a submission form, on the Yahoo! website, so that Yahoo!'s editors can consider it for inclusion. Yahoo! also provides conventional search engine results if its directory can't match your request. The site has also grown to become a portal site, offering free e-mail and auctions, and by the time you read this it will probably be offering singing lessons and veterinary advice.

References

Allen, G., 1995: 'Information superhighway - the key to reinventing democracy'. Letter to the *Guardian* 24 February, 25.

Anderson, B., 1991: *Imagined Communities: Reflections on the Origins and Spread of Nationalism*. London: Verso.

Appadurai, A., 1990: 'Disjuncture and difference in the global cultural economy' in Featherstone (ed.), *Global Culture: Nationalism, Globalization and Modernity*, London: Sage, 295–310.

Appadurai, A., 1996: *Modernity at Large: Cultural Dimensions of Globalization*. Minneapolis, MN: University of Minnesota Press.

Arlidge, J., 1997: 'Scotland plans tele-democracy'. *Guardian* 18 August, 5.

Arterton, F.C., 1987: *Teledemocracy: Can Technology Protect Democracy?* Newbury Park, CA.: Sage.

Augé, M., 1998: *A Sense for the Other: The Timeliness and Relevance of Anthropology*. Stanford, CA: Stanford University.

Baecker, R., 1997: 'The web of knowledge media design'. Paper delivered at the Knowledge Media Design Institute, Toronto, Canada.

Bailey, C., 1996: 'Virtual skin: Articulating race in cyberspace' in Moser, M.A. (ed.), *Immersed in Technology: Art and Virtual Environments*. Cambridge, MA: MIT Press, 29–49.

Banks, M. and Morphy, H. (eds), 1997: *Rethinking Visual Anthropology*. London: Yale University Press.

Barlow, J.P. 1995: 'What are we doing online?', *Harper's*, August, 35–46.

Bass, D., 1998: 'Portal? What's a portal? The latest, hottest internet stocks', *Fortune*. 26 October, 143–44.

Baym, N.K., 1995a: 'From practice to culture on Usenet', in Star, S.L. (ed.), *The Cultures of Computing*. Oxford: Blackwell Publishers, 29–52.

Baym, N.K., 1995b: 'The emergence of community in computer-mediated communication', in Jones, S.G. (ed.), *CyberSociety: Computer-Mediated Communication and Community*. Thousand Oaks, CA: Sage Publications, 138–63.

Baym, N.K., 1997: 'Interpreting soap operas and creating community: Inside a computer-mediated fan club', in Kiesler, S. (ed.), *Culture of the Internet*. Mahwah, NJ: Lawrence Erlbaum Associates, Publishers, 103–20.

Becker, H., 1998a: 'Visual sociology, documentary photography, and photojournalism: It's (almost) all a matter of context', in Prosser, J. (ed.), *Image-based Research: A Sourcebook for Qualitative Researchers*. London: Falmer, 84–96.

Becker, H., 1998b: *Tricks of the Trade: How to Think About Your Research While You're Doing It*. Chicago, IL: University of Chicago.

Benjamin, W., 1968 in Arendt, H. (ed.), *Illuminations: Walter Benjamin, Essays and Reflections*. New York: Schocken.

Benton Foundation, 1998: *Losing Ground Bit by Bit: Low-Income Communities in the Information Age*. Washington DC: Benton Foundation and National Urban League. http://www.benton.org/low-income report/Low-Income.html.

Berry, C., 1996: 'Seoul man: A night on the town with Korea's first gay activist', *Outrage* 159, August, 38–40.

Birkerts, S., 1994: *The Gutenberg Elegies: The Fate of Reading in an Electronic Age*. Winchester, MA: Faber and Faber.

Birt, J., 1999: 'The prize and the price: the social, political and cultural consequences of the Digital Age', *The New Statesman* Media Lecture, Banqueting House, Whitehall, London, 6 July. www.bbc.co.uk/info/speech/index.shtml.

Blankenship, L., 1985: 'The conscience of a hacker', *Phrack*, 1:7, Phile 3.

Bogdan, R., 1990: *Freak Show: Presenting Human Oddities for Amusement and Profit*. Chicago, IL and London: University of Chicago.

Bolter, J.D., 1991: *Writing Space: The Computer, Hypertext, and the History of Writing*. Hillsdale, NJ: L. Erlbaum Associates.

Borsook, P., 1996: 'The memoirs of a token: An aging Berkeley feminist examines *Wired*' in Cherney, L. and Weise, E.R. (eds), *Wired Women: Gender and New Realities in Cyberspace*. Seattle, WA: Seal Press, 24–41.

Brants, K., Huizenga, M. and Van Meerten, R., 1996: 'The new canals of Amsterdam: an exercise in local electronic democracy', *Media Culture and Society* 18, 233–47.

Briggs, A., 1979: *Governing the BBC*. London: BBC.

Briggs, A., 1985: *The BBC: The First 50 Years*. Oxford: Clarendon.

Bright, S., 1992: *Susie Bright's Sexual Reality: A Virtual Sex World Reader*. Pittsburgh, PA: Cleis Press.

Brown, G., 1996: 'In the real world', *Guardian* 2 August, 13.

Bruckman, A., 1992: 'Identity workshop: Emergent social and psychological phenomena in text-based virtual reality'. ftp://ftp.cc.gatech.edu/pub/people/asb/papers/identity-workshop.ps.

Budge, I., 1996: *The New Challenge of Direct Democracy*. Cambridge: Polity.

Buten, J., 1996: *Personal Home Page Survey*. www.asc.upenn.edu/USR/sbuten/phpi.htm.

Butler, J., 1990a: *Gender Trouble: Gender Trouble: Feminism and the Subversion of Identity*. London: Routledge.

Butler, J., 1990b: 'The force of fantasy: Feminism, Mapplethorpe, and discursive excess', *Differences: A Journal of Feminist Cultural Studies* 2:2, 105–25.

Bynner, J., 1997: *It Doesn't Get Any Better*. London: Basic Skills Agency.

Califia, P., 1994: *Public Sex: The Culture of Radical Sex*. Pittsburgh, PA: Cleis Press.

Camp, L.J., 1996: 'We are geeks, and we are not guys: The systers mailing list', in Cherney, L. and Weise, E.R. (eds), *Wired Women: Gender and New Realities in Cyberspace*. Seattle, WA: Seal Press, 114–25.

Canzian, F., 1999: *The Fake Counter Home Page*. www.geocities.com/SiliconValley/Heights/5910/counter.html.

Case, S.E., 1997: *The Domain-Matrix: Performing Lesbian at the End of Print Culture*. Bloomington, IN: Indiana University Press.

Cassidy, S., 1999: 'Civics to be put on timetable', *Times Educational Supplement* 26 February, 2.

Chandler, D., 1997: *Writing Oneself in Cyberspace*. http://www.aber.ac.uk/~dgc/homepgid.html.

Chandler, D., 1998: *Personal Home Pages and the Construction of Identities on the Web.* http://www.aber.ac.uk/~dgc/webident.html.

Chandler, D. and Roberts-Young, D., 1998: *The Construction of Identity in the Personal Homepages of Adolescents.* http://www.aber.ac.uk/~dgc/strasbourg.html.

Chao, A., 1996: 'The Performative Context of the T Bar' in *Embodying the Invisible: Body Politics in Constructing Contemporary Taiwanese Lesbian Identities,* PhD Dissertation, Cornell University.

Chen, C., 1997: 'Are you Gay, Ku'er, or Tongzhi?: Notes on the politics of hybrid sexual identity'. Paper presented at the Second International Conference on Sexuality Education, Sexology, Gender Studies and LesBiGay Studies, organized by the Center for the Stiudy of Sexuylaity and Difference, 31 May–1 June.

Cherny, L. and Weise, E.R. (eds), 1996: *Wired Women: Gender and New Realities in Cyberspace.* Seattle, WA: Seal Press.

Cisler, S., 1993: 'Community computer networks: Building electronic greenbelts'. http://bcn.boulder.co.us/community/resources/greenbelts.txt.

Clarke, R., 1999: *The Willingness of Net-Consumers to Pay: A Lack-of-Progress Report.* Paper presented to *Electronic Markets* conference. http://www.anu.edu.au/Roger.Clarke/.

Cohen, E., 1997: 'For Native Americans, the net offers both promise and threat', *The New York Times on the Web.* www.nytimes.com/library/cyber/week/041697natives.html.

Cohen, R., 1996: *Global Diasporas: An Introduction.* Seattle, WA: University of Washington Press.

Cohill, A.M. and Kavanaugh, A.L. (eds), 1997: *Community Networks: Lessons from Blacksburg, Virginia.* Norwood, MA: Artech House, Inc.

Coleman, S., 1999: 'Can the new media invigorate democracy?', *Political Quarterly* 70, 16–22.

Collins-Jarvis, L.A., 1993: 'Gender representation in an electronic city hall: Female adoption of Santa Monica's PEN system', *Journal of Broadcasting and Electronic Media* 37:1, 49–66.

Consalvo, M., 1997: 'Cash cows hit the web: Gender and communications technology', *Journal of Communication Inquiry* 21:1, 98–115.

Cornford, J. and Robins, K., 1999: 'New media' in Stokes, J. and Reading, A. (eds), *The Media in Britain: Current Debates and Developments.* London: Macmillan, 108–25.

Correll, S., 1995: The ethnography of an electronic bar: The lesbian cafe. *Journal of Contemporary Ethnography* 24:3, 270–98.

Cumings, B., 1997: *Korea's Place in the Sun: A Modern History,* New York: W.W. Norton & Co.

Danet, B., Ruedenberg-Wright, L. and Rosenbaum-Tamari, Y., 1997: 'Hmmm . . . Where's that smoke coming from?: Writing, play and performance on internet relay chat', *Journal of Computer-Mediated Communication* 2:4. http://jcmc.huji.ac.il/vol2/issue4/danet.html.

Dawson, J., 1998: *Gay and Lesbian Online: Your Indispensable Guide to Cruising the Queer Web.* Los Angeles, CA: Alyson.

Dawson, M. and Bellamy Foster, J., 1998: 'Virtual Capitalism: Monopoly capital, marketing, and the information highway' in McChesney, R., Wood, E. and Bellamy Foster, J. (eds), *Capitalism and the Information Age.* New York: Monthly Review Press, 51–67.

Delap, C., 1998: *Making Better Decisions: Report of an IPPR Symposium on*

Citizens' Juries and Other Methods of Public Involvement. London: Institute for Public Policy Research.

Denzin, N., 1997: *Interpretive Ethnography: Ethnographic Practices for the 21st Century*. London: Sage.

Denzin, N. and Lincoln, E. (eds), 1994: *Handbook of Qualitative Research*. London: Sage.

Dibbell, J., 1993: 'A rape in cyberspace; or how an evil clown, a Haitian trickster spirit, two wizards, and a cast of dozens turned a database into a society', *The Village Voice*, 36–42.

Dibbell, J., 1998: *My Tiny Life: Crime and Passion in a Virtual World*. New York: Henry Holt.

Dietrich, D., 1997: '(Re)-Fashioning the techno-erotic woman: Gender and textuality in the cybercultural matrix' in Jones, S.G. (ed.), *Virtual Culture: Identity and Communication in Cybersociety*. London: Sage Publications, 169–84.

DiGiovanna, J., 1996: 'Losing your voice on the internet' in Ludlow, P. (ed.), *High Noon on the Electronic Frontier: Conceptual Issues in Cyberspace*. Cambridge, MA: MIT Press, 445–57.

Dodson, S., 1999: 'A riot from cyberspace', *Guardian* 24 June.

Doheny-Farina, S., 1996: *The Wired Neighborhood*. New Haven, CT: Yale University Press.

Donath, J. and Robertson, N., 1994: 'The sociable web', *Proceedings of the 2nd International World Wide Web Conference, Chicago*. http://judith.www.media.mit.edu/SocialWeb/SociableWeb.html.

Donath, J., Karahalios, D. and Viegas, F., 1999: 'Visualizing conversation', *Journal of Computer Mediated Communication* 4:4 June. http://www.ascusc.org/jcmc/vol4/issue4/donath.html.

Downey, G.L. and Dumit, J. (eds), 1998: *Cyborgs and Citadels: Anthropological Interventions in Emerging Sciences and Technologies*. Santa Fe, NM: School of American Research Press.

Downing, J.D.H., 1989: 'Computers for political change: PeaceNet and Public Data Access', *Journal of Communication* 39, 154–62.

Dreyfus, M., 2000: *A Simple Guide to Creating Your Own Web Page*. London: Prentice Hall.

Dworkin, A., 1981: *Pornography: Men Possessing Women*. New York: Perigee.

Dworkin, A., 1987: *Intercourse*. New York: Free Press.

E! (Entertainment) Television, 1998: *Cyberwomen*.

Ebben, M. and Kramarae, C., 1993: 'Women and information technologies: Creating a cyberspace of our own' in Taylor, H.J., Kramarae, C. and Ebben, M. (eds), *Women, Information Technology, and Scholarship*. Urbana, IL: Women, Information Technology, and Scholarship Colloquium, 5–27.

Ebo, B., 1998: 'Internet or outernet?' in Ebo, B. (ed.), *Cyberghetto or cybertopia?: Race, class, and gender on the Internet*. Westport, CT: Praeger, 1–12.

Echols, A., 1983: 'Cultural feminism: Feminist capitalism and the anti-pornography movement', *Social Text* 7, 34–53.

Economist, 1999a: 'The BBC: online and in a mess', *Economist* 8 May: 35–36.

Economist, 1999b: Britain: Secret Society: The government's freedom of information bill makes a mockery of the idea of more open government. *Economist* 29 May: 32.

Elshtain, J., 1982: 'Democracy and the QUBE tube', *The Nation*. 7–14 August, 108–10.

Erickson, T., 1996: *The World Wide Web as Social Hypertext*. www.pliant.org/personal/Tom_Erickson/SocialHypertext.html.

Escobar, A., 1996: 'Welcome to cyberia: Notes on the anthropology of cyberculture' in Sardar, Z. and Ravetz, J.R. (eds), *Cyberfutures: Culture and Politics on the Information Superhighway*. New York: New York University Press, 111–37.

Fielding, N.G and Lee, R.M., 1998: *Computer Analysis and Qualitative Research*. London: Sage.

Firth, S., 1998: 'Woman puts herself and her apartment live on internet'. www.nando.net/newsroom/ntn/info/091797/info7_22171_body.html.

Fiske, J., 1992: 'The cultural economy of fandom' in Lewis, L. (ed.), *The Adoring Audience: Fan Culture and Popular Media*. London and New York: Routledge, 30–49.

Flanders, F. and Willis, M., 1998: *Web Pages That Suck: Learn Good Design By Looking at Bad Design*. California, CA: Sybex.

Foster, D., 1997: 'Community and identity in the electronic village' in Porter, D. (ed.), *Internet Culture*. New York: Routledge, 23–37.

Foucault, M., 1980: *Power/Knowledge: Selected Interviews and other Writings, 1072–77*. Gordon, C. (ed. and trans.), New York: Pantheon.

Fox, J., 1999: 'Net stock rules: masters of a parallel universe', *Fortune* 7 June, 26–31.

Gaiser, T., 1998: *On-line Focus Groups. An Interview with Ted J Gaiser*.

Garland Thomson, R., 1996: *Freakery: Cultural Spectacles of the Extraordinary Body*. New York: New York University.

Garland Thomson, R., 1997: *Extraordinary Bodies: Figuring Physical Disability in American Culture and Literature*. New York: Columbia University.

Gauntlett, D., 1995: *Moving Experiences: Understanding Television's Influences and Effects*, London: John Libbey.

Gauntlett, D., 1997: *Video Critical: Children, the Environment and Media Power*, Luton: John Libbey Media.

Gauntlett, D., forthcoming: *Media, Gender and Identity: A New Introduction*, London and New York: Routledge.

Gauntlett, D. and Hill, A., 1999: *TV Living: Television, Culture and Everyday Life*, London and New York: Routledge.

Gibson, W., 1984: *Neuromancer*. New York: Ace Books.

Gillett, S.E. and Kapor, M., 1997: 'The self-governing internet: Coordination by design' in Kahin, B. and Keller, James H. (eds), *Coordinating the Internet*. Cambridge, Mass. and London: MIT Press, 3–38.

Glover, J., 1999: *Top Ten Ways to Tell if You Have a Sucky Home Page*. http://jeffglover.com/sucky.html.

Goffman, E., 1959: *The Presentation of Self in Everyday Life*. London: Penguin (page references are to 1990 edition).

Goguen, J., 1999: *The Ethics of Databases*. Notes from an invited presentation at the 1999 Annual Meeting of the Society for Social Studies of Science, San Diego. http://www-cse.ucsd.edu/users/goguen/papers/4s/4s.html.

Goldhaber, M.H., 1997: 'The attention economy and the net'. http://www.firstmonday.dk/issues/issue2_4/goldhaber.

Gómez-Peña, G., 1996: 'The virtual barrio @ the other frontier (or the chicano interneta)' in Leeson, L.H. (ed.), *Clicking In: Hot Links to a Digital Culture*. Seattle: Bay Press, 173–79.

Gore, A., 1995: Speech to the international telecommunication union in Buenos Aires. www.eff.org/pub/GII_NII/Govt_docs/gii_gore_buenos_aires.speech.

Graham, A. and Davies, G., 1997: *Broadcasting, Society and Policy in the Multimedia Age*. Luton: University of Luton Press.

Grossberg, L., 1992: 'Is there a fan in the house?: the affective sensibility of fandom' in Lewis, L. (ed.), *The Adoring Audience: Fan Culture and Popular Media*. London and New York: Routledge, 50–65.

Grumer, A., 1999: *Employment Agencies That Suck*. www.users.interport.net/~avram/natter/19980612.html.

Gulker C., 1999: 'The Future? Just remember, you read it here first', *The Independent*, 20 December, 12.

Gurak, L., 1997: *Persuasion and Privacy in Cyberspace: The Online Protests over Lotus Marketplace and the Clipper Chip*. New Haven, CT: Yale University Press.

Gurley, J.W., 1998: 'Getting in the way on the net', *Fortune* 6 July, 188–91.

Habermas, J., 1989: *The Structural Transformation of the Public Sphere*. Cambridge: Polity.

Habermas, J., 1991: 'The public sphere' in Mukerji, C. and Schudson, M. (eds), *Rethinking Popular Culture: Contemporary Perspectives in Cultural Studies*. Berkeley, CA: University of California Press.

Hafner, K. and Lyon, M., 1996: *Where Wizards Stay Up Late: The Origins of the Internet*. New York: Simon & Schuster.

Hall, K., 1996: 'Cyberfeminism' in Herring, S.C. (ed.), *Computer-Mediated Communication: Linguistic, Social and Cross-Cultural Perspectives*. Amsterdam: John Benjamins Publishing Co., 147–70.

Hall, S., 1980: 'Encoding/decoding' in Hall, S., Hobson, D., Lowe, A. and Willis P. (eds), *Culture, Media, Language*. London: Hutchinson, 128–38.

Hall, S., 1992: The question of identity. In Hall, S., Held, D. and McGrew, T. (eds), *Modernity and its Futures*. Cambridge: Polity Press.

Harasim, L., 1993: 'Networlds: Networks as social space' in Harasim, L.M. (ed.), *Global Networks: Computers and International Communication*. Cambridge, MA: MIT Press, 15–34.

Harcourt, W, 1999: *Women@internet: Creating New Cultures in Cyberspace*. London: Zed Books.

Harper, D., 1994: 'On the authority of the image: Visual methods at the crossroads' in Denzin, N. and Lincoln, E. (eds), *Handbook of Qualitative Research*. London: Sage, 403–12.

Hauben, R., 1998: 'Report from the Front': Meeting in Geneva rushes to privatize the internet DNS and root server systems.

Hauben, R., 1998: *The Internet - an International Public Treasure A Proposal*. http://www.columbia.edu/~rh120/other/.

Heath, D., Koch, E., Ley, B. and Montoya, M., 1999: 'Nodes and queries: Linking locations in networked fields of inquiry' in Lyman, P. and Wakeford, N. (eds), *Analyzing Virtual Societies: New Directions in Methodology.. American Behavioral Scientist*: 43:3, November/December, 450–63.

Herman, E., 1998: 'Privatising public space' in Thussu, D.K. (ed.), *Electronic Empires*. London: Arnold, 125–34.

Herman, E. and McChesney, R., 1997: *Global Media*. London: Cassell.

Herman, G. and Holly, J. 2000: 'Trade unions and the internet' in Lax, S. (ed.), *Access Denied: Exclusion in the Information Age*. Basingstoke: Macmillan.

Herring, S., 1996a: 'Gender and democracy in computer-mediated communication' in Kling, R. (ed.), *Computerization and Controversy: Value Conflicts and Social Choices*. San Diego, CA: Academic Press, 476–89.

Herring, S., 1996b: 'Posting in a different voice: Gender and ethics in computer-mediated communication' in Ess, C. (ed.), *Philosophic Perspectives in Computer-Mediated Communication*. Albany, NY: State University of New York Press.

Herring, S., 1996c: 'Two variants of an electronic message schema' in Herring,

S.C. (ed.), *Computer-Mediated Communication: Linguistic, Social and Cross-Cultural Perspectives*. Amsterdam: John Benjamins Publishing Co., 81–106.

Herring, S. (ed.), 1996d: *Computer-Mediated Communication: Linguistic, Social and Cross-Cultural Perspectives*. Amsterdam: John Benjamins Publishing Co.

Hinsch, B., 1990: *Passions of the Cut Sleeve: the Male Homosexual Tradition in China*, Berkeley, CA: University of California Press.

Hirschkop, K., 1998: 'Democracy and the new technologies' in McChesney, R.W., Meiksins Wood, E. and Foster, J.B. (eds), *Capitalism and the Information Age*. New York: Monthly Review Press.

Hobbes Internet Timeline, 1999: http://www.isoc.org/guest/zakon/Internet/History/HIT.html.

Horn, S., 1998: *Cyberville: Clicks, Culture, and the Creation of an Online Town*. New York: Warner Books.

Hossfeld, K.J., 1994: 'Hiring immigrant women: Silicon Valley's "Simple Formula"' in Baca Zinn, M. and Thornton Dill, B. (eds), *Women of Color in US Society*. Philadelphia, PA: Temple University Press, 65–93.

House of Commons Select Committee on Culture, Media and Sport, 1998: *The Multimedia Revolution*. London: HMSO. www.parliament.uk/commons/selcom/cmshome.htm.

Howe, C., 1999: 'Cyberspace is no place for tribalism', rptd from *Wicazo-Sa Review* 13:2. www.ualberta.ca/~pimohte/howe.html.

http://www.bc.edu./bc_org/avp/csom/cwf/newsletter/archives/winter99/boundary.html.

Hung, L., 1997: 'Identity politics ends/and its own lack: From the interaction within Taiwanese cyberspace to the dynamics/visibility of queer politics/discourse.' Paper presented at the Second International Conference on Sexuality Education, Sexology, Gender Studies and LesBiGay Studies, organized by the Center for the Study of Sexuality and Difference, National Central University, 31 May-1 June.

Jeffreys, S., 1990: *Anticlimax: A Feminist Perspective on the Sexual Revolution*. London: Women's Press.

Jeffreys, S., 1993: *The Lesbian Heresy: A Feminist Perspective on the Lesbian Sexual Revolution*. North Melbourne, Australia: Spinifex.

Jenkins, H., 1992: *Textual Poachers: Television Fans and Participatory Culture*. London and New York: Routledge.

Johnson, T., 1995: 'The dealer's edge: Gaming in the path of Native America', *Native Americas* 12, 16–24.

Jones, S.G. (ed.), 1995a: *CyberSociety: Computer-Mediated Communication and Community*. Thousand Oaks, CA: Sage Publications.

Jones, S.G., 1995b: 'Understanding community in the information age' in Jones, S.G. (ed.), *CyberSociety: Computer-Mediated Communication and Community*. Thousand Oaks, CA: Sage Publications, 10–35.

Jones, S.G., 1997: 'The internet and its social landscape' in Jones, S.G. (ed.), *Virtual Culture: Identity and Communication in Cybersociety*. London: Sage Publications, 7–35.

Jones, S.G. (ed.), 1999: 'Studying the net: Intricacies and issues' in Jones, S.G. (ed.), *Doing Internet Research*. Thousand Oaks, CA: Sage Publications, 1–27.

Jordan, D.K., 1994: 'Changes in postwar Taiwan and their impact on the popular practice of religion' in Harrell, S. and Chün-chieh, H. (eds), *Cultural Change in Postwar Taiwan*, Taipei: SMC Publishing.

Jordan, G., 1998: 'Politics without parties: A growing trend?', *Parliamentary Affairs* 51, 314–28.

Kapor, M. and Barlow, J.P., 1990: 'Across the electronic frontier'. www.eff.org/ pub/EFF/Frontier_Files/EFF_Files/EFF_Info/electronic_frontier.eff.

Keck, M.E. and Sikkink, K., 1998: *Activists Beyond Borders: Advocacy Networks in International Politics*. Ithaca, NY: Cornell University Press.

Keegan, P., 1995: 'The digerati!', *The New York Times Magazine*, 38–45, 84–88.

Kelly, K., 1995: quoted in Ward, D., 'All power to the cybernauts', *Guardian* 22 February, 20.

Kelly, K. and Wolf, T., 1997: 'Push! Kiss your browser goodbye: The radical future of media beyond the Web', *Wired 5.03*. http://www.wired.com/wired/ archive/5.03/ff_push_pr.html.

Kempadoo, K., 1998: 'The Exotic Dancers Alliance' in Kempadoo, K. and Doezema, J. (eds), *Global Sex Workers: Rights, Resistance, and Redefinition*. New York: Routledge.

Kibby, M., 1997: 'Babes on the Web: Sex identity and the home page', *Media Information Australia* 84.

Kim, A.J., 1999: *Community Building on the Web: Secret Strategies for Successful Online Communities*. Berkeley, CA: Peachpit Press.

Kinney, J., 1996: 'Is there a new political paradigm lurking in cyberspace?' in Sardar, Z. and Ravetz, J.R. (eds), *Cyberfutures: Culture and Politics on the Information Superhighway*. New York: New York University Press, 138–53.

Kling, R., 1996: 'Hopes and horrors: Technological utopianism and anti-utopianism in narratives of computerization' in Kling, R. (ed.), *Computerization and Controversy: Value Conflicts and Social Choices*. San Diego, CA: Academic Press, 40–58.

Kollock, P., 1996: 'Design principles for online communities'. Paper presented at Harvard Conference on the Internet and Society, Cambridge, MA.

Kollock, P. and M. Smith., 1996: 'Managing the virtual commons: Cooperation and conflict in computer communities' in Herring, S.C. (ed.), *Computer-Mediated Communication: Linguistic, Social and Cross-Cultural Perspectives*. Amsterdam: John Benjamins Publishing Co., 109–28.

Kotamraju, N.P., 1999: 'The birth of web site design skills: Making the present history' in Lyman, P. and Wakeford, N. (eds), *Analyzing Virtual Societies: New Directions in Methodology. American Behavioral Scientist*: 43:3, November/ December, 464–74.

Labour Party, 1995: *Communicating Britain's Future*. London: Labour Party.

Landow, G.P., 1992: *Hypertext: The Convergence of Contemporary Critical Theory and Technology*. Baltimore, MD: Johns Hopkins University Press.

Landow, G.P., (ed.), 1994: *Hyper/Text/Theory*. Baltimore, MD: Johns Hopkins University Press.

Lather, P., 1993: 'Fertile obsession: Validity after post-structuralism', *The Sociological Quarterly* 34, 673–93.

Lem E., 1999: *The Anti-Personal Home Page FAQ: Your Guide to the Anti-Irrelevant Information Revolution*. www.ultranet.com/~mrlou/Anti-Personal_ Home_Page.html.

Levins, H., 1999: 'Indian immigrants have won acceptance in US through affluence, official says; many arrive here with lots of skills and quickly obtain high-paying jobs', *St Louis Post-Dispatch* 5 October.

Levinson, P., 1997: *The Soft Edge: A Natural History and Future of the Information Revolution*. New York: Routledge.

Levy, S., 1984: *Hackers: Heroes of the Computer Revolution*. New York: Dell.

Lyman, P. and Wakeford, N., 1999: 'Going into the (virtual) field' in Lyman, P. and Wakeford, N. (eds), *Analyzing Virtual Societies: New Directions in Methodology. American Behavioral Scientist*: 43:3, November/December, 359–76.

McChesney, R., 1999: *Rich Media, Poor Democracy: Communication Politics In Dubious Times*. Urbana-Champaign, IL: University of Illinois Press.

McChesney, R., Meiksins Wood, E. and Bellamy Foster, J. (eds), 1998: *Capitalism and the Information Age: The Political Economy of Global Communication*. New York: Monthly Review Press.

McDonough, J.P., 1999: 'Designer selves: Construction of technologically mediated identity within graphical, multiuser virtual environments', *Journal of the American Society of Information Science*, 50:10, 855–70.

McElroy, W., 1995: *A Woman's Right to Pornography*. New York: St Martin's Press.

MacKinnon, C.A., 1987: *Feminism Unmodified: Discourses on Life and Law*. Cambridge, MA: Harvard University Press.

MacKinnon, C.A., 1993: *Only Words*. Cambridge, MA: Harvard University Press.

MacKinnon, C.A. and Dworkin, A. (eds), 1997: *In Harm's Way: The Pornography Civil Rights Hearings*. Cambridge, MA: Harvard University Press.

MacKinnon, R., 1995: 'Searching for the leviathan in Usenet' in Jones, S.G. (ed.), *CyberSociety: Computer-Mediated Communication and Community*. Thousand Oaks, CA: Sage Publications, 112–37.

MacKinnon, R., 1997: 'Punishing the persona: Correctional strategies for the virtual offender' in Jones, S.G. (ed.), *Virtual Culture: Identity and Communication in Cybersociety*. London: Sage Publications, 206–35.

MacKinnon, R., 1998: 'The social construction of rape in virtual reality' in Sudweeks, F., McLaughlin, M. and Rafaeli, S. (eds), *Network and Netplay: Virtual Groups on the Internet*. Menlo Park, CA/Cambridge, MA: AAAI Press/MIT Press, 147–72.

McKinsey *et al.*, 1999: *Public Service Broadcasting Around the World: Report to the BBC*. London: BBC.

McLaughlin, M., Goldberg, S.B., Ellison, N. and Lucas, J., 1999: 'Measuring internet audiences: Patrons of an on-line art museum' in Jones, S. (ed.), *Doing Internet Research: Critical Issues and Methods for Examining the Net*. Thousand Oaks, CA: Sage, 163–78.

McLaughlin, M.L., Osborne, K.K. and Ellison, N.B., 1997: 'Virtual community in a telepresence environment' in Jones, S.G. (ed.), *Virtual Culture: Identity and Communication in Cybersociety*. London: Sage Publications, 146–68.

McLaughlin, M.L., Osborne, K.K. and Smith, C.B., 1995: 'Standards of conduct on Usenet' in Jones, S.G. (ed.), *CyberSociety: Computer-Mediated Communication and Community*. Thousand Oaks, CA: Sage Publications, 90–111.

McLaverty, P., 1998: 'The public sphere and local democracy', *Democratization* 5, 224–39.

McLean, R. and Schubert, R., 1995: 'Queers and the internet', *Media Information Australia* 78.

McLuhan, M., 1994 (first published 1964): *Understanding Media: The Extensions of Man*, fourth edition. Cambridge, MA: MIT Press.

Mander, J., 1991: *In the Absence of the Sacred: The Failure of Technology and the Survival of the Indian Nations*. San Francisco, CA: Sierra Club Books.

Mantovani, G., 1996: *New Communication Environments: From Everyday to Virtual*, London: Taylor and Francis.

Marcus, G., 1995: 'Ethnography in/of the world system: The emergence of multi-sited ethnography', *Annual Review of Anthropology* 24, 95–117.

Martin, F. and Berry, C., 1998: 'Queer'n'Asian on the net: Syncretic sexualities in Taiwan and Korean cyberspaces', *Critical InQueeries* 2:1, 67–93.

Miller, H., 1995: *The Presentation of Self in Electronic Life: Goffman on the Internet*. www.ntu.ac.uk/soc/psych/miller/goffman.htm.

Miller, L., 1995: 'Women and children first: Gender and the settling of the electronic frontier' in Brook, J. and Boal, I.A. (eds), *Resisting the Virtual Life: The Culture and Politics of Information*. San Francisco, CA: City Lights, 49–57.

Mitra, A., 1997: 'Virtual commonality: Looking for India on the internet' in Jones, S.G. (ed.), *Virtual Culture: Identity and Communication in Cybersociety*. Thousand Oaks, CA: Sage, 55–79.

Mitra, A. and Cohen, E., 1999: 'Analyzing the Web: Directions and challenges' in Jones, S. (ed.), *Doing Internet Research: Critical Issues and Methods for Examining the Net*. Thousand Oaks, CA: Sage, 179–202.

Mogelonsky, M., 1995: 'Asian-Indian Americans' in *American Demographics* 17:8, 32–39.

Morley, D., 1980: *The 'Nationwide' Audience*. London, British Film Institute.

Morley, D. and Robins, K., 1995: *Spaces of Identity: Global Media, Electronic Landscapes and Cultural Boundaries*. London and NY: Routledge.

Morris, C., 1999: *Amateur Web Sites - the Top Ten Signs*. http://webdevelopers-journal.co.uk/columns/abc-mistakes.html.

Mukta, P., 1995: *The Politics of Religious Nationalism and the New Indian Historiography: Lessons for the Indian Diaspora*. Coventry: University of Warwick, Centre for Research in Ethnic Relations.

Mulgan, G., 1997: *Connexity: How to Live in a Connected World*. London: Chatto and Windus.

Muller, M.J., Kuhn, S. and Meskill, J.A. (eds), 1992: 'PDC '92: Proceedings of the Participatory Design Conference'. Cambridge, MA.

Nader, R., 1999: *A Framework for ICANN and DNS Management: Initial Proposals*. Keynote address to 'Governing the Commons: The Future of Global Internet Administration', Computer Professionals For Social Responsibility Conference, Alexandra, Virginia, 24–25 September.

Naficy, H., 1993: *The Making of Exile Cultures: Iranian Television in Los Angeles*. Minneapolis, MN: University of Minnesota Press.

Nakamura, L., 1999: 'Race in/for cyberspace: Identity tourism and racial passing on the internet' in Vitanza, V.J. (ed.), *CyberReader*. Boston, MA: Allyn and Bacon, 442–53.

National Telecommunications and Information Administration, 1995: 'Falling through the net: A survey of the 'have nots' in rural and urban America'. www.ntia.doc.gov/ntiahome/fallingthru.html.

National Telecommunications and Information Administration, 1998: 'Falling through the net II: New data on the digital divide'. www.ntia.doc.gov/ntiahome/net2/falling.html.

National Telecommunications and Information Administration, 1999: 'Falling through the net: Defining the digital divide'. www.ntia.doc.gov/ntiahome/digitaldivide/.

Negroponte, N., 1995: *Being Digital*. London: Hodder & Stoughton/Coronet.

Nielsen, J., 1996: 'Top ten mistakes in Web design', http://www.useit.com/alertbox/9605.html.

Nielsen, J., 1999: 'The top ten new mistakes in Web design', http://www.useit.com/alterbox/990530.html.

O'Leary, M., 1998: 'Web directories demonstrate an enduring online law', *Online*, July/August, 79–81.

Oelson, V., 1994: 'Feminisms and models of qualitative research' in Denzin, N. and Lincoln, E. (eds), *Handbook of Qualitative Research*. London: Sage, 158–74.

Office of National Statistics, 1997: *Adult Literacy in Britain*. London: The Stationery Office.

Oxman, J., 1999: *The FCC and the Unregulation of the Internet*. Federation Communications Commission (FCC). OPP Working Paper 31. http://fcc.gov/.

Pai, H.-Y., 1995 (first published 1983): *Crystal Boys* (trans. Howard Goldblatt), San Francisco, CA: Gay Sunshine Press.

Palmer, S.J., 1986: *Korea and Christianity*, Seoul: Seoul Computer Press.

Parks, M.R., 1996: 'Making friends in cyberspace', *Journal of Computer Mediated Communication* 1:4, www.ascusc.org/jcmc/vol1/issue4/parks.html.

Parry, G., Moyser, G. and Day, N., 1992: *Political Participation and Democracy in Britain*. Cambridge: Cambridge University Press.

Patton, C., 1998: 'Stealth bombers of desire: The globalisation of "alterity" in emerging democracies', unpublished manuscript.

Penley, C., 1991: 'Brownian motion: women, tactics, and technology' in Penley, C. and Ross, A. (eds), *Technoculture*. Minneapolis, MN: University of Minnesota Press, 135–61.

Percy-Smith, J., 1996: 'Downloading democracy? Information and communication technologies in local politics', *Policy and Politics* 24, 43–56.

Phillips, D., 1996: 'Defending the boundaries: Identifying and countering threats in a Usenet newsgroup', *The Information Society* 12:1, 39–62.

Poster, M., 1995: *The Second Media Age*. Cambridge: Polity.

Poster, M., 1997: 'Cyberdemocracy: Internet and the public sphere' in Porter, D. (ed.), *Internet Culture*. New York: Routledge.

Postman, N., 1987: *Amusing Ourselves to Death*. London: Methuen.

Potter, D. (ed.), 1996: *Internet Culture*. New York: Routledge.

Poulter, A., 1997: 'The design of World Wide Web search engines: a critical review', *Program: electronic library and information systems* 31, 131–46.

Preston, J., 1993: *My Life as a Pornographer and Other Indecent Acts*. New York: Masquerade Books, Inc.

Radhakrishnan, R., 1994: 'Is the ethnic authentic in the diaspora?' in Juan, K.A. (ed.) *The State of Asian America: Activism and Resistance in the 1990s*. Boston MA: South End Press, 219–33.

Raymond, E.S., 1998a: 'A brief history of hackerdom', http://earthspace.net/~esr/faqs/hacker-hist.html.

Raymond, E.S., 1998b: 'Homesteading the Noosphere', *First Monday* 3, http://www.firstmonday.dk/issues/issue3_10/raymond/index.html.

Red Eagle, P., 1999: Online discussion. NativeLit-L@raven.cc.ukans.edu.

Rheingold, H., 1993a: 'A slice of life in my virtual community' in Harasim, L.M. (ed.), *Global Networks: Computers and International Communication*. Cambridge, MA: MIT Press, 57–80.

Rheingold, H., 1993b: *The Virtual Community: Homesteading on the Electronic Frontier*. Reading, MA: Addison-Wesley Publishing Co.

Rheingold, H., 1994: *The Virtual Community*. London: Secker and Warburg.

Richardson, L., 1994: 'Writing: A method of inquiry' in Denzin, N. and Lincoln, E. (eds), *Handbook of Qualitative Research*. London: Sage, 516–29.

Roeder, L., 1997a: *Homepage Stats Update*. http://personalweb.about.com/library/zArchivez/070198/saved/ff090897.htm.

Roeder, L., 1997b: *A Survey Of Online Diarists: Part Two*. http://personalweb.about.com/internet/personalweb/library/zArchivez/070198/ff120197.htm.

Rosenzweig, R., 1999: 'Live free or die? Death, life, survival, and sobriety on the information superhighway', *American Quarterly* 51:1, 160–74.

Ross, A., 1991: *Strange Weather: Culture, Science and Technology in the Age of Limits*. London: Verso.

Rotundo, E.A., 1998: 'Boy culture' in *The Children's Culture Reader*, Jenkins, H.

(ed.), New York: New York University Press, 337–62.

Rushkoff, D., 1994: *Media Virus: Hidden Agendas in Popular Culture.* New York: Ballantine.

Russell, D., 1993: *Against Pornography: The Evidence of Harm.* Berkeley, CA: Russell Publications.

Rutt, R., 1969: 'The Flower Boys of Silla (Hwarang): Notes on the sources', *Transactions of the Korea Branch of the Royal Asiatic Society* 38, 1–66.

Sack, W., 1999: *Conversation Map Version 0.01: An Interface for Very Large-Scale Conversations.* http://www.media.mit.edu/~wsack/CM/index.html.

Sale, K., 1995: *Rebels Against the Future: The Luddites and Their War on the Industrial Revolution: Lessons for the Computer Age.* Reading, MA: Addison-Wesley Publishing Co.

Saul, M., 1999: *The Boodle Box.* www.jwp.bc.ca/saulm/html/award.htm.

Scannell, P. and Cardiff, D., 1982: 'Serving the nation: public service broadcasting before the war' in Waites, B., Bennett, T. and Martin, G. (eds), *Popular Culture: Past and Present.* London: Croom Helm, 161–88.

Schmitz, J., 1997: 'Structural relations, electronic media, and social change: The public electronic network and the homeless' in Jones, S.G. (ed.), *Virtual Culture: Identity and Communication in Cybersociety.* London: Sage Publications, 80–101.

Schuler, D., 1994: 'Community networks: Building a new participatory medium', *Communications of the ACM* 37:1, 39–51.

Schuler, D. and Namioka, A. (eds), 1993: *Participatory Design: Principles and Practices.* Hillsdale, NJ: Lawrence Erlbaum Associates, Publishers.

Schwartz, E.I., 1999: *Digital Darwinism: Seven Breakthrough Business Strategies for Surviving in the Cutthroat Web Economy.* London and New York: Penguin.

Segal, L., 1993: 'Introduction', *Sex Exposed: Sexuality and the Pornography Debate.* New Brunswick: Rutgers University Press, 1–11.

Semans, A. and Winks, C., 1999: *The Woman's Guide to Sex on the Web.* San Francisco, CA: HarperCollins Publishers, Inc.

Shaw, D.F., 1997: 'Gay men and computer communication: A discourse of sex and identity in cyberspace' in Jones, S.G. (ed.), *CyberSociety: Computer-Mediated Communication and Community,* Thousand Oaks, CA: Sage.

Shneiderman, B. and Rose, A., 1997: 'Social impact statements: Engaging public participation in information technology design' in Friedman, B. (ed.), *Human Values and the Design of Computer Technology.* Cambridge: Cambridge University Press, 117–33.

Silver, D., 1996: 'Parameters and priorities: The formation of community in the blacksburg electronic village'. Unpublished MA thesis, Department of American Studies, University of Maryland.

Silver, D., 1999a: 'Localizing the global village: Lessons from the blacksburg electronic village' in Browne, R.B. and Fishwick, M.W. (eds), *The Global Village: Dead or Alive?* Bowling Green, OH: Popular Press, 79–92.

Silver, D., 1999b: 'Communication, community, consumption: An ethnographic exploration of an online city' in Kolko, B.E. (ed.), *Virtual Publics: Policy and Community in an Electronic Age.* New York: Columbia University Press.

Silver, D., in press: 'Margins in the wires: Looking for race, gender, and sexuality in the blacksburg electronic village' in Kolko, B.E., Nakamura, L. and Rodman, G.B. (eds), *Race in Cyberspace: Politics, Identity, and Cyberspace.* New York: Routledge.

Silverstone, R. and Hirsch, E., 1992: *Consuming Technologies: Media and Information in Domestic Spaces.* London: Routledge.

Smith, M. and Kollock, P. (eds), 1999: *Communities in Cyberspace*. London: Routledge.

Sobchack, V., 1993: 'New age mutant ninja hackers: Reading *Mondo 2000*', *South Atlantic Quarterly* 92:4, 569–84.

Song, B.N., 1990: *The Rise of the Korean Economy*, Hong Kong: Oxford University Press.

Spurgeon, C., 1998: 'National culture, communications and the information economy', *Media International Australia* 87, 23–34.

Star, S.L., 1994: *Misplaced Concretism and Concrete Situations: Feminism, Method and Information Technology*. Working Paper 11, Series: Gender-Nature-Culture, Feminist Research Network. Odense: Odense University.

Star, S.L., 1999: 'The ethnography of infrastructure' in Lyman, P. and Wakeford, N. (eds), *Analyzing Virtual Societies: New Directions in Methodology*. *American Behavioral Scientist* 43:3, November/December, 377–91.

Sterling, B., 1992: *The Hacker Crackdown: Law and Disorder on the Electronic Frontier*. New York: Bantam.

Stoll, C., 1995: *Silicon Snake Oil: Second Thoughts on the Information Highway*. New York: Doubleday.

Stone, A.R., 1991: 'Will the real body please stand up?: Boundary stories about virtual cultures' in Benedikt, M. (ed.), *Cyberspace: First Steps*. Cambridge, MA: MIT Press, 81–118.

Suchman, L., Blomberg, J., Orr, J.E. and Trigg, R., 1999: 'Reconstructing Technologies as Social Practice' in Lyman, P. and Wakeford, N. (eds), *Analyzing Virtual Societies: New Directions in Methodology*. *American Behavioral Scientist* 43: 3, November/December, 392–408.

Svennevig, M. and Morrison, D., 2000: 'Needs not nerds: People's reactions to the digital world' in Lax, S. (ed.), *Access Denied: Exclusion in the Information Age*. Basingstoke: Macmillan.

Svennevig, M., Brown, R., Houltham, M., Towler, R. and Firmstone, J., 1999: 'Researching the process of change' in Byfield S. (ed.), *Media Research*. ESOMAR Monograph Series Vol. 6. Amsterdam: European Society for Opinion and Marketing Research.

Tacchi, J., 1998: 'Radio texture: between self and others' in Miller, D. (ed.), *Material Cultures: Why Some Things Matter*. Chicago, IL: University of Chicago Press, 25–45.

Taylor, J., Bellamy, C., Raab, C., Dutton, W.H. and Peltu, M., 1996: 'Innovation in public service delivery' in Dutton, W.H. (ed.), *Information and Communication Technologies: Visions and Realities*. Oxford: Oxford University Press.

Thussu, D.K. (ed.), 1998: *Electronic Empires*. London: Arnold.

Toffler, A., 1980: *The Third Wave*. London: Collins.

Trahant, M.N., 1996: 'The power of stories: Native words and images on the internet', *Native Americas* 13 :1, 15–21.

Trigg, R., Anderson, S.I. and Dykstra-Erickson, E. (eds), 1994: 'PDC '94: Proceedings of the Participatory Design Conference'. Chapel Hill, NC.

Tsagarousianou, R., Tambini, D. and Bryan, C., 1998: *Cyberdemocracy: Technology, Cities and Civic Networks* London: Routledge.

Tsang, D.C., 1996: 'Notes on queer 'n' Asian virtual sex' in Leong, R. (ed.), *Asian American Sexualities: Dimensions of the Gay and Lesbian Experience*, New York: Routledge.

Turkle, S., 1995: *Life on the Screen: Identity in the Age of the Internet*. New York: Touchstone.

Turkle, S., 1997: 'Multiple subjectivity and virtual community at the end of the Freudian century', *Sociological Inquiry* 67, 72–84.

Valverde, M., 1989: 'Beyond gender dangers and private pleasures: Theory and ethics in the sex debates', *Feminist studies* 15:2, 237–54.

Wachman, A.M., 1994: *Taiwan: National Identity and Democratization*, Armonk, NY: ME Sharpe.

Wakeford, N., 1999: 'Gender and the landscapes of computing in an internet café' in Crang, M., Crang, P. and Dey, J. *Virtual Geographies*. London: Routledge.

Wallace, J., 1997: *Overdrive: Bill Gates and the Race to Control Cyberspace*. New York: John Wiley.

Wellman, B., 1997: 'An electronic group is virtually a social network' in Kiesler, S. (ed.), *Culture of the Internet*. Mahwah, NJ: Lawrence Erlbaum Associates, Publishers, 179–205.

Wellman, B., Salaff, J., Dimitrova, D., Garton, L., Gulia, M. and Haythornthwaite, C., 1996: 'Computer networks as social networks: Collaborative work, telework, and virtual community', *Annual Review of Sociology* 22, 213–38.

Wheeler, M., 1998: 'Democracy and the information superhighway', *Democratization* 5, 217–39.

White, P.B., 1996: 'Online services: the emerging battle for transactional space', *Media International Australia* 79, 3-9.

Whittle, D.B., 1997: *Cyberspace: The Human Dimension*. New York: WH Freeman and Co.

Wilbur, S.P., 1997: 'An archaeology of cyberspaces: Virtuality, community, identity' in Porter, D. (ed.), *Internet Culture*. New York: Routledge, 5–22.

Wilhelm, A.G., 1998: 'Virtual sounding boards: How deliberative is on-line political discussion?', *Information Communication and Society* 1, 313–38.

Wise, R., 2000: *Multimedia: A Critical Introduction*. London: Routledge.

Witmer, D.F., Colman, R.W. and Katzman, S.L., 1999: 'From paper-and-pencil to screen-and-keyboard: Toward a methodology for survey research on the internet' in Jones, S. (ed.), *Doing Internet Research: Critical Issues and Methods for Examining the Net*. Thousand Oaks, CA: Sage, 145–61.

Wolf, A., 1998: 'Exposing the great equalizer: Demythologizing internet equity' in Ebo, B. (ed.), *Cyberghetto or Cybertopia? Race, Class, and Gender on the Internet*. Westport: CN: Praeger, 15–32.

Wolmark, J. (ed.), 1999: *Cybersexualities: A Reader on Feminist Theory, Cyborgs and Cyberspace*. Edinburgh: Edinburgh University Press.

Wong, W., 1998: 'Search engine companies seek partners', *Computer Reseller News* 14 September, 79–80.

Woolgar, S. (ed.), 1988: *Knowledge and Reflexivity: New Frontiers in the Sociology of Knowledge*. London: Sage.

Wynn, E. and Katz, J.E., 1997: 'Hyperbole over cyberspace: self-presentation and social boundaries in internet home pages and discourse', *The Information Society* 13:4, 297–328. www.usyd.edu.au/su/social/papers/wynn.htm.

Yang, L., 1997: 'Virtual space and the flow of sexual discourse'. Paper presented at the Second International Conference on Sexuality Education, Sexology, Gender Studies and LesBiGay Studies, organized by the Center for the Study of Sexuality and Difference, National Central University, 31 May-1 June.

Yawakie, M.P., 1997: 'Building telecommunication capacity in Indian country', *Winds of Change* 12, 44–46.

Zeff, R. and Aronson, B., 1999. *Advertising on the Internet*. New York: John Wiley & Sons.

Index